THE FUTURE of PRIVATE ENTERPRISE

Challenges and Responses
Volume 1
1984

Edited by
Craig E. Aronoff, Ph.D.
Chair of Private Enterprise
Kennesaw College

and

John L. Ward, Ph.D.
Ralph Marotta Professor of Free Enterprise
Loyola University of Chicago

Sponsored by the
Association of Private Enterprise Education
with a grant from the
Scholl Foundation

Business Publishing Division
COLLEGE OF BUSINESS ADMINISTRATION
GEORGIA STATE UNIVERSITY
Atlanta, Georgia 30303

Library of Congress Cataloging in Publication Data

Main entry under title:

The Future of private enterprise.

"Sponsored by the Association of Private Enterprise Education."
1. Capitalism—Addresses, essays, lectures.
2. Economic policy—Addresses, essays, lectures.
3. Industry and state—Addresses, essays, lectures.
4. Laissez-faire—Addresses, essays, lectures.
I. Aronoff, Craig E. II. Ward, John (John L.)
III. Association of Private Enterprise Education (U.S.)
HB501.F83   1984   338.6'1   83-25386
ISBN 0-88406-164-7

Published by:
Business Publishing Division
College of Business Administration
Georgia State University
University Plaza
Atlanta, Georgia 30303
Telephone: 404/658-4253

© 1984 by The Association of Private Enterprise Education

All rights reserved, including the right to reproduce this publication, or portions thereof, in any form without prior permission from the publisher.

87 86 85 84   4 3 2 1

Georgia State University, a unit of the University System of Georgia, is an equal educational opportunity institution and an equal opportunity/ affirmative action employer.

Printed in the United States of America

Cover design by Marcia Lampe

This book is fondly dedicated to Robert L. "Bill" Milligan whose vision and tenacity made it all possible.

Contents

Preface ix

Contributors xi

Introduction xxi

SECTION I: Toward a Philosophy of Private Enterprise

1 The Judeo-Christian Values That Characterize Economic Freedom 5
  Michael Novak

2 Philosophical Norms for the Integrity of the Economic System 33
  Irving Kristol

3 The Coming Idea Revolution 43
  George C. Roche III

4 A New Philosophy for Corporate Management 51
  Kenneth Mason

5 The Constitutional Setting for a Free Enterprise Economy 65
  James M. Buchanan

SECTION II: The Role of Free Markets in Democratic Capitalism

6 Command vs. Market: Across the Centuries 81
  William H. McNeill

7 Government and Income Distribution: Its Effects
   on the Private Market **95**
   Yale Brozen

8 Constitutional Limits on the Role of the Federal Government
   in the Economy **111**
   Jerry Jordan and Paul H. Rubin

9 Wealth: Its Creation and Growth **133**
   George Gilder

**SECTION III: Roles of Business, Government, and Labor
in a Private Enterprise Society**

10 The Responsibility of Government to Guarantee
   Economic Freedom **143**
   Gerald R. Ford

11 Economic Freedom in Developing Countries **149**
   Edward Seaga

12 Economics, Private Enterprise, and the Workers **155**
   Phyllis A. Wallace

13 New Business Initiatives for Public Policy **169**
   George F. Will

14 The Business Role: The Visible Hand in Our Economy **181**
   Norma Pace

SECTION IV: Challenges to Private Enterprise

15 Retirement Security: Perspective for Reform **195**
   Colin D. Campbell

16 Employment Security: Government, Union,
   and Market Protection **213**
   James T. Bennett

17 Public Lands Policy: What Legacy for the Future? **231**
   John Baden

18 The Decline and Fall of the Welfare Industry **247**
   Charles D. Hobbs

19 New Initiatives for the Urban Environment **261**
   James W. Rouse

SECTION V: Solutions to Problems of Private Enterprise

20 Balancing Economic Growth and Income Distribution **271**
   Herbert Stein

21 Human Resources: What's the Solution? **283**
   William J. Baroody

22 Health-care Costs: The Competition Prescription **291**
   Karl D. Bays

23 Restoring Our Prosperity **303**
   Paul W. McCracken

Preface

During the 1981-82 academic year, ten colleges and universities were selected by the Association of Private Enterprise Education (APEE) to host Forums on the Future of Private Enterprise. These forums took the form of lecture series that explored current and future challenges to private enterprise, focused public attention on private-enterprise-related issues, and fostered college and university efforts toward private enterprise education. The host institutions were selected through a rigorous competition in which nearly 100 schools submitted proposals. The Scholl Foundation made it possible to provide each winning school with $25,000, the cooperation and support of the association, and extensive professional public relations assistance in coordinating, producing and promoting its series.

In all, sixty-three lectures were delivered to audiences totaling over 20,000 people. The lecturers included many of the finest minds in economics, social philosophy, politics, business, and academia. In this volume we have selected the best lectures from the series in an effort to collect and organize them and make them accessible to a still broader audience of opinion leaders in business, academia, and public life.

We have organized the book in five sections, each exploring a fundamental facet of the future of private enterprise. These themes were suggested by the lectures themselves as concerns and interests common to those who are scrutinizing our system. As we saw it, the crucial themes and concerns related to: the philosophy of private enterprise; the nature of the market mechanism; the appropriate roles for business, government, and labor in the system; specific contemporary challenges to private enterprise; and certain solutions to problems currently besetting the system.

You will recognize the names of many of the lecturers represented here. Some will be less familiar. All, however, make genuine contributions to the intellectual climate in which private enterprise is most likely to flourish.

The APEE is the entity through which the Forums on the Future of Private Enterprise and this book came to fruition. Founded in 1978, APEE seeks to put into action accurate and objective understanding of private enterprise by advancing teaching and research in free-market economics; helping communication and cooperation between academia and business; encouraging the creation of private enterprise education programs; and assisting in making existing programs more effective. We wish to thank all of our colleagues in APEE, especially Charles Myers of Vanderbilt University, Frank Chew of the University of Southern California, and Paul Goelz of St. Mary's University, all of whom served as president of the Association at various times during this project.

Particular recognition must be given the institutions who hosted Forums on the Future of Private Enterprise and the individuals who shepherded each undertaking. Our deep appreciation to: Dr. Lucille G. Ford, Ashland College; Dr. Gerald J. Lynch, Ball State University; William J. Sutton, Benedictine College; Dr. Ervin Williams, Georgia State University; Dr. John M. White, Howard University; Duane M. Bonner, National College of Education; Dr. Jules Backman, New York University; Dr. Paul C. Goelz, St. Mary's University; Dr. Lee E. Preston, University of Maryland; and Dr. Dolores T. Martin, University of Nebraska.

Special thanks must be given to Mary McCleary Posner of Posner Public Relations who brought the sum of her experience, skill, energy, and devotion to this effort.

Kathy Aronoff provided invaluable editorial skill in the preparation of this book. Many others, too numerous to mention, made important contributions. You know who you are and how we feel.

Our final recognition must be reserved for the man to whom we dedicate this book. The forums were his dream. Not content to dream, however, he provided the wherewithal that resulted in the means to make that dream a reality. In doing so, he convinced many that his dreams are worth sharing.

Contributors

JOHN A. BADEN has long been an advocate of the efficient management of natural resources. As Director of the Center for Political Economy and Natural Resources at Montana State University, he has written and lectured extensively on the need for scrutinizing how government and private interests manage this country's natural resources and how it can be done more efficiently and productively.
  Mr. Baden has a long history of interest in natural resource issues. He has been a logger, a Forest Service consultant, and the director of an environmental study program. He has published widely in such journals as *Public Choice*, the *Journal of Law and Economics*, *Environmental Law*, and *Policy Review*. He is also co-editor of *Managing the Commons*, *Bureaucracy vs. Environment: The Environmental Cost of Bureaucratic Governances*, and *Natural Resources: Bureaucratic Environmental Myths and Management*.

WILLIAM J. BAROODY, JR., is president of the American Enterprise Institute for Public Policy Research (AEI), an organization which for forty years has assisted the nation's legislators and educators by providing factual analyses of important national policy issues.
  Mr. Baroody assumed his present position in July 1978 after serving for a year and a half as AEI executive vice president.
  In his capacity as assistant to President Gerald Ford, Mr. Baroody organized and was the first director of the Office of Public Liaison. Before joining the White House staff, he served in the U.S. Department of Defense and in a staff capacity in Congress.

Mr. Baroody is a member of the Boards of Trustees of the Woodrow Wilson International Center for Scholars, the Center for the Study of the Presidency, and the John Carroll Society.

KARL D. BAYS is board chairman and chief executive officer of the American Hospital Supply Corporation.

Mr. Bays also serves as a director of International Harvester Corporation, Standard Oil Corporation (Indiana), Delta Air Lines, Northern Trust Corporation, and the Jewel Company.

He was the recipient of the Trojan MBA Achievement Award from the University of Southern California in 1972, the Horatio Alger Award in 1979, and the Distinguished Alumni Service Award from Indiana University in 1977. He was also named the Outstanding Alumnus at Eastern Kentucky University in 1973, where he received the Bachelor of Science degree in 1955 and Doctor of Laws in 1977. Mr. Bays holds a Doctor of Commercial Science Degree from Union College in Kentucky.

Mr. Bays is the Chairman of the Advisory Council for Northwestern University's Graduate School of Management and is a lifetime member of the Lake Forest Hospital board of directors.

Mr. Bays was nominated as the Marketing Man of the Year by the Sales and Marketing Executives Association of Chicago in 1977. He was also named Outstanding Chief Executive Officer in the drug products and hospital supply industry by the magazine *Financial World* in 1975 and 1981.

JAMES T. BENNETT is a professor of economics at George Mason University in Virginia where he has been since 1975.

Mr. Bennett's main teaching and research interests are in the fields of labor/manpower economics, political economy, macroeconomic theory, and public choice. His books include: *The Political Economy of Federal Government Growth: 1958-1978* (1980); *Better Government at Half the Price* (1981); *Deregulating Labor Relations* (1981); and *Underground Government: The Off-Budget Public Sector* (1983). Mr. Bennett has also published several monographs and contributed numerous articles to professional journals including: *Journal of Labor Research*, *Public Choice*, *Economic Inquiry*, the *Journal of Finance*, and the *Journal of Political Economy*.

YALE BROZEN is professor of Business Economics in the Graduate School of Business at the University of Chicago, directs the school's program in applied economics, and is an adjunct scholar at the American Enterprise Institute for Public Policy Research.

An internationally known economist, his articles have frequently been reprinted in collections and inserted into the Congressional Record and have been translated into French, Italian, Spanish, Portuguese, and Japanese for reprinting abroad. His books include *Advertising and*

Society (1974); *The Competitive Economy* (1975); *Textbook for Economics* (1948); *Automation: The Impact of Technological Change* (1963); *Mergers in Perspective* (1982); and *Concentration, Mergers, and Public Policy* (1982). The latter book received Emory University's Law and Economics Center 1982 award for scholarship in law and economics.

He has served as a consultant to major corporations and to various governmental agencies, trade associations, and foundations.

JAMES M. BUCHANAN is the director of the Center for the Study of Public Choice at George Mason University. His books include *Price, Income, and Public Policy* (1954); *Public Principles of Public Debt* (1958); *The Public Finances* (1960); *Fiscal Theory and Political Economy* (1960); *Public Finance in Democratic Process* (1966); *The Demand and Supply of Public Goods* (1968); and *Cost and Choice* (1969). He has also been editor of several other books including: *Theory of Public Choice* (1972); *LSF Essays on Cost* (1977); *Freedom in Constitutional Contract* (1978); *What Should Economists Do?* (1979); and *The Power to Tax* (1980). Mr. Buchanan also has contributed numerous articles to professional journals.

After receiving his Ph.D. at the University of Chicago in 1948, he taught economics at the University of Tennessee, Florida State University, the University of Virginia, and the University of California, Los Angeles. He was a Fulbright Scholar in Italy in 1955-56 and a Ford Faculty research fellow in 1959-60.

COLIN D. CAMPBELL is a Loren M. Berry Professor of Economics at Dartmouth College, where he has been a faculty member since 1956. He has also been an adjunct scholar at the American Enterprise Institute since 1974.

Mr. Campbell has served as an economist for the Central Intelligence Agency and the Federal Reserve System. He has been a director of the Dartmouth National Bank since 1961.

Mr. Campbell has contributed numerous articles to professional journals, and published *Introduction to Money and Banking* with his wife, R.G. Campbell, in 1981.

GERALD R. FORD, during his twenty-five years as the Republican representative from Michigan's Fifth Congressional District, acquired a reputation among his colleagues as an amiable, reasonable, accessible, politically conservative, thoroughly public spirited, and innately decent man.

Mr. Ford was the House Minority Leader from 1965 to 1972, where he tried to change the negative image of the Republicans by offering constructive alternatives to legislation proposed by Democrats. He served as vice president under Richard Nixon in 1973-74 and on August 9, 1974, Mr. Ford took the oath of office as thirty-eighth president of the

United States under "extraordinary circumstances, never before experienced by Americans," as he himself described them.
In confronting his inherited problems of inflation, recession, soaring unemployment, and the related energy shortage crisis, President Ford sought long-range solutions that would limit federal spending and reduce the government presence in the economy. Mr. Ford was defeated by Jimmy Carter in the 1976 election, and ended his term of presidency on January 20, 1977.
Mr. Ford is chairman of the board of the Academy for Educational Development and is a distinguished fellow of the American Enterprise Institute. He also participates in a series of seminars and conferences on university and college campuses under the institute's auspices as part of its academic outreach program.
Mr. Ford has published two books, *Portrait of the Assassin* (with John R. Stiles) and *A Time to Heal* (memoirs, 1979).

GEORGE F. GILDER is the program director of the International Center for Economic Policy Studies, a nonprofit organization dedicated to promoting conservative economic ideas, and chairman of the Economic Roundtable at the Lehrman Institute.
The largely self-taught economist and social philosopher has emerged as the most widely read of the American supply-side theorists. Mr. Gilder's books include *The Party That Lost its Head* (1965); *Sexual Suicide* (1973); *Naked Nomads* (1974); *Visible Man* (1978); and the recent *Wealth and Poverty* (1981). *Time* described *Wealth and Poverty* as "a bible for supply-siders" and as an "ode to the economic and moral benefits of unfettered capitalism."
In addition to writing books, Mr. Gilder is a regular contributor to the *Wall Street Journal*, the *Washington Post, Harpers, Commentary*, the *National Review*, the *New York Times, Playboy*, and numerous other publications.
Mr. Gilder served as speechwriter for Michigan Governor George Romney in 1967 and for Richard Nixon in 1968. He held a fellowship with the Kennedy Institute of Politics at Harvard University in 1970-71, and during the same period served as editor of the *Republican Ripon Forum*.

CHARLES D. HOBBS has owned and managed Charles D. Hobbs Incorporated, an independent public policy and management consulting firm, since 1973. His clients have included federal, state, and local government agencies; private companies and universities; and nonprofit research institutes.
In 1973-74 Mr. Hobbs was a member of the California Governor's Task Force on Local Government Reform. In 1972-73 he served on the California Governor's Tax Reduction Task Force, where he analyzed the impact of twenty years of growth of federal, state, and local taxes on state and local government programs, business development, and individual tax burdens in California.

From 1970 to 1972 he served as chief deputy director of Social Welfare in California, and was one of the principal architects of the California Welfare Reform Program.

Mr. Hobbs is also the author of two books and numerous articles on government structure and programs.

JERRY L. JORDAN has served as chief economist at the Pittsburgh National Bank and as an officer of the Federal Reserve Bank in St. Louis. He was the Dean of the Andersen School of Management at the University of New Mexico, until President Reagan named him to his Council of Economic Advisers in 1981. At the council, Mr. Jordan took the lead on forecasting and developing monetary and fiscal policy issues. He is considered a strong monetarist, which dictates that steady, moderate growth in the nation's money supply is the key to controlling inflation and ensuring stable economic growth.

Mr. Jordan is a member of the American Economic Association, the Western Economic Association, the National Association of Business Economists, and the World Affairs Council of Pittsburgh. He received his Ph.D. in economics from the University of California, Los Angeles, in 1969.

Mr. Jordan resigned from the Council of Economic Advisers in July 1982 to go back to his post as dean of the Andersen School of Management.

IRVING KRISTOL is professor of social thought and the Henry R. Luce Professor of Urban Values at New York University's graduate school of business.

A senior fellow at the American Enterprise Institute, Mr. Kristol served as an executive vice-president of Basic Books from 1962-69, was a founder and an editor of *Encounter Magazine*, and served as managing editor of *Commentary Magazine*. He is also a member of the *Wall Street Journal's* board of contributors and of the President's Commission on White House Fellowships.

His books include *On the Democratic Idea in America* (1972); *The American Commonwealth* (1976); *The Americans* (1976); and *Two Cheers for Capitalism* (1978).

KENNETH MASON retired as president of the Quaker Oats Company in October 1979 at age 57.

Mr. Mason joined Quaker as advertising director in 1963. He was named group vice president for U.S. grocery products and a member of the board of directors in 1968. In 1974 he was appointed executive vice president in charge of Quaker's worldwide grocery business and was elected president and chief operating officer in 1976. The Quaker Oats Company is an international marketer of foods, pet foods, toys, and chemicals.

A longtime supporter of the cause of public broadcasting in the United

States, Mr. Mason is a former president of Chicago's public television station WTTW, and was a member of the Carnegie Commission on the Future of Public Broadcasting.

Mr. Mason remains a member of the board of directors of the Quaker Oats Company. He is also a director of Rohm and Haas and of Harper and Row.

PAUL W. MCCRACKEN, the current chairman of the International Committee of Economists and former chairman of the President's Council of Economic Advisers, is noted around the world for his expertise in economic and financial matters. A highly recognized educator, he is the Edmund Ezra Day University Professor of Business Administration at the University of Michigan, where he began teaching in 1948.

In addition to being chairman of the International Committee of Economists, which makes recommendations on Western economic policy, Mr. McCracken is president of the Assembly on U.S.-Japan Economic Policy and chairman of the Academic Advisory Board of the American Enterprise Insitute for Public Policy Research. He is also a member of the *Wall Street Journal's* board of contributors.

A winner of awards and the author of many papers and monographs on economic and financial policy, Mr. McCracken is a member of the American Economic Association, the American Finance Association, and the Royal Economic Society. He has lectured throughout the world and has participated on economic commissions, task forces, and advisory boards.

WILLIAM H. MCNEILL is Robert A. Millikan Professor of History at the University of Chicago.

His books include: *Greek Dilemma, War and Aftermath* (1947); *History Handbook of Western Civilization* (1969); *America, Britain, and Russia, Their Cooperation and Conflict, 1941-46* (1954); *Past and Future* (1954); *Greece: American Aid in Action* (1957); *Rise of the West, a History of the Human Community* (1963); *Europe's Steppe Frontier, 1500-1800* (1964); *A World History* (1979); *The Contemporary World* (1975); *The Ecumene: Story of Humanity* (1973); *Venice, The Hinge of Europe* (1974); *The Shape of European History* (1974); *Plagues and Peoples* (1976); *Metamorphosis of Greece Since World War II* (1978); and *The Human Condition: An Ecological and Historical View* (1980).

He received the National Book Award, Gordon J. Laing Prize, in 1963 for *The Rise of the West, a History of the Human Community.*

MICHAEL NOVAK, resident scholar in religion and public policy at the American Enterprise Institute in Washington, D.C., is considered one of the "groundbreaking intellectuals" in the neo-conservative movement.

Mr. Novak joined the American Enterprise Institute in 1978. Previous to that he was the Ledden-Watson Distinguished Professor of Religion at Syracuse University, where he continues to serve as an adjunct professor. He has also taught at Harvard University and at Stanford University. But Mr. Novak's "intellectual odyssey," as some have called his span of endeavors, includes antiwar activism, and service as a speech writer and adviser to Sargent Shriver, Edmund Muskie, and George McGovern.

In 1982, Mr. Novak served as chief of the U.S. Delegation to the Human Rights Commission in Geneva, Switzerland. He has written two novels and several influential books which are translated into all major languages. These include: *Belief and Unbelief* (1965); *The Experience of Nothingness* (1970); *The Rise of the Unmeltable Ethnics* (1972); *Choosing Our King* (1974); *The Joy of Sports* (1978); *The Guns of Lattimer* (1978); *The American Vision* (1978); and *The Spirit of Democratic Capitalism* (1981).

Mr. Novak was educated at Holy Cross Seminary (Stonehill College) and at the Gregorian University in Rome, where he received his Bachelor of Arts and Bachelor of Theology, respectively. He completed his graduate studies at Harvard University, where he received his Masters of Arts, Doctor of Laws, and Doctor of Human Letters.

NORMA PACE is the senior vice president and chief economist of the American Paper Institute. She is also a director of Sears, Roebuck and Company, the Sperry Corporation, the Milton Bradley Company, Chase Manhattan Corporation and Chase Manhattan Bank, 3-M Company, and Vulcan Materials.

Ms. Pace was with the U.S. Economics Corporation's business advisory consulting service from 1944 to 1971, serving as its president for two years. She was the vice president and director of industrial economics at Lionel D. Edie and Company prior to joining the American Paper Institute in 1973.

GEORGE C. ROCHE III is president of Hillsdale College, a school that has become recognized as a bastion of intellectual endeavor associated with freedom and enterprise. His books include *Power* (1967); *American Federalism* (1967); *Education in America* (1969); *Legacy of Freedom* (1969); *Frederic Bastiat: A Man Alone* (1971); *The Bewildered Society* (1972); *The Balancing Act: Quota Hiring in Higher Education* (1979). He has also written numerous newspaper articles and columns.

JAMES W. ROUSE retired in 1979 as chief executive officer of the company that bears his name. He has remained chairman of the board of Rouse Company, famed for its innovative work in urban planning and design.

As chairman of the Enterprise Foundation, Mr. Rouse recently has launched a charitable corporation to provide support for nonprofit housing groups across the country, helping the poor to rehabilitate slum housing to fit and livable conditions. He is raising $25 million for this work.

Mr. Rouse was a member of President Eisenhower's Advisory Committee on Housing and chairman of the subcommittee that recommended the urban renewal program embraced in the Housing Act of 1954. He was also a founder and president of the American Council to Improve Our Neighborhoods (ACTION), and president of Urban America. In 1982, Mr. Rouse served as a member of President Reagan's Task Force on Private Sector Initiatives.

Mr. Rouse is a member of the Johns Hopkins University board of trustees; the MIT-Harvard Joint Center for Urban Studies advisory committee; and the Harvard University Public Policy and Corporate Management Program advisory board. He is also a trustee of the Council on Foreign Relations and a director of the Institute for World Order.

PAUL H. RUBIN is a professor in economics at Baruch College, University of New York. His major interests include microeconomic theory, industrial organization, public choice, and law and economics.

Mr. Rubin served as a senior staff economist for the President's Council of Economic Advisers and taught economics at the University of Georgia. He was the 1967-68 recipient of the Herman Krannert Fellowship, Purdue University.

Mr. Rubin is the author of *Congressmen, Constituents and Contributors* (1982). He has also contributed numerous articles to professional magazines, especially to the *Journal of Legal Studies* and *Public Choice*. *Public Choice*.

EDWARD SEAGA, the fifth prime minister since Jamaican independence in 1962, has been a leader in his party for more than twenty years. On October 30, 1980, in an election with implications for the entire Carribbean region, the people of Jamaica decisively rejected the programs and policies of the pro-Cuban People's National Party in favor of Mr. Seaga's moderate pro-Western Jamaica Labour Party. A banker by profession, Mr. Seaga put his financial skills to work in ministerial posts in two previous labor governments. Since taking office on November 1, 1980, Mr. Seaga, who also serves as his country's Minister of Finance, has devoted himself to repairing Jamaica's devastated economy by advocating a greater reliance on private enterprise and free market economics.

In his earlier position of Minister of Finance and Planning, Mr. Seaga earned a reputation for fiscal expertise. Determined to restore Jamaica to solvency, he established several important local financial institutions, among them the Jamaica Development Bank, the Jamaica Unit Trust, and the Jamaica Stock Exchange. He introduced a tax reform plan to strengthen local industry, and oversaw the transfer of many foreign-owned companies to Jamaican hands. To erect adequate housing and provide thousands of jobs, he organized the Urban Development Corporation.

On the international scene, Mr. Seaga serves as a governor of the

World Bank, and as a delegate to the Inter-American Development Bank, the Carribbean Development Bank, and the International Monetary Fund.

HERBERT STEIN is currently the A. Willis Robertsen Professor of Economics at the University of Virginia, Charlottesville, and a fellow at the American Enterprise Institute.
Mr. Stein was a member of the President's Council of Economic Advisers from 1969 to 1974 and served as its chairman from 1971 to 1974.
Mr. Stein is a member of the Board of Contributors of the *Wall Street Journal*, and he also writes a weekly column, "The Economy Today," which appears in the Scripps-Howard newspapers. At the American Enterprise Institute, Mr. Stein is editor of the monthly newsletter *The AEI Economist*, and contributes to the institute's annual volume, *Contemporary Economic Problems*.
Mr. Stein's books include: *Jobs and Markets* (1946); *The Fiscal Revolution in America* (1969); *Economic Planning and the Improvement of Public Policy* (1975); *The Economic System in an Age of Discontinuity* (1976); *On the Brink* (1977); and *Money Power* (1980). Mr. Stein received his Ph.D. from the University of Chicago in 1958.

PHYLLIS A. WALLACE is a professor at the Massachusetts Institute of Technology's Sloan School of Management.
She serves as a director of State Street Bank and Trust Company, Stop and Shop, the Boston Museum of Fine Arts, and the Manpower Demonstration Research Corporation. Ms. Wallace is also a trustee of the Brookings Institution.
Ms. Wallace has served as an economist and statistician at the National Bureau of Economic Research, the Equal Employment Opportunity Commission, and in other government posts.

GEORGE F. WILL is an editor and political columnist for the *Washington Post* and a regular columnist for *Newsweek*. He was the recipient of the Pulitzer Prize for Commentary in 1977, and named a Young Leader by *American Time* magazine in 1974.
Mr. Will has taught politics at several universities including Michigan State University, the University of Illinois, and the University of Toronto.
Mr. Will has published *The Pursuit of Happiness, and Other Sobering Thoughts*, a collection of columns.
Mr. Will was educated at Trinity College (Oxford University) in England and at Princeton University.

Introduction

What is the future of private enterprise in our nation and in the world? For the first time since the Great Depression, private enterprise is on the public agenda, being examined as a means by which to solve some of American society's most difficult problems—jobs, productivity, urban poverty, the high costs of health, and even peaceful international interdependence. Public opinion now seems more open to free market operations as an answer to tough questions. Entrepreneurship, competition, incentives, savings, sacrifice, and investment are seen by many as prescriptions for better personal and societal futures.

The enthusiasm for private enterprise is fragile. The public at large is not well informed of the economic complexities, social implications, or philosophical strength of any political-economic system. The current appeal of private enterprise lies mostly in rejection of, or dissatisfaction with, other approaches to governance and growth. Students—the opinion leaders of tomorrow—embrace private enterprise on pragmatic grounds as they seek jobs and livelihoods. Their grasp of the economics and philosophy of private enterprise remains questionable.

Students, in particular, and many other elements of society still need a more solid understanding of how and why private enterprise works if they are to effectively evaluate complex policy alternatives. Private enterprise and its advocates themselves require a positive theory—beyond economic efficiency—of the benefits of free enterprise. What is it that is special about private enterprise? Why can it be expected to meet the challenges of the future?

As a collection of essays, the book's approach is necessarily eclectic. Still, we have made every effort to produce a thematically cohesive volume that explores fundamental challenges to private enterprise as a way of life. The book has been rigorously edited, so that it is a highly readable collection of twenty-three carefully selected lectures by the most current and stimulating thinkers on the future of private enterprise society. These lectures have stood the tests of being well received by large audiences of economic lay people and, at the same time, have been endorsed by academic scholars. The book includes the thinking of three business chief executive officers, three past chairmen of the President's Council of Economic Advisers, a former president of the United States, the prime minister of a developing country, several journalists, and many leading economists. It is our hope this book will be useful to business, government, and professional leaders who are called on to explain private enterprise to others. It also serves as an excellent collection of readings for students of free market economics. Libraries will find the book a valuable reference to the ideas of twenty-four acknowledged, articulate leaders of private enterprise thought.

The greatest challenge to the future of private enterprise is to justify and rationalize its strengths and weaknesses relative to social and moral values and the ideals of political democracy. How can an impersonal economic system governed by a money-driven free market mechanism be consistent with other, well-accepted social traditions and norms? The first section of the book presents several papers relating free enterprise as a business and managerial system to philosophical goals.

The second section of the book deals with the effectiveness of free markets—the backbone of our private enterprise system. Two papers give a historical background and summary of our free market experience to date, information rarely found in any book on current economics. Then, some of our nation's leading economists explain free market solutions to current problems.

The third section of the book explores the appropriate roles for government, business, and labor in seeking solutions to societal and global problems. These papers acknowledge the importance of government and labor participation in our economy and politics, but reserve for business leadership the greatest responsibility for preserving and extending private enterprise. Business management, it is suggested, must aggressively direct its own enterprises in ways that provide fewer reasons for government intervention or solutions.

The fourth section of the book addresses five specific, but timely, challenges to private enterprise. These essays show how private enterprise can significantly contribute to the resolutions of the problems of retirement security, employment security, welfare, public land management, and urban decay.

The fifth and concluding section of the book presents hopeful arguments that the basic strengths of private enterprise, political democracy, and the American people create the resiliency and capability needed to cope with both broad and unforeseen challenges for the future. Competition, decentralization, and the selfless heritage of our people combine for a powerful reservoir of vitality. The book ends with an exciting scenario of growth, low inflation, and improved unemployment for the decade ahead.

SECTION I
Toward a Philosophy of Private Enterprise

Don't bother me with theory! I'll leave that to the philosophers! Get to the bottom line! The practitioners of private enterprise have had little desire and have seen little need for philosophy or theory.

This lack of philosophical perspective is at the root of the difficulty faced by those who seek to defend private enterprise or to transfer its meaning across the generations. Perhaps the greatest challenge facing private enterprise is to justify and rationalize its strengths and weaknesses in cultural and moral terms. We must seriously deal with questions like: How can an impersonal economic system governed by a money-driven, free-market mechanism be consistent with accepted social traditions like compassion and equality? What are the appropriate relationships between political, economic, and cultural institutions?

While none of the authors in this section provide final answers, they do provide perspectives and insights that carry us forward "Toward A Philosophy of Private Enterprise," the basis of private enterprise's future.

Theologian Michael Novak seeks the basis for democratic capitalism in Judeo-Christian tradition by exploring relationships between political, economic, and cultural aspects of the social order. Social commentator Irving Kristol further explores the relationship between cultural and economic institutions, seeking a means to make capitalistic theory as attractive as its reality.

Hillsdale College President George Roche is optimistic. He believes America's second major idea revolution will be centered on the notion of individual freedom.

Former Quaker Oats President Kenneth Mason takes a philosophical view of the corporation, which he considers the central institution in American society. Mason takes a new look at the proverbial "bottom line" and redefines it as "return on assets employed." Then he explores the meaning of this perspective.

Finally, political scholar James Buchanan suggests a way to put philosophy into practice through constitutional reform. His premise is that only constitutional protection can safeguard the competitive economy against political manipulation.

Does the democratic capitalism of the United States have a basis in Jewish and Christian intellectual traditions? That is the fundamental question raised by MICHAEL NOVAK *in "The Judeo-Christian Values That Characterize Economic Freedoms." To answer the question, he explores the relationships between the three fundamental aspects of social order: political, economic, and moral-cultural.*

Novak maintains that few themes are more common in Western intellectual history than the denigration of capitalism, in part because it lacks a moral theory. Philosophers and theologians have yet to study the real experience of capitalism with the close attention that it deserves. Novak is one who begins to correct this deficiency.

1

The Judeo-Christian Values That Characterize Economic Freedoms

MICHAEL NOVAK

You are advancing in the night, bearing torches toward which mankind would be glad to turn; but you leave them enveloped in the fog of a merely experiential approach and mere practical conceptualization, with no universal ideas to communicate. For lack of an adequate ideology, your lights cannot be seen.
—Jacques Maritain, *Reflections on America*[1]

What is our nation's vision? What is its philosophy—its theology, even? The question applies to all Americans, to the nation as a whole, and to both major political parties. Many concede that the ideas dominating discourse for the past half-century are tired. It is not useful in any case to be merely nostalgic. The proper question concerns the future. By what ideal of political economy ought the United States manage its internal affairs and commend its vision to the world?

The language of vision and ideals is inherently philosophical and theological. When anyone asks, "Who am I?" or "Who are we? What may we hope? What ought we to do?" such a person appeals to a broad framework of understanding—to a symbolic picture of the world, history, and meaning. Some will understand such symbols in language that is assiduously secular and agnostic. We may call such a symbolic language philosophical. Others will understand such symbols in languages inherited from religious traditions. We may call such symbolic languages theological. Questions of fundamental symbols and meanings, in any case, nearly always stimulate religious persons and religious institutions, and provoke even secular persons into modes of thinking that are at least analogous to religious modes. Such questions

---

Portions of this paper are based on Michael Novak's "The Economic System: The Evangelical Basis of a Social Market Economy," *The Review of Politics*, 43 (July 1981), 355-380.

soon involve public policy in religion and religion in public policy.

It is no wonder, then, that one of the striking features of public policy discourse during recent years has been the increased prominence of religion. Iran has been convulsed by an Islamic revolution. The role of "liberation theologians" in Nicaragua and elsewhere in Latin America has been widely noticed. Religious leaders of the American left—long active in the antiwar movement—once again became visible in highly publicized trips to Iran. Religious leaders of the center and right have slowly learned to imitate the tactics, organizing efforts, and public relations maneuvers of the religious left. The Institute for Policy Studies, the Center of Concern, the Interfaith Center for Corporate Responsibility, and many other institutes provide literature, speakers, and, in some cases, organizing efforts in religious communities throughout the land. Because the various churches have organizational capabilities, buildings, regular meetings of various sorts, and a sort of innocent credibility, organizers on behalf of virtually every possible public policy idea have richly targeted the churches as instruments of rapid dissemination. Lobbies of every sort have appeared, and newsletters proliferate. The churches are in a maelstrom of ideological struggle.[2]

Whether or not this is good for the churches, these developments have certainly affected both the course of public policy and the ways in which public policy must be addressed.

In one sense, all these activities cast doubt upon widely held theories of "secularization." The discovery of the churches as effective mediators suggests their enormous vitality and potential.[3] Far from disappearing, religious impulses and institutions seem to be at least as active as any others in modern society. But there is a second type of "secularization." Some critics believe that the churches are abandoning their primary concern about the life of the spirit in order to become political action groups of a character rather more ideological than religious.[4] The churches, these critics hold, are being secularized internally, even while becoming more active in the world. Earlier theories of secularization held that religious institutions may be failing, while religious vitalities are becoming "privatized." The later theory holds that religious institutions are remarkably vital, while their internal vitalities are becoming secular.

For what remains of the twentieth century, we need some guidance about the religious component of public policy. This paper, then, seeks vision. It also seeks theory—but with a practical purpose. The question to be addressed is this: Does the political economy of the United States—democratic capitalism and, more particularly, its economic component—have a basis in Jewish and Christian intellectual traditions? May its vision and theory be expressed in religious terms and, accordingly, its present practices brought under apposite judgment? The subject is vast and no one paper can adequately cover the topic. My task will be to inspire—and to focus—a fruitful competition of ideas. Each of the following sections is designed to bring to light an important problem.

Deficiencies of Intellect

Naturally enough, writers tend to write for readers. At higher levels of theory there is, then, a largely unconscious bias toward events and movements that occur within the fairly specific culture of those who read—the intellectuals and their immediate public. For the sake of simplicity, we may note that magazines like *Time* and *Newsweek* reach approximately one out of ten Americans (about 22 million); magazines like *Harper's* and *The Atlantic* about 400,000; journals like *Commentary, The New York Review of Books*, and *The New Republic* about 100,000; and journals like *Commonweal, Christian Century, Christianity Today*, and many others fewer than 50,000. Perhaps it is legitimate to speak of a rather highly educated, literate "culture" that represents only a fraction of American culture. The gap between this culture and the rest of the culture is frequently a matter of concern, always implicit and often explicit, in the pages of such journals.

It is not an exaggeration to hold that this literary culture tends to use an idiom rather more national, nondenominational, ecumenical, and secular than that of specific regional or religious cultures like those in which most Americans daily live. It seems accurate to hold that secularization is more pronounced within this literary culture than outside it; that many ordinary citizens spontaneously employ the particularities of native religious idioms of their upbringing; and that a certain sophistication is required even to comprehend, let alone to be in tune with, the preoccupations, passions, and interests of the literary culture. Not only is a mastery of a body of written materials and intellectual-verbal skills required, but also a training of sensibility. Certain forms of speech or sensibility may easily reveal a novice to be uninformed, unenlightened, and unsophisticated. One needs a sufficiently "raised consciousness" if one is to give "no offense."[5]

In *The Socialist Phenomenon*, Igor Shafarevich observes that the dominant form of the religious imagination in the twentieth century is the socialist dream, which his friend Aleksandr I. Solzhenitsyn describes as "a vague, rosy notion of something noble and good, of equality, communal ownership, and justice; the advent of these things will bring instant euphoria and a social order beyond reproach."[6] Socialism is the oldest and most common way of organizing society: "The majority of states in the history of mankind have been 'socialist.' "[7] In talking or thinking about religion and public policy, therefore, one inevitably finds that two concepts more than any others operate like magnetic forces attracting to themselves all other concepts and words, setting up a field of meanings. One of these concepts is "socialism," more commonly in the West, "democratic socialism." This concept has been voluminously studied by legions of thinkers, propagandists, and activists; books upon it number in the thousands. The other concept has been virtually shunned by religious thinkers, philosophers, and humanists; most of those who treat it have been economists. I call that concept "democratic capitalism," by which is meant a triple system of liberty: economic liberty, political liberty, and liberty of spirit. Only a handful of nations in history have found their way to a threefold system—an economic system, a political system, and a moral-cultural system—that institutionalizes such liberties.

In applying religious thought to public policy, religious thinkers unavoidably draw upon political and economic *ideas* and necessarily have in mind some *ideal* political economy. It is in this way that the ideal of socialism most powerfully exerts its—often unconscious—attraction. By contrast, the inadequate statement of the ideal of democratic capitalism, so long neglected by theologians, philosophers, and humanists, leaves a symbolic vacuum. The power of myth, symbol, and narrative appears, by default, to lie with socialism.

No task is more fundamental than the formation of a vision for the future. Such a vision must, of necessity, deal with the alternative dreams: the dream of socialism and the dream of democratic capitalism. Each of these dreams suggests a quite different practical future. During recent decades, American public policy thinkers have tried to avoid ideology. They have tried not to argue about vision or metaphysics. This deliberate neglect has some practical advantages. It enables one to concentrate upon immediate practical tasks, to be concrete, to compromise, and to work with a certain flexibility. But such deliberate neglect also has costs. It abandons to the partisans of socialism the entire battlefield of ideas, symbols, dreams, and appeals to the human spirit. The war of ideas on the international level degenerates, in that case, into a kind of universal, uncritical "vulgar Marxism."[8] The process of "semantic infiltration" affects entire institutions such as the United Nations, the international institutions of the churches, the press, and all conventional thinking.[9]

In such a climate, clear thinking is not possible. Yet to think clearly is the first moral obligation of human beings. Unless that duty is acquitted, choice is blind.

I wish to argue, then, that the government and public of the United States are obliged by present international circumstances to modify their long tradition of mere practicality in order to clarify alternative philosophies—and theologies—of public policy. In particular, we need to overcome our present ignorance about the ideals of democratic capitalism. For our own system embodies—although now in a largely unreflected way—our own most original contribution to human intellectual history. We need to be able to distinguish these ideals from the quite different ideals of democratic socialism. We need to do so both for our own morale and for guidance in practical perplexities. We need to do so because these ideals belong also to all others of the human race who would choose to realize the fruits of liberty. Liberty such as ours is not solely a goal, but also a means. It does not come after plenty. It is a means of achieving plenty. The system was intended to embody ideals open to all.

I propose to proceed rather modestly, by concentrating on one significant Christian thinker in the field of public policy, the one-time French ambassador and architect of the United Nations Declaration of Human Rights, the author of *Integral Humanism, Man and the State* and other profound works, Jacques Maritain.

Maritain: The Need for Theory

> The industrial regime inherited from Europe has now become unrecognizable in this country. It has been superseded by new economic structures which are still in the making, and in a state of fluidity, but which render both capitalism and socialism things of the past. Free enterprise and private ownership function now in a social context and a general mood entirely different from those of the nineteenth century.[10]
> —Jacques Maritain, *Reflections on America*

The world is entering yet another age of economics. Virtually all the major problems that preoccupy governments today are economic problems—employment and inflation, problems of growth and limits, food and fuel, productivity and expanding populations, development and justice. The official documents of the churches since *Rerum Novarum* (1891) seem more and more preoccupied with economics. Yet there is hardly a less developed area in the tradition of Christian thought, whether in philosophy or in theology, than the relation of Christianity to economics.

Only rather late in Christian history, in fact, did there develop an exposition of the evangelical roots of democracy. In his little classic *Christianity and Democracy* (1948), Jacques Maritain has shown once and for all the consonance between democracy and Christianity.[11] He showed how Judeo-Christian conceptions of the individual, the community, and sin led over time to the state of mind and practice—to the *ethos*—that made the recognition of the inalienable rights of individuals practicable in the worldly polity. Thus, in that book, Maritain dealt with two of the three fundamental and coordinate systems of a modern, fully differentiated society: its political system and its moral-cultural system. At that stage of his development he was not ready to deal with the third significant system, the economic system. Since the most grievous problems in the governability of democracies today appear to arise in the economic system, it seems necessary to carry Maritain's thought further at precisely this point. We may well be encouraged by Maritain's brief but penetrating chapter on the transformation of capitalism in *Reflections on America*.[12]

In his earlier period, Maritain had asked about the political systems with which Christianity is compatible. Specifically, he asked whether democracy is a natural expression of the Christian ethos. By analogy, we must ask with which economic systems Christianity is compatible. Specifically, we must ask whether an economic system based upon markets and personal incentives is a natural expression of the Christian ethos. We may also ask a further question. With which economic systems is *democracy* compatible? Is capitalism the natural economic expression of a democratic polity?

Implicit in these questions is a three-part concept of social order. This three-part social order makes democratic systems different from all traditional and socialist societies. In traditional and nondemocratic socialist societies,[13] the social order is unitary. One authority is granted powers over political, economic, and moral-cultural matters. In fully differentiated societies, these three systems are kept distinct, autonomous, and interdependent but separate. So our underlying question has a very general nature first. Is it a natural expression of the Judeo-Christian tradition that a society ought to be differentiated into three united and yet distinct systems? As I have shown in my book *The Spirit of Democratic Capitalism*, my purpose here is to inquire into the biblical roots of but one of the three systems: the economic system.[14] Does an economic system based upon markets and incentives have biblical roots?

In my own intellectual life, as in that of Maritain, I was early led to believe that democratic socialism or social democracy was more in tune with Judaism and Christianity, at least in the order of ideals, than capitalism. Few themes are more common in Western intellectual history than the denigration of capitalism.[15] Among "the despised and abject" things of this world (Isaiah 53), capitalism ranks high. There are multiple reasons why this is so. First of all, capitalism has many faults, distortions, and ill effects (as do all rival systems). Secondly, as Maritain has pointed out,[16] it lacks a theory, in particular a moral theory. Its theory has been left predominantly to economists, whose professional concerns lie less with the political system and the moral-cultural system than with the economic system alone. Even there, economists tend to overlook the political and moral-cultural dimensions of economic realities, confining themselves as narrowly as they can to economic dimensions. In abstraction, such a narrow focus may be useful. In real life, it distorts understanding. In practice, capitalism has political and moral-cultural dimensions of greater intellectual significance than any existing theories about it have articulated. Philosophers and theologians have yet to study capitalism with the close attention to real experience that it deserves.

In the third place, the intellectual history of capitalist ideas suffers from two internal flaws and sources of distortion. Unfortunately, the theory of capitalism was first developed in the Anglo-Saxon intellectual context of individualism and utilitarianism. In some ways, this context was favorable to economists. But it led to serious misunderstandings among humanists. The distinctive social organism produced by capitalism is not individualistic at all. It is a corporate organism, the business corporation. In addition, the inherent motive of capitalism as a system is not the well-being of the individual. It is the well-being of the entire human race. This underlying motive is expressed in the title of the most important document in the history of capitalism, Adam Smith's *An Inquiry into the Nature and Causes of the Wealth of Nations* (1776). As its title plainly states, its intention goes far beyond the question of individuals, beyond the question of Scotland or Great Britain; it aims to assist all nations. Adam Smith is the inventor of the idea of sustained economic development. His point of view embraced the entire world in all its cultures. His book on the economic system must, moreover, be read in the context of his earlier book on the moral-cultural system, *The Theory of Moral Sentiments* (1769), and his work on the political system which he left unfinished at his death. The three dimensions of intention were present from the beginning.[17]

Regrettably, the tradition of individualism and utilitarianism in Great Britain prevented these larger perspectives from becoming better known. Capitalism grew up together with democracy in Great Britain and the United States, in an ethos heavily saturated in a Judeo-Christian, pluralistic, humanistic moral-cultural system. Its practice was, therefore, more complex and far richer than the individualist, utilitarian theory in which it was embedded. In addition, after 1870, the ignominious tradition of Social Darwinism—"the survival of the fittest"—did immeasurable damage to the theory of capitalism. It was the transformation of capitalism beyond the bounds of individualism, utilitarianism, and Social Darwinism, in fact, that so surprised Maritain in America and arrested his attention. In practice, capitalism is not what these early cocoons in which it was embedded had led him to believe that it is. It is a practice in search of an accurate theory. Maritain appealed urgently for such a theory. Yet, aside from a few brief notes, he did little to supply it. One may note a similar evolution in the thinking of the great American theologian, Reinhold Niebuhr.[18] It will be the task of our generation to carry these tentative beginnings to fruition in a theory worthy of the actual practice. Then, in that light, reformers may lead the system to a larger fulfillment of its own dreams of liberty, equality, and justice.

Consider, first, the economic system.

The Economic System

It is a typical mistake to think of capitalism as merely an economic system. Analogously, it is a typical mistake to think of an economic system apart from its *political* and *moral-cultural* dimension. In actual life, each one of us is an economic agent. But each is also a citizen. And each of us seeks God, and follows conscience and the pursuit of truth and understanding. Human beings are simultaneously economic animals, political animals, moral-cultural animals. On the other hand, it is often useful, in Maritain's phrase, *distinguer pour unir*, to distinquish in order to unite. This is true for intellectual inquiry, in which one must proceed step by step; one cannot do everything at once.

It is also true in the proper organization of concrete social life. One of the great discoveries of modernity is the possibility—even the necessity—of differentiation in social institutions. It is a social *good* to practice a certain separation of church and state; to empower a free press, to maintain universities free from state control: that is to say, to differentiate the *political system* from the *moral-cultural system*—to allow each a certain autonomy, while recognizing that each system in a sense depends upon the other. In the same way, it was an important social good when human beings began to separate the economy from state controls and to protect the state from control by economic interests. It is as important to separate the *economic system* from the state as to separate the church (and other moral-cultural institutions) from the state. Like the political system and the moral-cultural system, the economic system, too, is entitled to a certain autonomy, even while we must recognize that it, too, depends upon the other two systems, as they depend upon it. It is good for human beings to have a trinity of systems, each distinct from the other two even when united with them to form a single social order.

Each of these three systems has its own institutions, rituals, procedures, social base, and social strength. Each has characteristic tendencies, ambitions, achievements, and distortions. Each for its own well-being requires the health of the other two. Each requires a certain balance and coordination with the other two. Each has a tendency to seek its own aggrandizement at the expense of the other two. Each needs to be watched closely—and checked—by the other two.

It is sometimes pointed out that a healthy democratic polity depends upon the *separation of powers* (executive, legislative, and judicial). Analogously, a healthy and fully differentiated social order depends upon the *separation of systems* (political, economic, and moral-cultural). As it happens, different personality types are commonly attracted to each of these different systems. In this way, each type develops, as it were, a psychological interest in checking the other two, a kind of native suspicion and hostility to the type of persons involved in the other two. Thus, it often happens that poets, priests, philosophers, and literary intellectuals cherish excess of admiration for neither men of commerce and industry nor for politicians; the reverse is also true.

In a healthy society, then, there are three different routes along which the will-to-power may be exercised. Some individuals move to the top of the economic system; a different type (generally speaking) to the top of the political system; and a third type (again generally speaking) to the top of the moral-cultural system. It is a rare human being, indeed, who moves comfortably in all three spheres. This systematic diffusion of the will-to-power is accomplished, in the long run, for the good of society. Each type of person, summoning up the powers of his or her own sphere of accomplishment, has both external and psychological interests in preventing persons of other types, representing other bases of power, from wholly dominating society. History affords many sad examples of domination by one sector only. The case of Iran under the Ayatollah Khomeini and the mullahs is a recent instance. Domination by emperors, popes, and ideological parties in other times and places are other instances. The differentiation of systems is intended to prevent such unitary domination, through the checks and balances of the three relatively autonomous systems.

No thinker has been as clear about these structural distinctions as Daniel Bell who, in his major studies *The Coming of Post-Industrial Society* (1973) and *The Cultural Contradictions of Capitalism* (1976), has decisively broken with all merely unitary or holistic schemes of social theory.[19] Human life, Bell notes, cannot be understood merely within a single scheme or on a single plane. Three quite different systems, operating with different rhythms and in different frames of time, affect every human being. Our economic system is focused along an axis of *utilitarian or functional* rationality. Our political system, according to Bell, has now come to be focused along an axis of *equality* and *entitlements* (often group entitlements). Our cultural system is focused along the axis of the *self*. From Bell's point of view, it is an error to try to think of social systems along one of these axes only. Furthermore, each of these axes points in a rather different direction from the other two. For both society as a whole and for individuals, therefore, they are fraught with "contradictions." Each axis in some respects contradicts and frustrates the other two. On a daily basis individuals are pulled first one way, then another, by the contradictory demands of the three systems within which all live. The search for self-fulfillment is not easily conducted when one's attention must be fixed upon the functional tasks of one's economic position. Nor can a political system concerned with equality and entitlements easily be reconciled with the imperatives of economic rationality, or even with the manifest differences in the personality, efforts, desires, and demands of each individual.

There are many questions to be raised about the exactness of Bell's definitions and concepts. I have several important criticisms to make of particular points. Yet for our present purposes his scheme is quite helpful. For Bell stresses the different "rhythms" and time-spans involved in each of these axial imperatives. At times, the imperatives of self-discovery and self-fulfillment are instant, spontaneous, and immediate. In another sense, they span an entire lifetime and occupy those many private and personal hours of the day on which the political system and the economic system make relatively little, if any, impact. The time horizon within which political leaders work (in democracies, at least) is notoriously different from the time-span of industry and commerce. Politicians are tempted to seek immediate benefits, whose costs other politicians in later administrations may have to pay. The question politicians are regularly asked by voters is "What have you done for me lately?" The demands made by economic systems often cut across personal desires and inclinations and respond poorly, if at all, to political manipulation. The three axial systems, in other words, affect individuals in different ways.

One essential point may be drawn from these reflections. No economic system represents the whole of life. An economic system may be as autonomous as the moral-cultural system and enjoy its own proper liberty and separation from the state. Still, the individuals who work within it are subject to imperatives that arise from axial principles, whose origin lies outside the economic system itself. They are subject to imperatives arising from political life and to others arising from moral-cultural life. There is really no such thing as "economic man." No economic system lives (or can live) in a vacuum apart from a political system and moral-cultural system. When we speak of an economic system, therefore, we must take pains to speak of its concrete, living connections with the political system and the moral-cultural system in which it is embedded.

In this respect, one cannot speak of capitalism solely as an economic system. Historically (and inherently) it grows up in concert with the imperatives of a democratic polity. Its own imperatives are not identical to the axial principles of democracy. Yet the two feed upon and require each other in fascinating ways. Similarly, as Max Weber pointed out, the rise of capitalism is inconceivable apart from the power of a specific moral-cultural system, an *ethos* that gives it shape, meaning, and motivating force. One may disagree with Weber's exact diagnosis of that *ethos*; it was, clearly, far less Protestant, far less Calvinist than he thought.[20] But he is surely right in seeing that buying and selling, which are immemorial economic activities as ancient as the Mediterranean civilizations and the desert caravans of biblical times, did not constitute capitalism until a specific moral-cultural system had reached a certain level of development. An economic system must always be studied in conjunction with the political system and the moral-cultural system in which it is embedded.

Let us concentrate upon the interplay between an economic system based on markets and incentives and a moral-cultural system based on Judeo-Christian understandings of liberty, the individual, the community, sin, and the like. Throughout history, most economic systems were relatively stagnant. Few showed sustained growth. All experienced cycles of prosperity and famine. The very concept of sustained economic development was lacking. The figure of the miser represented a certain quintessential evil, for in a no-growth economy anyone who hoarded gold or other goods subtracted from the common store. In order for sustained economic development to become possible (or even conceivable), individuals needed to believe that they could alter the future—and indeed, had an obligation to do so. The techniques for releasing their economic activism needed to be invented. The formation of a new economic system depended on changes in the moral-cultural system. Individuals had to begin to believe that they could improve their own economic position. They needed liberty. They needed law and stability. They needed patterns of social cooperation. They needed systems of long-term accounting. They needed new institutions in which risks could be shared and enterprises larger than those sustainable by single individuals might be launched. They needed to be willing to defer present gratification, to invest, and to labor for the sake of future rewards. They needed to concentrate on small savings and small gains, cumulatively recorded. Many parables in the gospels express some of the required attitudes of good and wise stewardship (even while pointing out that Christianity, as a more than this-worldly religion, imposes still more stringent axes of judgment). Sustained economic development, therefore, rests decisively upon moral-cultural values of certain sorts.[21]

In some ways, then, economic systems are dependent on moral-cultural systems. Where certain attitudes, habits, beliefs, aspirations, and exertions are lacking, economic development is unlikely to occur. Inversely, even among peoples who lack material resources or favorable natural conditions, strong moral-cultural traditions of certain sorts may give rise to amazing economic development. To some extent, such phenomena have appeared in Japan, Hong Kong, Taiwan, and elsewhere. The ethos of particular peoples is of exceeding—perhaps primary—economic significance.

On the other hand, economic systems impose demands on moral-cultural systems. At times, cherished magic, taboos, beliefs, customs, and attitudes must be set aside, or else an economic system of the modern, developing sort simply cannot take root. An economic system is necessarily a teacher and reinforcer of some moral virtues, and utterly dependent on the strength and vitality of others. Where monetary dishonesty, bribery, and corruption are a way of life—where even economic reporting and accounting are unreliable—economic systems are penalized as they are not where opposite qualities are more common. (Such virtues are never perfectly and universally practiced.) Where individuals lack the initiative or the talent for self-starting enterprise, the economic situation is quite different from one in which opposite talents frequently appear. Moral-cultural systems are not equal. Economic systems are much affected by such variations. The axial imperatives of a new form of economic system often evoke cultural resistance from those who live by other imperatives.

Thus economic systems are not *merely* instrumental. They carry some moral imperatives of their own, and these are often rather different from those which prevail in the moral-cultural institutions to which they are joined. Some philosophers or theologians tend to think that the moral-cultural system defines the kingdom of ends, while economic systems play a lowly instrumental role in the kingdom of means. This is not quite true. An economic system, too, necessarily incarnates certain goals and purposes. These goals and purposes are not merely materialistic. Thus, a people that would choose as one of its social goals sustained economic growth is choosing not solely an increase in the abundance of material goods but also a set of moral disciplines, habits, and activities—a way of life. Such a way of life may have among its specifications a love for liberty, for noble behavior, for highly developed character, for justice and compassion, and the like. The economic system of the Greek city state, for example, had among its purposes, at least for its elites, such ideals as Aristotle set forth in the *Nicomachean Ethics*. Some analogous qualities are compatible with an economic system of sustained economic growth; some are not. Sustained economic growth does not consist solely in material abundance; it springs from and it continues to demand the exercise of moral character of certain sorts. Should such character disappear, so would sustained economic growth. A hedonistic, narcissistic culture is not likely to invest in its own future or to make the necessary sacrifices for its own posterity.

There is a further matter. From the point of view of the concrete individual, one's participation in an economic system does not exhaust the whole of one's life nor is it merely a means to an end. Work is not merely a means for "making a living." Work is in itself a mode of living, and may even be a mode of praying. I have worked at many menial jobs, including mass-production jobs and tedious farm jobs. Every sort of job takes something out of you. One's substance passes into it. The job affects one's being. Much is written about the alienation in modern work, capitalist or socialist. More ought to be written about the alienation in *every* form of work (writing a paper, for example) and, also, about the contribution of every form of work to one's own being. Many writers suggest that not having any work is even worse than having alienating work. Philosophers, theologians, and others need to grasp the extent to which working is living, and hence not merely a means. On the other hand, work is not the whole of life. No human is defined by his or her economic activities alone.

A similar point must be made with regard to wealth. Wealth is neither an end in itself nor solely a means. The medieval maxim runs: *Radix malorum cupiditas*. This maxim blames *cupiditas*, not money. By contrast, the modern version runs: "*Money* is the root of all evil." The latter version is not true to experience. Power also corrupts. The roots of evil cannot really be said to lie in money. Man is seldom so innocently occupied, Samuel Johnson has written, as in the getting of money. Indeed, the moral meaning of wealth lies not in its *possession* but in its *use*, in the passions and interests it serves. To have wealth is to exercise a more ample liberty than is available without it. One's moral hazards are thereby magnified. ("It is easier for a camel to pass through the eye of a needle than for a rich man to enter into the kingdom of heaven.") To use wealth wisely and well may be to make of it a moral good, but to use it badly is to call down on oneself harsh moral condemnation. Neither poverty nor wealth guarantees virtue; neither suffices for salvation. The wealthy, however, acquire moral obligations toward the poor that are asymmetrical; they have greater obligations than the poor. On the other hand, wealth is in itself a good of liberty, which it much enlarges. "The wealth of nations" is to be esteemed, not for its own sake, but for the misery it may alleviate and for the liberties it may enlarge.

Thus, economic systems are properly to be judged not only in light of how much wealth they produce, although that is in itself good, but also in light of *how* their wealth is *used*. There are not an infinite number of economic systems in the historical experience of the human race, but a few: slavery, barter, trade, feudalism, mercantilism, capitalism, socialism, communism. Alternatively, one may speak of economies based on hunting, fishing, agriculture, land, exchange, industry, state control, intellect, services, and other characteristics of this sort. History may reveal new forms of economic life, as it often has. But we should not become bemused by fantasies of limitless possibility. The ways are relatively straight and few—as compared, for example, to languages and cultures.

Who can doubt that the major field of interest for governments and peoples today lies in this relatively narrow sphere of economics? Between 1900 and 1950, the population of the world doubled. Since 1950, it has doubled yet again. This planet must now be made to yield more food, clothing, building materials, medicines, school books, and all the other necessities of our complex life than ever before in history. The primary problem facing the human race is one of production, but it is followed by problems of distribution, scarcity, and, in certain directions, limits. Yet we must not lose sight of the preeminence of the problem of production, even if our moral purpose is distributive.

From ancient times, the primary emphasis in philosophical and religious thought has fallen on *distributive justice*. The problem of *productive justice* was understandably neglected, even though it has obvious priority, both logically and in reality. This truth did not acquire force until Adam Smith invented the theory of sustained economic development. Once it is shown that human beings with intelligence, organization, and effort have the capacity to unlock riches of creation never imagined by the ancients—oil, chemicals, alloys, foods, even the silicon of the sands of the sea—and once it is clear that millions (indeed, billions) of persons remain in need, then (and only then) does the responsibility to produce what can be produced become a clear moral imperative. Thus, only in modern times has the moral imperative of production come to precede the moral imperative of distribution and to be grasped as its necessary precondition. In the centuries before 1800, a famine occurred, on the average, once every fifteen years, and the earth supported only 890 million persons.[22] Today, enough is known to make famines unnecessary. They are no longer God's responsibility, but man's.

Governments can govern only insofar as they meet the material needs of their peoples. Given the new historical possibilities, the economic policies of governments will be rejected if their peoples cannot glimpse the real probability of a future better than the past. Governments depend on the productivity of their economic systems. The promise of democracy depends on high levels of economic productivity more than philosophers and theologians have recognized in the past.

What, then, have Christian philosophers and theologians to say about the available economic systems? There already exists a large body of Christian reflection on socialism, particularly in Latin America and in Europe. Ironically, even in the United States we already have a big book by a Jesuit, *Marxism: An American Christian Perspective* (1980),[23] but we do not yet have a single examination by a theologian or philosopher of democratic capitalism. Indeed, in *Reflections on America*, Jacques Maritain confessed his own biases against the images conjured up in his mind by the word capitalism. There is no denying that, rhetorically, it is easier to stand before the intellectual class as a socialist. In many circles, it is almost unforgivable to declare oneself to be in favor of capitalism. Yet this situation is odd. There are, as yet, no examples of socialist states becoming democratic. All existing democracies depend on substantial economic liberties. How can we properly defend democracy, if we overlook its inherent relationship to capitalism? How can democratic governments govern, unless they have a compatible economic vision?

It is not necessary for a people or a culture to be Jewish or Christian in order to develop a market economy. A market economy is inherently open to persons of every culture, faith, race, and philosophical point of view. It is altogether fitting that such a system should have been first invented and given spiritual legitimation under the impulse of the Old and New Testaments. Such a confluence of cultural currents occurred rather late in European history. It occurred first among the Erasmian Christians, both Catholic and Protestant, and among Jews and others described by Hugh Trevor-Roper.[24] It occurred in the visions of Adam Smith and James Madison.[25] It occurred gradually in the social systems of perhaps a dozen or a score of the nations on this planet. Jacques Maritain was the first to see the need for a new theory about the transformation of capitalism. Let us learn from him first.

Christianity and Democratic Capitalism

> The democratic impulse has arisen in human history as a temporal manifestation of the inspiration of the Gospel. The question does not deal here with Christianity as a religious creed and road to eternal

life, but rather with Christianity as leaven in the social and political life of nations and as bearer of the temporal hope of mankind . . . as historical energy at work in the world.[26]
—Jacques Maritain, *Christianity and Democracy*

Reflect on these words of Maritain. Cannot an analogous claim be made about capitalism—about *the economic system* based on respect for the rights of the individual, on markets, and on incentives? This is, after all, the economic system that grew up stride by stride alongside democracy in Great Britain, the United States, and then a score and more of other nations after 1776. To be sure, in the annals of social revolution, democracy has long carried a favorable reputation (so favorable that even the least democratic of nations insist on calling themselves by the name that most condemns them). By contrast, capitalism has almost everywhere been held in disdain.

When Maritain first came to America during World War II, he came with a European intellectual's negative judgments on capitalism. To him, capitalism connoted unchecked greed, atomistic individualism, and a merely mechanical view of human relations in the marketplace. The reality surprised him. Transformations must have occurred within the American economic system, he thought, during recent generations.[27] He described these as revolutionary. They startled him by their depth and scope. He believed that a "new reality" had appeared, for which there was as yet no suitable name or even an adequate theory.

In too many people's minds, Maritain noted, capitalism "stands for the primitive economic system of the nineteenth century." But something new had appeared. The new system, too, remained "imperfect, but always improving, and always capable of further improvement." In this new system, "men move forward together, working together, building together, producing always more and more, and sharing together the rewards of their increased production."[28]

"This new social and economic regime," Maritain wrote in 1958, "is still in a state of full becoming, but it has already brought human history beyond both capitalism and socialism." This "new social and economic regime is . . . a phenomenon which gives the lie to the forecasts of Karl Marx, and which came about not by virtue of some kind of inner necessity in the evolution of capitalism which Marx had overlooked, but by virtue of the freedom and spirit of man, namely by virtue of the American mind and conscience, and of the American collective effort of imagination and creation."[29]

Maritain had always been a great believer in human experience, in obscure ways of knowing, in "creative intuition," and in that wisdom which is barely if at all articulate in its profound workings. So it is not surprising that he was able to discern more at work in humble reality than anyone before him had discerned. He wrote: "Here we have a decisive fact in modern history; and this fact is a considerable success of the experiential approach dear to the American mind." He called the chapter in which his reflections on this theme unfolded "Too Much Modesty—The Need for an Explicit Philosophy," and was explicit: "But now I return to my point, namely to the need for an adequate ideology, or philosophy. And I ask: who in the world is aware of this decisive fact which we have just discussed?" He saw the necessity of a new name for this misunderstood system, and proposed, among others, "the new capitalism," "democratic capitalism," "economic democracy," "mutualism," "distributism," "productivism." He himself preferred "economic humanism," as a term "more pleasing to the ear, and more accurate." [30]

Let us assume for the moment that Maritain had his facts correct; that there has been, in fact, an inner transformation in the very nature of capitalism, not only in the United States but around the world. He traced the roots of this transformation to "the freedom and spirit of man" in "the American mind and conscience." But this "American" mind and conscience has profound Jewish and Christian roots. Despite its reputation for secularism, pollsters and scholars have long observed that the United States is perhaps the most religious country—in its practices and explicit attitudes—of any modern nation. Is democratic capitalism in its transformed state, then, like democracy itself, biblical in its roots? Democratic capitalism cannot be understood apart from an ethos of a specific sort; in some cultures of the world it would make no sense, could hardly be realized. A market economy may be as much an expression of the Judeo-Christian "historical energy" in the economic order as democracy is in the political order. Indeed, democracy itself may not be able to be realized apart from a market economy and personal incentives.

Until now, democratic socialists and social democrats have tried to capture the moral élan of democracy in order to steal it away for socialism. Socialism has many attractive moral qualities. But as the governing philosophy of a social system it has three grievous difficulties. First, it runs a very great risk of recreating the ancient patterns of state tyranny. Second, even in its democratic forms, it runs the risk of endowing collectivities, especially the best organized ones, with excessive power at the expense of individual liberties. (This is a real threat in all welfare democracies.) Third, paying too little attention both to markets and to incentives, it runs the risk of slowing productivity and raising the level of inefficiencies, thus reducing societies to a zero-sum game, in which factionalism and other forms of discontent multiply. Social democracy has had a relatively long period of trial in Western Europe. Its successes are many. Yet it has fallen short of the dreams of its founders. It can go forward toward socialist ideals only at great peril to its liberties. Are there not, then, other ideals? Is there no alternative to "democratic socialism"?

It seems intellectually useful and even urgent at the present time to look with fresh eyes at the experience of democratic capitalism.

Christian thinkers have for many years emphasized the connections between Christianity and democracy. But they have neglected the connections between Christianity and capitalism. Yet questions of economics are of urgent concern to governments today. What ought governments to expect of economic systems? How ought democracies to govern their economic systems? Above all, what have Christian ideas, values, and inspirations to say about economic systems?

It is important to note that capitalism and socialism are not symmetrical concepts. Under the theoretical framework of democratic capitalism, there are three distinct systems, each with its own autonomy and yet each also in part dependent upon the other two: an economic system, a political system, a moral-cultural system. By contrast, socialism is unitary. It tends to collapse these three systems into one. Socialism fuses the economic system and the political system into one, under the aegis of a single, collective moral-cultural system. Socialism is more like a religion or moral vision than capitalism is. Socialism proposes to produce the "new man" who will spring forth (like Venus from the sea) under "socialism with a human face." Capitalism has never been so morally pretentious. Morally, it has spoken of itself with what Maritain describes as excessive modesty. By and large, it has left moral visions to the poets, the philosophers, the archbishops. It thinks of itself as only one of three systems. These three systems are relatively autonomous. Each is *coordinate* with the other two. None is *subordinate* to the others.

In this respect, capitalism is not an alternative to democracy or to a Judeo-Christian culture. It is not so pretentious. It plays only one of three roles. It is compatible with democracy, on the one hand, and with the Judeo-Christian tradition, on the other. But it does not exhaust either the democratic or the Judeo-Christian ideal. The coalescence of all three systems into one unitary system, as in the socialist model, may at first seem to be in keeping with the Judeo-Christian ideal of social harmony and social unity. It certainly attracts a certain type of person. But unitary systems are especially vulnerable to tyranny, whether by a majority or by the seizure of collective powers by a small elite.

As has been shown earlier, a truly differentiated and fully humane social system is based upon the *separation of systems* (political, economic, moral-cultural). Democratic capitalism is such a system of systems. The warrant for this separation of systems is found in Judeo-Christian views of the nature of the individual, of social life, of history, and of sin.

Biblical Roots

Solzhenitsyn has argued that Western ideas of progress and revolution took a wrong turn at the time of the Enlightenment.[31] He attributes to secularism and to materialism modern beliefs in progress (especially material progress), the legalism of democratic life, the free press, the cult of the individual, narcissism, and other modern vices. He holds an ancient Russian Orthodox view of the sinfulness of human beings. In this view, dreams of progress are doomed never to come true. Solzhenitsyn places his trust in Christian virtue—in the power of such virtue in the lives of rulers and among whole peoples who follow in the ways of justice, charity, and peace. He seems at once too pessimistic and too optimistic.

One sympathizes with the great Solzhenitsyn's intentions. Yet his views on the relation of democracy and Christianity are not historically correct. As Maritain shows, it is not the Enlightenment which is the yeast that made the democratic idea grow. It is not the Enlightenment which, as Robert Nisbet has shown in the *The Idea of Progress*, taught the West that the future may be different from the past.[32] It is not the Enlightenment which instructed Adam Smith, James Madison, Thomas Jefferson, Benjamin Franklin, and others about the sinfulness of every human being. It is not the Enlightenment which counseled the invention of checks and balances against every form of tyranny, even the tyranny of "good" rulers, "benevolent" dictators, and "philosopher kings." It is not the Enlightenment which taught that one must not trust the virtue of the common people.

Without by any means intending to do so—exactly when trying not to do so—Solzhenitsyn, in wishing for a regime of virtuous Christian leaders, apart from democratic constraints, may be paving the path for a regime all too like that of the fabled Grand Inquisitor. Out of compassion for others, one may seek to make men virtuous by depriving them of liberty. There are too few protections in Solzhenitsyn's vision of the future to protect humankind against the tyranny of virtue.

Thus Solzhenitsyn, like many others, in seeking the true ground and origin of democracy, attributes too much to the Enlightenment, too little to Christianity. Yet, like democracy, capitalism grew out of specifically Judeo-Christian soil. Its preconceptions are also Judeo-Christian. Its ethos is in some substantial measure—but not entirely—Judeo-Christian. Its roots are in significant particulars biblical. Space is brief, but we may at least suggest a few themes for further study.

The Communitarian Individual—The corporation is the characteristic social invention of democratic capitalism in the economic sphere. The corporation is a social construct that springs, however, from individual initiative. Virtually every economic corporation of the present day is founded on an invention or, at least, on an organizing idea. In all cases, the idea originated in the mind of a single individual or a small team of individuals. Around this idea, such persons gathered colleagues, pooled investments, organized enterprises, and risked their resources. The risk was in every case a social risk. One individual alone would have been powerless. Founders of corporations necessarily rely on cooperation, trust, covenants, and compacts. Usually, the corporation is independent of the state. It is a collective of individuals who "incorporate themselves" and place at risk not public funds, but their own funds.

The history of the communitarian individual thus generated by the institutions of capitalism has not yet been written. Such an individual is a new social type. We are accustomed to think of such persons as "robber barons," thus imagining them to be like an *old* social type—that of the feudal aristocracy. We thus omit from consideration precisely what is new about them. When historians one day turn to examining the communitarian individual, however, they will have to turn to the emphasis that Adam Smith placed upon *benevolence, sympathy, fellow feeling,* and the spirit of *fair play* which he explored in his pregnant book, *The Theory of Moral Sentiments* (1759), which set the stage for his invention of the economics of development. The founder of a corporation does not, like a baron, rely on troops of his own enlisting. He does not seek military adventure or glory. He relies on persuasion, legal compacts, and the productivity of an idea in an economic enterprise.

The fundamental nature of capitalism as Adam Smith expressed it in the beginning, and as has been realized before our eyes since his time, is *not* "the wealth of individuals," or "the wealth of Great Britain," but "the wealth of nations"—*all* nations, without exception. The driving force of capitalism is social, indeed, universal. (Smith would have been cheered, one thinks, by the immense successes of Japan—and even of OPEC—since World War II, and by the "economic miracles" of Germany and Italy. The world has been transformed by the driving force he liberated.)

Moreover, capitalism proceeds even in particular localities only through the organizing of collaborative efforts. It is true that the ideas and initiatives of the individual are important. But the individual alone is not a corporation. Buying and selling are activities as ancient as the human race; they do not constitute capitalism. What constitutes capitalism is an organizing ethos, a corporate enterprise, a collective effort. Capitalism is far more social in character than its enemies—or its friends—have yet grasped. The growth of organized labor, of collective management, of profit-sharing and pension plans (the transformations that so struck Maritain) have been implicit in the ethos of capitalism from the beginning. It is true that these advances were won only through struggle, but so were many important victories in the history of Christianity and those of democracy, too. These victories could be won in relative peacefulness and with internal consistency, however, precisely because those characteristics are inherent in its inner logic. If, for example, a wage contract is conceived of as a voluntary exchange, both parties to it are entitled to renegotiate it constantly. The original historical weakness of the position of labor was bound, over time, to become a position of strength. The idea of "contract" remains intact as the contract becomes more favorable to labor, as well it ought. Future transformations in the relation of capital and labor are also likely.

The Social Nature of Man—British utilitarianism provided a limited intellectual framework for understanding the true import of capitalism. Social Darwinism, which followed utilitarianism by nearly three-quarters of a century, led understanding still futher astray. Nonetheless, the early conception of "economic man" was self-consciously designed to be an abstraction, not so much in order to deny the existence of "political man" or "moral-cultural man," as to allow analysts to concentrate on one aspect at a time. The economic system was never imagined to be coincident with the whole of human social nature. Capitalism was designed to be for the economic system what democracy is for the political system, and what the family, churches, universities, and the media are for the moral-cultural system. Since it is part of human nature for human beings to require one another's assistance, capitalism was designed to be a complex system in which there is a division of labor, a division of purposes, and a division of talents. It was conceived as a vision of interdependence—not only at the work site, but in an entire world of "free trade." Adam Smith, James Madison, and others argued explicitly that a world made interdependent through commerce, trade, and industry would, of necessity, become more lawlike and pacific.[33] They showed no particular respect for, or trust in, men of commerce and industry; quite the opposite.[34] But they observed that both in their typical temperament and in their typical self-interests such men were unlike the military rulers, clergymen, and feudal lords of the past who delighted in and benefited from abstract causes, adventures, and conquest. Sinful and lower class as men of commerce and industry might be, the entire scaffolding of their activities depends on systems of law, stability, and predictability. Lenin would one day taunt capitalists for selling the communists rope for their own hanging. It was precisely this ideological indifference of the men of commerce and industry which Smith, Madison, and others found hopeful. The interests of such men lie in interdependence, not in barriers or in strife.

Similarly, an economic system based on markets and personal incentives seemed to them singularly apt as a companion to a system of democratic pluralism. No test of faith or metaphysics is required for entrance into markets. None is appropriate for a pluralistic democracy. This does not mean that faith and metaphysics are matters of indifference. Rather, it means—as Maritain pointed out—that practical cooperation among men of good will does not need to wait upon prior resolution of all philosophical or theological disputes.[35] In order for democracy to function, it is not necessary for all to become converted to the same vision of reality. In order for a capitalist economy to function, it is not necessary for all who take part in it to share the same faith or metaphysics. Indeed, the notion that each *person* should be free to make his or her own economic decisions is intended to reinforce the ideal of

personal integrity in every sphere. This notion in the economic sphere matches that in the moral-cultural sphere which defends each person's conscience, and that in the political sphere which defends each person's human rights.
To be sure, liberty is dangerous. Any free society offers plenty of evidence of sinfulness. Some persons will use their liberty as saints, others as sinners. A market system protects their economic liberties as democracy protects their political liberties. Alas, their moral liberties will be used as humans will use them.
It follows, furthermore, that political liberties without economic liberties are empty. Totalitarianism may be just as effectively enforced through complete control over economic transactions as through police surveillance.[36] If presses must depend on state control of newsprint, numbers of copies printed, and systems of distribution, such presses are not free. Political liberties require economic liberties. Moral-cultural liberties depend on both. Thus religions whose essence lies in the free acts of individual conscience—as do narrative religions like Judaism and Christianity—require systems of political liberty and economic liberty for their natural expression in human social life.

Emergent Probability—Some thinkers have held that human progress is illusory, since history is inevitably caught in cycles of eternal recurrence. Others have held that human history is determined by forces beyond the liberty of individual human beings. Judaism and Christianity teach a quite different vision of history. Bernard Lonergan has described it in abstract philosophical terms as a vision of "emergent probability." [37] In this vision, human history is open to new futures, yet any one future depends on the fulfillment of prior conditions. Human liberty may affect the fulfillment of such conditions. Thus, choices made by humans today affect future probabilities. Humans may fulfill the necessary conditions for future Y, or fail to fulfill them. They are partly responsible for the emergence or non-emergence of Y. At times, even a single individual may invent new possibilities or set in motion new sets of occurrences that dramatically alter the probabilities faced by others. The world that humans face is, therefore, open, uncertain, not perfectly stable, and subject both to progress and to decline. Ideas count. Moral energies count. For want of them, whole societies may perish. Especially gifted societies may flourish in unprecedented ways. The Lord of History thus respects the liberty of his creatures in the long, disorderly pilgrimage of history.
Both democracy and capitalism were experiments. Their founders were not certain that either experiment would endure, and they recognized many hazards. They were obliged to argue against heavy opposition. They succeeded, at times, only through the force of arms. Their own sins and failings at times placed the entire experiment in jeopardy—as Abraham Lincoln observed during the Civil War in the

United States (1861-1865). Every market democracy has experienced the risk of failure or collapse, in one form or another, since its founding. Nothing in the stars guarantees the survival of either democracy or capitalism. Both are creatures of liberty. Both are subject to laws of emergent probability.

Sin—Perhaps the most important contribution of Judaism and Christianity to democratic capitalism is a theory of sin. According to this view, no human is without sin. In social systems, the most destructive expression of human sin is the will-to-power. Democracy is founded on a theory of sin which holds that, because of the dangers of tyranny, all forms of political power must be diffused. Political power is more dangerous than economic power, since it has at its disposal the coercive strength of the state. In order to attain other social goods, however, modern democracies have judged it necessary to expand the powers of the twentieth-century state beyond those of the nineteenth-century state. The dangers of tyranny are growing once again. On the other hand, it is the inevitable tendency of economic agents to expand and to solidify their economic power. As Adam Smith warned from the beginning, society and state alike must be ever vigilant to prevent economic monopolies, however irrepressible the tendency toward them. Modern technology and mass production have dramatically expanded the scope and economic power of the largest corporations. The contest between the expanded powers of the central state and those of the corporations—often operating in an international framework—bears the closest scrutiny. Those concerned to protect human liberty must worry both about the corporations and about the state. Both are creatures of sin, like all things human.

The theory of sin invites us to be vigilant about our liberties. It suggests that the wrong solution to our perplexities would be to increase the power of either one of these giants in an effort to contain the other. This is why the socialist solution appeals less and less to thinking persons today. If the eleven major oil companies of the United States, for example, are already too powerful, the creation of a single U.S. government agency to subordinate all of them hardly seems to diminish that threat.

Conclusion

My aim has been to extend the work of Jacques Maritain, who showed that democracy has its source in the Judeo-Christian leaven active in Western history and now in the entire world. I propose a hypothesis for further investigation—that is, that capitalism, like democracy, has biblical roots. Both democracy and capitalism breathe vital air from a moral-cultural system based on powerful ideas about the communitarian individual, the social nature of human life, emergent probability, and sin.

The implications of this hypothesis for public policy are many. Here are three: (1) In order to move beyond current practices, religious activists may appeal to specific, democratic, capitalist ideals of a profound and transforming biblical power. (2) In domestic affairs, biblical religion nourishes private-sector as well as public-sector initiatives, social inventiveness, and activism. (3) In international affairs, whether of peace, justice, or development, the ideals of democratic capitalism may be seen to be superior to statist alternatives in their promise, in their effectiveness, and in their liberties. One can imagine either of our two major political parties clarifying its own vision so as to become an effective force for the progress of democratic capitalism toward such ideals at home and abroad.

In any case, democratic capitalism, such as the world has until now experienced, is not yet at the end of its pilgrimage nor in the final stages of its testing. We will need all the energies our religious traditions offer to us, and all the clearsightedness and courage of which we are capable, if we are to be as inventive as our predecessors were. We have much to do.

Endnotes

1. Jacques Maritain, *Reflections on America* (New York: Charles Scribner's Sons, 1958), 118.

2. John C. Cort points out that the left, in particular, has begun to exploit the churches: "There is also a growing awareness among radicals and liberals that the churches have been, are now and will continue to be one of the best sources of recruitment for movements that are interested in social justice and structural change." "The Changing Face of Capitalism," *America*, 16 September 1978, 156. Cort, the editor of *Religious Socialism*, also explained to an Italian audience the leaning of American elites: "What is remarkable about Christian socialism in the USA is the large number of sympathizers who are reluctant to identify themselves as socialists, partly because socialism has such a bad name in this country and is so closely linked to Leninist varieties of Marxism in Russia, China and Cuba. For example, it is evident from the editorial policy of most of the influential Catholic and Protestant magazines—influential, at least, among the more intellectual circles of the Christian churches—that the editors are what we call over here 'closet socialists.' " "Christian Socialism in the USA," *ASCE News* (July-October 1980): 49.

3. See Peter L. Berger and Richard John Neuhaus, *To Empower People: The Role of Mediating Structures in Public Policy* (Washington, D.C.: American Enterprise Institute, 1977), Chapter 4; J. Philip Wogaman, "The Church as Mediating Institution," *Democracy and Mediating Structures: A Theological Inquiry*, ed. Michael Novak (Washington, D.C.: American Enterprise Institute, 1980), 69-105.

4. Among others, Edward Norman, *Christianity and the World Order* (New York: Oxford University Press, 1979). Five articles mostly attacking Norman appeared in *Christianity and Crisis* 39, nos. 4 and 6 (19 March and 16 April 1979). Notably, most of the authors attacked Norman's politics and defended their own without discussing the specific religious, spiritual quality of Christianity. In this, they appeared to concede Norman's central thesis. See also, Ernest W. Lefever, *Amsterdam to Nairobi: The World Council of Churches and the Third World* (Washington, D.C.: Ethics and Public Policy Center, 1979).

5. The allusion is to John M. Cuddihy, *No Offense: Civil Religions and*

Protestant Taste (New York: Seabury Press, 1978).

6. Trans. William Tjalsma, with a foreword by Aleksandr I. Solzhenitsyn (New York: Harper & Row, 1980), viii.

7. Ibid., ix.

8. See Raymond Aron, *In Defense of Decadent Europe,* trans. Stephen Cox (South Bend, Indiana: Regnery/Gateway, 1979), Chapter 20.

9. See Daniel Patrick Moynihan, "Words and Foreign Policy," *Policy Review* (Fall 1978): 69-71.

10. Maritain, *Reflections on America,* 101.

11. Maritain states his thesis in the following way: "The important thing for the political life of the world and for the solution of the crisis of civilization is by no means to pretend that Christianity is linked to democracy and that Christian faith compels every believer to be a democrat; it is to affirm that democracy is linked to Christianity and that the democratic impulse has arisen in human history as a temporal manifestation of the inspiration of the Gospel." Jacques Maritain, *Christianity and Democracy,* trans. Doris C. Anson (New York: Scribner, 1948), 37.

12. Maritain, *Reflections on America,* 101-120.

13. In practice, democratic socialist societies like those of Sweden, West Germany, and Israel retain large components of a democratic capitalist society. Intellectual and political traditions differ and moral-cultural resources differ, so that these different societies approach similar structures by different routes. Yet they remain variants of a democratic capitalist order because of their three-part systems.

14. I offer such reasons in Novak, *The Spirit of Democratic Capitalism* (New York: Simon & Schuster, 1982).

15. Among the small but growing literature on the intellectual biases against capitalism, I cite the following: *Capitalism and the Historians,* ed. F.A. Hayek (Chicago: University of Chicago Press, 1954); Ludwig von Mises, *The Anti-Capitalistic Mentality* (South Holland, Illinois: Libertarian Press, 1972); *Capitalism: Sources of Hostility,* ed. Ernest van den Haag (New Rochelle, New York: Epoch Books, 1979); *The Denigration of Capitalism: Six Points of View,* ed. Michael Novak (Washington, D.C.: American Enterprise Institute, 1979), especially the chapter by Edward R. Norman, "Denigration of Capitalism: Current Education and the Moral Subversion of Capitalist Society," 7-23.

16. Concerning the need for a theory of the American "transformation of the economic system," Maritain wrote: "This country should never, and will never, give up the experiential approach, which is a blessing for it; but . . . it would be quite beneficial for it to develop, at the same time, an adequate ideological formulation, an explicit philosophy, expressing its own ideal in communicable terms. This does not mean, of course, that it would be advisable to manufacture an ideology for the sake of propaganda, God forbid! It means that the development of a greater general interest in ideas and universal verities is a presupposed condition without which no genuine possibilities of intellectual communication can emerge." *Reflections on America,* 101, 118.

17. See especially, William Letwin, "Adam Smith: Re-reading *The Wealth of Nations,*" *Encounter,* March 1976; Garry Wills, "Benevolent Adam Smith," *The New York Review of Books,* 9 February 1978; Irving Kristol, "Adam Smith and the Spirit of Capitalism," in *The Great Ideas Today: 1976* (Chicago: Encyclopaedia Britannica, 1976); Jacob Viner, *Religious Thought in Economic Society,* eds. Jacques Melitz and Donald Winch (Durham, North Carolina: Duke University

Press, 1978); *The Market and the State: Essays in Honour of Adam Smith*, eds. Thomas Wilson and Andrew S. Skinner (London: Oxford University Press, 1976).

18. See the chapter, "Reinhold Niebuhr: The First Neo-Conservative," in Michael Novak, *The Spirit of Democratic Capitalism* (New York: Simon & Schuster, 1982). For Niebuhr's mature view of socialism, see especially *The Children of Light and the Children of Darkness* (New York: Scribner, 1944), Chapter 33; "Why Is Communism So Evil?" in *Christian Realism and Political Problems* (New York: Scribner, 1953), 33-42; *Our Moral and Spiritual Resources for International Cooperation* (New York: U.S. National Commission for UNESCO, 1956); "Biblical Faith and Socialism: A Critical Appraisal," in *Religion and Culture*, ed. Walter Leibrecht (New York: Harper, 1959), 44-57. On Niebuhr's abandonment of socialism, see John C. Bennett, "Reinhold Niebuhr's Social Ethics," and Arthur Schlesinger, Jr., "Reinhold Niebuhr's Role in American Political Thought and Life," both in *Reinhold Niebuhr: His Religious, Social and Political Thought*, eds. Charles W. Kegley and Robert W. Bretall (New York: Macmillan, 1956), 46-77, 125-150; John C. Cort, "Can Socialism Be Distinguished from Marxism?" *Cross Currents* (Winter 1979-1980): 427-428.

19. Daniel Bell, *The Coming of Post-Industrial Society* (New York: Basic Books, 1973), 12-13; and Daniel Bell, *The Cultural Contradictions of Capitalism* (New York: Basic Books, 1976). See especially the Introduction. Bell writes: "Against the holistic view of society, I find it more useful to think of contemporary society (I leave aside the question of whether this can be applied generally to the inherent character of society) as three distinct realms, each of which is obedient to a different axial principle. I divide society, analytically, into the *techno-economic* structure, the *polity*, and the *culture*. These are not congruent with one another and have different rhythms of change: they follow different norms which legitimate different, and even contrasting, types of behavior. It is the discordances between these realms which are responsible for the various contradictions within society." (Italics in original), 10.

20. For the best treatments of Weber's famous thesis, see H.R. Trevor-Roper, "Religion, the Reformation and Social Change," in *The European Witch-Craze of the Sixteenth and Seventeenth Centuries and Other Essays* (New York: Harper, 1969), 1-45; David Little, *Religion, Order, and Law* (New York: Harper, 1969). Also among the classic secondary literature, see R.H. Tawney, *Religion and the Rise of Capitalism* (New York: Harcourt, Brace, 1926); Ephraim Fischoff, "The Protestant Ethic and the Spirit of Capitalism: The History of a Controversy," *Social Research*, 11 (1944): 53-77; and Anthony Giddens, "Marx, Weber, and the Development of Capitalism," *Sociology* 4 (1970): 289-310.

21. "An economy consists of people whose performance determines its material advancement. Economic achievement depends primarily on people's aptitudes and attitudes (e.g., interest in material success) and their social institutions and political arrangements (e.g., in encouraging people to take long views). Societies, groups, and individuals differ widely in these matters. . . . Differences in these human determinants largely account for differences in economic achievement and rates of progress." P.T. Bauer, "Foreign Aid, Forever?" *Encounter*, March 1974, 17.

22. See Henry Hazlitt, *The Conquest of Poverty* (New Rochelle, New York: Arlington House, 1973); *Food and Social Policy I*, ed. Gary H. Koerselman and Kay E. Dull (Ames, Iowa: Iowa State University Press, 1978). On population, see Colin Clark, *Population Growth and Land Use*, 2nd ed. (London: Macmillan, 1977), table III.i.

23. Arthur J. McGovern, S.J., *Marxism: An American Christian Perspective* (Maryknoll, New York: Orbis Books, 1980).

24. Trevor-Roper, "Religion, the Reformation and Social Change," 24-33.

25. See Adam Smith, *An Inquiry into the Nature and Causes of the Wealth of Nations* (New York: Modern Library, 1937); cf. James Madison, *The Federalist*, no. 47; and *The Mind of the Founder: Sources of the Political Thought of James Madison*, ed. Marvin Meyers (Indianapolis: Bobbs-Merrill, 1973).

26. Maritain, *Christianity and Democracy*, 37.

27. Maritain described transformations in the unions, the corporations, the political system, and the beliefs of individuals in *Reflections on America*, 105-111.

28. Maritain, *Reflections on America*, 112-113. He is here quoting the words of William I. Nichols in "Wanted: A New Name for Capitalism," *This Week*, 4 March 1951.

29. Maritain, *Reflections on America*, 114-115.

30. Ibid., 113, 115-116.

31. Aleksandr Solzhenitsyn, *A World Split Apart* (New York: Harper, 1978), 47-51. See also *Solzhenitsyn at Harvard*, ed. Ronald Berman (Washington, D.C.: Ethics and Public Policy Center, 1980).

32. Robert Nisbet, *History of the Idea of Progress* (New York: Basic Books, 1980).

33. Ralph Lerner, "Commerce and Character: The Anglo-American as New-Model Man," *The William and Mary Quarterly* 36 (January 1979): 16.

34. In *The Wealth of Nations* Adam Smith, criticizing mercantilist theories of political economy, decries the "mean rapacity" and "monopolizing spirit of merchants and manufacturers"; he goes on to say that they "neither are, nor ought to be, the rulers of mankind" (460). Later, in his criticism of certain agriculturalist theories of political economy, he paraphrases the commonly held belief that "proprietors and cultivators...[exhibit] liberality, frankness, and good fellowship," while "merchants, artificers and manufacturers ... [exhibit] narrowness, meanness, and a selfish disposition, averse to all social pleasure and enjoyment." (632-633). He neither disputes nor endorses this view, but he does find a "capital error ... in ... representing the class of artificers, manufacturers, and merchants, as altogether barren and unproductive." (638-639). Cf. Duncan Forbes, "Sceptical Whiggism, Commerce, and Liberty," *Essays on Adam Smith*, ed. Andrew S. Skinner and Thomas Wilson (London: Oxford University Press, 1975), 197.

35. Addressing the Second International Conference of UNESCO in 1947, Maritain remarked: "How is an agreement conceivable among men ... who come from the four corners of the earth and who belong not only to different cultures and civilizations, but to different spiritual families and antagonistic schools of thought? Agreement ... can be ... achieved ... not on the affirmation of the same conception of the world, man, and knowledge, but on the affirmation of the same set of convictions concerning actions." *Man and the State* (Chicago: University of Chicago Press, 1951), 77.

36. See Michael Novak, "A Lesson in Polish Economics," *Washington Star*, 15 December 1979.

37. Bernard Lonergan, *Insight*, revised edition (New York: Philosophical Library, 1958), 121-128.

The American system of democratic capitalism works well in reality but sounds awful when we try to explain and defend it. This situation is the opposite of that faced by socialism which is beautiful in theory, but which fails in practice. IRVING KRISTOL *says that this should offer us small satisfaction, however, because theory generally wins over reality.*

To deal with this problem, Kristol maintains that we must bridge the gap that has emerged between our economic and cultural institutions. Cultural institutions must provide transcendent meaning that goes beyond the mundane notion of the good life of reasonable prosperity. He sees this volume as a part of that effort.

2

Philosophical Norms for the Integrity of the Economic System

IRVING KRISTOL

Recently Michael Novak was invited by a very well-known midwestern Catholic university to take part in a conference that was sponsored by the business school and the law school. The topic he was addressing was: "Can a Christian work for a corporation?"

In a moment of inspiration, I told him to go there and say "No," that only Jews and Moslems should work for corporations.

It is interesting to me that this question was asked in that way, at that place, in a conference sponsored, or at least co-sponsored, by the business school. It indicates the deep sense of unease felt by people about the moral, religious, and political aspects of our system, and how those aspects are related.

This unease was considerably diminished during the recent recession. If they were lucky, the graduates of that unnamed college went to work for a corporation. Their faculty knew that very well. But as times got better, those nagging questions have reemerged and again become of crucial significance. The question really involves our system of democratic capitalism and how it fits into a good human life. After all, the ultimate purpose of an economic system, of a social system, and of a political system is to produce certain kinds of human beings. It is not to produce wealth. It is not to produce military conquest. It is to produce certain kinds of human beings. If the kinds of human beings a civilization produces are not as admirable as many of us think ought to be the case and can be the case, then that system is delinquent and will run into deep trouble.

What is delinquent about our system? To begin to understand our system of free enterprise, one must understand that it is without precedent in the history of the human race.

In the year 301 A.D., the Roman Emperor Diocletian issued an order freezing wages and prices—wage and price controls. The first sentence of his edict read, "Unregulated economic activity is the religion of the godless," an idea that was—and I suppose is—the standard for every single civilization the world has ever seen except our own. The civilizations of antiquity, the Orient, and the Middle Ages all agreed that unregulated economic activity is the religion of the godless.

Why? For the same reason that unregulated sexual activity, unregulated political activity, or unregulated military activity are the religion of the godless. All of these human activities, unless they are shaped by something superior to them, become a form of idolatry, and thus the religion of the godless.

Economic life is always regulated. There is no such thing as unregulated free enterprise. The key question is, regulated by whom? Or, perhaps, regulated by what? Diocletian obviously thought it appropriate that it should be regulated by government, an idea that has achieved some popularity in our own time. In the Middle Ages it was thought appropriate that economic activity should be regulated by the church and that the church should be free or have the authority to establish the just price at which trades would take place.

Free enterprise as we understand it—namely, the system that has evolved over the past three centuries—is unique in world history because it said at various times and in different ways: Let us not regulate economic activity by the government. Let us not regulate it by the church. Let us regulate it in other ways. And, essentially, three approaches emerged historically on how to cope with free enterprise and contain it and shape it so that it is part of a civilization that produces worthy human beings.

The first is what historians called "the Protestant ethic," a peculiar title and a misnomer, but that does not really matter here. What Max Weber meant by the Protestant ethic—he was the first one to coin that phrase in our current usage—was the attitude of the Puritans who settled in American colonies and believed in a tie between economic activity and the religious life.

If you were a merchant or a worker, you were pursuing a vocation that had a divine sanction. Therefore, you had to pursue it in such a way that when you went home every night and examined your conscience you could say, "I have done well and I am worthy of salvation."

The original idea of how to regulate a civilization based on commerce was for individuals to internalize the regulations—all of the forces that shape economic activity. That is a very powerful force if you get it working. But, obviously, this approach only applies to small homogeneous communities. It does not work in a large heterogeneous society where it is unreasonable to expect everyone to be committed to a continual examination of conscience to assure that all economic activity is actually intertwined with the spiritual life. Internalization of regulation was a rare and transient phenomenon, though in certain small communities it may still exist.

The second and much more popular view was established by Adam Smith. He said that the market itself regulates economic activity; thus, you cannot do wrong in the market without paying a penalty. The market constrains you to do the right things. However, Adam Smith lived in a rather provincial culture, eighteenth-century Scotland, and it never occurred to him that concepts of right or wrong could be challenged the way we are challenging them today.

Essentially, he assumed that the churches existed, the people were relatively pious, and that the Judeo-Christian moral tradition was unchallenged. Adam Smith was not a particularly religious man, but he was not a particularly anti-religious man either. And certainly as far as the moral tradition was concerned, he was completely orthodox. And he assumed that the free market with all its own checks and balances would be surrounded by churches—educational institutions that would shape people's thinking about economic activity.

The question of business ethics just doesn't arise when you have ethics derived from some authority. And if it is not derived from your own conscience, it is derived from an outside authority. The outside authority that Adam Smith had in mind and which he simply took for granted was culture—specifically, the churches, educational institutions, what we would now call the media, and the educated classes.

But gradually things began to change. In part under the pernicious influence of economists, the system that we call free enterprise liberated itself from all moral constraint. But worse, it liberated itself from morality in theory.

Gradually what developed is what is taught in most of our colleges. Students study the workings of the system in nonmoral terms and it is assumed that there is no connection between what is called free enterprise and the moral life. Moral life is one thing. If you want the moral life, you take a course in morality. If you want to be in business, you take a course in business. How the two interface, no one tells you, except sometimes in court. But that, of course, is not morality; it is legality.

This sharp division occurred during the last century. Economic life simply became a completely independent, autonomous sector of human activity, not part of a whole civilization. Until economics became independent, the question of the purpose of economic activity did not arise.

It is possible to say, yes, the purpose of economic activity is to create wealth. But what do you want the wealth for? Economics does not itself dictate the ends of human existence, only the means whereby you can achieve a superior human existence in material terms. Economic enterprise produces wealth. That is what it does. The wealth can be badly used; it can be abused. We see it abused in all sorts of ways. It can be abused without conscience.

People can lead empty lives creating wealth. People can encourage others to lead empty lives creating wealth. In the end, economic activity that creates wealth has to be an organic, essential part of a way of life that is more than economic activity; otherwise, you do not have a defensible civilization. You do not have a civilization which you can transmit in good conscience to your young people, your children. In any case, you have a civilization that many of your children will find repugnant, as we have seen in our own lifetimes.

Capitalism is full of iniquities. But it was not those iniquities that led so many bright young students of the 1960s to the insane radicalism that had such a catastrophic effect on our universities. They found that the life offered to them was empty. That was the problem. It was not that they did not want to work. Of course they wanted to work. Young people like work. They just did not see any meaning in the existence offered to them, because work in itself, when it is disconnected from other values, becomes meaningless.

Those of us who are over a certain age have always managed to maintain a connection between work and those other values. But even for us, that connection has become considerably more tenuous.

The movie *The Graduate* symbolized much of what happened in the 1960s. What that movie expressed was a sense of intense dissatisfaction—vague and undefined, but dissatisfaction with a mode of living that seemed to lack important human dimensions.

I want to emphasize the importance of theories as opposed to fact. In fact, the lives of those people were not meaningless. Most businesspeople I know lead lives full of human satisfaction. They lead perfectly humane lives. Most people in this country with its system of free enterprise lead perfectly humane and full lives. But without a theory of free enterprise, without an idea of it, we have no way of explaining it to ourselves, to our children, or to the world.

In that sense, our position is absolutely opposite from the socialists. Socialists have a terrible problem, too. Their problem is that their system works worse than it is supposed to. Their system, in fact, works badly, but the idea of it is very attractive. Our system works quite well, even in terms of the kinds of human beings it produces, but the idea of it is terrible. We cannot explain our system to young people. We do not have the language. We have lost the knack of explaining to young people why they should like the system, aside from the fact that they might make money out of it. Money is much less important to young people than you think. Some of them manage astonishingly well without money. I do not know how, but they do.

Socialists all over the world—intelligent and thoughtful socialists who write, think, and argue—are trying to save the socialist ideal. They are trying to save it from socialist reality, which is ugly, hideous, and a great disappointment and frustration to everyone.

Capitalistic reality, on the other hand, suffers from the bad ideas that are expressed in defense of it. It is the explanation of capitalism that is so indefensible and is so unacceptable to many people.

We have an extraordinary situation in this country when you think about it. We know that the capitalistic reality is good. If we abolished our immigration quotas tommorrow, practically the whole world would come to the United States. So there is an inherent judgment in that. *They* know the reality is good. On the other hand, if you go to their countries and you ask them what they think about the United States, you get negative opinions. When they talk about the United States, they are talking about American capitalism. They are talking about what we call free enterprise.

There is a huge gap between our capitalistic reality and our inability to present it in meaningful terms—and I do not mean in public relations terms. I mean in moral terms, human terms, or even religious terms—that is, in its ideal dimension.

Every society must have an ideal dimension. Every society must fall short of that ideal dimension. It is inevitable. But it must have the ideal dimension. People respond to that ideal dimension. That is why people do not want to immigrate to Russia, but they are willing to admire it from afar. Russia has an ideal dimension and a terrible reality. In the case of the United States, people are willing to come to us to experience our reality, but they do not like our ideal dimension and do not accept whatever weak explanations we offer for it. This is a serious problem. It is a problem for the business community.

It is especially a problem for the business community, which keeps urging me, an academician, to sell free enterprise. I have to explain that if you really want to persuade people of the merits of the system, you do not sell anything. You persuade. The way you persuade is to have good arguments. The way to have good arguments is to have truthful arguments. The way to have truthful arguments is to have a system that you point to and say, "That's the way it is."

Let me give you a very homely instance of the kind of problem we run into. I have been to Dallas many times. I once had the privilege of speaking to the leading members of the business community of Dallas, and I decided to test them on this whole issue.

I asked them, "What do you think of the television show 'Dallas'?" They looked at me blankly. Why was I asking them that silly question?

And I said, "That show is of some importance."

And they said, "Well, what is the importance? Do you think it will stop people from investing in Dallas?"

I explained that "Dallas" is the most popular television show in the world. Not only in the United States—in the world. All over the world people watch a television serial that describes American business—corrupt, dishonest, and colorful, but in a disgusting sort of way.

I said, "How do you go home and face your kids at night?" If the black community was portrayed the way the business community in Dallas is portrayed, the Urban League and the NAACP would be up in arms. And I can tell you if the Jewish community were portrayed the way the Dallas business community is portrayed, the B'nai B'rith Anti-Defamation League would be up in arms and something would be done.

But there you have this quite untruthful portrayal of the Dallas business community which persuades everyone that the system of free enterprise is not something any decent human being wants to get too deeply involved in. That's the only message that comes through on that program. It is the only lesson you can learn from it.

"Dallas" is part of our culture. This is what we are saying about ourselves. This is what we are saying about ourselves to our children and to the world. We once had Horatio Alger, we now have "Dallas."

One can get indignant on a trivial level and say, "Let's stop it." But that is not the point. You have to present a better picture. You have to somehow understand the importance of pictures in general. In truth, the trouble with the Dallas business community, like most business communities, is that it does not take ideas seriously. It is *toasty*. It is not anti-intellectual. It respects intellectuals—perhaps, too much. But it does not take ideas seriously.

Take for another example the song, "Take This Job and Shove It." This song and others like it stem from people's perception of the system's own definition of itself. It is not that they have terrible jobs and do not like them. In fact, they often have jobs they are very happy with. And when all of those people at that unnamed midwestern university go to work in the corporation, they are going to discover that corporations are really, on the whole, quite nice places—very civilized places. Corporations are not at all like "Dallas." And if you think that they are, you do not last long.

In essence, we do not know how to present ourselves except as a caricature of ourselves. This is because the business community has left the world of culture, the world of ideas, to other people. This has not been the business of business. These other people, of course, with their own interests at heart, have been eager to point out their own problems with the system. And in all candor, democratic capitalism has problems—deep, inevitable, necessary problems.

There are awesome benefits to every civilization, including democratic capitalism. One of the nicest things about democratic capitalism, one of its truly ideal components, is that it is such a wonderful system for ordinary men and women. It is the one system among all the systems that the world has ever seen that is most attentive to the desires and ambitions and even appetites of ordinary people. It gives them the freedom and opportunity to satisfy those ambitions. That's great.

On the other hand, a problem exists, because it is such a mundane civilization. It is a worldly civilization. It exists for common men and women and permits them to lead good, decent, and relatively prosperous lives by historical standards. It is not a civilization that generates transcendent ideas. It is not in the nature of a capitalist democratic civilization to generate the desire to be a saint, a sage, or a heroic figure.

This civilization promotes men and women who are good husbands, good mothers, good workers, good citizens, and good friends. That is good enough. No more is asked. Consequently, intellectuals and artists have always found this a rather uninteresting and boring civilization. It is hard to write about ordinary people doing nothing more than leading ordinary lives. You would have to be a very good artist to write about people leading ordinary lives.

In our prosaic society we must work at fostering its transcendental elements. They have to be there. We must have a society that offers more than the satisfaction of the common ambitions of common people. Transcendental elements are supposedly the responsibility of our cultural institutions, above all our churches and educational institutions. That is their function. But these institutions have failed in that respect because they have not worked at it. We simply have not taken seriously the task of somehow integrating within the worldly, mundane civilization we call democratic capitalism the ideal elements that every civilization must have if it is to be self-respecting, if it is to be respected by its children, and if it is to survive.

We try to cope with this failing in patchwork ways. We have courses in business schools on business ethics—a complete absurdity. There is no such thing as business ethics that is worth studying academically. Ethics might be worthy of study. But the study of business ethics does not produce honest businessmen, and the study of ethics does not produce honest young people.

Ethics is a matter of character formation. If you want to make a young person ethical and moral, you do it by example, you do it by precept, you do it by penalty. You know how to raise small children. You do not tell them to take a class in ethics in the local school. First you teach a young boy how to make his bed and then insist that he make it every day. That is the introduction to ethics—teaching responsibility. It is a practical matter of forming character and shaping habits. Once that is done, then you can enroll him in a course in ethics; it probably would not do any harm.

Studying ethics is a confusing matter. It is not as if you take a course in ethics and you learn what is ethical. You take a course in ethics and you learn to question what is ethical, which is the way it is supposed to be. But what is the point in questioning if you do not know the answer or plan? You will end up muddled.

I was on the Council of Humanities for a time. Suddenly, grant requests came in for the teaching of ethics in agricultural schools. Everyone understood that this was a big gravy train, and every institution of higher or lower learning in the country wanted government money to study ethics. The key person was called a ethicist. That term did not exist until about eight years ago. It came into existence in response to all these programs financed by the federal government. So now we have a new profession. There really is an academic professional called an ethicist—a person who goes around teaching—no, not teaching—ethics, but giving courses in ethics.

When you have reached a situation where you are parodying—simply caricaturing—what a truly alive and vital civilization should be doing naturally, you know that something is wrong. You know that somehow or other our civilization as it has developed over the past 150 years has suffered an acute schizophrenia or inhibition.

We have an economic system that does very well in purely economic terms. Our economic system is a very good economic system. Then we have a cultural system at war with the economic system. The cultural system does not understand the economic system and does not want to; it feels that the economic system is something alien and hostile to it. Then you get these courses in ethics trying to bridge the gap, and you get everything else trying to bridge the gap.

But nothing can bridge the gap unless we work at recreating that unity that existed in Adam Smith's time. He took it for granted that the churches and the educational institutions all functioned in a way that linked the economic system to the moral system. Cultural institutions linked the economic system to traditional moral values in an unquestioning way so that when it was necessary to defend the system, one could do so articulately. Our problem is that we cannot provide an articulate defense.

We have a great country that everyone wants to come to, only no one can explain why it is a great country. Many people, including those who come and live here, spend half of their time vilifying the country.

The integration that has to take place has to be worked at. Somehow, we must bridge the gap that has emerged between the business sector and the cultural sector—between economics and all those things that shape attitudes and basic values and provide one with a sense of life's meaning and purpose and that permit one to cope with the crises of life.

The symbiosis between the cultural sector and the economic sector is absolutely indispensable if the economic sector is going to survive.

I gave a talk at Harvard, and I said, "How many here think that most business executives are immoral?" About two-thirds of the class raised their hands.

Then I asked, "How many of you have fathers who are business executives?" About two-thirds of the class raised their hands.

I said, "How many of you believe your fathers are immoral?" No hands were raised.

When a tremendous gulf exists between the abstract attitude and the concrete attitude the abstract will always win. Words will always win over reality. At the moment, socialism is the force in the world, even though it does not work and capitalism is on the defensive even though it does work, because ideas are more important than reality. To put it another way, there cannot be a bad horse with no horse. There cannot be a wrong idea with no idea. You can only meet it with another and, one hopes, have a more truthful idea.

If you want a free market, you need a free market that is enveloped in a whole set of ideas that are not produced by the free market but are produced by the agencies and institutions whose job it is to produce that enveloping atmosphere—mainly churches, educational institutions, and the media.

The legitimacy of the free market—that which defines what living a humane life is and the kind of person one is as a result of participating in a civilization centered on a free market—cannot be produced by the free market itself. For that you need those other agencies, and I am especially pleased to be a part of this volume produced under the auspices of such an agency.

The American market system is the result of a revolution in ideas that occurred 200 years ago. GEORGE ROCHE *maintains that another, similar revolution is at hand.*

Offering a history of the development of free enterprise in the United States, Roche shows how freedom benefited the common man, particularly the millions of European immigrants who came to the United States by 1920.

Somewhere along the line, however, Roche says that Americans lost their confidence in individual freedom. This lead to their reliance on collective political power with disastrous results.

A new coalition, anchored in the idea of individual freedom, is emerging. Its intellectual strength has left collectivist forces in disarray in the battle of ideas. While recognizing that the battle is not over, Roche feels that we are privileged to live during the formative stages of America's second major idea revolution.

3

The Coming Idea Revolution

GEORGE C. ROCHE III

The American market system is best understood as a revolution in ideas which occurred in this country 200 years ago. A similar revolution in ideas is occurring today. Let me try to explain what I mean. First, let's take a look at our American past.

Unlike Europe, which, by the seventeenth century was largely free of feudalism but where noncapitalist institutions and attitudes continued to survive, America was a land where capitalism was able to establish itself from the beginning. Capitalism was accepted morally, legally, and socially in the British mainland colonies of North America without reservation; in consequence, there was no question about its employment as the only organizing principle for the production of goods and services, the distribution of the social product, and the employment of accumulated funds.

The governmentally planned economy and social structure which went under the name of mercantilism in seventeenth-and eighteenth-century Europe was far more vigorously applied on the European continent than in its colonies. As the eighteenth century wore on, however, the "period of salutary neglect" which had allowed the colonies to prosper in the absence of government regulation was drawing to a close. Mercantilism and the economic planning that accompanied it were applied with increasing effectiveness throughout all aspects of American colonial life.

It is in this context that two events occurred in 1776.

In 1776 Adam Smith's *Wealth of Nations*, an economic treatise that had grown out of its Scottish author's preoccupation with the wider problems of free choice as a foundation of moral philosophy, was first published. That same year Thomas Jefferson, a man whose predilection for free choices had endowed him with many accomplishments (he could "calculate an eclipse, survey an estate, tie an artery, plan an edifice, try a cause, break a horse, dance a minuet, and play a violin"), retired for seventeen days to an upstairs room in a bricklayer's home in Philadelphia where he produced the Declaration of Independence. Between these two events there was more than a casual relationship of coincidence. Each document was the summary of an epoch, the distillation of what hundreds of people had been thinking and saying, usually with considerably less felicity. Each had come out of the same forcing house, an open defiance of the effects of a "planning" George III and his effort to remake the world in a mercantile planner's image.

The truly important connection between the two documents lay in the future, not in the past. The one was a prophetic economic blueprint, not without its flaws, for a vast outpouring of human energy that was to create the modern world; the other was a simple guarantee that the blueprint could be made possible within the physical growing space of a new continent.

We all recall that the Declaration of Independence refers quite directly to the American reaction to the planned economy: "He has erected a multitude of new offices and sent hither swarms of officers to harass our people and eat out their substance. He has combined with others to subject us to a jurisdiction foreign to our constitution and unacknowledged by our laws."

The American revolution was a successful effort to end such intervention in the colonies. We know about Jefferson's revolution. What is less commonly understood is that Adam Smith's ideas were equally revolutionary. America was about to build a new economic society as well as a new political society.

Smith was concerned with the promotion of the wealth of the entire nation. And wealth, to Adam Smith, consisted of the goods that *all* the people of society consume. This is a democratic and hence radical philosophy of wealth. Gone is the notion of gold and treasures; gone the prerogatives of merchants or farmers or working guilds. For the first time we were looking at a modern world where a flow of goods and services consumed by everyone constitutes the ultimate aim and end of economic life.

Adam Smith's laws of the marketplace are basically simple. They tell us that the outcome of a certain kind of behavior in a certain kind of environment, in a certain social framework, will bring about perfectly definite and foreseeable results. Specifically they show us how the drive of individual self-interest in an environment of similarly motivated individuals will result in competition; and they further demonstrate how competition will result in the provision of those goods that society wants, in the quantity that society desires, and at the price that society is prepared to pay. Let's see how this comes about.

It comes about in the first place because self-interest acts as a driving power to guide men to whatever work society is willing to pay for. "It is not [from] the benevolence of the butcher, the brewer, or the baker that we expect our dinner," says Smith, "but from their regard to their self-interest. We address ourselves not to their humanity, but to their self-love, and never talk to them of our necessities, but of their disadvantages." But self-interest is only half the picture. It drives men to action. Something else must prevent the pushing of profit-hungry individuals from holding society up to ransom. A community activated only by self-interest would be a community of ruthless profiteers. This regulator is competition, the socially beneficial consequence of the conflicting self-interest of all the members of society. For each man, out to do his best for himself with no thought of social cost, is faced with a flock of similarly motivated individuals who are in exactly the same boat.

It is important to remember that Adam Smith was not an economist, but a *moral philosopher*. Free choice, individual liberty, private property—these are the moral elements that Adam Smith, the moral philosopher, wedded to the economic ideal of the market, and that, together with the ideal of political freedom, constituted a mighty new source of productive power and creative vitality about to be released.

While the Founding Fathers could not have possibly blueprinted the future in detail and would have been the last to have made such an attempt, they knew that freedom would be equal to any contingency. They knew the connections between the "freedom to use" life, liberty, and property, and an energy system that would function without impediment. By accident, they were good economists.

Once begun, and once grounded upon the sound policy in monetary and credit matters, the superstructure of achievement could quickly be erected. The history of the nineteenth century is the history of the extraordinary climb of real wages without state intervention, and of all the ancillary benefits in public health and education that have come about as the result of the increase in national income.

During this period of unexampled expansion, the country's national income rose from $2,380 million in 1850 to $19,360 million in 1900. At the same time, the real per capita income almost doubled, from $787 to $1,388.

This was the work and accomplishment of America's first generation of industrial capitalists who owned and managed their own concerns, took risks, made enormous profits, and reinvested most of them in new and improved plants, the acquisition of raw materials, and the financing of market agencies. They were enterprisers, adventurers, and innovators; forward strides of technology were possible only as the result of their risk taking. They lowered costs, reduced prices, and kept wages high. In the process they made enormous profits. Real wages were rising, productivity was rising, and prosperity was becoming steadily more widely diffused.

The America consensus in favor of free enterprise and free men had demonstrated its workability.

The really significant point of the nineteenth century of free market prosperity in the United States is not that a few people made a great deal of money, but that the economic opportunity and improvement in standard of living available to the average American citizen was superior to any previous social experiment in the entire history of the world. The real beneficiaries of freedom in the United States were the generations of European immigrants who flocked to the United States by the millions.

Those Europeans coming to this country were fleeing the repression of planned European economies, where employment and upward mobility were becoming increasingly scarce. They came to a land that they termed "the land of opportunity," a country in which it was possible for the individual to work hard and to provide a better life and more opportunites for his sons and daughters than he himself had enjoyed. It is this opportunity and this growth that characterized nineteenth-century America under a system which emphasized individual freedom.

Even more important than the economic prosperity that Americans enjoyed was the dignity that accompanied the opportunity to make their own decisions and lead their own lives. America prospered greatly through the infusion of freedom which was the joint result of the political revolution of the Founding Fathers and the economic revolution pioneered by Adam Smith.

Unfortunately, the story does not end there. Somewhere along the line Americans lost confidence in their ability to solve their own problems and determine their own priorities. Politically, the twentieth century has shown a turn toward the collective idea, the timeworn, exhausted European belief that collective political power is a more effective problem solver than individual initiative and private, voluntary cooperation. This has brought an entirely new dimension to American political, economic, and social institutions. The disasters that have occurred were predictable. As Adam Smith suggested more than 200 years ago:

> The statesman who should attempt to direct private people in what manner they ought to employ their capital, would not only load himself with a most unnecessary attention, but would assume an authority which could safely be trusted to no council and senate whatever, and which would nowhere be so dangerous as in the hands of a man who had folly and presumption enough to fancy himself fit to exercise it.

Unfortunately, in recent years there seems to be no shortage of political figures who have folly and presumption enough to presume themselves capable of exercising power over all the actions and interactions of an entire social order. The results have been disastrous for our society.

As Samuel Lubell described it in his prophetic book *The Future of American Politics:*

> The expansion of government to its present scale has politicalized virtually all economic life. The wages being paid most workers today are political wages, reflecting political pressures rather than anything which might be considered the normal working of supply and demand. The prices farmers receive are political prices, the profits businesses are earning are political profits, the savings people hold have become political savings, since their real value is subject to abrupt depreciation by political decisions.

Earlier we discussed the Jeffersonian idea of limited government and the Adam Smith idea of free enterprise, and suggested how well these two ideas had fitted together to produce American prosperity and dignity. These founding fathers had their sights set on a vital point. In the last analysis an important truth has been painfully brought home to present-day American society. Political liberty and economic freedom are intertwined—they cannot be separated. Any system that deprives the individual of his economic freedom—by controlling his job, or how much he can earn, or what he can buy, or how he should live—takes away his basic freedom. And it is important to remember that throughout history, whenever bureaucrats controlled people's economic lives, they soon came to control their political freedom as well. It is essential for the survival of democratic government that economic power be separated from the political power. This is the *sine qua non* of democracy. It is the reason why the preservation of private capitalism is essential for the maintenance of a free society.

Freedom and prosperity go together—on principle. We cannot solve the problems that beset us until we recognize that fact.

Intervention is failing to solve our problems. In fact, it is strangling us. If we are to judge from present-day test scores, our schools no longer educate. If we are to judge from studies of the impact of financial policy, inflation drives old people and all those on fixed incomes to financial disaster with the rest of us not far behind. Meanwhile, our workers no longer want to work, our slums grow steadily slummier, the mail is no longer delivered. In recent years we have presented the alarming spectacle of a nation crying out to someone to take over our problems and responsibilities for us.

It is not my function here to explore the failings of collectivist society. Other chapters in this book will address the failures of collectivism and the damage that it does to our social order. Let me limit myself to a comment on just why such intervention, such unbridled use of political power in the lives of men, has disastrous consequences for any social order. The real point of freedom is not economic prosperity. Economic prosperity simply follows from freedom because of the dignity that it brings to men's lives in their freedom to choose their own priorities.

Unless men are left free to order their own existence, they are denied the very qualities that bring point and purpose to their lives, and prosperity to their social order.

The glory of the American experience was that we were blessed as a country to come on the scene at the precise moment when the moral case and the economic case for individual human freedom came together to produce a synergy unrivaled in the history of the world.

We Americans understood what it meant to live as free people and from that understanding flowed the dignity and the productivity that have made this society the envy of the world.

We Americans have always valued our independence and are on the verge of valuing that independence once again.

Americans of this generation are privileged to be living through the next great idea revolution in American history. The late Richard Weaver made one of the most profound points in intellectual history in the title of one of his early books, *Ideas Have Consequences.* Ideas do indeed have consequences and the intellectual revolution through which we are now living is the clearest possible demonstration of that fact. The idea of socialism, which has increasingly dominated American society for most of the twentieth century, is now drawing to a close and is steadily being replaced with applications of the case for moral, economic, and political freedom. This case has been increasingly made since World War II and has had its most recent political expression in the national elections of 1980. The battle is far from over, but the forces of interventionism are in sad disarray. The faith in a dominant collectivist ideal is simply no longer sustained in the face of the terrific problems that our social order faces. There is the strong likelihood that a new coalition, firmly rooted in the idea of individual freedom, will become the dominant entity in the world of ideas for America's twenty-first century.

We are privileged to live during the formative stages of this second major revolution in ideas which may well again make America the hope of the world.

The corporation is the central institution in American society. It has tremendous social and economic power and attracts the best and brightest young people to its ranks. According to KENNETH MASON, *this is what makes consideration of "A New Philosophy for Corporate Management" so important. No institution in human history, he maintains, has been better equipped to do tangible good than today's typical multinational corporation.*

While maintaining that "the bottom line" should be the primary concern of corporate managers, Mason points out that the meaning of that term has changed from "net profit after taxes" to "earnings per share" to "return on invested capital" to "return on equity" to "price/earnings ratios." He believes that the true bottom line is "return on assets employed," including all assets—financial, physical, environmental, intellectual, technological, and human. This standard retains the crucial discipline of profit but reminds us that there is more to management than turning a good profit.

4

A New Philosophy for Corporate Management

KENNETH MASON

I'd like to begin this discussion of a new philosophy for corporate management by relating a true story which, to me, demonstrates that the understanding of basic business economics by Washington officials leaves a lot to be desired. It involves the Fisher-Price toy division, one of the world's leading toy companies. Quaker acquired Fisher-Price in 1969, when it was a small company doing only about $35 million worth of business. Today it is a big company, doing close to $500 million worth of business.

During the early 1970s, as Fisher-Price was growing, its growth came from some very ingenious marketing efforts. The company had invented a toy called the "play family house." It was simply a house with a fence around it and little people that you could position around a little dog and a little cat. It was a very successful toy and sold well. The next year Fisher-Price expanded that idea and came up with the "play family farm." This was the same idea, except now instead of a suburban house, it was a farm and a barn; and instead of a dog and a cat, it had a cow and a goat. Kids loved it. The next year Fisher-Price marketing people extended the idea one step further and came up with the "play family city parking garage." You wound up the car and it parked itself. The kids loved that.

About this time, the marketing director of Fisher-Price was invited by the Federal Trade Commission (FTC) to talk about matters pertaining to the toy industry. It wasn't an investigation; they were just exchanging ideas. But since Fisher-Price is located near Buffalo, New York, and Quaker, the parent company, is located near Chicago, Quaker thought it would be smart to send one of their high-priced lawyers down to sit in with the Fisher-Price man just to make sure that everything was going to be all right. So these two fellows went down, one from Buffalo and one from Chicago, and met with the FTC in that wonderful building. At the end of the day the two men were riding down the elevator and the lawyer from Chicago said, "Gee, Jack, we have been so busy all day long talking to the FTC that I haven't had a chance to ask you how business is. How are things going?" And Jack said, "Well, despite the recession, business really isn't bad at all. So far this year, we have sold 600,000 houses, 500,000 farms and 450,000 city parking garages."

At that moment, they noticed that there was another man in the elevator who was looking at them curiously. When the elevator reached the main floor, this fellow cleared his throat and said, "Gentlemen, I don't want to be rude, but I happen to be in the real estate business . . . ." He didn't need to finish his sentence.

We at Quaker took that story and put it into our regular lexicon. We use it to demonstrate the aphorism: When in Washington, expect to be misunderstood.

When you think of the serious problems that are facing our nation today—the precarious state of the economy, the difficulty of getting agreement in the government, the escalating tension between the United States and a number of other countries, the belligerency in Latin America—you have to wonder why anyone would be attracted to a subject of such apparently miniscule importance, at least in a global sense, as the philosophy of corporate management in the United States. There are some very good reasons for anyone interested in the future well-being of this country to be concerned about what the American multinational corporation has become during the last twenty-five years and to ponder what this means for our society, our culture, and our economy.

First, consider the financial power that is concentrated in a handful of American corporations. Just 500 companies do more than half of all the business done in this country. Fewer than 1,000 corporate entities control the use of $2 trillion in assets, and that is in an economy where the annual gross national product is only $3 trillion. There is tremendous financial power in the American corporation.

Next, consider the social power of the American corporation. One thousand corporations provide the payroll for 20 million workers and, perhaps more important, they provide the workplace for 20 million workers—their physical and intellectual environment for forty hours or more a week. And these companies produce not only the products and services we use; they also produce the advertising that affects the way we think and feel about these products and services. And as psychologists have shown us, in some cases the advertising affects the way we feel about ourselves as well. Moreover, no one should forget that it is the American corporation that provides the financial support for commercial television in this country, the most single important cultural influence in America for the last fifty years.

So, you have tremendous financial power and tremendous social power. But in my view, the real key to corporate power in America, more important than the financial and social power and the thing that makes the corporation the central institution of our time, is the rich and varied lifetime career that it offers to young people from all walks of life. By "central institution" I mean such as the church in the Middle Ages, or the army in Roman times, or certain royal courts and certain great universities in other eras. I don't think there is a career in society today to compare with it. I don't think that any other career offers a wider variety of intellectual challenge or a greater opportunity to learn how the real world works than a successful career in middle management in a typical multinational business corporation.

I'll use Quaker Oats, a modest size company, as an example. Quaker is a company with annual sales of less than $3 billion. We rank 161 on the fortune 500. It is an average company, not an especially big or important multinational company. Much of our sales come from familiar brand names—Quaker Oats, Captain Crunch, Aunt Jemima, Kennel Ration, Flako, Puss N' Boots, Celeste Pizzas. However, Quaker is also the largest sardine producer in Brazil and the largest chocolate company in Mexico. Quaker makes laundry bleaches in Venezuela and scouring pads in Colombia. In Italy, Quaker sells more than $100 million a year in salad oil. In France, Quaker is a major factor in the pet food business. In Holland, Quaker is important in the manufacture of honey. Quaker's Fisher-Price toy division is the largest maker of preschool toys in the world. Our Magic Pan restaurant division was one of the most successful restaurant developments in the 1970s. Our Brookstone division is one of the leading mail order houses in the country. Joseph A. Bank is also a Quaker subsidiary, and one of the best men's and women's clothing retailers and mail order companies in the East. We have a chemicals division that is the world's leading supplier of furfural alcohol, a binding agent that is important in the foundry industry.

I went through this list not to urge you to buy Quaker stock, but for another reason. It is to suggest what it might mean to be a manager in a company even as small and innocuous as Quaker Oats, because managers in companies like that spend most of their business lives on the very cutting edge of the major technological and social developments that occur all over the world. I am talking about developments in such areas as the genetic engineering of plants and chemicals, the improvement of nutrition for both humans and animals, the utilization of energy in manufacturing and transportation, the demographic trends and developing life-styles in a dozen countries around the world. So a career in middle management, even in a company as small as Quaker, stimulates the development of expertise in very diverse and important subjects—subjects such as new techniques of steel production, the chemistry of rice hulls, the creation of computer software, and the learning capabilities of children. Here you have corporations that, of necessity, are the center of the latest technological developments in the world, and that have the financial resources and informational expertise to act on them. A moderately successful career, an average career, in a company like Quaker, can include managing people in a cereal plant, managing technology in a research lab, managing information in a corporate planning department, managing money in a financial department, or managing a self-contained operating unit in South America or in Europe. And you can have a career like that all within the space of a few years.

I don't think there has ever been an institution to equal the modern corporation in providing society with superb financial, physical, technological, and human assets all brought together under one management. And I don't think there is any equal for the opportunities it offers people with brains and ambition, opportunities to develop and put to use skills and knowledge that used to be available only to the rich and socially privileged. I think the case can be made that in all of human history there has never been an institution better equipped to do some tangible good in this world than the typical multinational corporation of today.

Think about the American corporation in this light—in the light of its economic power, its daily impact on our culture, its development of our best and brightest minds, and its bringing those minds into play on the major technological and social issues of the age. Then consider the belief of the current Washington administration that the business sector should begin to shoulder some of the social burdens that government would like to lay down. I would submit to you that what the five hundred chief executive officers of America's largest corporations think their responsibilities are is every bit as important to you and to me as what the five hundred congressmen and senators who work on Capitol Hill think their responsibilities are.

If you ask these five hundred congressmen and senators what they think their number one responsibility is, you are going to get a number of different answers. You may get answers ranging from "My number one responsibility is to represent my constituency," to ". . . voting my conscience." But if you ask five hundred executives what they think their number one responsibility is, you are going to get just one answer from all five hundred, and that answer is, "My number one responsibility is to bring a satisfactory number down to the bottom line."

Now, I want to say quickly, I think that answer is absolutely right. I have given a number of talks around the country, and on occasion they have been reported in the business section of the newspaper the next day. Reports of my speech frequently state that I said that business was giving too much attention to the bottom line. That is not what I had been saying. I think the bottom line is what business should be paying attention to. It is business's great distinguishing feature. It is what separates the private sector from the public sector. It is what makes businesspeople see the world differently from others—government people, for instance. It is what makes American executives so different from their European counterparts. It is a great compliment, not only to a manager but to anybody trying to get a job done, to be described as "bottom-line oriented." That description means that the person is perceived as someone who doesn't equivocate, isn't easily diverted from his goals, and isn't likely to make excuses for his failures. I think those are great qualities in any undertaking, not just in business.

It is interesting to see the bottom line as a concept creep into our language. Listen to Howard Cosell, for instance: "What's the bottom line on today's game, coach?"

On Capitol Hill you sometimes hear: "Would you like me to bottom-line that for you, Senator?" It is a part of our language; everybody understands what it means.

I am all for the bottom line as the definitive measure of performance in business. My quarrel with American corporate philosophy, and my great disappointment in the business leadership of my generation, is not that we have been too concerned with the bottom line, but that we are drawing the bottom line in the wrong place. We haven't kept pace with the important changes in where the bottom line really is. In our society over the last twenty years, the bottom line has continually moved lower and lower on the corporate income statement. I think few corporate chief executives have kept pace with that movement.

When I started in business, the bottom line was net profit after taxes. There wasn't any other concept involved. The net profit after taxes was the objective of all the plans that we worked on at Quaker, and everybody else that we knew did the same. At that time you said: Here is our net profit for the year, and next year we've got to beat that. And we did; we beat our net profit figures, and our net profit kept going up year after year, and that was great. Then one year our net profit went up, but our earnings per share went down. The reason was that we had acquired some companies, and thus had put out more stock than we had before. Our net profit total was going along fine, but we had begun to dilute the stock.

All of a sudden the bottom line in our company changed. Our plans were no longer focused on net profit after taxes, they were focused on earnings per share. This involved a different calculation. Our bottom line dropped a notch. Now we had this new target and so we said, "Okay, we are going to make our earnings per share go up every year." We did that for a while, and then one day the financial man came in and said, "Fellows, this is just terrific with these earnings per share figures up each year, but what you don't realize is that this is a much bigger business now. You've got all these inventories over here, and all those receivables over there; and you've got a lot more capital in this business. It is nice that earnings per share keep going up, but the return on invested capital is going down, and we've got to do something about that."

Well, we suddenly had a new bottom line on the income statement—

return on invested capital. That became the new name of our game. And, of course, no sooner did some of us operating guys get that through our heads than in comes the company's treasurer, and he says, "Fellows, return on invested capital is indeed important; but what the security analysts are looking for is return on equity. That is the number to look for." So our bottom line dropped another notch, and return on equity became the key figure that we built our plans around.

However, I don't think we came to the bottom line there either. The only reason the company treasurer wanted return on equity was to please the security analysts, and he wanted to do that to raise our price/earnings ratio, so that the price/earnings ratio was what he thought the bottom line was. But the price/earnings ratio itself isn't really what you are after; what you are after is to make your stock price higher, so the bottom line was actually the price of your stock on the stock market.

That is just a rudimentary example of how the bottom line falls lower and lower in the financial area. My point is that the bottom line is falling in other ways as well. All of those measures are clearly important. Net profit is important, as is return on invested capital, return on equity, stock market prices, and so forth. These all, of course, have to be taken into consideration by corporate managers. But I have come to the conclusion that there is another measure, more important than those. I think that farther down the page there is a *true* bottom line for business corporations, and I think it should be called "return on assets employed." By that phrase, I mean *all* the assets employed in the business, not just the financial assets, but the human assets, the intellectual assets, the physical assets, the technological assets, and the environmental assets.

The reason that I am convinced that I am right about this, that return on all assets employed is really the bottom line, is that if it weren't, I think we would all be in the pornographic film business. In terms of net profit as a percent of sales, you simply can't beat a pornographic film. The same is true of return on capital, and of earnings per share (if there are shares in it), and of return on equity. The initial investment in pornographic films is so low, and the earnings life of a successful pornographic film is so long, that the return on investment of just a routinely successful pornographic film is astronomical. In addition to that, when you think of the rapidly increasing presence of video players in American homes, and you think of the increasing availability of cable television channels in cities all over the country, pornographic films may well be the fastest growing consumer market in America today.

Why aren't all the hotshot, blue-chip consumer goods companies in there fighting for a share of this new market? Aren't growth and high returns on investment exactly what every red-blooded chief executive officer is looking for? We think Quaker Oats is a hot marketing company; why didn't we go into the pornographic film business? Well, we are interested in growth and we are interested in high returns, but the reason we aren't interested in pornographic films is that we know, even if we haven't articulated it, that the pornographic film industry produces an unacceptably bad return on some of the most important assets corporations possess. Assets like brains, character, personal integrity, and the desire to do some good in this world; assets that most businesses, even though they don't state it openly, prize dearly and are determined not to waste.

I think that the concept of return on assets employed as a bottom line for business operations makes a great deal of sense. It maintains the crucial discipline of profit, because you can't get a good return on all assets without a return on the financial assets. At the same time, it reminds those of us who have been given the privilege of managing America's assets that there is a lot more to good management than turning in good profit figures.

The most glaring example I know of management turning in good profits but getting an incredibly bad return on assets employed is the commercial television industry in this country. By any kind of financial ratio, it is one of the most profitable businesses in the world, particularly the children's segment. Children's television delivers the highest profit margins that the networks get. Now I will defy any reasonable adult who is not currently employed in the television industry to sit down in front of a television set next Saturday morning for three or four hours, the way so many of our children do, and not be appalled at the way the United States of America, which is still the richest nation in the world, has chosen to use this powerful medium on young children.

The question I keep asking is, why is the intellectual and aesthetic quality of children's television in this country so disappointing? Certainly it isn't due to lack of money. American corporations spend well over $100 million a year just on Saturday morning television, just for those programs. Is it possible that what we see on the screen is the best that America's writers, directors, and producers can do with $100 million dollars? Obviously it's not. We have seen what public television can do for children with much less money. Why is children's television the shame of the nation today? I think it is because television executives think that the huge profits they make on Saturday morning television mean Saturday morning television is a huge success. The truth of the matter is that much better programs could have been produced with the same amount of money. And when you factor into the equation at least some nominal value for the future potential a young child's attention represents, then I would submit that children's television in America is an economic disaster, and America's television executives are the most dismal failures in American business. I just don't see how anyone who cares about the future of this country can fail to be concerned about the negative effect that television is having on young minds.

I would think those who would be most concerned would be the business community, for it has the largest stake in the free enterprise system. The research on television is telling us that the commercial networks' preoccupation with crime and violence and sex is infecting the youth of the country with the very diseases that businesspeople decry the most: cynicism, apathy, lack of personal values, and lack of respect for America and its political heritage. Who gets hurt the most by that kind of an attitude? American business corporations. I think the case can be made that the commercial networks' use of television has been the most devastating and successful attack on the moral fiber of the nation ever conducted from within. The mounting evidence suggests that the most serious threat to the continuing success of the free enterprise system is not that it may lose its freedom, but that it may lose its enterprise. If it does, I think that those business corporations that spend $5 billion a year to enable the networks to put this kind of programming on are going to have to accept a large portion of the blame.

You may think that in talking about the networks I am getting far afield from my topic. I think I am still close to the point, because the misuse of this country's television medium, the failure of the business executives in television to get a good return on those important assets, is just one example of many I could cite where American management is getting shockingly poor returns on important resources.

Consider another example, the American labor force. For most of this century, it has been the best-educated, best-paid, and most competent labor force in the world. Clearly, the labor force is among the most important assets any company can have. And this asset is not being managed by the government; it is managed by the free enterprise system. What kind of results has American management received from this labor force? Have we created worker loyalty? Do we have worker identification in this country with the free enterprise system? Do workers in America understand and respect corporate problems and objectives? Do American workers take pride in their jobs and the products they make? The evidence suggests they do not.

Take the advertising industry. American corporations spend $60 billion a year in consumer advertising. What does this $60 billion a year expenditure get for American business? For one thing, we get some help in selling merchandise that might not sell quite so well if it weren't advertised. But we also get, according to recent polls, the persuasion of more than 50 percent of all adult Americans that consumer advertising is misleading and untrustworthy. In a 1977 Gallup inquiry about the honesty and ethical standards of people in twenty different occupational groups, the advertising practitioners ranked dead last. Now, most of the ad agencies that created the advertising that has produced these results, both for the advertising industry and for the corporations, are quite profitable. But can you think of a worse return on investment for America's advertisers than to have made a $60 billion annual expenditure to convince the public that advertisers are dishonest? If businesspeople had known in advance that this would happen, do you think they would still have hired those agencies? And would those agencies have still thought of themselves as successful businesses? I don't think they would.

Look at the environmental situation. The environment is an important asset in any economy. In fact, it is the source of all economic activity. What have America's business leaders done to assure the public that we are going to manage this precious asset wisely? In general, the American business community has dismissed those who raise environmental issues as kooks, cranks, and bleeding hearts who have no understanding of economics and who would throw millions out of work just to save a few trees in the woods or fish in a river. This response can hardly give concerned citizens the feeling that they're in good hands with American business.

There has been a great deal of discussion in recent years about the concept of corporate responsibility, and a great deal of progress, I think, in getting corporations to embrace that concept. It is now commonplace for the boards of directors of most corporations to have a corporate responsibility committee that is chaired, almost always, by an outside director. That is a good sign. The annual reports of corporations now almost without exception cite examples of how the corporation has performed as a citizen of the community; and we cite with pride how we give to charity, support the arts, and help the community to solve some problems. Recently the Business Roundtable, an organization of chief executive officers of 250 of the nation's most prestigious corporations, published a "Statement of Corporate Responsibility" which states unequivocally the belief that business activities must make social sense.

This is a healthy sign, and should be applauded and encouraged. But supporting the arts isn't really what corporate responsibility is all about. It is what corporate philanthropy is about, and that is wonderful. But I don't think that true corporate responsibility is about the arts, giving to charity, or helping the community solve problems. I think the real responsibility of corporations in our free enterprise system is to get good returns on all the assets we employ. Not just the assets we legally own, like the money, the buildings, and the machinery, but the assets that belong to the nation—people, air, water, and so on. It is my belief that if we don't get a good return on these assets, then the private enterprise system will have lost not only its claim to fame but also its reason for being. Then someone else, government or labor, will—and I think should—take over.

In this obligation to get a good return on assets employed, corporations are no different than any other organization, or any other organism, for that matter. Because whether we are managing a big business or a little one, whether we have a big family or a small one, whether our health is good or bad, whether our IQ is at the genius level or just normal, there is really just one universal yardstick that measures all of us: How well did we do with whatever assets the good Lord happened to give us to work with? The quantity and quality of those assets varies enormously from individual to individual. It varies enormously from nation to nation, from species to species; it varies enormously from corporation to corporation. But I think the evidence is that we are all playing the same game. We are all trying to get some kind of sensible return from the assets that are under our control. My career in business has convinced me that only a few institutions in the entire history of the world have been given so many magnificant assets to work with as the American business corporation. And it is my belief that only to the extent that America's business leaders seek returns commensurate with the superb quality of those assets will the capitalism that has served this country so well in the past continue to serve it in the next century.

Discussion

Question: How can we operationalize that concept for corporations and the people who run them, since everything seems to be based on measurable and quantifiable performance? In other words, how do we get a handle on the return to all assets employed and on corporate responsibility in general?

Mr. Mason: I am impressed with how we have gotten a handle on corporate social responsibility in general. There is an unquantifiable concept, but the Business Roundtable statement is an amazing step. Look at the oil companies and the power they have if they want to use financial power. But there isn't an oil company in the country today that is in the marketplace, in the media, saying, "I'm trying to make profits, that is my only responsibility." They don't brag about their profits. They are saying, "I have to make this money because if I don't make the money I can't explore for oil, and I need to explore for oil because the country needs it." They have embraced the concept. They are afraid to come to the country and say, "We have no responsibilities." They have accepted those. The Business Roundtable is the most prestigious organization in American corporate life today; and it has gone on record as saying, "We believe that business activity must make social sense." Now social sense may not be quantifiable in dollars and cents, but once you have said "We must make social sense," it means that you are committed. So I am hopeful. I don't see the conflict with profits. I don't think it changes the fact that a company has its profit obligations. You either make the money or you go out of business; there is no change in that. But I think there is general agreement in this country now that you can't ignore the environment. And I hope we are going to get to the point where you can't go on the air and ignore what television is doing to our culture. The fact that the concept can't be quantified doesn't mean that it hasn't been embraced. And I think we will see a lot of activity, a lot of changes, in corporations from what has already happened in this country. But probably not in my lifetime.

Question: What precisely is your criticism of advertising?

Mr. Mason: I have two criticisms. One is the result. These surveys show that 50 percent of the adults interviewed believe that advertising is misleading. Those have to be very unproductive expenditures. With all that money to spend, how much more productive it would be if people didn't think it was misleading. I could run fewer ads, and my profits would be higher; or I could price my products lower, if one commercial would sell you. I think it has been an expenditure of money, an unproductive, lax expenditure. We criticize labor—the unions—and say, "You are featherbedding, and there is a lot of unproductive activity." But here is a $60 billion expenditure that has been proven by surveys to be unproductive.

The second objection is that this country has been built, in my opinion, by two things: a fine system of government and a fine system of economic activity. And our free enterprise system is wonderful; it is a magnificent thing. What disturbs me is that since television came in it has lost its voice. The people of the United States don't hear from business, they hear from Hollywood. The commercials, the exposure to business and business products in this country, come from television; and what we are hearing is the voice of Hollywood. It's how Hollywood thinks we should talk about our soaps and our cereals and our cars. I think some of the lack of respect for business arises because business has treated its products in a very Hollywoodish fashion on the national media, rather than making sober, sensible comments about the products. I know the advertising people say, "Fine. That will be a dull ad you want to write, nobody will listen to it, and it won't work." I know the alternatives. I am not saying it is simple.

Those are my two complaints: that we abdicated our voice as business leaders to Hollywood scriptwriters to write 30-second commercials, and that the results show that people don't have much respect for advertising or its practitioners.

Question: What difference do you see in the bottom-line concept, between foreign corporations and American corporations?

Mr. Mason: I think it is universally agreed that foreign corporations are in a position to take a longer range view than American corporations. They are not so wedded to the short-term effect of their price on the stock market. The foreign stock markets don't seem to be judging individual companies by market appreciation on a daily basis, so that they can take a much longer point of view. The real way to take a long-range point of view is to look for return on all assets employed, but let's talk about the financial assets only—the return on financial assets employed over a period of time. If you are getting a good return overall, it shouldn't matter at all if your earnings vary from period to period. The American business leader has abdicated his leadership to security analysts in the brokerage firms, and he has let himself be locked into a rigid pattern of earnings increases with no deviation. This is a bad way to run a business. It just adds one more hurdle and you have enough without that. There is no reason for business to have a rigid pattern. Businesses should have cycles. There is no reason for this year's first quarter necessarily to be over last year's fourth quarter. Doesn't mean a thing if it is over; doesn't mean a thing if it isn't over. What matters is, are you getting a good return on your assets over any length of time and does your future look good? Have you brought the products along? Are you going to get a good return over a ten-year period? One quarter is meaningless. You have no idea the number of executives involved, and how much time they spend three days before that report goes out. Absolutely unproductive time. Foreign companies have it much easier.

What about the companies that are not publicly held; how do they compare with European companies? The publicly held company is at a great competitive disadvantage compared to the nonpublicly held company. The nonpublicly held company can make all kinds of short-term investment, can let its earnings grow on a cycled pattern, because it isn't reporting to the public. Its stock price is its own concern, and if you run your own business, it doesn't matter what price your stock might be worth on any given day unless that is the day you plan to sell it. The American stock market has come up with an investment theory that doesn't make sense. It is that the return on your investment in stock should come in two forms, dividends and market appreciation, of which market appreciation is the greatest and most important. There are many theories that say corporations shouldn't pay dividends, that they should reinvest the money so that the market appreciation is greatest. This puts a short-term pressure on all executives to see that the stock price goes up, and that it never goes down. They are afraid to report lower earnings for fear that the market price will go down, even if it only goes down for three months. This is the short-term pressure that is causing bad business decisions.

Question: What incentive do managers have to follow your advice?

Mr. Mason: Actually, what they have is a disincentive, because they have the great incentive for the reverse. The problem is that the stock market in America has become a speculative stock market. It is interested in short-term results; and most corporation leaders are reluctant, even afraid in most cases, not to turn up short-term earnings as the market anticipates. I am sympathetic with their problem. I think there are ways to change that. One way would be to reduce the supposed dependence of American industry on security analysts' judgments. One way to do that would be to have a different taxation system for dividends, one which favored dividends over capital gains. This would enable corporations to give you a return on your money through dividends, and you wouldn't keep looking at the stock market thinking, "I've got to sell tomorrow because that is where most of my return is going to come."

Question: Why haven't you made your criticisms of advertising more effective?

Mr. Mason: I have expressed them as a person, and I have expressed them for the Quaker Oats company, which is not the largest advertiser but is a significant advertiser. But it is difficult to move the broadcasting industry. One of the disappointments of my business career was that the people at Kellogg's, General Mills, and General Foods missed a great opportunity to join in when Quaker, some years ago, was making a strong plea for self-regulation in the cereal industry with respect to advertising. It would not have violated the antitrust laws at all, but would have enabled us to almost force the networks to put on better programming and a better style of commercial for children. We made a clear proposal and the other companies were reluctant to join us. I think self-regulation is the answer, and more business leadership and more business followership. It doesn't do any good to get business leadership if nobody comes along.

In "The Constitutional Setting for a Free Enterprise Economy," JAMES BUCHANAN *maintains that a free enterprise economy cannot survive a totally politicized society. Only through constitutional protection can the competitive economy be safeguarded against the inroads of politics.*

Buchanan suggests that since the 1930s the United States has suffered a piecemeal politicization of the marketplace due to inadequate constitutional protection, severely hampering economic efficiency. Western European countries, lacking any constitutional protection, have experienced "wholesale politicization" placing them at economic disadvantage.

Economic efficiency is an inadequate political argument to stem the tide threatening free enterprise. Buchanan poses arguments for constitutional reforms, like absolute protection of the right of adults to enter into contracts, as a means of combating injustice.

Realizing that proposed constitutional alterations will be difficult to achieve, Buchanan finds cause for optimism in efforts to introduce constitutional changes related to balanced federal budgets and monetary rules. He is concerned, however, that the Reagan presidency will suggest that effective change can be achieved by electoral rather than constitutional means.

5

The Constitutional Setting for a Free Enterprise Economy

JAMES M. BUCHANAN

In this paper, I shall concentrate on the *constitutional* setting within which both political and economic activities are carried out, and particularly on that setting within which we might predict that a reasonably free economy can emerge and develop. By constitutional setting, I refer to the whole set of rules and institutions that constrain governmental or collective decisions along with the comparable set of limits or boundaries for the range and scope of governmental operations.

In the inclusive sense, every society has a "constitution." But my emphasis here is on much more explicit restrictions on governmental operations than such general terminology might suggest. I do not think that anything that can be appropriately described as a free enterprise economy can survive in a totally *politicized* society, by which I mean a society where *all* elements of economic activity are subject to potential governmental interference, whether this interference takes the form of taxation, subsidization, regulation, control, takeover, confiscation, or operation.

An effectively operating competitive economy must be *constitutionally protected* against the inroads of politics. Without such protection, any politically orchestrated attempt to revive or to promote the market or the free economy is almost certain to be at best temporarily successful. In other words, my message is that it is necessary to do more than elect politicians and governments who declare support for free enterprise principles and competitive markets. On occasion, such politicians and such government may generate major changes in the "right" direction, but electorally channeled efforts will be wasted until and unless they are accompanied by the implementation of enforceable guarantees against the prospects that other politicians and other governments cannot as quickly undermine the "good" that "right-thinking" predecessors might have accomplished.

Great Britain offers an almost classic example of this point. In Britain, the constitution does not effectively limit the range of governmental economic intervention. In post-World War II decades, we have witnessed several programs of nationalization by labor governments followed by programs of denationalization by conservative governments. Once elected to office, a government's powers are almost unlimited. And we now seem to be witnessing a comparable total reversal in economic policy by the Mitterrand government in France. In contrast to these European examples, in the United States—despite the overburdening weight of governmental regulation in almost every detail of private business operations—the constitutional structure would have surely prevented a comparable record of total reversals or revolutions in economic policy. The United States economy is less than totally politicized largely because of existing *constitutional* protection.

The Constitutional Attitude

Before plunging into a discussion of what the constitution for a free economy should contain, it is essential to secure some acceptance of what I have in several places called *the constitutional attitude*. At its simplest, this attitude amounts to little more than a willingness to acknowledge the elementary distinction between *the rules of the game* and *play within the rules*, along with some acknowledgment of the fact that play becomes chaotic in the absence of any rules.

Unless one makes this crucial distinction, and especially with respect to the social order, I do not see how sense can be made, conceptually, of the whole web of social-economic-political relationships that describe modern societies. We carry on our activities within an existing structure of law, and while we recognize that the law can be changed through certain appropriately defined procedures, we also recognize that there are limits beyond which ordinary legislation cannot go. These limits are defined by the presence of a higher law, that of the Constitution. Without some understanding of the distinction between rules and play within rules, what is the alternative conceptualization of social-economic-political reality?

At one level, of course, almost everyone accepts the distinction I have noted, and, correspondingly, almost everyone will, if put to it, acknowledge the desirability of genuine constitutional protections for the so-called "basic freedoms"—speech, press, association, religion, and electoral franchise. Almost everyone will acknowledge the desirability of having such freedoms made immune from the foibles of day-to-day strategic politics. None of us would like to see governments, elected for short periods of tenure in office, empowered to impose restrictions (or even executions) on minorities just because these minorities failed to support the majority coalition that happened to be electorally successful. Indeed, the presence of genuine constitutional protection for the basic freedoms is commonly hailed as the characteristic feature of a free society.

It is surprising, therefore, that the prevailing orthodoxy does not extend the simple logic of constitutional protection for basic freedoms to the equally important freedoms of the marketplace—the freedom to choose employment, to enter into voluntary contracts, to enter and to exit from industry, to buy and sell to whomever one chooses. Apparently, the dominant mind set of this century (unfortunately including the judiciary, which must make ultimate interpretative decisions) has, for some reason, placed economic freedoms beyond the range of constitutional protection. Hence, individuals' economic rights have effectively been up for grabs in the day-to-day partisan political struggles, with few limits on the grabbing game.[1] In the United States today, the constitutional protection against overt politicization of the whole economy lies in the structure of the government which is constitutionally emplaced, rather than in any explicitly protected range for economic enterprise.

Piecemeal Politicization of the Market

In any crossfire of partisan democratic politics, the market economy is likely to be destroyed. I shall concentrate on what we may call *piecemeal politicization* which is more characteristic of United States experience, rather than on *wholesale politicization*, which would be illustrated by the 1981 French nationalizations. Political choices to be confronted in the 1980s include choosing between control and decontrol of natural gas prices, between restricted and free entry of new firms in the trucking industry, between lowering the minimum wage for teenagers and maintaining uniform minimums for all workers, between control and decontrol of rents in California cities, and between federal control and decontrol of cable television.

In each choice, the collective outcome for the relevant governmental jurisdiction will depend on the political coalition that can be constructed for each of the relevant choice options. The motivations for the politicization or control alternative may vary widely. The teamsters' union may seek to ensure a regulated and cartelized trucking industry in order to protect its own monopoly power. Labor unions, largely controlled by workers with seniority, generally may seek to maintain uniform minimum wages to prevent potential competition from low-wage, less-productive workers. Established television networks and their outlets may want to maintain monopoly rents that would be threatened by unregulated cable television.

In these particular instances, the theory of politicization is reasonably straightforward. A group of beneficiaries can directly pressure legislative representatives, congressmen, and senators—pressure that is not specifically offset by countervailing pressures from the larger group of constituents who would be damaged by the politicization of the activity in question. Consumers, generally, would benefit from lower minimum wages for teenagers, from free entry into trucking, from unregulated cable television. But, for any single consumer, the benefits would be relatively small; hence, the individual is unlikely to spend much time and effort trying to convince his or her representative in Congress to oppose the proposed control legislation. Sensing the absence of such consumer pressures, the politician responds naturally and predictably to the more concentrated pressures of the groups who stand to make direct and measurable gains from the politicization. As a result, the market principle goes by default; we observe how legislatures impose ever-widening political controls while, at the same time, legislators spout effusive rhetoric about the virtues of free enterprise.

Two of the examples that I noted in my initial list cannot be brought directly into this explanatory model, however. It is not possible to explain the pressures for control over natural gas prices and over rents by the simple concentrated-beneficiary-group pressures model of political action in democracy. A different model must be introduced to explain these two cases, and other actions of politicization that are similar. The concentrated-beneficiary-group model would, in this case, yield the prediction that natural gas producers could exert political pressures to ensure that prices would not be controlled, and that housing interests would ensure that rents be left free to market determination. An amended interest-group model of politics is, however, applicable to these cases. Existing consumers of natural gas and existing occupants of housing face potential monetary loss if gas prices and rents are decontrolled, or potential pecuniary gains if prices and rents previously uncontrolled are brought under a control umbrella. In both cases, the items in question make up relatively large shares in consumer budgets. Existing consumers are a much larger group numerically than producers, and, hence, they are more important constituents for legislators subject to election. Those who are damaged by the imposition of controls are *potential consumers*—those persons who might secure access to the scarce supplies under the operation of a free market but who will necessarily be unable to consume the items in question under control. But a potential consumer is virtually ineffective as a political force for the simple reason that such a person will not be cognizant of his deprivation. The opportunity loss that the potential consumer suffers will not be felt as a loss in any subjective sense relevant for behavior. The potential consumer will have no incentive at all to complain to his or her legislative representative.

In either of these explanatory models, no political force can meaningfully organize in support of the principle of the market, of free enterprise, of competition, of Adam Smith's "system of natural liberty." As noted above, politicians will act in response to interest-group pressures, and at the same time espouse free enterprise rhetorically. The result is, of course, a gradual erosion of the effective operation of the organizing principle of the market in the economy as a whole. As more and more activities become subject to politicized regulation and control, the area of operations over which the market is allowed to work in relatively nonpoliticized fashion shrinks. This history describes the United States economy in this century, and notably since the Roosevelt New Deal in the 1930s.

Efficiency and Justice

This historical record has been made during a period when economists have, for the most part, quite consistently argued and demonstrated that increased politicization reduces the overall efficiency with which the national economy performs. With relatively few exceptions, economists have continued to demonstrate that rent controls destroy a housing stock. With relatively few exceptions, and especially since the 1960s, economists have agreed that uniform and increasing minimum wages explain much of the high and persistent teenage minority unemployment. With relatively few exceptions, economists have agreed that free entry into trucking would promote efficiency in the economy.

The advice of the economists has largely been ignored because politicians respond to the interest-group pressures placed on them. Efficiency, as an abstract objective for policy, simply does not command constituency support. We can observe relatively few demonstrations that involve participants carrying banners that read "For Efficiency."

What can be done? I suggest two separate avenues for constructive reform. The first involves no basic change in constitutional structure, and involves only a shift in the *form of the arguments* made by economists. The second and much more important avenue for reform involves basic changes in the constitutional rules, changes that will limit the ability of rotating governmental majorities to politicize the economy.

Let me first discuss a change in the way economists argue their case. As noted, efficiency does not carry with it powers of potential political persuasion. By showing that some existing or proposed institution generates inefficient results, the economist has not made much of a dent in the pressure-group dominance of the politician's attention span. Many of the same institutions that can be shown to be inefficient can, however, be shown to be *unjust*, by widely accepted criteria for justice. And, as an argument, charges of injustice can be orchestrated in such a manner as to make them politically persuasive.

Existing constitutional rules might be modified in two separate ways minimum wage versus a lowered minimum wage for teenage apprentice workers. Economists have shown conclusively that the uniform minimum causes high unemployment among teenaged workers, a grossly inefficient utilization of this part of the potential labor force in the economy, yet despite these demonstrations, the uniform minimum wage remains as law. But consider the vulnerability of the uniform minimum wage to a carefully orchestrated argument based not on efficiency at all, but on the injustice to teenaged minority workers who would be able, ready, and willing to work at wage rates somewhat below the coercively imposed uniform minimum.

The argument that any political or governmental control imposed on the freedom of persons to enter into voluntary contracts, one with another, violates a basic human right can be persuasive, or at least relatively so in comparison with the argument from efficiency. Almost all of Adam Smith's "system of natural liberty" can be defended in terms of principles or precepts of justice, quite apart from defenses based on efficiency of results.[2] In one sense, it is unfortunate that economists came to concentrate their attention almost exclusively on the wealth-generating properties of the free market system, and, in the process, distracted public, political, and legal attention away from more fundamental properties of the free market that meet widely accepted precepts of justice.

In the United States, *freedom of contract* was considered one of our constitutionally protected rights for many years. Unfortunately, modern courts have almost totally abandoned efforts to protect such rights against political abrogations.[3] For this reason alone, a simple change in economists' arguments would have a primary or short-run effect on the behavior of politicians within existing constitutional interpretations. But legal understandings that have shifted once can shift again, and not necessarily in the direction of weaker constitutional protections for basic liberties.[4]

Government with Different Rules

As I noted earlier, however, the primary emphasis must be placed on *changes in the basic rules* through which political decisions are made rather than on any changed argument within existing rules. The rules of modern democracies are necessarily biased toward producing political interferences with the operation of markets, and improved results can only be ensured through changes in the rules that constrain the behavior of governments. Unlimited government, no matter how democratic it may be in some electoral sense, is not consistent with the long-range viability of a free economy, and, by necessary inference, with the long-range viability of a society embodying individual liberty.

Consider only one of the examples listed above, that of the uniform to provide protections for the economic freedoms. The first involves changes in the rules for making political decisions, without specification of the limits over which such decisions might be applicable. I shall call these *procedural* changes in the Constitution. The second way in which constitutional rules might be changed involves drawing limits to the intrusion of political controls. These I shall call changes in the *limits* of application. I shall discuss these two ways of changing the rules separately.

Procedural Changes in Collective Decision-making Rules—
Earlier, I referred to the constitutional differences between the United States governmental structure and the parliamentary structures of European nations. These differences, described by the more distinctive separation of powers, and the more effective two-house legislature in the United States, are procedural in the two-part classification mentioned earlier. And, as previously suggested, the differences in constitutionally authorized procedures for reaching collective decisions tend, in this case, to make overt politicization of the economy more difficult in the United States than in European parliamentary democracies. This difference in institutions alone, and not necessarily any difference in ideological tradition, may be sufficient to explain the differential size of the public sector in the United States and in European countries.

As I also noted, however, even within a more effectively constrained set of procedures for making political decisions, the United States government has engaged in increasingly detailed piecemeal interference with market processes, and the overall size of the governmental sector has grown dramatically in this century and notably since the 1960s. The trends that describe the politicization of the American economy in this century simply cannot be extended without total collapse of the central organizing principles of our society. Additional procedural constraints on the ways government makes political decisions would ensure that the trend be reversed or at least that the levels of governmental intrusion in the economy be stabilized.

Several forms of additional procedural constraints can be noted here. The first, and perhaps most fundamental, change is that made by Professor Hayek in the third volume of his *Law, Legislation, and Liberty*.[5] Hayek proposed a two-house legislature, but with quite separate functions for the two bodies. The lower house would function more or less as a parliament as currently organized in parliamentary democracies. But its functions would be constrained by basic laws that would be laid down by an upper house, which is the law-making body as opposed to the governing body. For example, the upper house would settle the distribution of tax shares in the collectivity, while the lower house would be allowed to move tax rates (and spending) up and down, but always within the tax-share distribution laid down in law by the upper house. In making these proposals for constitutional reform, Hayek was thinking primarily of reform in parliamentary structures rather than of reform in structures like the United States republic. Some, but surely not all, of the features of the Hayek proposals are embodied, directly or indirectly, in the United States Constitution, as noted above.

A second proposal for a fundamental procedural change in the rules draws on the proposals made by the great Swedish economist, Knut Wicksell, as early as 1896.[6] Wicksell sought reform in the fiscal arena of politics; he proposed that governments be required to consider expense items simultaneously with the taxes necessary to finance such items, and that each item be separately considered in this two-sided fashion. The practical implication here would be a multi-sector government budget, with each sector standing on its own feet with respect to earmarked revenue sources, and with political decisions being made separately for each sector. Further, Wicksell proposed that near unanimity among the members of the legislature be required for approval of *any* fiscal action.

Various proposals for requiring greater than simple majority approval in legislatures have been made as a means of constraining the proclivity of majorities to introduce legislation aimed at providing specific benefits or even direct transfer to designated groups at the expense of the general taxpaying constituency. Any such change would, without doubt, be effective in the direction indicated. It would be harder for any proposal to be approved if, say, a two-thirds majority in the legislature were required rather than a simple majority.

A third procedural change is a variant on the Wicksell approach, but one that does not require modification of the principle of majority voting, a principle that is held sacrosanct in many strands of modern opinion. If a constitutional requirement for full compensation were introduced, many of the grossly inefficient regulatory interferences of modern governments might be eliminated. If all persons and groups who suffer damages as a result of governmental regulation were guaranteed compensation for such damages, and if legislators knew in advance of the legislation that such damages would have to be paid—from tax sources if necessary—these legislators would think twice about introducing inefficient regulations that benefit isolated groups in the economy at the expense of consumers.

Constitutional Rules to Limit the Range and Scope of Governmental Interference in the Economy—The second basic means of changing the rules would not involve direct modification of the procedures through which legislatures and other governmental bodies make decisions. Instead, the Constitution would be modified so as to declare certain types and forms of action illegitimate or unconstitutional. One such rule would be that already noted. The Constitution might be modified to make the right of freedom of contract between competent adult individuals inviolate. So long as a teenager is of a competent age to make contracts, if that teenager chose to engage in employment, he or she must be protected in his or her right to do so. A minimum wage restriction would be unconstitutional under this changed rule. Government would be prohibited from setting wages, prices, rents, interest rates, or any terms of trade between freely contracting parties or groups.

If such a constitutional provision were implemented, governments would also have to be prevented from accomplishing indirectly what they were prohibited from doing directly. Some supplementary rules would be required, rules designed to prevent indirect controls over terms of trade through taxes and subsidies. For example, if government chose to keep rents below market-determined levels, but was prohibited constitutionally from imposing direct controls over rents, it could accomplish the same purpose by overtly subsidizing rental housing. Explicit uses of fiscal powers for regulatory purposes would be a necessary accompaniment to any constitutional prohibition of direct interferences in the economy.

More direct limits may be imposed on the government's fiscal authority, on the powers to tax, and on the powers to spend. A fiscal constitution also may take several forms. The bases or sources of taxation may be limited, and hence indirectly limit the overall size of the governmental sector in the economy.[7] Or, the level of outlay can be constitutionally tied to the size of the national product and to its rate of growth. A proposal that probably has a somewhat greater chance of securing public acceptance in the 1980s involves a constitutional amendment that would require the federal government to balance the budget. This amendment gained increasing support in the period 1978-1981, and the widespread public association between deficit financing and inflation almost guarantees that this particular constitutional dialogue will accelerate in the 1980s.[8] Such attempts to control the size of the overall governmental or public sector through constitutional provisions may, however, make politicians resort to more direct interferences with markets. At best, controls on the fiscal powers should be accompanied by some attempt to enshrine freedom of contract in the Constitution.

Even more urgently needed than reform in the fiscal constitution, however, is reform in the *monetary constitution*. We have, in effect, a totally unconstrained, quasi-independent monopoly agency (the Federal Reserve Board) empowered to issue fiat money. It is hard to imagine a structure that could generate more unpredictability in the course of money issue, and, of course, there has never been an explicit constitutional or political decision to set up such a monopoly of issue. The Federal Reserve Board was established for the purpose of assisting in regional credit flows in a banking structure where the monetary regime was a gold exchange standard. As the gold standard was replaced, in part in 1934 and finally in 1971, the Federal Reserve Board simply became the residual monopolist of money issue, tied to no rule for issue and to no commodity base.

Dialogue and debate are very active now on alternative monetary arrangements and alternative monetary constitutions. Active support is being voiced for a return to a gold-related currency. Other proposals involve a commodity bundle as the monetary base. Some include a specific constitutional rule that states the allowable rate of increase in base money. My own fear is that debates among the proponents of the different schemes, between the "gold bugs" and their adversaries, will be allowed to distract attention from the more basic requirement that *some* monetary constitution be installed before the inflationary history of the 1970s extends sufficiently to produce the Latin American results.[9]

Is Constitutional Reform a Possible Dream?

I have argued that the political environment for a free enterprise economy must embody genuine and effective constitutional guarantees against undue political-governmental interferences with the workings of free markets, either directly or indirectly via the absence of fiscal and monetary discipline. Such constitutional guarantees do not now exist, either in the United States Constitution or in the written or unwritten constitutions of other Western countries. Can modern governments be harnessed under new constitutional rules? Can constitutional reform be accomplished? And, if introduced, can constitutional rules be enforced?

There is no point in my pretending that these are easy questions, or that the answer is necessarily affirmative to any one of them. As I have said on numerous occasions, however, I think those of us who work primarily in the realm of ideas have a moral obligation to think and to act as if the answer to each of the three questions is affirmative. I must refuse to believe and act as if I did not also acknowledge that there are tremendous barriers to the achievement of any effective change in constitutional rules in America or elsewhere.

There will be resistance to any basic constitutional change in part because of change itself, but primarily because any change must threaten the economic positions of those individuals and groups who secure net rents from the existing structure of government and all of its arms and agencies. Any increase in governmental involvement in economic affairs quickly generates its own clientele, including the dominating bureaucracy that has now reached previously undreamed of levels of power in all Western countries. Members of this bureaucracy will not allow rules changes to be made without putting up a fight.

Nonetheless, times are changing. I can now seriously discuss constitutional reform in forums that would have been impossibly hostile only a decade past. I can seriously present arguments for a constitutional amendment requiring the United States government to balance its budget to an audience of economists who might have laughed me out of court in 1965, or even 1970. Much the same thing applies for those who argue for basic constitutional changes in monetary rules, including some return to a relationship between fiat issue and a commodity base (gold).

One slightly negative note I should add is that the landslide victory of Reagan in 1980 probably reduced the momentum of the movement for basic changes in constitutional rules. This victory (which, of course, I welcomed) lends some support to those critics of constitutional reform who have argued, from the outset, that the forces of electoral competition are sufficient to keep governmental proclivities toward excessive growth and regulation within control. These critics can say to those of us who have been in the forefront of the constitutional reform advocacy: "Look, see what we told you! Electoral competition is working. Government got too big, and the people, through normal electoral processes, have called a halt. There was no need to change the rules, which are now proven to be working well." The argument is superficially plausible, but, at base, I think that such a faith is delusory. Until and unless the basic rules are changed, the forces working toward governmental expansion, along all margins, seem to be inexorable, regardless of which party or which men are in positions of power. At best, a shift of politicians toward those who might support free-market principles, at least in the abstract, and who might possibly attempt to implement these principles in political reality, can generate temporary holding actions against what seems to be the underlying trend patterns for political development.

The accession to office of such parties and politicians may, however, occasion the opportunity to design, construct, and secure general support for changes in the rules of the game that future politicians and parties can violate only at some considerable cost. To expect a constitutional change to be self-enforcing, however, raises another host of issues. Without the widespread adherence to the constitutional attitude referred to in this paper, constitutions remain paper documents, as the evidence from several non-Western countries surely suggests.

My final comment is that there is much, much work to be done by those of us in the academy before getting too involved in day-to-day practical policy advocacy. Constitutional reform is a possible dream; indeed, it must be so, but it is not a dream that is likely to be realized by street-level advocacy in the here and now. We must recognize that we need to turn around intellectual errors of a century; we must make right the fallacies that have pervaded elementary political theory since the early nineteenth century. We must recover the eighteenth-century skepticism about the operations of government and about its potential for doing good.

But let us take heart; men once were wise. They need not remain the twentieth-century idiots that we now observe. Whether or not the required transformation in ideas, which might then allow the transformation in institutions, can be accomplished before matters get much worse than they are now—this is the question that our time will answer, one way or the other.

Endnotes

1. For a good history of the judicial repeal of the "economic constitution," see Bernard Siegen, *Economic Liberties and the Constitution* (Chicago: University of Chicago Press, 1980).

2. For a full discussion on this point, see James M. Buchanan, "The Justice of Natural Liberty," *Journal of Legal Studies* (January 1976): 1-16.

3. Siegen, *Economic Liberties.*

4. Indeed, some evidence suggests that judicial attitudes are changing. "Substantive due process" may be reemerging in a meaningful way. I base this statement on an unpublished lecture presented by Christopher DeMuth at a Liberty Fund Conference in Snowbird, Utah, June 1981.

5. Chicago: University of Chicago Press, 1979.

6. *Finanztheoretische Untersuchungen* (Jena: Gustav Fische, 1896).

7. For a thorough analysis, see Geoffrey Brennan and James Buchanan, *The Power to Tax* (Cambridge: Cambridge University Press, 1980).

8. For a thorough discussion of the development of the economic and political ideas that produced the modern regime of perpetual deficits, making such a constitutional reform needed, see James M. Buchanan and Richard E. Wagner, *Democracy in Deficit* (New York: Academic Press, 1977).

9. For a general discussion of the points made in these two paragraphs on the monetary constitution, see Geoffrey Brennan and James Buchanan, *Monopoly in Money and Inflation* (London: Institute of Economic Affairs, 1981).

SECTION II

The Role of Free Markets in Democratic Capitalism

Free enterprise, private enterprise, and free markets are often used synonymously. As we build toward a philosophy of democratic capitalism, the distinct economic and philosophical nuances of each need to be explored. What is the core drive and value of capitalism—competition or self-interest? What comes first: entrepreneurial creativity, private incentive, or the miracle of efficiency and equity in free markets? What elements of capitalism must meet the tests of philosophy and morality?

In the first reading of this section, University of Chicago scholar William McNeill traces the history of free markets and government intervention. He illustrates with examples from Chinese dynasties one thousand years ago through Western Europe and the United States the social benefits gained from increased reliance on freely competitive markets. His bold historical summary explains the forces that have limited free markets and ultimately effected government intervention. If free markets are to be preserved, McNeill maintains, we must recognize the challenges of national defense, changing technology and, now, modern management methods.

McNeill's philosophical colleague at Chicago, Yale Brozen, provides persuasive contemporary examples of the elegance of free markets. By studying several applications of government intervention, Brozen shows its implicit social disadvantages. Society pays more for intervention than a few special interests gain, he claims. He disputes the justice of the minimum wage law, unemployment taxes, and the progressive income tax.

President Ronald Reagan's economic advisers Jerry Jordan and Paul Rubin discuss one of the tenets of "new federalism": that our Constitution calls explicitly for limits to federal government market intervention. They explain the many common rationales for a government role in our economy—including macroeconomic stability, monopoly, public goods, externalities, and income redistribution. Their point is that the government's role also has many costs. They elaborate on the disadvantage—"government failures"—noted by Yale Brozen. They challenge the public sector to use the inherent strengths of the free market to meet the demands for government participation.

George Gilder declares that focusing on the pros and cons of free markets misses the boat. The backbone to wealth and overcoming poverty is in the unbridled basic humanity of entrepreneurs and businesspeople. Successful businesses—and therefore wealth and jobs—depend on human impulses to save, to fill the needs of others, and to make everyone better off. Public policy and moral philosophy must appreciate the primary role of this entrepreneurial spirit in building or destroying a society. Businesspeople must first of all be free in order to create the value that free markets exchange efficiently.

In these times of high unemployment it is probably no coincidence that all of the authors in this section argue that their solutions are beneficial to the poor. Whether through free markets or through private enterprise, the authors claim more income is created for all.

Obedience to command behavior has deep psychological roots and occasional social benefits; but the impulse to seek personal advantage is always with us too. WILLIAM MCNEILL *boldly describes the evolution of the effectiveness of and limitations on this market principle over more than one thousand years of history.*

He explains that the social benefits of free enterprise were apparent as early as 1000 A.D. in the Chinese Sung Dynasty. There, however, the Confucian moral disdain and distrust for profiting merchants ("human parasites") limited their economic development. As the primacy of market over command spread to northern Italy and then to northwest Europe, the benefits of market economies grew and the limits and destructive forces to free markets changed. McNeill discusses the inherent counterpressures (defense, technology, and modern management) to acceptance of private wealth and unregulated prices. He ponders how the basic simultaneous drives for command and competition will be resolved.

6

Command vs. Market: Across the Centuries

WILLIAM H. MCNEILL

Throughout history two ways of getting things done have rivaled one another. Before about 1000 A.D. the command principle dominated. Large-scale enterprises were undertaken in obedience to someone's orders and transmitted to the work force, often as not, through a hierarchy of subordinate officers and straw bosses. This was the way Stonehenge and the pyramids were built; it is the way the Great Wall of China was constructed. Innumerable temples and other public works were built and maintained by this method of command.

The market principle relied on self-interest in a more direct and private way, motivating people to perform work by offering them the chance to gain. Buying, selling, and exchanging goods and services in response to a perceived advantage to each of the parties involved was harder to organize and more difficult to sustain. For that reason, really large-scale enterprises long remained beyond the reach of market behavior. But from the very earliest time, long before civilized skills evolved, human beings did exchange rare and valued objects—obsidian flakes, cowrie shells, and nuggets of gold and copper, for example.

The rise of civilization enhanced the importance of command since it was on the orders of priests and kings that the monumental works of civilization were constructed. But it also enhanced the scale of trade and long-distance exchanges, since civilized skills often required commodities obtainable only at a distance. Ancient Sumer, for example, the earliest seat of civilized society, had to import building stone and timber, and all early civilizations sought metal from afar. Such dealings were sometimes a result of personal, private responses to market possibilities but such behavior affected relatively few persons directly. Only highly valued commodities could bear the cost of transportation. The great majority of the population were simple farmers, consuming what they themselves produced, paying rents and taxes in kind to their superiors, and sometimes working or fighting at the command of their superiors as well. For this reason the command principle remained predominant. It was the way to get things done.

Human beings are fundamentally attuned to obedience as the basis of common action. Children begin life under the command of their parents, who know more and have greater strength than their offspring. Obedience is expected and in extreme cases can be enforced. Later in life, as adults, they assume their own autonomous roles in the family. But beyond the family circle, it is easy to reaffirm and perpetuate childhood behavior patterns. Whoever exercises authority successfully and issues orders that are obeyed usually does know more than the ordinary fellow who does what he is told; and in any ordered political society the leader will also have superior force at his disposal to coerce any recalcitrant individuals. Yet effective command does not rest primarily on force or the threat of force. Coercion comes into play only exceptionally and by way of example. Far more important on a day-to-day basis are the altruistic sentiments of social solidarity which hold every family together. Extended to a wider circle, such sentiments require each moral individual to share good and bad times with his fellow. Obedience to duly constituted leaders and willing participation in common enterprises as defined by public authorities are part of such sharing. Not to play one's part willingly is therefore felt to be wrong as well as dangerous if it invites punishment.

As a result, command behavior has deep and abiding psychological roots in all of us. Twentieth-century families, as well as modern business corporations, athletic teams, armies, and governments, depend on the aptitude of ordinary people to work together and obey orders willingly.

Yet the impulse to seek personal advantage by making a deal with someone else is also deeply rooted and widespread. This aptitude began to find greater expression after about 1000 A.D. when transport costs were lowered to a point at which regions of diverse natural resources and climatic conditions and with varying local skills could start to trade with one another. Water transport was always much cheaper than overland transport; and ports fronting on quiet seas, like the Mediterranean, had been the foci of far-ranging trade from the time men learned to construct sailing ships—shortly before 3000 B.C. Seaborne trade in the Indian Ocean and in the seas that bathe the coasts of Arabia also originated in ancient times. In the first centuries of the Moslem era, sailors and merchants, operating from such centers as Baghdad and Cairo, wove a commercial network throughout this expanse of quiet sea and supplemented sea trade with overland caravan routes.

But risks remained high. Consequently, trade for the most part was confined to luxuries and items of high value in proportion to their bulk. A decisive change in this pattern, concentrated initially in China, came after about 1000 A.D. Items of everyday consumption began to enter channels of trade, so that common people, ordinary peasants, and a much expanded class of artisans began to depend for their daily livelihood on the circulation of goods and services through the marketplace.

The canalization of China's rivers made this remarkable change possible. That enormous work took centuries to complete and was initially designed more to ensure irrigation and to drain potentially fertile land than for transport. But as the network of canals and canalized river courses was linked into a single system, so that simple boats and barges could convey tons of goods for several hundreds of miles from north to south and inland from the coast, transport costs dropped as never before. Even quite small, local differences in price soon made it worthwhile to carry grain and many other items of everyday consumption up and down the waterways of China. The effect was to increase the country's wealth spectacularly. All the advantages of specialized production, which Adam Smith later analyzed so persuasively in *The Wealth of Nations*, asserted themselves. The population approximately doubled, and China's cities grew to a size that dazzled and amazed such sophisticated world travelers as Marco Polo and Ibn Battuta, the Moslem.

China's commercial transformation was an advantageous departure from earlier subsistence patterns of life. It was also precarious, for any interruption of the circulation of goods and services could lead to acute shortages and swift starvation for millions. But the benefits were so great that every time the trade pattern broke down, the Chinese people speedily set out to reestablish the system by seeking out advantageous exchanges once again, wherever a good deal could be contrived.

Adjacent lands and peoples soon began to share in China's eleventh-century commercial upsurge. Caravans and ships distributed silks, porcelain, and other products of Chinese artisan workshops far and wide and returned with various raw materials and curiosities. The network of shipping that began to connect the south coast of China with the Indian Ocean penetrated even more diverse landscapes and linked up peoples who had entered into commercial relations with one another long before. But there is reason to suppose that the spice trade, so important in medieval Europe, assumed a new scale when Chinese ships and trade goods began to circulate in the Indian Ocean as a supplement to the older trade patterns.

From the Indian Ocean it was no great jump to the Mediterranean. Not surprisingly, therefore, the late eleventh century saw a notable upsurge of Mediterranean trade. Italian merchants and mariners became the principal organizers of that trade, displacing Arab and Byzantine ships and crews from their earlier commercial and piratical primacy. Three factors seem to have allowed the Italians to take over. First of all, they had access to timber in the Apennines and Alps that was superior to anything dwellers on the southern side of the Mediterranean could enjoy. This raw-material advantage was driven home when Italian carpenters developed a cheaper way of building seaworthy ships by substituting a rib and plank construction for the cabinet-work methods then in use. This lowered the cost of shipbuilding substantially. In addition, the Italians discovered a cheap way of protecting their vessels by stationing a handful of crossbowmen in the crow's nest at the top of the mast. Three or four archers could defend a ship against most marauders at the cost of a few crossbow bolts. The combination of a cheap and abundant timber supply, cheaper construction, and inexpensive protection put the carrying trade of the Mediterranean into Italian hands very quickly after about 1100 A.D.

Throughout the world, political protection costs were quite as critical as transport costs for the success of commercial dealings. Within the Chinese empire, officials of the Sung Dynasty (960-1279) fostered and protected trade, and found it advantageous to shift from taxation in kind to a cash basis—thereby, of course, forwarding the rise of the market, since taxpayers now had to sell something to meet their obligations to the state. Nevertheless, as Confucians they believed that a man who got rich from trade did so by cheating others. (Confucius had classed merchants with soldiers as human parasites because they bought cheap and sold dear without adding anything to the value of the goods they dealt in.) Good government therefore required that no one should get conspicuously rich from trade. That made private accumulation of capital very risky in imperial China. The officials' greed and sense of duty coincided, making it their business to prevent anyone from profiting too much. They had the power to check commercial accumulation by imposing confiscatory taxes or by setting "just" prices for what must be sold. In doing so, officials could count on popular support, since ordinary people shared the Confucian distrust and suspicion of anyone who got rich at others' expense. The result, therefore, was to confine trade and manufacturing in China to comparatively small-scale enterprises, usually managed by the members of a single family. Anything requiring large capital investment remained an affair of state, launched, if at all, in response to political decisions and in obedience to official commands.

In this fashion, the commercial transformation of Chinese society was kept within bounds. Rich merchants survived only when they connived with officials, either by paying heavy bribes, or by farming taxes, or by performing some other function at official behest. This set a ceiling on technical advance. Large fixed investment was too much at risk to attract private entrepreneurs. China therefore saw little private development of mining and shipbuilding, the two forms of economic activity that most conspicuously required relatively large capital investment. Not by accident, it was in these domains that the skilled and commercially sophisticated Chinese fell behind the comparatively unskilled Europeans about 1450. It is no exaggeration to suggest that the course of modern history turned on this reversal of the earlier relationship between the Far Eastern and the Western segments of the Old World. How it happened therefore deserves the most careful consideration.

Unfortunately, historians have not usually addressed this question, preferring to specialize in either European or Chinese studies. Nothing resembling a scholarly consensus therefore exists, and my thoughts on the question remain without benefit of systematic professional criticism and correction.

With this by way of apology, therefore, let me assert that Europeans conspicuously outstripped the Chinese and all other civilized peoples after 1500 because the market principle of marshaling the factors of production was protected from political interference in Europe for a longer time than elsewhere. This permitted relatively large accumulations of capital in private hands and opened up possibilities in mining, commerce, and industry that were beyond the resources of other societies that allowed comparably large private wealth only in the form of landholding.

The upper hand that market relations eventually won in Europe had an important side effect inasmuch as it stimulated technical innovation. Innumerable individuals, seeing a chance for gain, became eager to exploit new techniques, since any process or product that proved itself in the marketplace could be expected to enrich its propagators, even if the actual inventors and initial risk-takers often failed to reap the rewards they hoped for.

Why did Europeans tolerate private enrichment from buying and selling when other peoples did not? Nothing in Christian doctrine as interpreted by medieval moralists encouraged the private accumulation of wealth. Quite the contrary; the low opinion Confucius held of merchants was matched by the denunciations that Christian preachers delighted to make of those who imperiled their souls and grew rich at the expense of the poor by refusing to observe just (i.e., fixed and traditional) prices.

The critical difference was not in the realm of ideas but in that of institutions. The really successful European merchants and men of the marketplace were not dependent on the goodwill of political superiors. Instead, they looked after their own defense, and as their wealth increased businessmen became political masters of the cities in which trade and industry flourished most. In effect, the weakness and disruption that descended on the western Roman Empire in the Dark Ages paved the way for the emergence in the eleventh century of a unique new balance between merchants and artisans on the one hand and rural lords and their dependent peasants on the other. As imperial governance decayed and disappeared, local self-defense had become a necessity throughout western Europe. Townsmen who built protective walls and defended them by banding together to form a militia were therefore only doing what others had to do. City walls formed a collective carapace for Europe's townsmen, analogous to the armor that protected the individual knights who became dominant in the European countryside from the tenth century onward.

With arms in hand and city walls to defend, medieval European merchants and artisans found themselves in a different position from that which prevailed in China and other better-governed parts of the world. Outside Europe, officials, soldiers, and landowners everywhere held the upper hand, dividing political power differently in different times and places, and always keeping merchants, artisans, and peasants in subordinate, dependent positions. But in Europe, knights and kings could not surmount a resolutely defended wall at will; and seldom could a feudal army remain long enough in the field to starve out a properly provisioned stronghold. Consequently, European city folk became free to manage their own affairs, set their own taxes, make their own laws, and create local institutions to suit themselves. In those cities where merchants congregated and prospered, laws and institutions were soon adopted to fit their particular convenience. This meant that in such locations no political superior could seize the profits of trade by punitive taxation or fix prices at a level that deprived sellers of profit. Market behavior, responding to differential prices, had freer scope under these conditions than in lands where the moral disapprobation of profiteers, shared as much by Europeans as by other peoples, regularly achieved political expression in the form of confiscatory taxation and price regulation.

North of the Alps, European cities usually recognized some kind of political subordination to a king or other territorial ruler. Not so in Italy, however, where big business developed most vigorously and evolved new forms of military and fiscal management from the fourteenth century onward. For a while, in the thirteenth and fourteenth centuries, a critical weakness in civic self-defense threatened to destroy the independence of leading Italian cities. Internal differences between the rich and the poor became acute so that neither side quite trusted the other to do its share on the battlefield or even in defense of the city walls. Simultaneously, warfare intensified and became chronic. This made it more and more onerous for militiamen to fulfill their military duties. A few cities solved this difficulty by hiring professional soldiers and then inventing administrative methods by which pay could be regularly provided so as to minimize the risk of a *coup d'etat* by disgruntled, unpaid soldiers. By 1400 the best-governed cities of northern Italy had well-disciplined armies at their disposal, and a fiscal system that made it feasible to pay punctually for services rendered on the battlefield and in the frontier guardhouses as well.

As professional, standing armies came into being in Italy, cities were able to take the offensive against local rulers of the countryside. Then greater cities conquered lesser ones, until about a dozen states divided all of northern Italy among themselves, inaugurating an era of city-state war and diplomacy that lasted until after 1500. The remarkable thing about the mercenary armies that carried through this political transformation was that their existence both defended and reinforced the market economy on which the entire power structure rested. By spending their pay, the soldiers accelerated the circulation of goods and services, and made it relatively easy to collect taxes with which to pay their next month's salaries. A powerful feedback loop thus came into operation and made the marketplace safe for private enterprise against enemies abroad and against opponents at home. The successful establishment of mercenary armies coincided with the disfranchisement of the poor. Only thus could merchants, bankers, and men of affairs secure a clear field for self-enrichment and for the enrichment of their cities and of European society as a whole through the expansion of market relations and the specialization of production.

Such a system reversed the normal relationship between commerce and armed force. Everywhere else, merchants existed at the sufferance of local rulers and men of the sword. Kings and princes set the price of doing business. Sometimes they robbed and murdered, and sometimes they merely taxed. But always they had the power to decide just how much protection would cost the merchant who wanted to do business in the territories under their control. In the great commercial and industrial cities of northern Italy from the fourteenth century onward, it was merchants and men of the marketplace who decided how many soldiers they would hire, and how much they would pay for local self-defense. Their interest was to keep such costs to a minimum, and it is safe to assume that the costs for effective military protection in the Italian countryside were indeed less than would have been the cost if military men and the bureaucrats serving them had been free to set a protection price at will.

Careful administration and cost-conscious accountancy in military matters were fully compatible with the rapid technical evolution of weaponry and the art of war. In weapons technology, the Italian city-states engaged in a race between more and more powerful crossbows and better and more cunningly fitted plate armor. Indeed our ordinary image of a medieval knight encased in armor dates only from the latter stages of this race, when armorers learned to sheathe the complex contours of the human body in metal plate literally from top to toe.

The *art* of war was just as important in ensuring the success of Italian professional armies. Strategic and tactical maneuvers, in which pikemen, crossbowmen, and cavalry all played their part, required special skill and a centralized system of command and communications in the field. The bloodless or nearly bloodless battles and elaborate maneuvering of which Machiavelli was so disdainful were the fine fruit of the art. Military success could not be more cheaply attained; and it *was* successful. For some two centuries, Italian mercenaries were entirely able to hold their own against all comers, and they did so at minimal cost to all concerned.

What ended Italy's primacy in war and commerce was a gradual transfer of its administrative, commercial, industrial, and military skills to much larger territorial states located beyond the Alps. Beginning in 1494, first France and then Spain sent armies into Italy that were larger than anything a single city-state could afford. This escalation of numbers coincided with an important technological revolution that made guns decisive in battle. This put Italians at a disadvantage, for they lacked sufficient supplies of metals and fuel to compete on even terms with gunfounders north of the Alps. Perhaps, too, craft-guild inertia and vested interest in crossbow and plate armor manufacture hindered adaptation to gunpowder weapons in Italy and let Germans and Netherlanders take over primacy in the arms business.

At any rate, the evolution of military management beyond the Alps more or less paralleled that of Italy. In particular, the commercialization of war, consummated in the age of the Italian Renaissance, spread north, beginning in the fourteenth century as older feudal armies became outmoded. To be sure, there was some delay. Not until after 1648 did mercenary troops and bureaucratic management of a tax system capable of assuring regular pay become firmly implanted in trans-Alpine Europe. By that time, commercial exchanges had become so intense in many parts of northwestern Europe that the same feedback loop that had allowed Italian cities to sustain an efficient mercenary force indefinitely and without too heavy a strain on the taxpayers also became operative in such countries as France and the Netherlands, and in some German principalities as well.

Yet the trans-Alpine development was not simply a recapitulation of earlier Italian experience. For kings and noblemen continued to rule the states of northern Europe, and merchant oligarchies of the sort that controlled Venice, Milan, Genoa, and—less securely—Florence were never more than junior partners to the men who managed trans-Alpine governments. Nevertheless, the noble and well-born rulers of western Europe reluctantly learned from the course of events that if commerce was allowed to flourish freely and merchants were permitted to set their own prices and accumulate profits without fear of confiscation, then, and only then, could kings and princes hope to collect enough taxes to pay for a first-class army. The price of becoming and remaining a great military power was to tolerate and even to encourage trade and commerce, to foster industry and in general to create conditions under which rich merchants and capitalists could and would do business. A ruler like Philip II of Spain, who failed to observe these rules, saw the wealth and military capability of the lands under his control seep away. His enemies, the Dutch, let market relations prevail and turned desolate sand spits and water-logged bogs in the northern Low Countries into the world's most active center of commerce. They were therefore able to make good their revolt against King Philip's taxation by winning an eighty-year struggle against the imperial might of Spain in 1648.

The commercial prosperity that sustained well-managed politics in Europe was reinforced after 1500 by the fact that European ships were able to traverse all the oceans of the earth, thanks to improvements in shipbuilding and navigation, and to the geographical discoveries of bold captains like Columbus, Vasco da Gama, and Magellan. Stout construction, necessary to survive the storms of the north Atlantic, and cheap cannon, resulting from Europe's precocious development of mining and metallurgy, made European ships more formidable than others. Traders could go where they pleased, at little risk from local opponents and rivals who could neither match nor resist European guns. Europe's merchants were therefore free to explore the inhabited coasts of the earth, seeking profitable deals. Sometimes supremacy at sea was swiftly translated into territorial sovereignty, as happened in the New World and, on a lesser scale, in the East Indies. More often a few coastal forts sufficed to give European merchants the shore base they needed for the conduct of trade. This was the case in Africa and India before the eighteenth century.

But whatever the local political arrangements may have been—and they varied widely—the essential point was this: armed European merchants were able to weave an increasingly dense network of commercial exchanges around the shores of every inhabited continent, and to bring back to their home ports the profits of their dealings all around the world. Such wealth in turn encouraged further investment in ships and trade goods, and helped to support the political structures—themselves in perpetual competition and conflict—that protected the merchants and allowed them to engage in business without fear of crippling taxation. Moreover, as the scale of European trade increased, the invention of joint stock companies allowed business to transcend the limits of individual wealth.

Other peoples could not compete or catch up. Instead, sooner or later their defenses broke down in the face of ever-mounting European formidability. Most of India fell under English control by the end of the eighteenth century, for example. Similarly, almost all of North America and South America was partitioned among European imperial powers by the same date. Simultaneously, the vast expanse of Siberia and much of central Asia fell under the domination of Russia. Australia, too, saw the beginning of European colonization in 1788, and James Cook's voyages of exploration opened the vast and almost empty expanses of Oceania to commercial and colonial penetration.

For three centuries, Japan and China were able to hold Europeans at arm's length. Strict regulations imposed on foreign traders kept exchanges at a comparatively trivial level until after 1838. But Far

Eastern defenses, too, eventually failed. This became obvious when an expeditionary force sent to avenge insults to British commerce at Canton easily overcame the Chinese. After a few clashes that demonstrated their superior military power, the British compelled the Chinese government to sign a humiliating peace in 1841 that opened additional ports to British merchants.

Weaknesses within China certainly had much to do with this amazing demonstration of the superiority of the European armed forces by the fourth decade of the nineteenth century. But the incipient industrialization of war, which got into high gear during the 1840s, meant that for another full century western European governments were able to overpower resistance in Asia, Africa, and Oceania so easily that there is much truth in the gibe that the nineteenth-century British empire was acquired in a fit of absence of mind.

As long as Great Britain played the central role in European expansion, the sovereignty of the market as the regulator of large-scale economic effort seemed secure. Britain's eighteenth- and nineteenth-century greatness had been founded on a policy of fostering trade abroad and allowing free scope to individual initiative at home. The advantages of free trade had been persuasively analyzed by Adam Smith toward the end of the eighteenth century, and free trade became government policy in the 1840s. Thereafter, British diplomacy and British arms removed obstacles to trade and expanded its scope everywhere. Other peoples, too, saw the advantages to be had from allowing market prices to direct economic behavior, though most governments maintained protective tariffs against foreign goods, fearing the consequences of free competition.

Nevertheless, these surviving political obstacles to untrammeled operation of the price system were trivial in comparison to the enormous changes that came pell-mell as the industrial revolution made its way around the earth. The market principle seemed everywhere triumphant. Cheaper transport on a global scale allowed more and more persons to live by buying and selling goods and services. Optimists believed that economic interdependence would make war among the world's leading industrial states impossible, though an escalating arms race that pitted the world's leading industrial powers against one another from the 1880s argued otherwise.

All the same, World War I came as a great shock to all the participants. Expectations of quick victory were betrayed by the event. Instead, each principal belligerent had to harness the entire resources of society to the task of maximizing the national war effort. All of a sudden, command again took precedence over mere market considerations. Profiteering became wicked. Prices were fixed. Rationing deprived cash income of its accustomed value. The triumph of the market, so self-evident before 1914, went into escrow for the duration.

After the war ended, to be sure, western nations made an effort to return to prewar patterns of economic and social management. In Russia, however, the Bolsheviks set out to create a communist society, explicitly repudiating the market as a guide to action. For a while they, too, found it necessary to revert to a limited reliance on market incentives to induce peasants to bring their grain to market; but in 1928 Stalin inaugurated a new drive to industrialize "according to plan." To feed the industrial work force, the Soviet regime fell back on forcible requisitioning of grain from the peasantry. This reaffirmation of the command principle was soon followed in the western world by a partial reassertion of World War I patterns of state economic management. Severe depression, beginning in 1929, provoked this response, especially in Germany and the United States. Soon thereafter World War II broke out and once again each of the major belligerents set up a war economy, reaffirming the centrality of the command principle for successful waging of war. Peace in 1945 brought only a partial retreat from political management of the economy, even in the United States. Welfare supplanted warfare as the professed goal toward which politicians directed their efforts, but in the United States an arms race with the Soviet Union swiftly became a second powerful shaper of government economic action.

To be sure, in the post-war decades the deliberate manipulation of taxes, interest rates, and public expenditures did leave considerable room for privately set prices to rise and fall. Price regulation of individual and small-group economic behavior thus remained real enough in the so-called free world. But the framework within which such private activity was conducted became subject to change at the will of government authorities and elected officials. The market was no longer sovereign; instead its operation had become subject to command decisions emanating from the political process.

The change from the nineteenth century was remarkable. In retrospect one can see how new methods of business management, starting about the 1880s, paved the way for the restoration of the primacy of command over the market as the regulator of mass behavior. Assembly-line and other flow-through technologies proved capable of lowering production costs spectacularly. A few firms, by achieving such economies, grew to enormous proportions even before 1914. It therefore became a relatively simple matter for such firms, together with smaller and less efficient ones, to come together during World War I into what amounted to a national cartel, within which principles of management analogous to those developed in the best-run private firms could be applied on a nationwide basis to maximize war output. World War II enlarged the base by establishing transnational war economies; and in the postwar world, transnational corporations have shown that similar geographic range is well within the capability of private firms as well.

In retrospect, it seems plausible to believe that between 1914 and 1945 something like a millennium of growing market dominance was checked and reversed within the lifetime of a single generation. This is not really surprising. A majority have always disliked and feared the short-term impact of free operation of the market. Such popular, populist feelings probably intensified as technological change became more and more rapid and disrupted existing social relationships. Any political system that registers democratic wishes and pursues welfare as a short-term goal is therefore bound to inhibit and interfere with the untrammeled operation of the market.

But political pressure to protect the weak from the play of market forces is powerfully countered by persistent competition among states and other large, bureaucratized, private, sometimes quasi-governmental corporations. New techniques and new patterns of behavior that promise greater power, wealth, or prestige have enormous pulling power when survival of one or more of the competitors is, or seems to be, at stake. The plain fact is that deliberate interference with market relationships may accelerate social and technical change as well as obstruct it. Indeed, the rise of democracy, with its penchant for protecting the weak, and the rise of private and public technocratic management have been running a race since the 1880s, when scientific management of large-scale enterprises first began to foster systematic change in business and industry.

As long as individuals were free to enrich themselves by taking whatever advantage of market relationships they could, society remained open to technical improvement. Those injured by some new method of cheapened product were unable to stop others from making their fortunes by introducing a new and superior device. Of late, however, another, very powerful source of innovation by command has come into operation. Corporate research and development plans systematically seek new techniques from which profits may be derived—eventually. Many such plans are keyed to and largely sustained by the rivalries among mutually distrustful states which impel an almost frantic pace of weapons development. Apart from the technological marvels of modern weapons themselves, spin-offs from the arms race have become a principal and perhaps *the* principal source of technological advance. Consider the recent impact of airplanes, computers, atomic energy, lasers, and microchips, for example, none of which would have developed as they did without military origins. Costs scarcely mattered. Command situations, always seeking new and superior weapons, therefore seem to have taken over from the market as the principal promoter of technological change.

The days of rugged individualism and unregulated operation of the market are therefore unlikely to return. Perhaps the centuries of ever-expanding market sovereignty were only possible because, for nearly a millennium, cheap transport outranged effective administration, until in the last hundred years electromagnetic communications made administrative coordination on a global basis feasible. More recently, computers have made data retrieval remarkably rapid and easy. It has become correspondingly difficult for large-scale economic activity to escape governmental regulation, supervision, and management, though international corporations are still free to pick and choose whose regulations to submit to for at least some of their operations.

On the other hand, impulses to make a deal and acquire private advantage are presumably as strong and widespread today as ever in the past. Governmental management does not always work well; and ways to get around regulations, or to act outside the law by entering a black market, are as numerous as the regulations themselves. Mass obedience to official management undoubtedly depends on the pre-existing willingness of the population at large to abide by the rules. If official rules seem silly or unjust, enforcement soon becomes difficult or impossible.

Wartime experience of the possibilities of a command economy are perhaps deceptive, inasmuch as during World Wars I and II the great majority of the people under each belligerent government believed in the necessity and general righteousness of the cause for which their nation stood. Willing cooperation and obedience, even at heavy personal cost, were duties almost everyone accepted. In peacetime, when comparable public emergency does not impel cooperation and self-sacrifice, management of a command economy becomes far more difficult. The choice of goals is more ambiguous, and differences of opinion about priorities, prices, and the decision-making process itself may become serious. Recent experience in socialist countries illustrates the difficulty of managing a command economy efficiently and to everyone's satisfaction. The dilemmas of stagflation encountered by the United States and other western countries since the 1970s suggest that the free world's post-World War II version of politically managed economies has not escaped all the dilemmas of state planning that beset socialist countries.

I conclude that the interplay between command and market incentives as a basis for large-scale human cooperation has not achieved any final resolution in our time, even though the sudden and unforeseen upsurge of political management of society and the economy since 1914 has certainly altered the balance between the two principles very sharply. The market still has its power, as the rise of Japanese, Hong Kong, Taiwanese, and Korean export industries since 1950 shows. Tax havens still exist for private wealth. As long as the earth continues to harbor numerous independent states, with divergent tax and credit policies, capital can be expected to flow toward places where protection costs are lowest. Only the establishment of an empire of the earth could check that sort of capital migration. And even were such a global empire to arise, there would remain the black market. The age-old polarity between these two principles is therefore most unlikely to be resolved by any political act, however much public authorities may seek to control, channel, and limit market dealings to suit particular interests, popular feeling, and political pressure groups.

Brozen's Law: "Whenever the government attempts to redistribute income from the rich to the poor, it creates more poor people, impoverishes the nation, and decreases the portion of the tax burden borne by the rich."

YALE BROZEN *argues that any government interference with the free market allocation of wages and employment fails by ultimately increasing the demand for poverty. A few benefit; the nation and the majority of the poor lose. He develops his argument by analyzing selected data on minimum wage rates, progressive income tax rates, and unemployment tax legislation. He further asserts that U.S. auto and steel industry woes (as examples) are inspired by government-sanctioned union power and that the workers in the other industries absorbing the unemployed from auto and steel pay the price through reduced wages.*

Ultimately, productivity falls and unemployment grows. Following Brozen's Law, we need to decrease the rewards for not working.

7

Government and Income Distribution: Its Effects on the Private Market

YALE BROZEN

There are many so-called "laws of nature." Professor C. Northcote Parkinson, for example, the former Raffles Professor at the University of Singapore, through many years of painstaking research, discovered the law that "expenses rise to meet income." If he had spent a little time observing the federal government, he might have amended his law to read, "expenditures always exceed income, no matter how great income is."

Lee Loevinger, formerly of the Federal Communications Commission, discovered a very useful law that helps us to understand many things. His law might be called "the law of irresistible use." Loevinger's law says, "If a boy has a hammer, it proves something needs pounding. The political science analog is that if there is a government agency, this proves something needs regulating."

This paper proposes Brozen's Law: *Whenever the government attempts to redistribute income from the rich to the poor, it creates more poor people, impoverishes the nation, and decreases the portion of the tax burden borne by the rich.*[1]

First, what are the means used by government to redistribute income? They are many and varied in design. They range from minimum wage laws to welfare programs to a steeply progressive income tax structure that taxes high incomes disproportionately more than it taxes low income. A more complete list would have to include: rent controls and other price controls (such as those imposed on natural gas and the lifeline rates for telephone service); unemployment insurance; laws granting power to unions and exempting them from the antitrust laws and the laws against the use of violence; the bend in the formula relating Social Security benefits to the amount of Social Security tax paid; provision of educational services at no charge or at a nominal charge; Medicaid, housing, and urban renewal programs; toll-free waterways constructed or maintained by the federal government; overpayment of low-echelon civil servants and postal workers; agricultural and maritime subsidy programs; corporate earnings and property taxation; the subsidies provided to the Tennessee Valley Authority; the Rural Electrification Administration loans at 2 percent and 5 percent; and so forth. Even this very incomplete catalog of income redistribution programs is too long to analyze in one short paper. And, as you may be aware, some of these programs redistribute income from the poor to the rich while others redistribute in the opposite direction. The net effect of all these programs is to impoverish the nation without producing marked benefits for the poor. Some of the poor are helped, but most of the poor are worse off than they would be without the programs that are supposed to help them.

The minimum wage laws are an example of an attempt to help the poor that has backfired. There are four effects of these laws. One is that some people do receive an increase in their cash wage rate and in their total cash income. The increase is small, and for many, it is at the expense of their future income.[2]

Despite the increase in cash income, with a rise in the statutory minimum, the recipients of this largess suffer from a reduced utility of their total compensation. Employers compensate their workers not only with cash, but also in other ways. They provide training programs, other noncash income in the form of amenities on the job, and various fringe benefits (medical and dental insurance, contributions to pension plans, stability of employment, vacation and holiday pay, and so forth.) When an employer is forced to raise the cash wage rate for employees, he often reduces other elements in the compensation he provides, such as training programs, rather than laying people off or reducing the number of people hired.[3]

With less training provided for low-wage workers, they do not become as skilled. Their future compensation is reduced by the rise in their current minimum cash wage. A survey of the job experience of young male workers between 1966 and 1969 found that they received 38 percent to 58 percent of their compensation in the form of on-the-job training in 1966. The 1967 increase in the minimum wage reduced the amount of on-the-job training by 26 percent to 31 percent. As a result, the wage for these young male workers rose less rapidly in the following years. By 1969, their compensation was 14 percent to 17 percent lower than it would have been if there had been no increase in the statutory minimum wage in 1967.[4]

A second effect of minimum wage laws is to reduce the cash income of some low-wage workers by forcing them out of higher-wage jobs into lower-wage work. The federal minimum wage law does not cover all occupations. Whenever the minimum wage increases, the number of jobs in covered occupations decreases in comparison to what it would otherwise be.[5] Some workers forced out of covered occupations or prevented from entering these occupations by a rise in the statutory minimum wage have had to take jobs in noncovered occupations—for example, as busboys or in domestic service—at a lower wage that they had previously spurned.[6]

Since 1956, the coverage of the Fair Labor Standards Act has been expanded from 53 percent of all jobs to 84 percent.[7] The result is that workers who have been laid off can no longer find jobs, as they once did, in noncovered occupations at low-wage rates. This is the third effect of our minimum wage laws. Thus, each increase in the statutory minimum and its coverage has increased the unemployment rate among unskilled workers, and the number of unskilled workers is increasing because there is less on-the-job training.

This has produced tragic results for minority teenagers, who are among our least skilled workers.[8] Their unemployment rate is now 40 percent, a rate never before reached even at the depths of previous recessions. This scandalously high unemployment rate is a consequence of the new high level of the statutory minimums and, also, of the high entering minimums set by some unions.

The fourth effect of the minimum wage rate is a misallocation of capital and labor and a reduction in the rate of capital formation, causing a much slower rise in productivity. One of our major problems in this country is a declining rate of productivity growth. It has dropped continuously since the mid-1960s. From 1947 to 1966, output per worker hour grew by 3.2 percent per year. The output-per-hour growth rate dropped by one-third to 2.1 percent from 1966 to 1973. Then it fell by more than one-half to 1.0 percent from 1973 to 1978. Since 1978, output per hour has declined for many reasons. One reason is the rising statutory minimum wage rate, which has gone from $2.30 to $3.35 an hour plus legally required benefits since 1977. This has forced people into low-productivity, noncovered jobs instead of the high-productivity jobs that they otherwise would have found. As a consequence, average productivity has decreased.

Rather than elaborate further on the influence of the *statutory* minimum wage rate, let me turn to an illustration in terms of *collectively bargained* minimum wage rates, since their effect is the same as statutory minimums. Incidentally, those collectively bargained minimums would not be as high as they are in steel; auto, air, rail, truck, and ship transporation; mass transit; coal mining; and construction but for the power that we have given to unions on the basis of the misguided notion that giving power to unions would redistribute income to poverty-stricken workers.[9] The net result is the same as the effect of the statutory minimums. More workers have been impoverished by unions than have gained from union efforts. Attempting to redistribute income from the rich to the poor by giving power to unions has made the poor poorer than they would otherwise be.

For example, in the steel industry, workers in a free market would normally be paid about 15 to 20 percent more than an average manufacturing worker. Their skill level is somewhat higher than the average manufacturing worker and the steel industry invests more in worker training than does the average employer. When employers invest more in worker training, they pay higher wage rates in order to reduce the voluntary quit rate and avoid losing their investment through worker quits.

In the early 1950s, the premium received by steelworkers over the average manufacturing production worker was 18 percent. By the early 1960s, the premium mounted to 46 percent, and the steel industry began to be troubled by imports and a loss of export markets. The discipline imposed by imports dropped the premium back to 39 percent (see Exhibit 1). By the time the extended negotiating no-strike agreement was signed in 1973, the premium had returned to the 46 percent level. It then accelerated its rise, from a little over one percentage point per year (1952-1973) to nearly six percentage points, reaching 86 percent in 1980. The result of this superpremium pay in the steel industry relative to the pay of the average manufacturing worker is that employment in the industry is now about 400,000 less than it would be if a "normal" premium were paid.

What happened to the 400,000 workers who were frozen out of the steel industry by the minimum wage set in collective bargaining agreements? These workers have found jobs in other industries—jobs in which they are less productive than they would have been in the steel industry and in which they are paid less than they would have been paid in steel. In steel, absent the power of the union, workers would be paid 20 percent to 25 percent more than they are now earning and they would be employed more productively.[10]

Not only have the invisible 400,000 suffered as a result of the current pay scale in the steel industry. Other workers are also paid less. Employment in other industries expanded by 400,000, but only because pay rates are lower than they would have been if the invisible 400,000 were not competing for these alternative jobs. The high pay rates of steel industry workers who are employed come at the expense of all other workers.

Incidentally, this squeeze on opportunities for employment in high-productivity jobs is forcing workers into less-productive, alternative occupations. That is part of the reason for the decline in productivity in the last three years and the slowed growth in average productivity in earlier years. This is the reason I spoke earlier of the fact that the redistribution mechanisms we have employed, which were intended to redistribute income from the rich to the poor, have instead impoverished the nation and the poor. Productivity growth has been slowed in part by minimum wage laws and minimum wage rates set in collective bargaining agreements. As a result, our total output today is about 23 percent less than it would otherwise have been. Real wage rates are

Exhibit 1: **Relationship between steel and all-manufacturing employee compensation**

	Average hourly earnings[a]				Hourly employment costs[b]		
	Steel		All manufacturing (BLS)	Percent premium[c] (BLS)	Steel (AISI)	All manufacturing (BLS)	Percent premium
Year	(BLS)	(AISI)					
1947	$ 1.44	$ 1.46	$ 1.22	18	$ 1.56	$ 1.96(2.8)	18
1952	2.02	2.04	1.64	23	2.32	2.53(1.6)	27
1957	2.73	2.73	2.04	34	3.22	2.85(1.4)	46
1962	3.29	3.33	2.39	38	4.16(0.3)	3.43(2.3)	39
1967	3.62	3.66	2.83	28	4.76(0.8)	4.84(2.3)	46
1972	5.15	5.22	3.81	35	7.08(0.6)	5.26(2.8)	46
1973	5.56	5.69	4.07	37	7.68(0.9)	5.75(2.4)	58
1974	6.38	6.55	4.40	45	9.08(0.7)	6.35(1.4)	67
1975	7.11	7.23	4.81	48	10.59(0.2)	6.92(1.7)	70
1976	7.86	8.00	5.19	51	11.74(0.3)	7.59(1.8)	72
1977	8.67	8.91	5.63	54	13.04(0.4)	8.31(2.1)	72
1978	9.70	9.98	6.17	57	14.30(0.4)	9.08(2.0)	75
1979	10.77	11.02	6.69	61	15.92(0.4)	9.92(1.5)	86
1980	11.84	12.11	7.27	63	18.45(0.2)		

[a] Does not include pay for holidays not worked or vacation pay.

[b] Quit rate shown in parentheses (monthly quits per 100 employees). Employment cost includes holiday and vacation pay plus employee benefits.

[c] Percent by which steel hourly earnings or compensation exceed the corresponding figures for all manufacturing.

Source: U.S. Bureau of Labor Statistics, *Bulletin* 1312-11; *Employment and Earnings* (Washington, D.C.: Government Printing Office, March 1981); U.S. Council on Wage and Price Stability, *Prices and Costs in the United States Steel Industry* (Washington, D.C.: Government Printing Office, October 1977).

BLS data include all steel manufacturers in SIC 3312.

AISI data include only wage employees engaged in steel producing operations.

about 20 percent lower than they would have been if we had not installed various mechanisms to push wage rates up, such as minimum wage laws and unions and other income redistribution schemes. And unemployment has been mounting recently because collectively bargained wage rates have been rising at a 10 percent rate instead of the 6 percent rate that would have been consistent with the maintenance of full employment.

The wage and employment experience in the automobile industry is almost identical with that in the steel industry (see Exhibit 2). The same story can be repeated for automobile wage rates and employment. We can add an analysis of the experience in one state to provide further detail. From 1950 to 1957, wage rates in the auto industry rose 10 percent more in Michigan than they would have without a strong union. Employment in the auto industry fell by 88,000 in Michigan compared to what it would otherwise have been. The workers who would have found jobs in the auto industry went to work in other industries in Michigan. Wage rates in these other industries rose 6 percent less than they would have if wage rates had not been pushed to superpremium levels in the Michigan portion of the auto industry.[11] A large number of lower-paid workers suffered a 6 percent wage decrease and a small number of higher-paid workers enjoyed the 10 percent increase in their premium. As a consequence, workers as a whole in Michigan were worse off.

So far, I have discussed only indirect methods of income redistribution and the consequences of their distortion of wage rates in private markets. Turning now to some of the programs for direct redistribution of income, let us examine some of their consequences. First, let us look at the steeply progressive income tax structure that we have had.

In 1921, the income tax rate on top-bracket income was 73 percent. As a result, people did not choose to earn much income subject to such a high tax rate. Since most of our saving and investment in tools and equipment, which makes workers more productive and which enables them to earn high rates of pay, is done by upper-income groups, there was little high-bracket income produced and little saving and investment. Also, since there was little taxable high-bracket income, most of the taxes were paid by lower-income people. In 1921, 72 percent of all income taxes were collected from people making less than $100,000 per year. Those making over $100,000 were subject to income tax rates ranging from 60 percent to 73 percent on their marginal income, and they paid 28 percent of all income taxes collected. By 1926, the tax rate on income over $100,000 was reduced to 25 percent. With this steep reduction in top-bracket rates, incentives for earning taxable income in this bracket increased greatly. Instead of keeping only 27 cents out of each extra dollar earned, top-bracket-income taxpayers could now keep 75 cents.

A remarkable thing happened. Despite a nearly two-thirds reduction in tax rate on the top-bracket group, they paid 86 percent more taxes in 1926 than they paid in 1921 (see Exhibit 3). They earned so much more

Exhibit 2: **Relationship between motor vehicle and all-manufacturing employee compensation for wage earners**

	Average hourly earnings							Hourly employment costs				
	Motor vehicle[c]		All-manufacturing		Percent premium[a]			General Motors		All-manufacturing		Percent premium[a]
Year	Hours paid	Hours worked	Hours paid	Hours worked	Hours paid	Hours worked		Hourly employment costs	Quit rate[b]	Hourly employment costs	Quit rate[b]	
1952	—	2.11	$1.65	—	—	—		$2.26	—	$1.96	2.8%	15%
1957	—	2.64	2.04	—	—	—		2.90	—	2.53	1.6	15
1958	$2.64	—	2.10	—	26%	—		—	0.5%	2.64	1.1	—
1962	3.10	3.26	2.39	2.55	30	28%		3.71	0.6	2.85	1.4	30
1967	3.66	4.11	2.82	3.04	30	35		4.87	1.3	3.43	2.3	42
1972	5.35	6.00	3.82	4.14	40	45		7.58	0.8	4.84	2.3	57
1973	5.70	6.47	4.09	4.45	39	45		8.10	1.0	5.26	2.8	54
1974	6.23	7.20	4.42	4.83	41	49		9.52	1.0	5.75	2.4	66
1975	6.82	7.96	4.83	5.29	41	50		10.59	0.6	6.35	1.4	67
1976	7.45	8.72	5.22	5.72	43	52		11.23	0.7	6.92	1.7	62
1977	8.22	9.64	5.68	6.24	45	54		12.56	0.8	7.59	1.8	65
1978	8.98	10.56	6.17	6.79	46	56		13.76	0.8	8.31	2.1	66
1979	9.74	11.54	6.69	7.37	46	57		15.13	0.7	9.08	2.0	67
1980	10.66	13.34	7.20	8.02	48	66		18.44	—	9.92	1.4	86

[a] Percent by which motor vehicle hourly earnings or compensation exceed the corresponding figures for all manufacturing.

[b] Monthly quits per 100 employees in the motor vehicle industry and in all manufacturing.

[c] U.S. Bureau of Labor Statistics, *Bulletin* 1312-11, *Employment and Earnings* (Washington, D.C.: Government Printing Office, November 1980). BLS stands for data from the Bureau of Labor Statistics. Hourly employment costs are for General Motors production workers.

income in 1926 subject to the 25 percent rate than they earned in 1921 subject to 60 percent to 73 percent rates that they paid 51 percent of the total tax collected instead of only 28 percent (see Exhibit 3). Taxing the rich less resulted in their bearing a doubled share of the tax burden. We were on the wrong side of the hump in the Laffer Curve in 1921.

In the same period, 1921 to 1926, average annual earnings of employees rose by 12 percent and the consumer price index dropped by 2 percent. You might contrast that with the years 1975-80 in which weekly pre-tax earnings dropped by 6 percent measured in constant dollars[12] and, because of bracket creep resulting from inflation, after-tax real earnings and median family income dropped even more (see Exhibit 4).[13] During the first half of the 1920s, saving and investment barely kept up with the rise in the work force. They have been insufficient to increase the amount of tools and equipment available for each employee.

In our impatience to squeeze more out of the geese that laid those golden eggs, we have nearly strangled them with punitive tax rates and now have fewer golden eggs.

The 1921-26 experience is not unique. We were on the wrong side of the Laffer Curve in the early 1960s. In 1963, income over $50,000 was taxed at rates ranging from 59 percent to 91 percent. These rates were then cut to a

Exhibit 3: **Tax revenue collected before and after tax reduction during the 1920s**

Net income grouping	Tax revenue collected (in millions of constant 1929 dollars)			Percent of tax revenue collected	
	1921	1926	Percent change	1921	1926
Less than $ 5,000[a]	$ 89.0	$ 12.8	− 85.6	12.9	1.8
$ 5,000 to $ 10,000	66.1	19.7	− 70.2	9.6	2.8
$10,000 to $ 25,000	121.8	70.3	− 43.2	17.6	9.9
$25,000 to $ 50,000	108.3	109.4	+ 1.0	15.7	15.4
$50,000 to $100,000	111.1	136.5	+ 23.0	16.1	19.2
Over $100,000	194.0	361.5	+ 86.3	28.1	50.9
Total	$ 690.2	$ 710.2	+ 2.9	100.0	100.0

[a] Due to increases in the minimum filing income level and increases in the personal exemption allowance from $2,500 to $3,500 for joint returns ($1,000 to $1,500 for separate returns), the number of persons filing in this income class decreased dramatically during the period.

Source: Internal Revenue Service, *Statistics of Income* (Annual). Cited from James Gwartney and Richard Stroup, "Tax Reductions, Incentive Effects, and the Distribution of the Tax Burden," *Economic Review* (Atlanta, Georgia: Federal Reserve Bank of Atlanta, March 1982).

Exhibit 4: **Median family incomes before and after direct federal taxes and inflation, 1971-1981**

		Direct federal taxes			After-tax income	
Year	Median family income[a]	Income tax[b]	Social Security	Total	Current dollars	1971 dollars[c]
1971	$ 10,314	$ 933	$ 406	$ 1,339	$ 8,975	$ 8,975
1972	11,152	982	468	1,450	9,702	9,392
1973	11,895	1,098	632	1,730	10,165	9,264
1974	13,004	1,267	761	2,028	10,976	9,014
1975	14,156	1,172	825	1,997	12,159	9,149
1976	15,016	1,388	878	2,266	12,750	9,071
1977	15,949	1,466	933	2,399	13,550	9,056
1978	17,318	1,717	1,048	2,765	14,553	9,034
1979	19,097	1,876	1,171	3,047	16,050	8,955
1980	20,900[d]	2,197	1,281	3,478	17,422	8,563
1981	23,700[d]	2,801[e]	1,576	4,377	19,323	8,548

[a] Median income for all families with one earner employed full-time, year-round.

[b] Married couple filing joint return, two children.

[c] Adjusted by *Consumer Price Index* of the Bureau of Labor Statistics.

[d] 1980 and 1981 estimated by Tax Foundation.

[e] Assumes no change in current law.

Source: *Monthly Tax Features*, vol. 25, no. 6 (June-July 1981).

range of 50 percent to 70 percent. With these cuts, revenues from this group increased 34 percent in 1965 over 1963 (see Exhibit 5). The share of personal income tax revenues collected from the top 5 percent of taxpayers rose from 35.6 percent to 38.5 percent. This was not a result of bracket creep or inflation. The data were adjusted for the 3 percent increase in the consumer price index to measure what happened in constant dollars.

> Tax rates—particularly marginal tax rates—influence the reward structure confronted by individual taxpayers, and thereby exert an impact on the allocation of labor and capital resources.... When taxes are levied on an economic activity, the quantity of that activity undertaken will decline.[14]

In attempting to redistribute income from the rich to the poor, a high tax rate on the rich will, paradoxical as it may seem, result in less of the tax burden being borne by the rich. Reducing tax rates on our upper-bracket-income taxpayers increases the revenues collected from them and increases the share of the tax burden they bear.

Exhibit 5: **Growth rate of adjusted gross income (AGI) and tax revenues (income of $50,000 or more before and after 1964 tax cut) (in constant 1963 dollars)**

Year	Adusted gross income (billions of dollars)	Tax revenue collected (billions of dollars)	Average tax rate
1961	$ 13.75	$ 5.21	37.9%
1962	13.62	5.04	37.0
1963	14.60	5.38	36.8
1964	17.67	6.08	34.4
1965	21.33	7.20	33.8
1966	23.65	7.97	33.7
	Growth		
1961-1963	6.2%	3.3%	—
1963-1965	46.1	33.8	—

Source: *Statistics of Income: Individual Income Tax Returns*, Internal Revenue Service (Washington, D.C.: Government Printing Office, Annual). Cited from James Gwartney and Richard Stroup, "Tax Reductions, Incentive Effects, and the Distribution of the Tax Burden," *Economic Review* (Atlanta, Georgia: Federal Reserve Bank of Atlanta, March 1982).

Transfer Programs and the Labor Participation Rate

Let us turn now to the effect of governmental largess on the recipients. The largess is passed out through many channels—Social Security disability pensions, aid for families with dependent children, general welfare assistance, supplementary security income, food stamps, school lunch programs, basic educational opportunity grants, price support programs for farmers, maritime subsidy programs, mass transit subsidy programs, heating cost allowances for low-income families, and many more. Let us take Social Security disability pensions for analysis.

You would think that the supply of disabled people would be completely inelastic. To get a disability pension, you must have been unable to work for at least five months and there must be no prospect that your disability will be cured in the next twelve months. That would seem to fix the population eligible for disability with no possibility for expansion.

Disability pensions were first provided under the Social Security system in mid-1957 for workers aged 50 to 64. They were expanded to cover all workers late in 1960. In addition, the monthly payment has grown from $97 in 1961 to over $400. The monthly payment has gone up relative to the wage rate. As it did so, the number of disabled workers grew much faster than the total work force. From two million in 1961, the number expanded to five million.

Professor Donald Parsons investigated the phenomenon as part of a project in which he was trying to find out why so many men in the prime working age, 35 to 64, had dropped out of the work force. The number of men 35 to 44 years of age who do not participate has more than doubled since 1953, rising from 1.8 percent to 4.3 percent (see Exhibit 6). In the 45- to 54-year-old group, the number increased from 3.5 percent to 8.7 percent. And in the 55- to 64-year-old group the proportion increased from 12 percent to 27 percent.

Professor Parsons measured the effect of a number of factors. The primary factor causing an increase in the proportion of men withdrawing from the labor force was a rise in the pay for not workig. He found that a 10 percent increase in disability pensions increased the nonparticipation rate by 6 percent, other things equal. A 10 percent increase in monthly general welfare payments increased the nonparticipation rate by 3 percent.[15]

Parsons' findings are illustrative of a general principle. If we tax people for working and subsidize them to not work, we will create more poverty to be subsidized by income redistribution schemes. We see this effect at work in many areas. To illustrate with another example, we can look at the consequences of different levels of unemployment compensation. The higher the level of benefits relative to previous take-home pay, the longer workers remain unemployed and the more frequent their spells of unemployment. In the states that provide early unemployment benefits, that is, those in which no waiting period or only

Exhibit 6: **Rates of male nonparticipation in the labor force by age, 1948-78**

	Age		
	35-44	45-54	55-64
1948	2.1%	4.2%	10.5%
1953	1.8	3.5	12.1
1958[a]	2.1	3.7	12.2
1961[b]	2.4	4.4	12.7
1963	2.5	4.3	13.8
1968	2.9	5.1	15.7
1973	3.8	7.0	21.7
1978	4.3	8.7	26.5

[a] First full year in which Social Security disability pensions were available for male workers aged 50-64.

[b] First full year in which any age worker was eligible for disability pension.

Source: U.S. Bureau of Labor Statistics, *Handbook of Labor Statistics* (Washington, D.C.: Government Printing Office, 1981).

a short waiting period is required before unemployed workers can start drawing benefits, and also in states that provide benefits to voluntary quits and early benefits for people on strike, unemployment rates are higher than in states that are less liberal.[16]

The Decline in Self-support of Low-income People

The potpourri of "income maintenance" programs, which have only been highlighted in this discussion, has induced people to give up employment. Formerly, the majority of the lowest quintile of families (ranked by income) obtained income from employment. Now, only a minority do so, since income has become available on increasingly generous terms without work. In 1953, 58 percent of the heads of low-income families were employed. In 1978, a prosperous year, only 41 percent of the heads of low-income families chose to work. Income maintenance programs have been sufficiently generous that many households whose head does not choose to work are in the second quintile of families ranked by income despite that choice. The proportion of households in the second quintile whose head does not choose to work has doubled since 1960, rising from 12 percent of the households in the second quintile in 1960 to 24 percent in 1978. The proportion of families with a working head in this group has dropped from 81 percent to 69 percent.

The effect of the withdrawal of the male head of a household from the work force appears, from some very sketchy evidence, to reduce daily income by about one-third despite the replacement of lost income by other sources. In other words, our income maintenance programs have provided an incentive to become poverty stricken. Leisure is preferred by many to the income obtainable by working, even when it means some sacrifice of income—provided the sacrifice does not exceed one-half of the earnings obtainable from a job. The low-income population appears to have become less self-supporting and more dependent on government transfers over the past two decades.[17]

The consequence of this withdrawal from participation in the work force is that our capital stock is focused on a smaller work force. Because of this, the productivity of our tools and other equipment is reduced. With a less productive capital stock, the incentive to save and invest is dampened and the growth rate of our national income is slowed.[18]

Conclusion

The course down which public policy has been proceeding is one which has been increasing poverty, destroying capital,[19] and decreasing the rate of capital formation. People have been subsidized to be unemployed and to withdraw from the work force. Because we pay the unemployed and those in poverty so well, we are getting a rise in unemployment and in the number of individuals in poverty. The amount of unemployment responds to the demand for unemployment and poverty.

President Reagan is being criticized for reducing the generosity of the programs that subsidize unemployment and withdrawal from the work force. But if we do not decrease the rewards for not working, there will continue to be a decreasing participation rate, falling productivity, and declining real-wage rates. Poverty will increase because people do what they are rewarded for doing. As long as poverty pays well, the number in poverty except for the various "income-security" programs will continue to grow and our affluence will continue to decline. It is that slide into the abyss that President Reagan has worked hard to reverse by developing proposals for changes in government programs which, if installed, will turn the country around.

President Reagan has proposed the course of action that will *begin* to do that job.[20] In doing so, he has stepped on the toes of almost every group feeding at the federal trough. The proposals, *if enacted*, will cause some pain for a while as we adjust our expectations and rid ourselves of the "cargo cult" mentality that has grown up in the last two decades. But the reward will be greater affluence for everyone, with a reinvigoration of American industry and a reestablishment of American leadership in innovation and productivity.

Endnotes

1. The credit for this law belongs to many scholars. See James Gwartney, "Some Thoughts on the Economics of Redistribution," Working Paper, Department of Economics, Florida State University, 1981. See also, Henri Lepage, *Tomorrow, Capitalism: The Economics of Economic Freedom* (LaSalle, Illinois: Open Court Publishing Co., 1982).

2. Donald O. Parsons, *Poverty and the Minimum Wage* (Washington, D.C.: American Enterprise Institute, 1980).

3. Walter J. Wessells, *Minimum Wages, Fringe Benefits, and Working Conditions* (Washington, D.C.: American Enterprise Institute, 1981).

4. Masanori Hashimoto, *Minimum Wages and On-the-Job Training* (Washington, D.C.: American Enterprise Institute, 1981); Edward Lazear, "Minimum Wages versus Minimum Compensation" in *Report of the Minimum Wage Study Commission*, vol. 5 (Washington, D.C.: Government Printing Office, June 1981), 347-80.

5. Finis Welch, "The Rising Impact of Minimum Wages," *Regulation* 2, no. 6 (November-December 1978).

6. Yale Brozen, "Minimum Wage Rates and Household Workers," *Journal of Law & Economics* 5 (October 1962).

7. Welch, "The Rising Impact," Exhibit 1, 29.

8. Yale Brozen, "The Effect of Statutory Minimum Wage Rate Increases on Teenage Employment," *Journal of Law & Economics* 12, no. 1 (April 1969).

9. Unions are simply cartels of workers. Cartels—price conspiracies—are a per se violation of the antitrust laws, but unions are exempt from the application of the antitrust laws unless they overtly and explicitly conspire with employers to control product prices. In addition to this exemption, numerous pieces of legislation—ranging from the Norris-LaGuardia and Wagner Acts to the Walsh-Healy and Davis-Bacon Acts, and Section 13(c) of the Mass Transit Act—are designed and administered to empower unions.

10. Although the steelworker premium would be 15 percent to 20 percent over other manufacturing production workers, pay rates would be 20 percent to 25 percent higher than the workers now receive in other industries because expansion of steel employment would raise the wage rates in the job now occupied by those who would enter the steel industry if employment in the industry expanded.

11. Stephen Sobotka, *Profile of Michigan: Economic Trends and Paradoxes* (New York: Free Press, Macmillan, 1963).

12. *Economic Report of the President* (Washington, D.C.: Government Printing Office, 1981).

13. "Families with no earners . . . fared better than their counterparts with earners. Families with one or more earners showed declines in real median income, while the median for families without earners showed no change in real terms from the 1979 level." *Money Income and Poverty Status of Families and Persons in the United States: 1980* (Washington: Bureau of the Census, Current Population Reports, Series P. 60, no. 127).

14. James Gwartney and Richard Stroup, "Tax Reductions, Incentive Effects, and the Distribution of the Tax Burden," Federal Reserve Bank of Atlanta, *Economic Review* (March 1982).

15. Donald O. Parsons, "The Decline in Male Labor Force Participation," *Journal of Political Economy* 88, no. 1 (February 1980). See also, C. I. Brehn and T. R. Saving, "The Demand for General Assistance Payments," *American Economic Review*, 54, no. 6 (December 1964): 1017.

16. M. Feldstein, "Unemployment Compensation: Adverse Incentives and Distributional Anomalies," *National Tax Journal* 27 (June 1974). See also, Arlene Holen and Stanley Horowitz, "The Effect of Unemployment Insurance and Eligibility Enforcement on Unemployment," *Journal of Law and Economics* 17, no. 2 (October 1974).

17. Edgar K. Browning, *Redistribution and the Welfare System* (Washington, D.C.: American Enterprise Institute, 1975), 30.

18. J. Huston McCulloch, "Macroeconomic Implications of the Minimum Wage" in *The Economics of Legal Minimum Wages*, ed. S. Rottenberg (Washington: American Enterprise Institute, 1981).

19. Many plants are being shut down and the capital invested is being junked even though the plants could still be economically useful if resources were appropriately priced. Some steel mills owned by U.S. Steel are being junked, for example, because the overpricing of labor makes them uneconomic to operate.

20. *America's New Beginning: A Program for Economic Recovery* (Washington: Government Printing Office, 1981).

If in doubt, limit the role of the federal government in order to better "promote the general welfare!" JERRY JORDAN *and* PAUL RUBIN, *two of President Ronald Reagan's key economic advisers, discuss the "new federalism" and the constitutionally intended limits to government economic intervention. They sadly concede the judiciary's unwillingness to protect the Constitution's intent.*

Assuming the unwillingness by the courts to decentralize power to the states, they thoroughly explain the economic justifications—"market failures"—for some form of government economic intervention. But they claim there is much less understanding of the economic costs and imperfections of intervention—"government failures." They conclude with some bold recommendations that they propose will reduce the cost and likelihood of government failures when intervention is necessary. Creating incentives for compliance and cooperation (rather than penalties) and dismantling special-interest-group programs are among the several principles they advocate for limiting the role of the federal government.

8

Constitutional Limits on the Role of the Federal Government in the Economy

JERRY L. JORDAN and PAUL H. RUBIN

In principle, the economic policy of the federal government is constrained by the U.S. Constitution. The formal Constitution has changed relatively little since it was adopted, though interpretations have changed substantially. The economic role of the federal government, as delineated in the Constitution, was meant to be quite limited. Examination of changing interpretations of the Constitution reveals how these changes have contributed to the increase in the role of government in the economy in the past fifty years. Though constitutional interpretation is the responsibility of the Supreme Court, there are important economic principles in the document and much of the recent development of a theory of constitutions has been by economists.[1]

The Nature of the Constitution

The Constitution was envisioned by its authors as a contract between the federal government and the states. As in any contract, both parties gave something up and gained something. The states gave sovereignty to the federal government in some matters in return for the advantages of having a central government with sufficient power to govern effectively. The second side of the bargain needs no explanation; few people today are confused about the power of the federal government.

However, the other side of the agreement is more important in today's context, and less well understood. A basic purpose of the constitutional contract in the American context is to limit the power of government. Framers of the Constitution had recently fought a war against a government with too much power, and they endeavored to ensure that such a government did not arise in the new republic. Therefore, much of the language and purpose of the Constitution was aimed at controlling and restraining the federal government. This is apparent both in the mechanisms of government designed in the Constitution, in the specific functions authorized to the federal government, and more specifically in the Bill of Rights.

Every schoolchild studies the system of checks and balances among the executive, the legislative, and the judicial branches of the government. It is commonly argued that this system preserves liberty by not allowing any one branch of government to gain too much power. However, this system is aimed not only at constraining each branch of government, but also at restraint of the whole government. Any rule or law promulgated by government must have the implicit or explicit consent of all three branches; this will serve to constrain the overall level of government activity. One sometimes hears arguments about the difficulty of passing laws in our system, for example, when the president and the Congress are of different parties, and it is sometimes argued that this system leads to inefficiency. But this misses the point of the separation of powers; this doctrine was built into the Constitution specifically for the purpose of making it difficult to pass laws.

Other restraints on the power of the federal government are explicitly stated in the Constitution and the amendments. The Ninth Amendment, part of the Bill of Rights, states that "The enumeration in the Constitution, of certain rights, shall not be construed to deny or disparage others retained by the people," and the Tenth Amendment says that "The powers not delegated to the United States by the Constitution, nor prohibited by it to the states, are reserved to the states respectively, or to the people." These are two explicit statements of the limitations of the power of the federal government. Moreover, the entire Bill of Rights is a statement of such limits; each of these ten amendments imposes specific limits on the power of the government.

Federalism

Our governmental system is a federal system—one with different levels of sovereignty. The Constitution was essentially an argument among sovereign states. The earlier Articles of Confederation had established a central government, but it was felt that this government did not have sufficient power. One of the major debates in writing and ratifying the Constitution was over the amount of power which would be reserved to the states; as mentioned above, the Tenth Amendment specifically reserves to the states or to the people those powers that are not explicitly given to the central government.

Though the states do have sovereignty in many areas, one of the purposes of the Constitution was to set up a free trade area constituting the entire United States, and to this end the Constitution does place restrictions on the states. States are not allowed to impose tariffs or other trade barriers on commerce between them; the federal government is explicitly given the power to "regulate commerce . . . among the states. . . ." (Article 1, Section 8). However, there are many matters that are generally governmental in which the federal government was granted no specific role; these matters were left to the states. Most law, both civil and criminal, is state law rather than federal law.

Constitutional Provisions for Economic Activity

Though the Constitution is primarily a political document, there are several specific economic policies mentioned. Some of these are economic powers granted to the federal government; equally important, there are several types of economic rule making that are forbidden to it by the Constitution.

The federal government is given the power to collect taxes, subject to certain constraints. Congress is also given the power to coin money and regulate its value; to set up a system of patents and copyrights; to regulate commerce with foreign nations, among the states, and with Indian tribes; and to establish a post office.

Perhaps of more interest are the prohibitions on actions of either the federal or the state governments in the Constitution. Restrictions imposed on the states aimed at making the country into a free trade area have already been mentioned. In addition, Article I, Section 10 says that "No State shall . . . pass any . . . law impairing the Obligation of Contracts. . . ." The Fifth Amendment forbids the central government from depriving anyone of ". . . life, liberty, or property, without due process of law . . .," and the Fourteenth Amendment extends this ban to the states. These two clauses are consistent with sound economic principles; however, their interpretation by the Supreme Court has changed substantially over time in important and at times controversial ways.

The theory under which the Supreme Court invalidated certain laws regulating economic behavior, primarily in labor markets, is sometimes called *substantive due process*.[2] Essentially, this was a doctrine under which the Court scrutinized state laws regulating occupations, wages, and hours. The basic conflict was between rights of individuals to freely contract and the police power of the state. For example, many of the invalidated laws would present a public health justification for a law regulating hours of work. The Court would then go behind this justification, and attempt to determine if there was actually a relation between the law and health; if the Court was not convinced that health was the true purpose of the law, then it would be invalidated.

The period of substantive due process (or what some authors call *economic due process*) lasted from about 1905 to 1937. Beginning in 1937, the Court withdrew from its position in which it would scrutinize economic regulatory laws, and essentially began deferring to the legislature. The Court argued that its purpose was not to serve as a "superlegislature" and oversee the democratic will of the people as expressed in statutes. Of course, the Constitution, as discussed above, may be interpreted as giving the Court exactly this function, as the framers of the Constitution were aware of some of the problems of representative government. Moreover, the Court continues to examine carefully laws that deal with political and personal rights; a doctrine very much like substantive due process is essentially applied to these laws in that the justices will examine the purpose of laws dealing with these matters. It is primarily economic rights that are no longer consistently protected by the court.

The Economic Theory of Constitutions

The theory of constitutions begins with the following perspective: Assume there is a group of individuals who are contemplating establishing a government, and these individuals are assumed to be in a *state of nature*—that is, in a world with no government.[3] Moreover, assume they are *behind the veil of ignorance* about their own exact position when the government is established; that is, they do not know what job, income, or other personal characteristics they will have once the constitutional contract is established and begins operating. What characteristics will such individuals want in their government?

The exact answer to this question depends on matters such as the degree of risk aversion that is assumed for the individuals. Detailed models of various aspects of the constitutional contract have been explored by many analysts. However, all agree on certain matters that are relevant for this paper. For example, it generally is agreed that individuals would want to avoid interventions such as monopoly, tariffs, or direct subsidies that favor specific industries. Each individual knows that once the constitution is adopted and begins functioning he or she would like to be able to use government to obtain some specially favored position. However, by assumption, no one knows what industry or market he or she will be in, and therefore does not know which sector of the economy he or she would like to see benefited.

If the constitution allows legislation granting special-interest benefits, then each industry or trade will find it worthwhile to lobby government to grant such a position. This lobbying will itself use resources that will therefore not be available to produce real goods and services.[4] Moreover, though each individual will gain from the imposition of his or her own special-interest favor, each will lose from the imposition of all the other benefits that will be established. The sum of the losses will be greater than the sum of the gains; that is, the laws and the associated costs of establishing such benefits impose efficiency losses on the economy. Nonetheless, if such legislation is allowed in the constitution, then each group will have an incentive to try to gain its own benefits. The structure of the problem is the classic prisoner's dilemma in which each individual agent has incentives to take actions that are jointly disadvantageous.

The solution is a constitutional prohibition that prevents anyone from gaining such a protected position. If everyone knows that such behavior is prohibited, then no one will spend resources in trying to obtain a government sanctioned benefit, nor will the deadweight efficiency losses exist. Moreover, these arguments are not purely theoretical; it may be argued that the U.S. Constitution did prohibit exactly such regulations. Indeed, the period of substantive due process was a period in which the Supreme Court took essentially this view of the Constitution. This argument is also quite consistent with the view that an important purpose of the Constitution was to restrict the power of government; one important restriction was on the power of government to grant favors to special-interest groups. That this was known to the writers of the Constitution is made clear from the Tenth Federalist Paper, where Madison explicitly warns of the dangers of *faction* and explains that one purpose of the Constitution is to limit the power of such factions to gain at the expense of other citizens.

This view of government also is consistent with the federal nature of our government. One important check on the power of the government to impose costs on its residents is the ability of those residents to leave—to move out of the jurisdiction of the government.[5] It is costly to leave the United States; there are only a few other English-speaking countries, and moving to a country in which another language is spoken would require an expensive learning process. However, there are now fifty states, and migration from one state to another is relatively simple. Thus, one argument for federalism is essentially an argument for restricting the power of the government, since any state that passed laws that were sufficiently inefficient would find itself losing residents. The increase in power of the federal government in the past few decades at the expense of the state governments greatly weakened this constraint on governmental power.

The more traditional argument for federalism, given that the demands and costs of government services differ across regions, is that state and local governments are more likely to choose the level and quality of such services preferred by their voters. This argument has important implications for both the types of services that should be provided at the several levels of government and the structure of the tax system. The decisions on the level and character of services that provide benefits to people throughout the nation, such as national defense and the protection of basic constitutional rights, should be made by the federal government and such services should be financed by federal taxes. Similarly, the demand on services that provide benefits only or dominantly to residents of a specific region, such as urban transit and sewer systems, should be made by state or local governments and such services should be financed by taxes or user charges on the directly affected residents. Federal grants-in-aid to states and local governments should be restricted to those services provided by these governments that have significant benefits to residents in other regions of the country. The growth and proliferation of federal grants-in-aid in the last several decades, however, have not been focused on such services. These grants, by reducing the local tax price of these services, have increased the level of these services relative to that which local residents would prefer in the absence of these governments. The relative growth of federal financing of state and local services has both increased the total size of government in the United States and reduced the efficiency and responsiveness of the federal system.

The Competitive Model

In discussing the role of government in the economy, economists usually start with the model of a perfectly competitive economy, for such an economy can be shown to have desirable efficiency properties.[6] In a very rough sense, this refers to the ability of an economy to satisfy consumer wants to the greatest extent possible, consistent with the wants of others. However, for such an economy to exist, certain assumptions must be satisfied. In general, these assumptions are not satisfied by any real world economy. Therefore, it is often argued that intervention is justified in order to correct the inefficiencies that occur when the assumptions are not met. This provides a classification scheme in which to analyze intervention. It is important to note, however, that failure of an assumption to be satisfied is a necessary, but not sufficient, condition for government intervention. To show that a perfectly functioning government could correct some problem with a free economy is not enough, for government itself will not function perfectly. Even given this framework, however, it is true that many past interventions cannot easily be explained by any market failure argument; that is, on grounds of economic efficiency, many interventions could be justified only with great difficulty. This naturally leads one to ask how such interventions can be explained. This, in turn, raises constitutional questions; as we have argued, one function of a constitution is to prevent certain interventions from occurring.

Each individual in a competitive economy is characterized as being concerned primarily with his or her own welfare, including each person's sense of benevolence toward others. Moreover, there is no central direction in this economy; whatever results occur are the unintended consequences of millions of individual actions. Nonetheless, the outcome of this apparently uncoordinated, self-interested behavior is coherent and efficient in the sense mentioned above. Without any central direction, it can be shown that an order is generated and, moreover, that this order has certain desirable properties. This efficient order is responsive to individual wants; that is, efficiency is defined in terms of each economic agent achieving his or her own goals. This system relies on the ability of individuals to trade freely with each other, for a bargain entered into voluntarily by two individuals is expected to make both of them better off. There are two conditions that must be fulfilled for such trades to occur.[7] First, individuals must have the right to enter freely into whatever bargains they wish; that is, there must be freedom of contract. Second, property rights must be well defined and as extensive as possible, consistent with the costs of enforcement. Thus, the constitutional principles that may be interpreted as allowing freedom of contract and protecting property rights are necessary for the efficient operation of the economy; the legal doctrine of economic due process, discussed above, is consistent with sound economic principles.

There must be certain additional characteristics for efficiency to occur. For policy purposes, the most important of these characteristics are no externalities, no monopoly in the economy, and no public goods. Though such an economy is efficient in the sense just defined, this says nothing about the distribution of income which results from the process; by some criteria, the market-generated distribution of income may be unacceptable. Thus, government intervention may be justified to correct any of the market failures mentioned above, or to change the resulting distribution of income. It is also possible that such an economy may be less stable than is generally desirable.

Externalities—An externality is said to exist where some economic agent either does not bear the full marginal costs or does not gain the full marginal benefits of his or her action. Therefore agents may not undertake the optimal level of the activity. If there are external costs, then the agent may undertake too high a level of the activity; if there are external benefits, then the agent may not undertake enough of the activity.

In some cases, private transactions between parties may be adequate to solve externality problems.[8] However, this requires that transactions costs be low; in situations where there are many parties involved this requirement will not, in general, be satisfied, and some direct intervention may be necessary.

Monopoly—One of the conditions for efficiency in markets is that there be enough actual or potential buyers and sellers so that none of them is able to influence price. This condition is not always satisfied. Sometimes technical and cost conditions in an industry are such that there will be room for only one or a few firms in that industry. In these cases, some intervention may be appropriate. In the United States, two approaches have been taken to this problem. In the case of natural monopoly, direct government regulation is common. In the case of oligopolies, the antitrust laws are more generally used.

In recent years, the antitrust authorities sometimes behaved as if they viewed their function as protecting existing competitors; that is, they have tried to protect firms that are currently in the market from new entrants, as well as from each other. From an economic viewpoint, the purpose of antitrust is to maintain competition; effective competition will often lead to the elimination of firms that are inefficient. Such a process is desirable and should not be blocked by the government.[9]

Public Goods—There are several definitions of public goods in the economics literature. Here, we will call a good a *pure* public good if consumption of the good by one party does not reduce consumption of the good by others. The standard example of a public good is national defense. If someone deters a foreign aggressor from invading, everyone in the country benefits. This means that no one individual will have sufficient incentive to spend resources on defense, for each can benefit from his neighbor's spending. In this case, the only way in which the good can be provided is by some coercive action by the government to obtain resources—typically by taxation—and to use these resources to provide defense. Government intervention usually is necessary for the optimal provision of public goods.

Another good with public goods properties is information. If one person learns some valuable fact and tells someone else, then both know this fact; use of information by one individual does not reduce the use of the same information by another. Patents and copyrights are aimed in part at solving the problem of the public-good nature of information by giving inventors and writers property rights in their products, but there are still examples of cases where the private market will not generate sufficient information. This provides the rationale used to defend some government subsidization of research.

Income Redistribution—In a market economy, one's income depends on what one has to sell and on the amount that others are willing to pay for it. For most people, the primary good that they have to sell on the market is labor, and about 75 percent of the gross national product (GNP) is wages and salaries. Others have capital or land to rent on the market, and their return is interest, dividends, and rent. (Many people earn incomes from both capital and labor over their lifetimes.) However, in such an economy, some persons may have few or no valuable goods to sell, and such persons will have low incomes. For them, a decision may be made to transfer incomes directly through government. There are two economic justifications for government transfers—one based on insurance and one based on benevolence. We consider each.

It is possible for anyone to lose his or her earning ability. A worker may become physically disabled, or may find that technological progress has made his or her particular set of skills obsolete. An investor may find that changing market conditions have eroded the value of invested capital. In either case, income may fall to low levels. Individuals generally want to insure against such risks.

There are difficulties with the private provision of insurance against falling incomes. A major difficulty is what is called *adverse selection*. Assume that some insurance agency offers actuarially fair insurance against this risk. Since people are risk averse, they would prefer this insurance; this would be true even if the insurance had a premium that was somewhat greater than the expected cost because of the costs of writing the insurance. Some persons would know that they were better risks than the average, and insurance companies could come into being and compete with the initial company for these better risks. This would leave the original company insuring only the relatively bad risks; the process could continue until one class of persons would be unable to obtain any insurance. This would be an example of market failure. In this case, there may be an argument for government provision of the insurance since the private market could not provide it; government could force everyone to join the same insurance pool.[10] The appropriate form of transfer to serve this insurance function is a cash grant to those who experience a temporary loss of income. Welfare and unemployment compensation may be viewed as just this sort of insurance.

The second argument for government transfers to the poor is a public-good argument based on benevolence. Many people prefer living in a society in which there is no abject poverty. Thus, individuals who are not poor have some incentive to transfer resources voluntarily to the poor. However, if one non-poor individual performs such a transfer, then all non-poor individuals who dislike poverty would benefit. Everyone in the society thus lives in a society with the same income distribution. Each individual would have an incentive to reduce his or her contributions to the poor and rely on the contributions of others to achieve the desired level of transfers. In such a case, voluntary transfers will be too low, and overall welfare can only be increased by a program of mandatory government transfers.[11]

In those cases where transfers are desirable, economic theory can also indicate the most efficient form of the transfer. The goal should be to minimize interference in markets, and to rely as heavily as possible on markets to provide the desired level of transfers. For example, programs that directly interfere in markets for the purpose of helping the poor, such as price controls on gasoline, or minimum wages, are extremely inefficient forms of help.

The way in which resources should be transferred to the poor depends on the goals of the donors. If the goal is to simply improve the welfare of the poor, then the most efficient solution is a cash transfer, since the recipient will be best able to determine that pattern of spending which maximizes his or her own welfare. If the donor is concerned not with the welfare of the poor person, but rather with the specific bundle of goods that the recipient consumes, then some direct transfer of goods is preferred. In this case, an argument can be made for using some form of voucher in order to transfer the goods. A voucher is essentially a ticket usable for the purchase only of a specific type of good; an example is food stamps. Use of vouchers, rather than direct transfer of goods, allows the recipient to adjust his or her own consumption, but still constrains the recipient to purchase the type of goods that the donor desires.

No matter what form of transfer program is used, there is still an efficiency cost to income transfers. Transfers to the poor reduce the incentive of the recipients to work, and the taxes on the rest of society used to finance these transfers also impose efficiency losses. There are also costs of administering the program. Economists are able to give advice on efficient ways of transferring that may serve to minimize these effects. Given the necessary existence of these costs, however, the decision as to the level of transfers is a political, not an economic, decision.

Macroeconomic Stability—It is sometimes argued that a market system is subject to unacceptably large fluctuations in income. If this were true, it would have welfare implications. First, the level of incomes, averaged over the business cycle, might have smaller fluctuations than would be true if the level of activity were more stable. Second, even if the level of incomes was unaffected by such fluctuations, economic agents are generally risk averse; that is, most agents prefer a certain stream of income to a fluctuating stream, even if the expected values are identical. For these reasons, government might have a role in providing stability.

An alternative view is that a capitalist economy is inherently stable. According to this view, actions by the government frequently are destabilizing factors in the economy. Many fluctuations in income resulting from private sector actions are actually caused by attempts to second-guess government policies.

Of related interest is the role of money. There are several functions that money performs in an economy. It economizes on transactions costs and on information costs, since all persons accept the same money and are aware of its value. There also are arguments for a monopoly money supply, since the use of only one type of money in an economy will reduce information costs. The Constitution specifically gives Congress the power "to coin money, regulate the value thereof. . . ." (Article I, Section 8). However, the government (or, more specifically, the Federal Reserve) must be careful in its money-creating function not to exacerbate cyclical fluctuations; some economists have argued that the severity of the Great Depression of the 1930s was caused primarily by inappropriate Federal Reserve policies.[12] Placing constraints on the discretion of the Federal Reserve is consistent with the sort of constitutional restrictions described earlier.

Even if the government is the appropriate agent for stabilizing the economy, the limits of this policy must be understood. "Fine tuning" the economy—responding to every small fluctuation—is not a feasible policy. The information needed for such a policy is simply not available. What information is available is generally not accessible in time for such efforts to be successful; by the time information is available, it is quite likely that underlying conditions will have changed sufficiently so that the policy is as likely to be counterproductive as to be helpful. Also, there are lags in the system that are of variable and unknown length. This often means that policies will be responding to conditions that no longer exist, and may actually tend to exacerbate the conditions that they are aimed at alleviating. Though it is necessary for the government to have macroeconomic policies, including both monetary and fiscal policies, which are designed to achieve some desired growth of nominal income, such policies are not suitable for correcting small fluctuations in economic activity.

Limits on the Exercise of the Federal Role

This paper has summarized the theoretical reasons, both constitutional and economic, for a limited role of the federal government in the economy. Even when there is clear justification for some intervention by government, however, there are reasons for believing that the government will not do a perfect job; that is, just as there sometimes are reasons for expecting *market failure* as discussed previously, sometimes there also are theoretical reasons for expecting *government failure*. In this section, we discuss some of these reasons.

The Political Process—For several reasons, the political process is expected to be overly responsive to special-interest groups. One cause is high information costs. An example is a policy such as a tariff, which benefits some special interest. Such a program will give rather large benefits to a concentrated group of individuals, firms, and workers in the targeted industry. It will impose small costs on everyone else in the economy. For such programs, the sum of the losses is greater than the sum of the gains. However, each of the losers loses so little that it will often not pay for the individuals to spend even the resources necessary to learn about their losses. For example, a rather detailed study of law and of economics would be necessary for the average voter to determine how much cartelization of the trucking industry by the Interstate Commerce Commission costs that voter. It is quite rational for an individual citizen not to bother to learn about this cost, for the resources spent in learning would probably be greater than the costs of the government activity. This is commonly called *rational ignorance*.[13] On the other hand, the beneficiaries gain substantial amounts. It does pay for these beneficiaries to spend resources in learning. Thus, trade associations will hire lobbyists whose job it is, at least in part, to inform members of the industry about political decisions that might affect their industry.

Moreover, even if voters had the required information, it is not clear what effect this would have. Assume that some citizen knows that his representative has voted for a tariff that imposes a $50 cost on the voter. However, this same congressman has voted for some other bill that benefits the voter as a member of his own special-interest group, and gives him a benefit worth $500. What is the rational behavior of the voter? He should vote for the reelection of the congressman, since on balance he gains from the behavior of the congressman. That is, there are reasons for expecting the political process to be overly responsive to special interests. It is possible for a representative to obtain a sufficient plurality to be elected by favoring a set of special-interest policies, each of which appeals only to a minority of the electorate. Moreover, achieving a victory with such a *coalition of minorities* is possible even with complete information. This is because the gains from such special-interest policies will be concentrated only within the majority, while the costs will be borne by members of both the majority and of the minority. Therefore, it is possible for a majority coalition, made up of several special-interest groups, to form and gain benefits for themselves, even if the sum of the costs (which are borne by all in the society) are greater than the sum of the benefits that accrue to members of the winning coalition.

The same arguments that apply to voting by the citizens for congressmen and senators also apply to other aspects of political activity. It will pay for concentrated special interests (including both business and unions) to make campaign contributions to those representatives who vote for benefits for the individuals in the industry; it will not, in general, pay for citizens to make such contributions to congressmen who vote against such bills, because the size of the losses for each individual are small and because overturning inefficient legislation is a public good for citizens, and it does not generally pay to contribute voluntarily to the provision of public goods.[14] (A law benefiting an industry is a public good for members of the industry, but the larger size of benefits and the smaller number of beneficiaries make it sometimes possible to overcome such free-rider problems.)[15]

It is for reasons such as these that the political process responds to special-interest groups, and it is desirable for constitutions to attempt to limit the power of such special interests in obtaining legislation, as discussed earlier.

Supply by Government Bureaus—When the government undertakes some activity, the actual activity is performed by bureaucrats—by government employees. Bureaucrats are sometimes criticized for being inefficient; at other times, the implicit view of bureaucrats seems to be that they are dedicated public servants concerned with the public interest. Economic theories of bureaucracy make neither of these assumptions; rather, they assume that bureaucrats behave like other economic agents and are concerned with promoting their own interests, as are people in general.[16] Thus, to study the effect of bureaucratic provision of government goods, it is necessary to study the set of incentives that face bureaucrats.

There are several incentives for bureaucrats to increase the size and power of their agencies. First, the salary and promotion prospects of a bureaucrat depend in good measure on the size and influence of the agency, as does the power of the bureaucrat. Second, even if we assume that some bureaucrats are motivated by perceptions of the public interest, this would lead to the same result. Someone concerned with the public interest is likely to go to work for an agency that fulfills his or her vision of this interest; an environmentalist, for example, would be likely to work for the Environmental Protection Agency. Such an individual would then want to expand the power of this agency, independently of his or her own self-interest, because he or she would feel that such an expansion would benefit the public. Thus, for self-interest reasons or for reasons due to perceptions of the public interest, we would expect bureaucrats to want to increase the size of their agencies. This is a partial explanation of the relatively long life of agencies and the difficulty in terminating such agencies—those who work for the agency become a special-interest group. It is also an explanation for overspending on many goods provided by government.

The risk structure associated with government regulation has also created some perverse incentives for bureaucrats. For example, the drug regulations of the Food and Drug Administration (FDA) have been studied in this context.[17] In the case where some government employee must make a decision about approving some new drug, there are two errors that can occur. First, the official can approve a drug that is unsafe, in which case some persons will suffer harmful side effects. Alternatively, the official can fail to approve some safe drug, in which case some persons will needlessly suffer from a disease. Either type of error will lead to harmful consequences, and ultimately may lead to deaths. The potential errors are implicit in the structure of the problem; these types of errors will always be possible, no matter what decision-making process is used. However, the bureaucrat faces an asymmetric situation with respect to these errors. If the drug is approved and someone dies, then the bureaucrat will be blamed for approving the unsafe drug. Conversely, if the drug is not approved, those who suffer from the disease are not likely to know that a cure would have been available if only the FDA had approved this new drug. Thus, in this circumstance and many others, bureaucrats would be expected to be overly risk averse—not because of the nature of the person holding the job, but because the incentive structure facing this person would lead to this behavior.

Since these types of responses by bureaucrats are predictable, they must be considered in designing programs. More specifically, as has been argued several times, it is not enough to argue that a perfectly functioning government program could correct some market failure. Rather, we must realize that the government will not function perfectly, and then attempt to determine if a predictably imperfect government program is better than what results from an unregulated market.

Diversity of Conditions and Preferences—One advantage of a market economy, mentioned earlier, is that such an economy is responsive to varying consumer demands. Individuals have different preferences and desire different goods. If these desires are reflected by willingness to pay, then firms will find it worthwhile to satisfy them. The market will produce a diverse set of products in response to diverse demands.

If a good is a public good, however, this diversity cannot exist. We must all purchase the same amount of national defense, whether we are pacifists or hawks. This is the nature of public goods and, for true public goods, there is no alternative. However, one result of government behavior is sometimes to treat goods that could be private as if they were public goods. Thus, if government provides public schools, all students from families that are not willing to pay the full cost of private school tuition must consume the same bundle of educational service. Voucher plans for education are attempts to get around this problem, as are proposals for refundable tuition tax credits. Similar programs occur when government regulates product characteristics.

Detailed government regulation of technologies also reduces the responsiveness of the economy to changed conditions. Detailed regulation, by not allowing entrepreneurs to take advantage of new technologies, retards the technological progressiveness of an industry.

Limits on Information—For government policies to achieve their goals, they must be based on correct information, a condition that is not always satisfied. Examples of problems in formulating and implementing macroeconomic policy were discussed previously.

Sometimes the problem is that policymakers cannot predict the extent to which individuals will respond to their policies. The imposition of credit controls in 1980 had surprisingly rapid and perverse effects. Another example is the rapid increase in the cost of medical care as a result of Medicare and Medicaid; here, policymakers underestimated the extent to which the cost of medical care would rise, with very expensive consequences.

In general, it may be predicted that individuals will respond to new rules or regulations in such a way as to minimize the adverse impact of such regulations on themselves. However, it is generally difficult or impossible to predict the exact nature of this response, for there are millions of individuals affected by any given regulation and some of them will think of alternatives that did not occur to the policymakers.

The myriad of ways in which individuals subvert price controls is illustrative. One solution is to attempt to devise policies that make use of individual goals; too often, however, regulations take the form of specific rules that ignore these responses.

One advantage of a market economy is that it is *informationally efficient*. That is, a market will function well if each individual knows only his or her own preferences and opportunities.[18] Conversely, when the government controls an activity, much more information must be collected and centralized, but this information is expensive and sometimes not available. This places another limit on the ability of the government to achieve its goals.

Time Horizon—Elected officials are concerned with their prospects for reelection. Thus, in general, a policy that imposes costs today in return for benefits in the future will be discounted by elected representatives, even if the program has a positive present value. Conversely, programs with near-term benefits to some, and deferred costs, will be preferred by politicians and costs will not be well discounted and net benefits will be overstated. In the private market, since benefits can be capitalized and property rights sold, programs and projects with a positive present value will be undertaken; while government may undertake some such projects, we would expect a bias against long-term programs.

This short time horizon has other effects. Recently, for example, some analysts have detected a *political business cycle*—a phenomenon in which government spending projects are approved or programs are initiated just before an election, leading to higher taxes or inflation which, however, do not occur until after the election.[19] This is a predictable response to the time horizon in the political process. Wage and price controls, which might produce an apparent short-run moderation in the rate of inflation, lead to substantial deadweight losses because they reduce the responsiveness and flexibility of the economy. However, these ill effects occur long after the controls are imposed. Thus, there sometimes will be incentives to impose such controls just before an election, when the ill effects will not be detected until later. This problem of a short time horizon, inherent in a political process with nontransferable property rights, is another limitation on the effectiveness of government programs.

Principles for Limiting Federal Government

Several guiding principles will help constrain the activities of the federal government.

Emphasis on Personal Responsibility—Many government policies, such as detailed safety and health regulations or providing the poor with specific goods rather than money, can be best understood if we realize that government has in many respects behaved paternalistically. Paternalism occurs when the government is unwilling to let individuals make decisions for themselves, but rather protects them from the possible bad effects of their own decisions by outlawing certain actions. It is a policy which says explicitly that certain preferences cannot be allowed.

There is no reason for thinking that orders from the government or its agents can do a better job of maximizing some individual's welfare than individuals can do by making choices themselves. Moreover, a long-term cost of paternalism may be to destroy people's ability to make their own decisions. Many of the safety regulations of the past have been based on an implicitly paternalistic policy.

As we discussed earlier, there are economic arguments for transferring resources to the poor. However, if the primary concern is the welfare of the poor, then the most efficient form of transfers is simply cash, rather than benefits-in-kind. (Examples of benefits-in-kind are public housing, food stamps, and medical care.) If poor people are given money, then they can determine for themselves what goods to buy; if they are given goods, then such determinations are impossible. One justification for programs that give aid in kind is again paternalistic; such programs must be based on the argument that poor people are unable to spend their money correctly. Another justification is that the donors are concerned with the particular bundle of goods purchased by the recipients, rather than with their welfare. To the extent that decisions for the poor are made by government agencies, we would not expect recipients ever to learn how to spend their own money.

Role of Regulatory Authorities—From an economic viewpoint, the purpose of antitrust laws is to maximize consumer satisfaction by reducing monopoly power. However, in the past the laws often have served both to protect smaller business (as the Robinson-Patman Act does explicitly, and as some interpret the Sherman Act and the Clayton Act to do implicitly) and to penalize large business, even if size is due to increased efficiency. This should not be the direction of the antitrust laws.

Because property rights in air and water have not always been correctly defined, there is scope for government intervention to alleviate the problem of pollution. However, the form that such intervention has taken in the past can be clearly shown to be inefficient. In particular, regulation has been by direct specification of the technology of pollution control rather than by either defining property rights or by charging for polluting.

Another major effort by economists addressing the role of government is to emphasize the use of cost-benefit analysis in regulation. In many cases, this is a step in the right direction: regulation that does not compare costs with benefits is wasteful and inefficient, and will not even serve to accomplish its own goals efficiently. For example, if one industry is forced to spend $4.5 million in order to reduce expected fatalities by one person (a low estimate of the cost per life saved by the OSHA coke emission standard), while elimination of all railroad grade crossings would save lives at an estimated cost of only $100,000 per life saved, then we are passing up an opportunity to save more lives, because transferring the spending from the first to the second on the margin would serve to save 45 lives.[20] The only way in which to rationally make this sort of calculation (where the market, for some reason, fails) is through cost-benefit or cost-effectiveness analysis.

However, this tool is, at best, a second-best solution. At best, a decision based on cost-benefit analysis maximizes the interest of only the average person affected. The judgment of the market, where it is available, should be respected. Thus, in most areas of safety regulation, the best solution would be to rely on market judgments about the value of safety. Where this may not be possible, then cost-benefit analysis is preferred to blind reliance on regulations, but it is not an optimal solution. On the other hand, in areas such as environmental regulation where the market will not work unaided, cost-benefit analysis may be necessary. Even if we move toward a system of effluent charges, an analysis of costs and benefits will be necessary in order to determine the optimal charge; if we move to a system of the sale of pollution rights, then the amount of rights to be created will need to be determined in some similar way.

Decentralization—One important principle implied by a constitutional view of the federal government is an increased reliance on state and local governments, rather than on the central government. For example, the replacement of many direct transfers to the states with large block grants is such a program.

As discussed above, there are both constitutional and economic reasons for this reliance on state governments. States are more responsive to the people in their jurisdictions than is the federal government, and therefore they can take better account of the diversity of local conditions. More importantly, states have less monopoly power with respect to their citizens. Since an important check on government abuse is the opportunity to move, reliance on local levels of government will serve as a needed check on the power of government.

Reliance on Market-like Devices—One principle that has been mentioned several times in this paper is the increased reliance on market-like devices for those government interventions that are to be undertaken. Since this is an important principle, it seems worthwhile to indicate the ways in which it operates; this will demonstrate some relationships between seemingly disparate changes in forms of intervention.

First, consider the reasons for reliance on devices that try to simulate markets where intervention is the desired policy. The alternative is direct regulation. Direct regulation puts the government in an adversary position with respect to the party being regulated. Such an adversary relationship creates ill will between the government and business or other regulated parties. Ill will is also created when, for example, government employees monitor and control the spending of welfare recipients. Besides creating ill will, detailed monitoring of behavior is expensive and, because there are millions of regulated individuals and businesses, such detailed regulation generally will permit monitoring only a small fraction of the intended recipients, so that the goals will be reached imperfectly.

The advantage of markets or market-like devices is that such devices create incentives for agents to behave in the desired way. That is, if we can simulate an effective market in some area, we can rely on the self-interest of the economic actors to achieve the desired goals. This reduces the resource cost of achieving the regulatory goal; it also will increase the extent to which the goal will be achieved.

An interesting example is provided by comparing governmental safety regulation of firms with private market insurance against risks. In the case of government regulation, the only sanction for a violator is a fine, which creates incentives for regulated firms to conceal possible violations and to avoid cooperation with safety inspectors. On the other hand, if a firm that is insured can make its operations safer, then it benefits by obtaining a reduced premium from the insurance company. Thus, such firms have an incentive to cooperate with safety inspectors and adopt any recommendations that are made. This is but one example of a situation in which a market device, by eliciting cooperation, is more efficient at achieving desired goals than is regulation, which elicits conflict.

A Broad-based Approach to Scaling Back

As stressed throughout this paper, many federal government programs have tended increasingly to give benefits to special-interest groups; these programs are inefficient in that the gains to the beneficiaries are generally less than the losses to the losers. Nonetheless, the political process, if unconstrained, would tend to pass many such programs. However, under current Supreme Court interpretations, such a universal ban does not exist. It is true, nonetheless, that if these special-interest programs could be eliminated, then almost everyone could benefit because of the efficiency losses that the programs impose. However, it is extremely difficult to reduce such programs one at a time since, in each case, the particular beneficiaries would correctly perceive that they would lose from elimination of their program.

An alternative is to reduce a large number of programs simultaneously. If enough cuts in both spending and taxes can be made simultaneously, then individuals may feel that while they lose from the cuts in their specific program, they gain enough from cuts in other programs and in taxes to compensate them for their losses; if the cuts are sufficiently broad, then each individual may be correct in his or her perception. Thus, the principles of optimal constitutional design can be used to rationalize very broad cuts in spending and in benefits. A general reduction of special-interest programs is a necessary step to meet the constitutional charge to "promote the general welfare."

Endnotes

1. The classic discussion of the economic theory of constitutions is in James M. Buchanan and Gordon Tullock, *The Calculus of Consent* (Ann Arbor, Michigan: University of Michigan Press, 1962).

2. The material in this section is based on Bernard Siegan, *Economic Liberties and the Constitution* (Chicago, Illinois: University of Chicago Press, 1980).

3. Much of the work on the economic theory of constitutions has been done by James M. Buchanan. In addition to *The Calculus of Consent*, see, for example, *The Limits of Liberty* (Chicago: University of Chicago Press, 1975), and also the paper by Buchanan in this volume. For a similar approach by a philosopher, see John Rawls, *A Theory of Justice* (Cambridge, Massachusetts: The Bellknap Press of Harvard University Press, 1971).

4. This process recently has been analyzed as *rent seeking*. For a discussion, see *Toward a Theory of the Rent Seeking Society*, eds. James M. Buchanan, Gordon Tullock, and Robert Tollison (College Station, Texas: Texas A&M Press, 1980).

5. The basic source of this argument is found in C.M. Tiebout, "A Pure Theory of Local Expenditures," *Journal of Political Economy* 64 (October 1956): 416-24.

6. See, for example, Jack Hirshleifer, *Price Theory and Applications*, 2nd ed. (Englewood Cliffs, New Jersey: Prentice-Hall, 1980), Chapter 17.

7. For a discussion of the economics of legal rules, see Richard A. Posner, *Economic Analysis of Law* (Boston: Little Brown, 1977).

8. Ronald Coase, "The Problem of Social Cost," *Journal of Law and Economics* 3 (1960): 1-44.

9. For two discussions of the antitrust laws from an economic perspective, see Richard A. Posner, *Antitrust Law* (Chicago: University of Chicago Press, 1976), and Robert H. Bork, *The Antitrust Paradox* (New York: Basic Books, 1978).

10. An early argument that asymmetric information may lead to adverse selection and thus to market failure is in George Akerlof, "The Market for 'Lemons,'" *Quarterly Journal of Economics* 84 (August 1970): 488-500. See also, Mark Pauly, "Overinsurance and Public Provision of Insurance," *Quarterly Journal of Economics* 88 (February 1974): 44-62.

11. Harold M. Hochman and James D. Rodgers, "Pareto Optimal Redistribution," *American Economic Review* (September 1969): 542-57.

12. Milton Friedman and Anna Schwartz, *A Monetary History of the United States* (Princeton, New Jersey: National Bureau of Economic Research, 1963).

13. Anthony Downs, *An Economic Theory of Democracy* (New York: Harper and Row, 1957).

14. For an empirical analysis of contributions, see James B. Kau and Paul H. Rubin, *Congressmen, Constitutents, and Contributors* (Boston: Martinus Nijhoff, 1982).

15. Mancur Olson, Jr., *The Logic of Collective Action* (Cambridge, Massachusetts: Harvard University Press, 1966).

16. The standard source on the economics of bureaucracy is William A. Niskanen, *Bureaucracy and Representative Government* (Chicago: Aldine, 1971).

17. Sam Peltzman, "An Evaluation of Consumer Protection Legislation: The 1962 Drug Amendments," *Journal of Political Economy* 81 (1973).

18. Friedrich Hayek, "The Use of Knowledge in Society," *American Economic Review* 35 (1945): 519-530.

19. E. R. Tufte, *Political Control of the Economy* (Princeton, New Jersey: Princeton University Press, 1978).

20. These numbers are from Martin J. Bailey, *Reducing Risks to Life* (Washington, D.C.: American Enterprise Institute, 1980).

GEORGE GILDER *asserts that free markets are not the core or the backbone of wealth-creating capitalism. Rather, the key is unleashing and appreciating the basic moral impulses of successful businessmen. Successful businessmen are savers, self-deniers; they are inventors, givers; they fulfill the unmet needs of others. The marketplace is merely where transactions take place, where information is efficiently exchanged.*

Profit is not the greedy drive of the self-interested; profit is the result, the value of providing something that someone needs. Consequently, according to Gilder, the Adam Smith representation of avaricious capitalists misses the point. Instead, the business impulse of giving should be permitted to help create wealth—to overcome poverty. Welfare solutions to poverty strip away the moral foundations that encourage success: saving, self-denial, giving, inventing. High tax rates divert the talents of businessmen from creating new wealth to retaining old wealth.

Our social economic policies create poverty—probably for generations to come. The key is appreciation of the basic humanity of successful businessmen, not the perfections of free markets of exchange. Gilder is more a supporter of business than a supporter of markets.

9

Wealth: Its Creation and Growth

GEORGE GILDER

Wealth, I believe, is created in accord with and through the expression of moral and religious values. When there is a divorce of economics from the moral order, the kind of demoralization we find in western capitalism results.

I think the beginning of this problem comes not from the opponents or critics of capitalism, but from its supporters. The supporters have embraced a theory of capitalism that is fundamentally misconceived and adverse to economic growth. This theory of capitalism was best summed up by John Kennedy when he said, "Businessmen are bastards."

Kennedy's position is not very different from the position espoused by Adam Smith, the leading theorist on capitalism. This defender of capitalism once said: "It is from the luxury and caprice of capitalists that we gain that share of the necessaries of life that we would in vain have expected from their humanity." In other words, we cannot expect anything from the mere humanity of capitalists. He continued: "Though their sole aim be the gratification of their own vain and insatiable desires, they are led, as though by an invisible hand, to serve the interests of society."

This is not an uncharacteristic quotation from Adam Smith. Adam Smith was a rather typical British intellectual and aristocrat who was disdainful toward people in trade. People in trade were believed to be in a somewhat lower moral category than intellectuals and aristocrats. Today intellectuals still try to create a system of capitalism, a system for the generation of wealth, that avoids paying tribute to capitalists. It is a system of capitalism without capitalists. It is not businessmen themselves by their own creative activities who generate wealth, the intellectuals maintain, but the mystical workings of a free marketplace that magically transmutes the greed and avarice that businessmen display into a good society. This theory suggests a kind of Faustian pact, a deal with the devil whereby we gain wealth from giving in to greed and avarice. It is sort of a contemporary alchemy, popular among economists who want to imagine that self-interest alone fosters economic growth. Unfortunately, this theory is very unconvincing. It is this theory, however, that many of the leading analysts and defenders of capitalism maintain. Milton Friedman, for example, is forever saying he does not support business, he supports free markets. His is the characteristic stance. But this idea subordinates a higher level of activity—the creation of value through launching businesses, inventing new goods, and marketing them to the public—to a lower order of value, which is the mere exchange of goods in the marketplace. Indeed, the marketplace is governed by computations of self-interest that have nothing to do with avarice. Such computations are accomplished by the transmission of information about supply and demand. In effect, the marketplace itself is just the final denouement. It is the end of a long process that begins by the creative activities of capitalists inventing goods and services, creating jobs, building inventories, and learning how to market their products—all long before any return is received or any goods are actually brought to market to be sold.

It is this creative process that precedes the market exchange which is the crux of the creation of wealth. When one focuses on the creative process of starting a business, one realizes that it has nothing to do with the greed and avarice ordinarily ascribed to businessmen.

What does a businessman do? What the businessman has to do, long before there is any assured return at all, is save. He has to begin by saving in order to accumulate the disposable personal savings that are the source of initial capital for the majority of small businesses. Over 90 percent of all the funds that finance business come from disposable personal savings.

What are savings? Savings are forgone consumption. They are self-denial. The first act of the capitalist, saving, is not an expression of his own selfish desires, succumbing to his own greeds and appetites, as is often supposed. The initial act of the businessman is to suppress his own needs and desires in order to accumulate disposable funds he can use to launch his business. So his initial act is an act not of greed but of self-denial.

Then the businessman starts his company. He contrives a specific product, perhaps a new product; he hires people to produce it; he develops a marketing plan; and he devotes himself to a long process of work and investment before any kind of return is received or any goods are actually marketed. This process requires continual consideration of the needs of others.

After his initial act of savings, he then has to determine what the needs of others are, and if he can satisfy them at the right price. So the success of his business is dependent on his responsiveness to the needs of others.

This means that the crucial process in capitalism has virtually nothing to do with the caricature of capitalism that prevails in virtually all of the texts of the defenders of the system, beginning with Adam Smith and proceeding through the works of Milton Friedman.

The process I have just described occurred to me first from a peculiar source. I wrote several books about sex in society years back, and during the course of writing them, I studied anthropology. One thing I observed in studying primitive tribes was the ritual of gift giving. Levi-Strauss, the famous French anthropologist, said that gift giving is universal in all human societies. He and one of his followers, Marcell Marcuse, author of *The Gift*, are concerned that modern societies have succumbed to the impersonal marketplace in modern society and eschew this impulse of giving that is so prevalent in primitive society. Both of them are socialists because they believe that socialism somehow embodies the spirit of giving better than the impersonal capitalist marketplace.

But it seemed to me when I examined these primitive societies, what was really going on is the opposite of socialism. Primitive societies are reduced to barter because they have no money; they trade one thing for another. Barter is difficult to arrange. When one person has a horse and another person has a loaf of bread, somehow you have to figure a way through a complex arrangement of trading that helps get one person the horse and the other person the loaf of bread.

It seems to me that barter is essentially the same as socialism. Barter requires a planned society. Primitive societies using barter were essentially socialist societies since all exchanges had to be predetermined. There had to be some arrangement to assure that the horse got to the right person and the bread got to the right people. Essentially socialism is a return to the system of barter.

But what happened? In a lot of these primitive societies there were some guys who just said, "This is too much trouble, to try to figure out all the arrangements of barter. We just cannot find somebody who wants precisely the amount of bread or horse meat that I have available, so I will just give it away." In most primitive societies people began just giving their goods away, and this generated in the recipients of this gift a sense of obligation to the giver. Then the recipients would try to give something back. Ordinarily the recipient would try to better the initial gift with his reciprocal gift. He would try to give back the original gift with interest. This is really the way capitalism began. But it was these primitive leaders who decided they no longer had the patience to arrange all the details and artificial exchanges; they started giving their goods away in the expectation that other people would reciprocate.

What happens when capitalism is rejected is a return to planned economics that resembles the most primitive economics in the world—barter.

Giving is just as prevalent now in capitalistic societies as it was in primitive societies, contrary to what Levi-Strauss and Marcell Marcuse have said about modern society being dominated by impersonal modes of exchange in which gift giving is absent. I think that capitalism itself epitomizes a process of gift giving. In order to give something to somebody that will evoke a further gift, one has to understand the recipient. One has to understand others in order to give successfully; and, as a matter of fact, one has to begin by suppressing one's own interest.

The profit in the system is the difference between the value of the gift to the giver and to the receiver. It is the altruistic content of the gift. It is the extent to which the person has suppressed his or her own needs and interests in order to respond to others' needs and interests. The capitalistic process of building and maintaining a business corresponds closely to the process of giving in primitive societies. It is a process that depends on the responsiveness of the business to others' needs.

But there is a further sense in which the capitalist has to be altruistic—the capitalist has to hope that other people succeed. This is why the image of competition, which depicts people taking from one another in some sense, misconceives the essential process of capitalism. The capitalist hopes that other people succeed, because if other people succeed, then they provide markets for his goods. So not only does the capitalist begin by an act of self-denial, he continues by considering the needs of others. Finally, the capitalist wants others to succeed in order to expand the market for his own product. So throughout this long process there is very little greed and avarice.

I think that all people are self-interested in some sense, but to say that capitalism is based on self-interest is almost meaningless. If everybody is self-interested, then the extraordinary success of particular societies in creating wealth cannot be merely attributed to self-interest. So I believe that self-interest, as by an invisible hand, leads inexorably to an ever-growing welfare state because when individuals consider their own interests first, they tend to seek comfort, security, leisure, and consumption. In other words, they come to seek support from government; they want predetermined outcomes; they do not begin the long and risky processes of giving of their wealth and work in order to create a business.

This perception reached me first when I began to consider the advice of some of the libertarians. A lot of libertarians have the view expressed in the book *Looking Out For No.1*. They recommend that we buy gold and guns and retreat to rural areas; that we buy a lot of dry packaged goods and avoid productive activities and avoid the kind of risks and challenges that business entails. This view is like that of the "me generation," with which I was brought up and with which I went to Harvard. One of the key problems of capitalism in the world today is its demoralization. This demoralization results from capitalism's divorce from its religious foundations. Thus the restoration of a thriving, capitalist society entails a moral revival as well as a material one. That is really the essence of capitalism.

I began studying capitalism when I was writing about wealth and poverty. I began by studying poverty and wrote several books on that subject, one of which was based on a long series of interviews with the poor in Harlem; in Albany, New York; and in Greenville, South Carolina. I wrote a book called *Visible Man* based upon that analysis, and that became a critique of the welfare state.

I think the fundamental misconception of the welfare state is that giving is easy, that compassion is easy, that all you have to do is go out and distribute money and you are actually helping people. This is the failure of the welfare state. For decades we have been giving things to poor people in the slums, and the result has been to destroy their families and their motivations. In other words, this giving—which pretends to be charitable—ends up being vicious because it destroys the very people who it is designed to serve and it tends to serve the very people who purport to be compassionate.

The fact is that charity is very difficult. It depends on a close scrutiny of the needs of others; it depends on long devotion of wealth and work to this process. The most effective manifestation of charity comes through the normal operations of businesses that have to respond to the needs of others in specific ways, or fail.

The so-called poverty programs have intensified and perpetuated poverty everywhere they have been administered. Today the situation in the inner cities of America is far worse than it was when the Great Society programs were launched. Today about 55 percent of all black children are born out of wedlock; six out of ten black children are brought up without fathers; youth unemployment is worse than ever before. This is after twenty years of massively increasing funds and services into the ghettos. The more money that goes in, the worse the situation gets—the more crime, violence, demoralization, and broken families.

This is defended in the name of compassion, but the problem with all these programs is that they are based not on a realistic understanding of the needs of the people in the inner cities, they are based on some concept of redistribution contrived by Marxist professors of economics at M.I.T. These programs do not have a clue about how to actually help people, and thus they are not—from my point of view—charitable.

The operations of businesses do help people, because they are based on a real response to the needs of others. The chief reason that the ghettos are so poor is that no successful businesses are there.

Welfare programs generate failure. First, in order to qualify for benefits, you have to not save. If you have any savings, you must give up welfare. You cannot save if you are a welfare person; and if you cannot save, you cannot start a business. Since it is small businesses that everywhere have accounted for the emergence from poverty, this initial approach destroys the possibility of renewal in the inner cities. Immigrants continue to come to our shores in greater numbers than ever before and create jobs for themselves and others by launching small businesses. Certain immigrant groups collectively exceed white, Anglo-Saxon Protestants in per capita income. They have risen by starting small businesses. Poverty is overcome through the creation of small businesses.

That is the key to capitalist success. Capitalism does not succeed in creating wealth simply because it is a more homogenous arrangement of carrots and sticks or a shrewd arrangement of incentives. It succeeds ultimately because it mobilizes the fundamental moral impulses of society.

Capitalism also allows the conduct of experiments because this is what all business projects are. Each business project, whether it is big or small, is virtually a laboratory test of an entrepreneurial idea. When people analyze these laboratory tests, they usually focus on the profits. What were the earnings of this particular new business venture? But accompanying the financial profit is an increase in knowledge.

The very people who gain the knowledge through the entrepreneurial experiment also are granted the power to direct the future course of investment. In this way, accumulated physical capital is combined with metaphysical capital of knowledge, courage, and faith, and this combination of physical capital and metaphysical capital creates the synergic thrust of capitalist growth. It is the secret of the success of free economies.

The chief problem of high tax rates on which supply-side economists focus is that they destroy this knowledge. They not only destroy incentive but they also destroy knowledge, because they deny to the people who conduct successful entrepreneurial experiments the wherewithal to direct the future course of investment. When individuals operate in an economy with a high progressive system of tax rates, they are forced to eschew the knowledge and values that made it possible for them to earn this money and, instead, engage themselves in a long process of financial finagling in order to avoid taxation.

A businessman does not enter an enterprise and learn how to produce a product successfully in order to consult with lawyers and accountants about sending money to off-shore trusts. That is not an essential interest. But if levels of taxation mean that he cannot profit from his product, sustain his enterprise, and continue the process of reinvestment, he is virtually constrained to consider such tax options in order to continue his very business as an entrepreneur. High tax rates essentially destroy knowledge and stultify the economy as well as demoralize capitalists, because capitalists lose their sense of purpose and the exhilaration of creativity of enterprise if they spend two days with their accountants trying to figure out how to finagle tax savings. That is the reason why supply-side economists focus so much on reducing tax rates.

When one scrutinizes the results of having low taxes, one realizes that it helps the poor most. This surprising conclusion is contrary to what everyone tells us in the press these days, but the fact is that high tax rates on income do not tax being rich, they tax getting rich. People of wealth can easily escape these high tax rates. It is people who are getting rich—who are really involved in expanding their businesses—who get punished by these high rates.

High progressive tax rates create a static economy with less opportunity for the poor. When tax rates are reduced across the board, the rich pay more and the poor pay less. Just analyze any previous across-the-board tax cut that has been made in the United States or in any other country. Every tax cut shows this effect, but the biggest tax cut we ever had was during the early 1920s, when the top rate was cut from 73 percent to 25 percent in four years. Now, that's a tax cut, and everybody predicted, just as they do today, that the result of this tax cut would be to redistribute income from the poor and the middle class to the rich. This was the general assumption. But what happened? The result was that the rich paid 200 percent more taxes after the cuts than before and that the share of total taxes paid by the rich increased from 27 percent to 63 percent. In other words, the result of this slash of the top tax rate to 25 percent was to vastly increase the tax payments of the rich, and the rich moved their money out of tax shelters into taxable forms of income, while the poor—who usually have their income withheld at source—actually paid less. The result of having tax cuts across the board is to increase the taxes paid by the rich and to reduce the taxes paid by the poor.

In sum, the welfare state destroys the families of the poor, and the way to overcome our current predicament is to unleash the generous and altruistic impulses of a capitalist society and return to a system of work, family, and faith, which have been the foundations of all wealth creation in our history.

SECTION III

Roles of Business, Government, and Labor in a Private Enterprise Society

The "invisible hand" is not left uninfluenced in a society of democratic capitalism. Government, labor, and business seek roles to play to shape our future. Each must struggle with the tensions between long-term and short-term policies—between quiet and visible compassion.

Two heads of state, former President Gerald Ford and Prime Minister Edward Seaga of Jamaica, share the personal philosophies and the philosophies of government that shape their perspectives. Both propose that government must guarantee economic and personal freedom. Both suggest a similar role for government—though one is for a developing country and the other is for a developed country. Both strongly believe in the goodness of their people.

The concern for the quality of life and for market efficiency is clearly tested in the labor markets. Economist Phyllis Wallace addresses the role of labor in private enterprise. The challenge is with the "leftovers," those unable to compete for available employment. For them, who plays what role?

Columnist George Will and business economist Norma Pace urge business to play a more aggressive role in improving the standard of living of our country. They believe business is hardly without fault in our recent and current economic woes. If business is passive and unresponsive to the economy, private enterprise will again be threatened by public opinion. Business must return to what business does best: take risks, invest aggressively, assure productivity, and provide public leadership. The authors charge business with the responsibility to take the biggest chances.

Former President GERALD FORD *endorses the efforts of President Reagan to promote a stronger free enterprise economy. He applauds the attempts to (1) reduce the growth rate of federal spending, (2) reduce individual and business taxes to stimulate savings and investment, and (3) reduce government regulation. He views the economic policies since 1980 as significantly changing our economic direction after twenty years of excessively expanding social programs.*

Mr. Ford rebukes those who believe these policies demonstrate lack of compassion; he empathizes with those who are apprehensive and cannot yet feel the long-term benefits. He expects increasingly heated political debate—which is healthy in a system of democratic capitalism. He reminds us of our cherished tradition of "respect for the convictions of others and faith in the decency of others which allows us the luxury of rugged economic and political competition."

10
The Responsibility of Government to Guarantee Economic Freedom

GERALD R. FORD

For some 205 years, we in the United States have been the beneficiaries of what has become known as democratic capitalism. By any scorecard our system of government produced far more benefits for more people over a longer period of time than any other system in the history of mankind. By any standards, we in America have more freedom than any other group of people throughout the world. There is no question that we have the freedoms of speech, of worship, of the press, and countless other freedoms. No nation can compete with the United States in the availability of material benefits.

In stark contrast, we now see the utter failure of another ideology, Communism, as the tragedy of Poland unfolds. Communism in practice emerged about fifty years ago in the Soviet Union and was subsequently imposed on the eastern European nations after World War II. In the late 1940s, most unfortunately, Poland was one of those nations caught in the web of Communism behind the Iron Curtain. We now see firsthand the total failure of Communism both politically as well as economically.

The Polish people have lost all vestiges of freedom. They literally had none under the recent martial law. The Polish economy cannot provide enough food for its people. The Polish government owes the free world about $28 billion and cannot meet the current debt payments on those obligations. They are totally in default. Poland today is a showcase of failure—of failure of Communism, the government domination of individual lives, and the government domination of the economy.

The recent events, of course, in Poland are sad and tragic, but these developments should teach us that Communism does not work, and our system of democratic capitalism must be supported and strengthened.

Over the past three or four decades in America, many well-intentioned Americans have promoted the idea that government in our nation should be expanded and that the private sector should be more restricted and curtailed. Program after program was proposed by presidents and enacted into law by the Congress to solve our social problems and our economic difficulties. As a consequence, the cost of government at the local, state, and federal levels soared. The tax burden from the lowest level to the top skyrocketed. Our economy faltered as we became less productive and less competitive.

Let me give you a couple of figures to show how the parts of our government changed in the last twenty or thirty years. In 1960, out of the total pie of federal spending, the defense department was spending about 40 percent of every dollar. Domestic programs were spending roughly 30 percent. In other words, the heaviest concentration of the total federal expenditures in 1960 was for national security and a lesser percentage was for our domestic programs.

In 1980, the percentages had just about reversed. Out of the total federal expenditure pie, the slice for domestic programs was about 42 percent, and the defense department had dropped to about 24 percent. There was in about twenty years an almost total reversal of government expenditures from defense to social or domestic programs. There was a distinct change in the way our government was expending its resources. As a consequence, the American people—in my opinion—were frustrated and deeply concerned in 1980 and by their ballots voted for a change.

After the election in 1980, I was dumbfounded to read that some commentators were saying that the majority of the voters were less compassionate than those who voted in previous elections. I strongly disagreed with that conclusion. It was my impression that the voters, or a majority of them, were just as compassionate as the voters in previous elections. They were simply fed up with the failure of most of the social programs that had been undertaken over the previous twenty years, and they were demanding by their ballots a change in the way our government was operated.

All of our problems domestically, as I saw it, seemed to come to a head in 1980. Many of these well-intentioned social programs obviously had not produced the results that many had thought they would, and serious economic problems in our country also came to a head. The year 1980 by any standard was a bad year economically. Statistics for that year included an inflation rate of 13.4 percent; unemployment, 7.4 percent; and a prime interest rate of 21 percent. The home-building and automotive industries were flat on their backs; bankruptcies were at an all-time high; government regulation, primarily at the federal level, was overwhelming our business community. Federal budget expenditures were skyrocketing.

That last statement was a strong one, but let me illustrate what I mean. In fiscal year 1980 the federal government spent $580 billion. In fiscal year 1981, the federal government spent $660 billion. That is a lot of increase. Then in the proposed budget of fiscal 1982, it was recommended by President Carter that the expenditures for the government go from $660 billion to $740 billion, another $80 billion increase. And the net result, if that budget had been approved, would have been a $160 billion increase in the short span of twenty-four months. By any standard, that is a lot of increase. The net result was that federal expenditures were accelerating at the rate of about 17 percent on an annual basis.

If you extrapolated that kind of an increase until the year 2,000, you would find that by the turn of the century the federal government would be spending better than 50 percent of our total gross national product every twelve months.

The economic situation in this country in January 1980 was critical. Dr. Arthur Burns, former chairman of the Federal Reserve Board, said the circumstances were so dire that we needed shock therapy. And so the president, on the basis of his mandate at the election, proposed some very tough economic measures—measures, in my opinion, that are seeking to turn around the trends that had developed over time and to give to the free enterprise system an opportunity to operate effectively.
operate effectively.

We are in a tough time right now. But I remind you that the actual program that the president proposed is aimed at stimulating democratic capitalism in a period where pressures are great and statistics are discouraging. There is no question that many people are concerned on the one hand and encouraged on the other. As I travel around the country, I find that people are encouraged. They believe there has been a change in direction in our economic policy. They are encouraged that the right decisions have been made, but they also do not see the light at the end of the tunnel. The net result is some criticism and apprehension. But I found from personal experience that a president cannot change the direction of an economy overnight.

Let me illustrate the basic ingredients of what is under way in Washington that will give a new breath of life to the free enterprise system. Number one, the rate of growth of federal expenditures has been significantly reduced. Over the last three or four years, the rate of growth had been at 17 percent per annum. The president recommended and Congress approved a reduction in the rate of growth of federal spending from 17 percent per year to 7 percent.

The public might get the impression from the media that President Reagan cut 1982's budget below 1981's budget. That is not true. He reduced the budget recommended by President Carter at $740 billion to $700 billion, but that is still $40 billion more than 1981's budget. But it is a big step forward and a tremendous change in direction that I fully support. But to hear the bureaucrats scream, to hear some of the beneficiaries complain, you would have thought that 1982 programs were getting less money than they got in 1981.

Let me take an example. Suppose there was an agency or department in the federal government that in 1981 got $100 million. I might emphasize that this is a very small agency in the federal government. But supposing this agency got $100 million that year. Under former President Carter's proposed budget they would have gotten $117 million in 1982, a 17 percent increase. Under President Reagan's budget, they got $107 million, $7 million more.

But if we are going to get a responsible fiscal policy, if we are going to eventually control the expenditures of federal money, there had to be some reins tightened on the federal budget. And the change that was undertaken by the president is definitely in the right direction.

A handful of programs did get less than they got in 1981. But in about 90 percent of the cases, the department got more, not less, than it got the preceding year.

On the other side of the coin, to give our economy the kind of shot in the arm needed, there had to be some tax relief. There is no question that our tax policies in this country over a period of the last twenty years have placed an ever increasing burden on the individual taxpayer and our business society. The net result was that individuals could not save to invest and our businesses could not generate capital to expand and to modernize. Therefore, we were becoming less productive and less competitive on a worldwide basis.

So the administration wisely proposed tax reductions both for individuals as well as for corporations. The first tax reduction has been in effect since October 1981. The second reduction came in July 1982. It is a start in the right direction that is absolutely essential if we are going to generate the kind of savings that we need to provide the capital to invest.

The third change that is a stimulant to the expansion of our free enterprise system is deregulation. There is no question that through legislation over the last twenty years bureaucratic rules and regulations have exploded.

I am not talking about those that involve health and safety. I am talking about those kinds of rules and regulations that are in the imagination of the legislatures and bureaucrats and that are not justified on the basis of cost-to-benefit ratios.

At last some headway is being made to slow down the imposition of those rules that are unnecessary for the future and to pull back some of those whose initial justification cannot be warranted today. It is a tough process. But, nevertheless, if we are going to be competitive with the Japanese, with the West Germans, and with others, we have to more or less operate in the same business environment. I believe that our changed direction is a big step toward the goal of reviving the democratic capitalism that did so much for so many people over so many years in the United States.

It will not be easy. There will be pressures. There will be criticisms. I happen to believe the president is going to stand his ground, not capitulate to political expediency on the short-term basis.

A bright future in this country is predicated on our history as well as our traditions. Our nation, we must remember, was born in adversity. Our forefathers two centuries ago fought for and won our freedom. They gave their lives, their fortunes, and thank goodness, they have prevailed.

Those leaders in that perilous period gave us the Declaration of Independence and our Constitution—priceless documents as well as ideals. And those who followed that original group forge today a nation of fifty states and 230 million people.

Yes, we have had two world wars in this century. In our very best American tradition, we have helped friend and foe alike recover from the ravages of war. And in keeping with our desires to help those less fortunate than ourselves, we have sought to end poverty, to eradicate illiteracy, and to help those in less developed nations of the world.

Our nation has had some stormy seas at home—depressions, riots in our streets, and disillusionment in our hearts. At times there was public despair that made many lose faith in our economic as well as our political philosophies.

However, history tells us in the United States that our forefathers did more than just stand around and wring their hands. They were resilient, and they faced forthrightly the challenges of their day. They kept a steady hand on the tiller. They believed, as Abraham Lincoln did, that America is our last best hope.

There has been and still is a very fundamental belief in our society that the things that unite us as Americans are far, far more enduring than the things that divide us.

The Prime Minister of Jamaica traces the role of Marxism and free enterprise in his nation over the past twenty years. EDWARD SEAGA *is credited by many for the startling economic turnaround of Jamaica since his election in 1980. He concludes that it is the role of the private sector to improve a developing country's standard of living and the role of the public sector to improve the quality of life.*

Seaga explains that the challenging task facing leaders in the Caribbean is to find a judicious mix of industry and compassion. He stresses that the most powerful tool to combat poverty is economic freedom. He is an outspoken advocate of free trade, free markets, and personal freedom. He provides the recent history of Jamaica as testimony.

11

Economic Freedom in Developing Countries

EDWARD SEAGA

The test of any government is, in the final analysis, whether it attains a better standard of living for its people.

This is as true of developing countries as it is of developed societies. One may even say that governments have a moral obligation to ensure that the most deprived sectors of the population have access to opportunity and a chance to improve the quality of their lives.

In this respect, the objectives of good government are compatible with Judeo-Christian ideals in the widest sense. The validity of the free enterprise system can only be that it offers to society a better hope of improving the lot of the individual than does the Marxist system of social and economic organization. But because there is a concentration of poverty in the developing world, our countries are particularly vulnerable to the Marxist approach, especially since this approach is often represented by a moral argument that blames the accumulation of material wealth by individuals as the cause of poverty, and thus a bad thing. The argument has been seductive to many precisely because it is so simplistic. Resources are few; needs are many; disparity is great. Therefore, the answer is for the state to take command of the economy and to control and distribute resources, thus theoretically wiping out the disparities and poverty at the same time.

Reality, however, belies this theory. The fact is that recent history has shown clearly that this centrally planned and managed economy under its socialist Marxist system has simply not delivered the conclusion. It has not worked in eastern Europe; it has not worked in Africa or Asia; and it has not worked in the Caribbean. We all know what happened to Jamaica when the illusion of Cuba's advancement prompted the democratic socialist government between 1972 and 1980 to try to imitate this approach to economic development. It failed because, in the end, people were worse off than they were before. The recent Jamaican experience underscores what is by now a familiar story. By restricting economic freedom, production decreases and then the inevitable progression of tightening controls emerges in a vain endeavor to achieve by fear and rhetoric what can only transpire through free choice and the motivation of a system that rewards personal enterprise. Indeed, if improvement in standards of living is the absolute bottom-line test of successful development, the strategies that work best are those established on the principle of individual freedom operating within the market system of private enterprise. The industrial world and the newly industrialized countries are abundant testimonies to this success. So, too, are those countries that are successfully making their way up the ladder toward the point of take-off. There is no better example than Jamaica to illustrate how the forces of personal motivation, of enterprise, and of freedom of choice combine to generate economic growth or, conversely, how the diminution of perceived degradation of these forces combines to assault the quality of life. Over the period of a decade Jamaica was transformed from a market system economy with unthreatened individual freedoms and rights to a fearful, anxious country through the process of mutation to a Cuban satellite. The mechanisms of transformation were not always easy to perceive, but the rhetoric clearly defined much of the intent.

Since November of 1980, the process of recovery to establish the spirit of enterprise and to remove the fear of threatened rebound have effected a remarkable turnaround.

The 1960s were a period of economic stability for Jamaica. Caribbean inflation averaged 6 percent in real terms. On the foreign exchange, reserves grew annually. Budgetary outlays, by means of prudent judgment and management, were financed without special accommodation by the Central Bank, inflation rates were in single digits, and the value of the Jamaican dollar was higher than the U.S. dollar. The market system functioned, and the political system flourished in a climate of unthreatened freedoms and rights.

In 1972 a change in government took place. Socialism was introduced softly at first, but grew in intensity each year. The government changed hands in 1980. We lost 20 percent of our national income in those eight years, and more than 50 percent of our industrial capacity was idle. More than 50 percent of our hotel rooms were vacant; one-third of all bauxite mining capacity was idle; building construction fell to the level of the 1950s; and unemployment increased by 50 percent and reached levels of 78 percent and 54 percent among young people and women, respectively. All of this was reflected in the precipitous decline of the standard of living by 57 percent in U.S. dollar terms. The rate of inflation averaged a staggering 30 percent each year over the five-year period preceding 1980.

When it was all over, the Bank of Jamaica reeled from repeated attempts to support failed production. All foreign exchange reserves were wiped out, and the Jamaican dollar, worth more than the U.S. dollar only a few years before, was cut in half by a series of unilateral devaluations. The impact on the society was almost incalculable. Outages, stoppages, and shortages occurred with frustrating regularity. Public services broke down repeatedly, causing widespread confusion. Hospitals went without medicine, instruments, and bed linens; schools went without benches and books; buildings and roads went without repair; the police and military went without equipment; and bills went without payment. These were just some of the consequences, a few items in the long catalog of collapse. For the first time in recent memory basic supplies disappeared. Black markets appeared. The little shops in the hills of Jamaica were without groceries. Thousands of these shops went out of business, and the rural people in particular were without even basic groceries. While inflation and joblessness reached staggering heights, lack of goods paralyzed the economy, services collapsed, and social and political tensions in the country rose to the breaking point. Many lost hope and migrated, splitting families and separating friends. Others turned to crime, an undesirable way out that all of us want to forget. They were, without doubt, the most unproductive, frightening, and unforgettable years in this century.

It has taken one year to reverse this process of decay and to recover some of the slippage of those eight years. The return to a value system that rewarded enterprise and advanced personal freedoms showed immediate results with a return to growth in the first year—marginal but positive. Basic supplies of groceries have been fully restored; black markets, broken up; raw-material flows, significantly improved. Tourism is up to near capacity; services have generally improved; and shortages, outages, and stoppages are generally under better control. Best of all, unemployment is moving favorably downward and inflation, in relative terms, not unfavorably up. The inflation curve in 1981 reflected a return to economic sanity with an incredibly low rate of 4.7 percent, as compared to 28 percent in 1980.

These figures do not imply a recovery, but they do signal a turnaround and a move made in the right direction: the reversal of the process of decay. Why and how this turnaround took place is what I wish to address in this paper. The answer is not shrouded in the mysteries of dogma. It is simple; it is basic; it is understandable. The economic system that generated this turnaround is based on a strategy that is responsive to the dynamics of the personal motivations of the Jamaican people. These motivative forces are basically the intense desire to improve standards of living and to optimize economic rights and freedoms as the previous ingredients of an enhanced quality of life. The means to the end are to reward personal enterprise that achieves personal goals and to establish parliamentary democracy to ensure the right to freedom of choice.

Phrased in other terms, this is the classic prescription for a market-system economy motivated by enterprise and a democratic system of political and civil rights.

But this formulation would be oversimplistic if it ended there. The Jamaican psyche is also characterized by a respect for state intervention to assist the disadvantaged and the deprived sections of society, those who are not fully drawn into the mainstream of the development. The parameters of the private sector are, therefore, drawn to encourage growth and production, to ensure the ability of the treasury to mold social programs to deal with those who might be otherwise forgotten, and to respect regulations that protect the rights of workers and consumers. The balanced mix of interest has crystallized over the year into several roles and responsibilities that encourage private enterprise to perform successfully in response to both market and social forces, reflecting in this balance the fundamental Judeo-Christian value mix of industry and compassion.

You may gather from this that the Jamaican system features private-sector predominance in productive programs and public-sector predominance in social programs. The country looks to the private sector to improve its standard of living and to the public sector to improve the quality of life. Certainly Jamaica relies more on the developing structure, building on the needs of the individual moreso than on the needs of the state. It is this building block of human motivation, rather than state veneration, that induced the development strategy of the region to a special resilience to the standard, well-promoted, although illusory, objectives of Marxist-oriented indulgence. At some stage in the promotion of treatment, the hardheaded fathers, workers, and consumers of the Caribbean recognized the promised land of Marx to be a misconceived land of promises, and they continue to reject the Marxist system for the market system. It is against this background that the Caribbean Basin Initiative (CBI) has been framed to stimulate the spirit of enterprise, a basic building block of the society. To be sure, the CBI has existed between thrusts, as it must, reinforcing the ability of the public sector to develop the infrastructure and the capability of the private sector for production and growth. But the emphasis, without doubt, is on development mechanisms, investment, and trade moreso than on aid.

The Caribbean region is fertile ground for political stimulation. I will put it no stronger than that. Seeds have been known to fail and fertile growth, through neglect, to wither. It is for each country to seize the unprecedented opportunity of a tariff-free, quota-free regime backed by investment incentives. The successes of the CBI may one day be associated in economic terms with improvement of growth and production within the region, and more meaningfully, with improvement in the standard of living of the people.

However, I hope these successes will serve a deeper purpose, whether by design or otherwise: to strengthen the development strategy of the region, which has prevailed over four decades. This strategy features parliamentary democracy as the basis of the political system and as the basis of the economic structure. It is a market system appropriately regulated to protect workers and consumers, which has had remarkable success in its political objectives but a lesser effect in producing widespread economic benefits. The region can boast the richest concentration of democracy in the world—more than twenty proven democratic regimes—but it has failed in its economic mission to reduce unemployment and to improve standards of living. The reason is not hard to find.

The microsize of the unit countries, of which twenty in the Caribbean could fit into the King Ranch, provides a minimarketplace unable to support sufficient growth opportunities for the needs of the labor force. The answer must be to find a larger marketplace and to expand production to assist growth and employment, precisely what the CBI is designed to offer.

This reinforcement is timely. The force and the economic strengths of the Caribbean development strategy are the result of exposure to the alternatives of Marxist attractions provided by Cuba. This threat was defeated sizably in Jamaica and was further rejected as an alternative in half a dozen other elections in the region during 1980. But the threat that the politically sharp will gobble up the little fish has principally been averted by the distinct benefit of the democratic electoral system, not by the bountiful benefits of the economic system to date.

The future of the CBI is drawn in terms of its one-way free-trade area and its investment incentives. The Caribbean can become the next fast-growth area of the world. It can demonstrate that a judicious mix of industry and compassion in the sensitive structuring of national goals is the most powerful tool yet devised to combat poverty and the most proven and successful strategy to propel the developing nations of the western world to a new dimension of prosperity.

In a democratic society with humanitarian values, perhaps the most important test of the impersonal efficiency of free markets is in the workplace. How well do the forces of supply and demand of labor serve our economy and our people?

Professor PHYLLIS WALLACE *briefly traces the history of labor in the U.S. economy and explains how changes in the size, the age, and the skill distribution of our work force have affected our national productivity. She describes how computer-assisted technology and quality-of-work-life concerns will affect national productivity in the future. She also discusses current trends in government regulation of the workplace—especially through minimum wage legislation—and in union contract concessions.*

She concludes with a compelling look at the leftovers—that 15 percent of our work force not equipped to compete for available jobs. What responsibility does business have for these leftovers? What responsibility does government have? What responsibility do the workers themselves have?

12

Economics, Private Enterprise, and the Workers

PHYLLIS A. WALLACE

In establishing a capitalistic democracy, the United States has built a society on two differing foundations. The capitalistic foundation attaches top priority to efficiency—operating through market incentives for getting the economic job done in the way that obtains the most useful output from our labor, capital, and natural resources. The democratic foundation, in contrast, emphasizes egalitarian and humanitarian values of cooperation, compassion, and fraternity.

Because our society rests on both of these foundations, we encounter creative tensions and uneasy compromise.[1]

With such a broadly defined topic, one might investigate how different schools of economic thought from Adam Smith to present-day, human-capital theorists treat labor as a factor of production. Or from a shorter historical perspective, it might be more interesting to examine the role of labor within the framework of the American economy. From the early days, labor was in short supply in this country, and the emergence of the United States as a leading industrial nation was tied to the immigration of indentured servants (mainly from Europe); the flourishing of that peculiar institution, namely slavery for blacks; and the waves of immigrants who entered the country during the latter part of the nineteenth century and up to World War I.

The success of the factory system in the textile towns of New England; the assembly-line production in Detroit; and the expansion of basic manufacturing in iron and steel, meatpacking, and railroads were achieved through the creative implementation of the supply strategies noted above. The invisible hand of the market also induced labor supply adjustments through major internal migrations from farms to urban areas and from south to north and west. It also improved the quality of labor through education and training. Although the past might be a prologue, I believe that the decade of the 1980s will serve as a significant turning point in reshaping the relationship between American-style private enterprise and the worker. Some of the issues that will determine the rules of the workplace are: new technology, quality of work life, the growth of government regulation of the workplace, the declining influence of organized labor, productivity improvements, and employment and training programs. I have more questions than I have answers, and it is likely that my list of issues would not be identical with others who have a different set of values. Although these concerns are identified as problems, it does not mean that our over a trillion-dollar economy may not be able to adapt to structural shifts.

Characteristics of the Work Force

There were 107 million individuals in the American labor force at the beginning of the 1980s, and 83 percent of those workers were in the private sector. During the post-World War II period almost the entire growth in employment occurred in the private, nonagricultural sector. Now with over 60 percent of all wage and salary workers in nonagricultural industries such as communications, finance, retail trade, transportation, health services, and so forth, the United States has attained the status of a service economy. At the same time that the industrial shift away from basic manufacturing occurred, more than half the American work force became white collar workers in a variety of occupations from clericals to professionals and managers. Thus, a more educated, better qualified work force held different attitudes and expectations about work: that is, they were less driven by the work ethic than were their ancestors.

If we examine more carefully the demographics of this American work force, we can anticipate some of the stresses and strains in the workplace throughout this decade. They are associated with the aging of the baby-boom population and the increased labor force participation of women. Between 1946 and 1964 the United States experienced an enormous increase in its population (some 75 million births) and this sizable cohort has been seen by some as a disruptive force in the labor markets of the 1970s. These young and inexperienced workers in the 16-24 age group have been the fastest growing component of the labor force and may have helped to depress productivity. By 1990 there will be a decline of the youth population from 24 percent to 19 percent of the labor force, even as the total labor force is projected to grow. Nevertheless, by the end of this decade those in the prime working age group (25 to 44), those aging baby boomers, will account for 54 percent of the civilian labor force.[2]

What are some of the problems associated with the baby-boom

population? This is an exceedingly well-educated group with high expectations about the world of work. An oversupply of college educated workers may force some of them to settle for lower level jobs—far down in the occupational hierarchy. Many employers are worried about the bulge or promotion squeeze that will occur by the middle of this decade. If the "brightest and the best" find that there are severe restrictions on their upward mobility, other ways will have to be developed to motivate them and to reward them for their contributions to the firm. Many may demand costly fringe benefits such as vacation cashouts, contributions to ESOPS, profit sharing plans, bonuses, subsidies for child care, and expensive training arrangements. Thus the flexible benefits may become an accepted way of doing business in many firms. Many of these workers will belong to dual career families where the income provided by a working spouse might enable primary wage earners to have many more options about work—and so a new ethic may emerge.

A recent article in the *Wharton Magazine* noted that "young managers entering the Bell System today simply do not have the lust to climb the corporate ladder that management recruits had twenty years ago." Two of that company's psychologists noted that the new managers neither aspire to higher-level positions (even though they have the skills) nor defer to those who have them. They concluded by stating that their "studies of Bell System managers point to a potential crisis brewing as the next generation meets and replaces the last. A generally reassuring continuity in managerial abilities is matched by a disturbing discontinuity in managerial motivation. For the sake of our organizations, our economy, and our country, we hope a solution can be found."[3]

The increased labor force participation of women is expected to continue to provide most of the growth in the labor force, and their share of the total labor force will rise from 42 percent to 46 percent by 1990. Corporate policies will have to reflect the needs of women workers, many of whom will be single parents with concerns about flexible scheduling, child care subsidies, better medical packages, and, foremost, reducing the income gap between themselves and their male colleagues. However, nearly three-fifths of all women workers are married; many are under 35 years of age and have small children. Women workers, regardless of marital status, have forced employers to modify their pension benefits, pregnancy and maternity leave policy, and procedures for training and promotion.[4] More of the growth in female participation will occur in the nontraditional occupations for women.

Productivity

Since 1960 the United States has experienced one of the lowest rates of productivity growth of the industrialized countries. In the period 1960-79 the annual productivity growth was 1.5 percent for the United States as compared with 7.1 percent for Japan. American industrial productivity grew 3.3 percent a year from 1948 to 1965, by 2.3 percent from 1965 to 1972, by 1.8 percent from 1972 to 1977, and for the 1977 to 1980 period it was negative.[5] Lester Thurow asserts that with the enormous increase in the labor force of members from the baby-boom population and of women, employers tended to utilize more people and to not invest in capital. Capital/labor ratios (the amount of equipment per worker) fell. Michael Wachter notes that although a demographic adjustment for age and sex can explain the decline in productivity between 1965 and the early 1970s, this adjustment does not explain the major slowdown that began after that period.[6]

Other reasons for the decline in productivity may have been decreased spending on research and development, the impact of regulatory programs such as environmental protection laws, higher energy prices, tight money policies, and the shift in the industrial mix to the low productivity sectors such as some service industries. The good news for the latter part of this decade is that the labor force growth will be lower due to the arrival of the baby-bust group (those born after 1964). There will be a shortage of younger, less-skilled workers. Meanwhile, efforts to improve productivity will be accelerated, and I shall highlight two activities: (1) development of new technology, and (2) attempts to improve the quality of work life for employees.

Technology

The August 3, 1981, issue of *Business Week* carried a special report on the speedup in automation. This report stated that "after a decade of decline in the face of low-cost, high quality imports, U.S. industry is beginning to automate at a pace that will soon change the face of American factories and offices. Within reach are computer-controlled systems of robots and other sophisticated machines that will replace most humans on plant floors and produce unprecedented gains in productivity. Automated equipment is moving into the offices, too, and both trends portend a radical restructuring of work, with jobs becoming more technical and more complex than ever. Altogether these changes will affect more than 45 million American jobs, many of them during the next 20 years."[7]

One expert forecasts that purchases of computer-aided design (CAD) systems, the essential first step in integrated CAD/CAM (computer-aided manufacturing) systems, will climb 35 percent or more annually, to an estimated $2.5 billion in 1985 from $610 million in 1979. The United States dominates in CAD technology. With a devaluation of current work skills, some workers will have their jobs threatened—others who can be retrained as computer technicians will benefit. The new jobs will be for people with degrees in computer science, electrical and mechanical engineering, systems analysis, and computer design and programming. If 45 million jobs in factories and offices will be directly affected by automation this may produce considerable disruption and hardship, because no one has conducted comprehensive studies of the employment impact of the new automation. As the computer moves from being a product to being a component embedded in a whole range of end-user devices, the stakes in the game are high and displaced people represent the stakes. This may be the major social and cultural change to justify the term "postindustrial revolution." Where will all of the displaced people (even with fewer entering the labor force) find employment?

Quality of Work Life

There has been a debate over whether the growing educational levels of the work force, the shifting of the demographic makeup, and other factors have combined to produce a new set of employee needs, aspirations, and expectations toward their jobs. This debate spawned the quality of working life movement and led a number of firms to embark on experiments designed to test new forms of participation and management practices. The interest in developing more effective managerial strategies for encouraging employee participation, teamwork, loyalty, positive job attitudes, and so forth, increased toward the end of the 1970s as more Americans became intrigued by Japanese managerial styles and practices. The new managerial interest in both quality of working and in Japanese management practices stems from a belief that one means for improving the productivity of U.S. industry is by harnessing great individual and work-group effort and by achieving greater cooperation and consensus within organizations.

Today there are more than 1,500 U.S. companies with quality circles. A quality circle is a small group of workers from the same division who volunteer to meet regularly to discuss ways to improve the quality of the product, the production process, and the work environment. Quality circles have been successful in Japan but may hold little promise of short- or intermediate-term gains for the United States.

Workplace Regulation—The Case of Minimum Wages

Over the past two decades there has been growth in government regulation of workplace practices. In accordance with the neoclassical model of the labor market, these regulatory laws are seen as creating inefficiencies in the market. They supposedly increase labor costs, lower profits, and lead eventually to reduction in employment. My examination of the economic consequences of minimum wage laws would indicate that these outcomes are not so easily predicted.

Under the provisions of the Fair Labor Standards Act (FLSA) of 1938, the federal government established a minimum wage of 25 cents per hour for selected workers, set a premium for overtime pay, restricted child labor, and specified that the standard workweek would be gradually reduced to forty hours. The 1938 act applied to one-fourth of the work force. Now some forty-four years after the passage of the FLSA there have been six amendments to the law that have greatly expanded the coverage of the act to 90 percent—90 million workers—of the nonsupervisory workforce (63 percent minimum wage covered and 27 percent covered but exempt from minimum wage), and in January 1981 the minimum wage was increased to $3.35 an hour.

Even though the average hourly earnings (AHE) in the private nonagricultural sector in 1980 were approximately double the minimum wage ($6.66 nonagricultural; $7.27 manufacturing; $5.48 wholesale and retail), employers still had an incentive to try to mitigate the effects of increased labor costs. Wages were higher than what might have prevailed in an unconstrained labor market. For some labor intensive operations this shift could mean a significant increase in hourly earnings of those workers who were previously paid less than the new minimum wage. Because they have more low-wage workers, some industries will find their wage bill raised more than others by a minimum wage increase. Also, where there are workers who already are making more than the new minimum wage, the so-called ripple effect takes place. Employers' wage policies frequently are designed to maintain a relative wage level; thus changes at the bottom ripple throughout the system. The minimum wage shift spills over to income, output, costs, demand for goods, and factor demand as businesses adjust to the higher labor costs by attempting to raise their product prices, change the skill mix of labor, substitute machinery for workers, and not hire new workers.

At the time of the last amendment in 1977, the United States Senate and House were not able to resolve a number of controversial issues in conference and agreed to establish a Minimum Wage Study Commission (MWSC) to examine the economic, social, and political ramifications of FLSA of 1938. I served as a Commissioner on Minimum Wages from 1978 through 1981 when we submitted our final report to the Congress. The commission was mandated to investigate twelve topics including the effect on inflation of increasing the minimum wage, employment and unemployment, the economic consequences of automatic indexing of the minimum wage, the ability of the minimum wage to ameliorate poverty, the demographic profile of the minimum wage worker, the level of noncompliance, the exemptions from minimum wage and overtime requirements, the relationship (if any) between the federal minimum wage rates and public assistance programs, and—one of the most divisive issues—whether to provide for a special subminimum rate for young workers (the *youth subminimum*).

For years economists have argued about the *disemployment effects* of minimum wages. Simply put, with a higher minimum wage employment will be lower than it otherwise might be. The impact will be the greatest on low-wage workers. In 1980 roughly ten million workers or 12 percent of all wage and salary employees had jobs that paid the minimum wage of $3.10 or less. Forty-eight percent of these workers at minimum or below were adult women and 29 percent were adult men. Adult women are potential substitutes for youth in much of the low-skill job market. Minority workers carried a disproportionate share of the minimum wage burden—nearly one out of every five minority workers received the minimum wage or less. The MWSC had a sizable budget to conduct surveys and undertake research. One of the surprises revealed in the examination of the minimum wage workers was that 70 percent of the teenagers who were such workers were found in families with incomes greater than $15,000. This posed a dilemma for the commission as we tried to determine whether there should be a youth differential. Most of the teenage minimum wage workers were from affluent families and yet the public political debate focused on whether a youth subminimum wage could be used to reduce the extraordinarily high rates of unemployment mainly among minority youth. A review of teenage employment and unemployment studies found that a 10 percent increase in the minimum wage would reduce teenage employment by about 1 percent to 2.5 percent (80,000 to 200,000 jobs from a base of 8 million) and would *increase* teenage unemployment by one percentage point (nearly 100,000 more workers unemployed). Thus, it might appear that a youth subminimum would be desirable. Many have argued that the extension of the minimum wage was responsible for the increase in youth unemployment. Others have noted that the suburbanization of jobs, the increased labor force participation of women, and the entry of illegal aliens have also been important.

Since such a heated debate arose over the effects of lower minimum wages for youth, many people have overlooked the fact that at the present time there is a youth differential already in the law. Since 1961 full-time students working part-time during the academic year and full-time in the summer may be paid 85% of the basic minimum wage. The student certification program is restricted to employers in retailing, service jobs, and higher education. It would be difficult to determine whether a less restricted youth differential would be as successful. One researcher has noted that an unrestricted youth differential might encourage reverse substitution among teenagers by increasing the employment of nonstudent teenagers (who are on average from less affluent families) at the expense of full-time students (who are on average more affluent).

The minimum wage staff calculated that a 25 percent youth differential would increase teenage employment by about 400,000 to 500,000 jobs *but* at a cost of 50,000 to 150,000 adult jobs, so there could be a substitution of subminimum wage teenagers for minimum wage adults. In evaluating whether the trade-off of teenage jobs for adult jobs is a desirable one, it is important to know whether the additional teenage jobs go to disadvantaged inner-city youth or merely provide more regular employment for teenagers with few employment problems.

The commission recommended against the youth differential because of its limited potential for reducing unemployment. One of the most conservative commissioners noted in his statement that "one possibility of a youth subminimum wage is that it could cause the displacement of minority adults from low-income families by youth from wealthier families who can work at a wage below the minimum wage applicable to poverty adults. Given the large percentage of minimum wage workers from nonpoor families, one must be particularly concerned with income distribution effects on any changes in minimum wage laws. A national youth subminimum could have adverse effects in the sense of hurting adults from low-income families while helping youth from higher-income families."[8]

The final report of the MWSC was submitted to the Congress in June 1981 and was promptly placed on the back burner because of the need to pass the administration's budget and tax packages. Perhaps some of the priority issues (indexation, inflation) may have been resolved in other economic arenas. The demographics of the 1980s (baby-bust population enters the labor market) may even take care of the teenage employment problem.

Concession Bargaining

The 1980s may serve as another turning point in the relationship between workers and employers in the United States as the labor/management system shifts away from the adversarial toward the cooperative mode. There is a debate over whether the trend toward wage concessions by unions represents a major shift in power from labor to management and whether there will be a spillover to other industries. Concession bargaining occurs where a union agrees to reduce wages, delay cost-of-living allowances, or modify work rules under an existing contract. This type of negotiation usually takes place in response to management demands backed up by the threat of plant closures, layoffs, and even relocation of production outside of the country. Concession bargaining has occurred in several industries facing very stiff overseas competition, such as automobiles and steel, or in industries adjusting to deregulation, such as trucking or the airline industry. Unions trade off future economic gains for job security and the opportunity to share in future profits.

A recent contract between the Ford Motor Company and the United Automobile Workers (UAW) demonstrates how both labor and management can compromise. After more than a year of intense pressure from automobile companies (with the exception of Chrysler which had earlier gained more than one billion dollars in concessions in the deal to save the company), the UAW agreed to negotiate with Ford and General Motors prior to the expiration of their current contracts. Both companies claimed that American automobiles were no longer competitive with Japanese imports because of high labor costs. At the end of 1981 more than 211,000 auto workers were laid off with no definite date set for their return, and another 69,000 were on temporary layoff. So it was clear that thousands of jobs would be permanently lost in this industry.

In March 1982, Ford and the UAW signed a new 31-month contract (ending September 1984) that will save the company more than one billion dollars or about $2 per hour on labor costs and will guarantee job security for the most senior employees, those with fifteen years or more of service.

The Ford Motor Company:
    1. placed a two-year moratorium on plant closings;
    2. guaranteed employment for those employees with fifteen years or more of service. If such workers are laid off, a guaranteed income of 50 percent of their annual salary will be received until age 62;
    3. offered profit sharing for the UAW blue-collar workers and said that payments would be provided on a sliding scale depending on the ratio of profits to sales;
    4. agreed to establish training programs to prepare for the new technology; and
    5. strengthened its contribution to Supplemental Unemployment Benefits (SUB) for laid-off workers.

The UAW:
    1. gave up six paid personal days per year and bonuses for working on Sunday;
    2. deferred cost of living allowances for nine months;
    3. gave up its traditional 3-percent annual pay increase for a period of two and one-half years;
    4. will have a pilot program on "lifetime employment" at two plants where 80 percent of the work force will be protected against layoffs; and
    5. agreed to start new workers at 85 percent of the rate for a given job and gradually phase in benefits.

Is this a survival strategy where the cost savings will help to narrow the company's losses and preserve jobs for more senior workers, or is it a significant shift away from business as usual in collective bargaining? It may be too early to tell. We have certainly seen the decline of unions in the older industries so that at the present time the unionized segment of the work force is less than 23 percent of all workers. Over the past few years there has been an aggressive *union avoidance* effort by management. Even if these are tactics to reduce costs in a period of recession for such industries as airlines, trucking, meatpacking, retail, and rubber, it is likely that these exercises in shared power will be carefully reviewed by other employers whether they operate in unionized or nonunionized settings.

"Leftovers"

I have left the most difficult issue for last. My earlier discussions cover the activities of approximately 85 percent of the American work force. A simple model depicting the interactions between workers and the private enterprise system would show individuals endowed with certain productivity characteristics selling their services in different labor markets. Services might vary from those of a maintenance person to those of a senior manager. Although there are a number of imperfections in these markets, by and large the forces of supply and demand determine prices (wages and salaries). The compensation packages agreed on have become heavily weighted with a dazzling array of fringe benefits. Although most of the initial hiring and screening activities pit the individual seller against the representative from corporate personnel departments or a small business, unions have negotiated the terms and conditions of employment for groups of workers mainly in the manufacturing sector.

The apparent debates in the economics profession over segmented labor markets or dual labor markets are not as acrimonious as in prior years, and there is a general consensus that internal labor markets function quite differently from external labor markets. Once workers have been hired into primary labor markets, they strive to advance, and their rewards are tied to job performance. The literature of industrial sociology and social psychology documents the operation of the industrial work force and the deviation from the normal rules of hiring, promotion, layoff, transfer, training, retirement, and so forth.

There is a belief that the private sector (with some allowance for frictional, seasonal, or cyclical variations) will be able to provide jobs for all who present themselves to employers. Yet, the private sector has not served well the needs of the most disadvantaged groups in our society, and it is unlikely to do so in the future. In 1980 there were approximately 20 million persons participating in the labor market or who wanted to participate but were greatly handicapped by deficiencies in their education, skills, and work experience. Robert Taggart has called these low earners (less than poverty level even though they work full-time), unemployed, involuntary part-timers, and discouraged workers the *leftovers*.[9] They require major *remedial* training prior to a job assignment, and even if training programs are completed they are not equipped to compete for the types of technical jobs that are available today. Yes, the private sector spends enormous amounts on training, but it is primarily for those managers and highly specialized personnel where the payoff is likely to be significant.

As Sar Levitan notes, "Unlike Western Europe, there is little in the U.S. tradition for business undertaking an active role in formal programs designed to help the disadvantaged become economically independent. Long-range social goals do not easily fit into private sector objectives which must keep profits in the foreground."[10] Under the Private Sector Initiative Program (PSIP) launched in 1978, private industry councils (PICs) created in Title VII of the Comprehensive Employment and Training Act (CETA) were supposed to initiate placement and training programs for disadvantaged workers. Data for 1980 indicate a significant negative correlation between PIC private sector placement rates and the relative number of minority and disadvantaged groups served.[11]

How will we deal with those on the periphery of the labor market? The hundreds of millions that were spent on employment and training under CETA and predecessor programs did not *permanently* improve the economic status of this group. These programs were not targeted on the most needy individuals until just a few years ago and there were many difficulties in the implementation of programs. One of the most unfortunate outcomes was that program operators were under considerable pressure to produce spectacular results in a short period of time. At the present time it appears that the federal government, with a harshness that is unseemly for a democratic society grounded in Judeo-Christian ethics, is drastically retrenching and reducing the opportunities for these leftovers to survive. It behooves those of us in that safe 85 percent who have made it in the labor market to support appropriate employment and training programs funded by the federal government for those 15 percent who currently are the *rejects* from the private sector.

Endnotes

1. Arthur M. Okun, *Capitalism and Democracy: Some Unifying Principles* (paper delivered at the Columbia University/McGraw-Hill Lectures on Business and Society, 31 October 1978).

2. Howard N. Fullerton, Jr., "The 1955 Labor Force: A First Look," *Monthly Labor Review* (Washington, D.C.: U.S. Department of Labor, Bureau of Labor Statistics, December 1980); Ronald E. Kutscher, "New Economic Projections Through 1990—An Overview," *Monthly Labor Review* (Washington, D.C.: U.S. Department of Labor, Bureau of Labor Statistics, August 1981).

3. Ann Howard and Douglas W. Bray, "Today's Young Managers: They Can Do It, But Will They?" *Wharton Magazine* (Summer 1981): 23-28.

4. Phyllis A. Wallace, *Women in the Workplace* (Boston: Auburn House Publishing Co., 1982).

5. Lester C. Thurow, "Solving the Productivity Problem," *Strengthening the Economy: Studies in Productivity* (Washington, D.C.: Center for Democratic Policy, 1981).

6. Michael Wachter, "Economic Challenge Posed by Demographic Changes," *Work Decisions in 1980s* (Boston: Auburn House Publishing Co., 1981).

7. "The Speedup in Automation," *Business Week*, 3 August 1981, 58-67.

8. *Report of the Minimum Wage Study Commission,* Vol. I-VII (Washington, D.C.: Government Printing Office, June 1981).

9. Robert Taggart, "CETA Training: Past, Present and Future," in *CETA Results and Redesign*, ed. G. Mangum (Salt Lake City, Utah: Olympus, 1981).

10. Sar Levitan and Richard S. Belous, "Bridges to the Private Sector: Remedial Employment and Training Programs," *CETA Results and Redesign*, ed. G. Mangum (Salt Lake City, Utah: Olympus, 1981), 52.

11. Ibid., 61

For the business community this has been a time of unusual opportunity. Corporate taxes have been cut significantly; regulation has been lessened. According to journalist GEORGE F. WILL, *this time of opportunity is potentially one of crisis if business does not respond successfully to three reasonable demands: (1) invest aggressively in new productivity; (2) voluntarily donate more resources to public welfare needs; and (3) work to assure an increasing revenue base for the federal government.*

Will begins his argument with an analysis of our current economic woes. He traces their origin to the assumption begun after World War II that our economic growth would last forever. While this assumption has been shown false for a decade, our political system has been unable to adjust to reality. Entitlements run too deep; they are now a middle-class right.

Will applauds the effort of the Reagan administration to increase savings and stimulate the economy. He suggests that the federal government can be expected to do no more; it has neither the power nor the tools. The responsibility and hope must rest with business initiative.

13

New Business Initiatives for Public Policy

GEORGE F. WILL

When Elliott Richardson was a young man, just leaving Harvard, he came to work on the Senate staff for Leverett Saltonstall, one of the senators from Massachusetts. Leverett said to young Elliott, "What do you want to work on?" Elliott said, "I want to work on legislation, not politics." Saltonstall said, "It's all politics, son."

The preceding anecdote sums up the moral of this paper. There is not a single economic problem in this country that cannot be explained in terms of our political and social culture. That is why the problems are as deep-seated and intractable as they are—and in many cases, as alarming as they are.

To begin to understand the political climate in which economic decisions are going to be made for the rest of the 1980s, let us go back and look at what happened in November 1980. Obviously, President Reagan won an emphatic victory, but his margin of victory over Jimmy Carter was only the ninth largest margin of victory in this century. Obviously, the Republicans did well in the Senate. They gained, approximately, ten Senate seats. But Democratic candidates for the Senate in 1980 got more votes than the Republican candidates did, because while Republicans were piling up small victories in small states, Senator Alan Cranston in California and Senator John Glenn in Ohio were piling up enormous victories. The real message of the election was, I think, somewhat more clouded than people realized.

Furthermore, the misunderstanding of the current political climate in the country has been aggravated by a steady misinterpretation of events by my profession. The Washington press corps—especially, having underestimated Ronald Reagan for fourteen years—promptly went to the other extreme. We had a kind of apotheosis of Ronald Reagan in the summer of 1981: The belief that here was a man who, by the power of his considerable charm and his manifest rhetorical abilities, was going to melt what we in Washington called the Iron Triangles—those three-sided relationships that exist among the congressional committees that authorize, the bureaucratic groups that administer, and the client groups in the country that benefit from particular programs. Today, with the dawning of realism—tardy but welcome—it seems that the Iron Triangles are called "iron" for a good reason. They are much more durable than we realized, much less apt to melt beneath the sunshine of even a man with considerable charm and rhetorical gifts. Therefore, we are today, as we have been generally in the modern period of our politics, face-to-face with a peculiar kind of tough, interest-group-brokered liberalism by which we practice politics at the national level.

I am not for a moment denying that the country has moved emphatically to the right. Of course it has. Indeed, it has done so because of the delayed reaction to two wars. The first of these was World War II. Conservatism in America has always complained about the weight of government. Prior to Pearl Harbor that complaint lacked saliency, because prior to Pearl Harbor only one in ten Americans paid any income tax at all. By the end of World War II, the withholding tax and the weight of government were beginning to be felt. But so extraordinary and predominant was the American economy in the postwar world, so rapid and easy its economic growth—that we continued to build an enormous welfare state. We made enormous calls on the future wealth of this country, making generous promises to ourselves, on the assumption that the post-World War II growth would continue endlessly into the future. That assumption ended in 1973 with the Yom Kippur War and the extraordinary energy crisis. The problem is that it has now been ten years since we have had that kind of economic growth, and we still have the promises we made, making calls on the government's revenues on an assumption of economic growth that is invalid.

This brings us now to the texture of American politics and the peculiar climate in which the business community has to operate in this decade. I cannot think of a more educational, a more instructive, a more all-around interesting year in American politics in my lifetime than 1981. Indeed, I think we as a country learned three lessons in that year.

First, we learned, and especially the president learned, that you cannot take the country quite at its word. Woe to the political leadership who believes that the American public, or any public for that matter, says exactly and precisely what it feels and thinks. This country is not nearly as conservative as it talks.

The second lesson was that the middle class, which is the most vehement and articulate in condemning big government, is the big beneficiary of big government.

The third lesson we learned was that the conservative agenda for the United States costs as much money as the liberal agenda.

Let me go over these three lessons one at a time to illustrate the economic climate that will dominate the decade—no matter who is president.

There is always in a democracy a gap between the public's real expectations and its rhetorical expectations. You cannot judge any democracy by what the politicians say or what the people say. But the gap today is, I think, uncommonly wide.

I live in Montgomery County in Maryland. In 1978 someone was running for the school board and ran an ad on the radio that said, "If I am elected, the schools of Montgomery County will begin to produce some Beethovens and Einsteins." I would be pleased if upon leaving school my children have *heard* of Beethoven and Einstein.

Also in 1978, and this is a bit more germane, a man named Lee Dreyfus was elected governor of Wisconsin. I had lunch with him last week in Madison, and I reminded him that his campaign slogan at that time was that the federal government has three duties. "They ought to deliver the mail, defend the shores, and get the hell out of my life." It's a catchy slogan and it served him well, but I told the governor last week that I was bitterly disappointed that we have not seen him picketing the Agriculture Department begging to get dairy subsidies out of the lives of Wisconsin farmers, or outside Congress begging to get revenue sharing out of Milwaukee and Federal Aid to Education out of Oshkosh. My point is that if he tried to govern for ten minutes on the basis of the slogan that helped elect him, he would be impeached within the next ten minutes, because the people of Wisconsin, like the people of America generally, do not mean quite what they say about their government.

This is a country complaining about big government, yet a country in which one in seven Americans is a Social Security recipient. One in six Americans who works off the farm works for government; and 48 percent to 49 percent of America's families this year will receive some form of transfer payment from the government.

The president says, "We must get the government off the backs of the American people." And the American people say, "Yes, please, get the government off my back." Who do they think put it there? Well, I can tell you. It was put there, by and large, by legislators—elected and re-elected professionals who have ascertained the real desires, as opposed to the ephemeral rhetoric, of the American people.

In the 1970s the Congress of the United States passed 3,500 laws. That is nearly one law a day, seven days a week, for ten years. It is ridiculous. It couldn't happen if Congress had a simple rule that said, "You cannot vote for a law you have not read." The state legislatures—which are closer to the people, ostensibly more responsive to their real desires, and the depositories of so much conservative sentimentality—are worse. In the 1970s the state legislature of New York passed 9,500 laws and the fifty state legislatures combined passed a quarter of a million. They did not do this because legislators get up in the morning and say, "How can we be obnoxious to the voters today?" They did this because they believe, with reason, that the American people have a voracious appetite for public goods and services. The American people also have an unwillingness to pay for them, which makes being a politician difficult and explains today's conservatism. Hence the prayerful phrase, "It is time to cut my neighbor's subsidy."

The problem is, of course, that we are all heavily subsidized. I'll give you an example. If there is any single point on which economists today agree, it is that we save too little and consume too much. Why then are we subsidizing borrowing? We are subsidizing borrowing by the tax deductibility of interest payments on mortgages. We are even subsidizing by the deductibility of interest payments on consumer credit. Behind both of these provisions in the tax code are enormous interests, enormous lobbies, and pretty good arguments. Nevertheless, it is an example of how everyone benefits in some way or another from what can, without undue torture to the logic of the language, be called a federal subsidy.

The second lesson—the first was that the country is not nearly as conservative as it says it is—is that the middle class is the big beneficiary of these subsidies. This is a country in which about 80 percent of the country is in a meaningful sense in the middle class, and 90 percent of the country *says* it is in the middle class. The reality of politics revolves around that fact.

There was a mass throwback in American politics in summer 1981 for one moment when Reagan and Rostenkowski were competing with one another in the great bidding war for votes on the alternative tax bills. Rostenkowski, the chairman of the House Ways and Means Committee, came front and center on the Democratic tax bills and said, "We, the Democrats, are a party of compassion, because our tax bill looks after those earning between $20,000 and $50,000 a year." If you make $23,000 in the United States, you're about the median income. If you make $50,000 in the United States, you're in the top 5 percent of income earners. You're at the top, that is, of a rich country and are in some sense statistically, objectively rich. There's nothing an audience in America resents more than being told that it is rich. If you're earning $50,000 in this country, you're statistically rich and you're psychologically strapped. Indeed, many people now earning that much were not long ago undergraduates, and their political philosophy was *soak the rich*. Now they are the soakees. They've reached the social stratosphere of a country like this but have not found the kind of ease and gratification that you're supposed to find when you are statistically rich. There is a kind of aura of disappointment in the upper middle class.

What was revealed in that Rostenkowski statement was that American politics generally is a competition for the floating middle-class and upper-middle-class vote. After all, the argument in summer 1981 over the tax laws was taking place well to the right of the 1976 Republican platform. the president had moved the political argument in this country thoroughly to the right. This is not for an instant to say that the country has made a clear, unambiguous decision; nor has the administration. A lot of Republicans came to town in 1981 convinced that they could balance the budget by getting rid of waste, fraud, and abuse; that all the programs were valid and justified if they would only work efficiently. They were ignoring the fact that we may have made promises on economic assumptions that are no longer valid, and therefore promises we cannot keep.

The Republicans ignore the structural nature of our problem. The real essence of our problem can be summed up in one word. The word is *entitlements*. We have, as a society—Republicans and Democrats alike—been translating the concept of civil rights into a doctrine of economic rights and economic entitlements for twenty-five years. The mechanism for this has been the so-called transfer payment programs: Social Security, Medicaid, Medicare, food stamps, housing subsidies, and so forth. Transfer payments are payments made through the federal mechanism, generally shifting money from high producers to low producers or nonproducers. Entitlements are the essence of the welfare state.

The entitlement portion of the federal budget has been growing with remarkable constancy, about 8.5 percent a year, under the Republicans and Democrats alike, much faster than the economy that must pay the bills has been growing. This did not matter as long as the entitlements were a small portion of the federal budget. It matters tremendously nowadays when entitlements are nearly 48 percent or 49 percent of the budget, and I believe that when Reagan with his knife and Stockman with his ax get done trimming—the so-called *ruthless pruning* of the federal budget—that portion of the budget is apt to grow even more. The reason is that in a democracy demography is destiny; and the big demographic fact about the United States is that the population is aging. The elderly are disproportionate consumers of public goods and services, particularly pensions and medical care. The elderly are lobbying much better for their benefits. They're incomparably the strongest lobby in Washington.

If you walk down K Street in Washington you will see the ugly architecture of those new glass buildings, and in every pane of glass there are three elements of modern government: a fluorescent light, a telephone, and a lawyer. That is where the associations are. If you want to know how your government works, do not read the Constitution. Pick up a Washington telephone directory and read the pages that begin "National Association of. . . ." Those will be some of the 2,200 trade associations and other lobbies represented in Washington. After government and publishing in all its forms, they are the third largest employer in the metropolitan area. You've heard of all the big ones, the National Association of Manufacturers, the National Association of Broadcasters, and so forth. You may not have heard of the National Ice

Association or the National Crushed Stone Association or the National Association of Truck Stop Operators. We have a town loaded with professionals who bend public power to their private purposes. Half of them are called public interest groups, but that is a semantic camouflage.

The highest form of praise that we can bestow on a politician is to say that he or she is *responsive*. Well, if you have a government devoted solely to being responsive, you have a government technically incapable of leadership, because leadership is the ability to inflict pain and get away with it—that is, short-term pain for long-term gains. It does not take any leadership to respond to the desires that are quite apt to lead my children to McDonald's. Those are not partisan remarks; this is part of the political culture of the day in which both parties participate.

The worst example I can give you was in 1974 when Gerald Ford had just become president and he was asked at a press conference, "Do you favor a stiff tax on a gallon of gasoline as a form of price rationing to dampen demand?" Ford's answer was, "Today I saw a poll that shows that 81 percent of the American people do not want to pay more for a gallon of gasoline." Ford then said, "Therefore, I am on solid ground in opposing it." Well, all ground seems solid when you've got your ear next to it. And as Churchill said, "It is hard to look up to someone in that position." But it is almost philosophically the position of the American government today. The problem is not that our government is not responsive. Our government is too responsive, to a fault surely, or at least excessively responsive to the wrong forces.

Let me get back to K Street. One of the buildings on K Street is the American Association of Retired Persons. At the beginning of the 1970s, that organization had 1.5 million members. That is a lot of members. At the end of the decade it had 12.5 million members. You can get out your hand calculators and figure out for yourself how many members they got per day, seven days a week, for ten years. And that is when you will begin to understand why approximately one dollar in three on the domestic side of the federal budget goes to the elderly.

I am not saying that the elderly are any less publicly spirited than anyone else in America. On the contrary, the elderly have more reason than anyone else to be enraged and afraid—enraged because it is federal policy that has created the inflation that has debased their savings and mocked the virtue of thrift that they have practiced through their lives; and they are justifiably afraid of a future in which they have been robbed of the benefits of their thrift. Still, the fact is that this is a large demographic political pressure for maintaining the structure of entitlement programs, a structure with which I by and large agree.

I must give you some numbers to make this more real. In 1980 we elected a 26-percent president, which is to say that about 51 percent of the Americans eligible to vote voted, and about 51 percent of the 51 percent voted for Reagan. Sixteen percent of those who voted for Reagan were 65 years old or older. I'm not saying they are a single-issue constituency.

You can turn them into one, however, by touching Social Security. The president touched it lightly, decorously, at the margin, and jumped back as though he had touched a stove. What he learned was that the American people do not regard Social Security as just another benefit, but rather as expressing somehow the essence of our citizenship, the bonding of the generations, and American acceptance of an ethic of competent provision. This experience brings any president face-to-face with the political and demographic pressures that work to maintain an enormous in-place structure of promises of entitlements that we must pay for, unless the political system can or should summon the strength to take back the promises it has made.

Someone says, "Well, fortunately we can afford those expenditures now because the conservative agenda for America is less ambitious." Not true. The conservative agenda costs as much as the liberal agenda: $1.6 trillion for defense; $6 billion for new prisons; $6 billion revenue loss for tuition tax credits; and on and on it goes. As Everett Dirksen said, "A billion here, a billion there; it soon adds up to real money." That is why you hear today more people saying, "Well, we must talk about revenue enhancements." "Revenue enhancement" is to a tax increase what a "protective reaction strike" is to a bombing raid. That is the way government talks when it is uneasy about what it has to do. But what the government is trying to do is to attempt to break into a new or different future.

As recently as eighteen years ago, we were convinced in Washington that we had so mastered the management of the modern economy, so thoroughly understood macroeconomic forces, that we would ever after ensure economic growth so rapid that we could generate at constant tax rates an excess of revenues for the government—excess, that is, above and beyond the demands made by existing entitlement programs. The political task of the foreseeable future was going to be allocating abundance.

By the end of the 1970s, it was clear that the political task for the foreseeable future was to allocate pain, scarcity, and disappointment. No one in Washington knows how to do that; no one went into politics to learn how to do that. Therefore, there is a great bipartisan desire to break this cycle, to again get the economy growing fast enough relative to experiment, to be generous, and to be compassionate. The Reagan program was devised as a bold attempt to break through; and it was devised with heavy reliance on economic theory at precisely the moment when throughout the industrial world there was a collapse of confidence in economic theory.

But what in reality public policy people of all persuasions are up against is this: The federal government, which is expected to be held accountable for the aggregate economic condition of the country, has exactly two serious mechanisms for dealing with the economy. One is the Federal Reserve Board, which is statutorily, psychologically, politically, and every other way virtually independent. It has one great duty, to control the money supply, which it cannot do because honorable men and women cannot agree even on the definition of money supply. The second instrument is the federal budget, which the president manifestly does not control and the Congress is loathe to control. Thus, there is an enormous disproportion in our government between the expectations of what the federal government should do and the instruments at hand with which it can do it.

Here is a sample of what the Reagan program was supposed to do. First, it was to stimulate savings. As I said, we have this extremely low savings rate. It is perfectly clear why we do. The American people have looked at our political system—the voracious appetite for public services, the negligible willingness to pay for them—and recognized an intuitive inflationary bias, permanent and structural, in the economy. They see that inflation is not a problem to be solved; it is a permanent affliction of modern life. The currency is a wasting asset; therefore, it is only rational to turn the currency into goods and services above all debts, as fast as possible. The pile of debts in 1983 dollars will be paid back in 1983 dollars. A year ago at this time the average American family was spending one dollar in three of its disposable income on debt service. Perfectly sensible, but you cannot fund enormous deficits, and you cannot modernize an economy, if you are not saving more than that. The available investment pool is simply too small.

Well, that was the first thing the Reagan program was to do, to change the American attitudes and expectations toward an inflationary future in a radical way, and to generate a more saving attitude toward the future. The second thing the program was to do was stimulate the economy in the short run, so that you would have a gusher of revenues to the government at lower tax rates. This would prevent a ballooning of the deficit, a crowding out of private borrowers, a driving up of the prime interest rate, and hence a snuffing out of the recovery.

These two things, each of them difficult, were to happen simultaneously. Stranger things have happened, and I think we ought to give it a try. It is rather too late to try something else, and rather too early to judge the Reagan program either a success or a failure.

But there is a responsibility for the business community in all this. I think the business community is in somewhat the position that the Democratic Party was in, say in 1965. Let me explain what I mean. The Chinese character for "crisis" also means "opportunity." Let me turn that around. An opportunity can also be a crisis.

In 1965, as a result of the Goldwater landslide, there appeared in Congress for the first time since 1938 a liberal legislative majority, a terrific opportunity for American liberalism—and it damned near killed it. Seizing this opportunity, the liberal majority plunged ahead and got pretty much what it wanted for two years. It produced the Great Society legislative initiatives, which clearly promised more than they delivered, and began the disillusionment with the federal government—the effects of which we're still seeing today.

The business community is in a comparable position today. For years it has been saying, "Cut our taxes, cut taxes generally, and especially cut business taxes." Well, I do not know if you've noticed, but in the summer of 1981 to get votes for two tax bills, the Congress absentmindedly abolished the corporate income tax. I say absentmindedly because it didn't actually do it, but the net effect is that it did. In 1950, 30 percent of the federal revenues came from business. In 1980, before Ronald Reagan came to town, it was down to 12 percent; and as the revenue system now stands, in 1984 or 1985, it will be down to 2 or 3 percent. I am not saying that that is good or bad. Economists argue about who pays corporate taxes. Is it the shareholders of the corporations, the employees, the customers? One thing that I think most economists agree on is that corporations do not pay corporate taxes. Corporations collect taxes.

What I have sketched for you is what I take to be the political, which is to say the economic, pressures on this country. You can begin to see why on television and in my writings I am making myself a bit of a bore, saying that we need to face the fact that we are an undertaxed society. I support what the president did in lowering marginal tax rates which were clearly having a rational economic disincentive, but conservatives have for too long focused on one number. They said the crucial variable in the health of the economy is how what percentage of the gross national product is taken by tax revenues. By that measure, Germany has been worse off than Britain since World War II, which is crazy. The real and more complicated question is: How does this whole network, the web of taxes and expenditures, fall across the community, having various incentive and disincentive effects?

It is quite possible to support, as I do, lowering the marginal tax rate, which after all only will establish in 1984, when it's fully in place, the 1978 level of personal taxation. In 1984 you will be paying, as a percentage of your income, on Social Security and income taxes about what we were paying in 1978. Granting that, it seems to me we do need more taxes, and it is going to be up to the business community—which complains vociferously about deficits—to understand that restoring the revenue base of the federal government is a bipartisan, business, and labor prerequisite.

Do not just take my word for it. Do not take the Congressional Budget Office's word for it. Take David Stockman's numbers. In 1985 three categories of spending—social insurance programs, defense, and interest on the national debt—will consume 16 percent of the gross national product. The revenue system will only give the federal government 18 percent of the gross national product. It cannot run the rest of this government on the difference between those numbers, which is 2 percent.

The final dilemma that the business community faces is the need to understand that the public sector cannot wither away. It can be made more rational, but you cannot attack the basic structure of the welfare state in this country because the country demands that basic structure. Only once since 1933 has either party nominated a man perceived to be fundamentally out of sympathy with the New-Deal, welfare-state style of politics. It was Goldwater in 1964 and he carried five states. If Jimmy Carter had been successful in portraying Ronald Reagan as fundamentally hostile to the welfare state, which he manifestly is not, then Jimmy would have carried forty-four states, because that is not negotiable to the American people.

Let me add one more point. The real fundamental problem facing our political system in affecting the formulation of rational economic policy is a shortage. But it is not a shortage of energy; it is not a shortage of capital. It is a shortage of patience. We are a country in which the electoral cycles are overwhelming our policy cycles. Mitterrand in France has seven years to formulate and implement his policies rationally in an orderly manner, and then be fairly judged on their success. Mrs. Thatcher in Britain has five years, which is a lot longer in electoral life than four years, and she has party discipline. Ronald Reagan has only fleeting sporadic party discipline and he only has four years. Indeed, he doesn't have four years, because less than two years after his inauguration we have, in the off year, elections that will be viewed clearly but unfairly as ratifying or deratifying elections. If the American people under this president or any president cannot bring themselves to take a longer view, the kind of longer view that I'm challenging the business community to take in its own dealings, then a rational policy left, right, or center is impossible, because no policy produces results in the modern world as fast as our elections tumble upon us. It is only with the ability of the American people generally, and the business community in particular, that we can summon the maturity and the patience required to produce a successful free enterprise economy.

Economist NORMA PACE *continues the plea for business's need to invest in new productivity. She states that investment has always been the main responsibility of business. She proves that it has long been a neglected responsibility.*

The fault lies in great part in government policy and the social environment; we have since World War II thought of our economy as a spending system, not an investing system. The results are (1) inefficient production, (2) declining value of the dollar, (3) more costly exports, and (4) a shift in our economy from exportable production goods to less exportable services.

Supply-side economics is a beginning step to provide a better investing climate for business. But the author outlines many obstacles to be faced and overcome by business decision makers. With increased risk-taking by business, the free market will eventually reward and stimulate investing. Will the public be patient enough to allow the eventuality to occur? Or will it again intervene to overcome, mistakenly, some obvious, short-run market idiosyncrasies? The answer in large part depends on the aggressiveness of business investment.

14

The Business Role: The Visible Hand in Our Economy

NORMA PACE

The business world is evolving into an ever more complicated mechanism wherein specialization continues to subdivide the system and create greater uncertainty and suspicion. Individuals in this expanding business universe have a growing feeling of helplessness, complicated by the increased internationalization of many major industries. As we know, Japan has captured the lion's share of the auto market causing great distress among auto workers in practically all countries. But this is only part of the problem. Increasingly, domestic car manufacturers obtain their parts from an international pool of parts suppliers. Picture, if you will, an engine from the Philippines, an axle from Germany, and a chassis from the United States, and you have a U.S.-made automobile. Even management know-how has shifted from American to Japanese dominance during the past decade.

The proliferation in products and country of origin of goods and services sold to U.S. consumers may make the output of business more visible, but its complicated processes are still mysterious and its vastness occasions misconceptions and insecurity.

Business has been very conscious of this "tune-out" by its many publics—workers, customers, shareholders, and government employees who monitor the actions of businesspeople. Consequently, many businesses have turned to the part-science and part-art of communication in order to overcome fear and suspicion; to help individuals adjust to the growing complexities of the new economics system; and, of course, to vindicate their own actions.

This great need, this earnest desire by business to tell its story, accelerated in the 1970s and is now in full swing.

The communication urge gained momentum when it became clear to businesspeople that their processes were misunderstood, their motives misjudged, and their contribution to increasing the economic welfare of individuals totally ignored. The invisible role of business had to become visible because it had been totally eclipsed by the radiant role of government. Government took care of the sick, of the poor, of senior citizens, of homeless individuals, and of the unemployed. Business seemed to care only about profits.

The restlessness of college students in the 1960s over the chronic ills of the world and the repeated failures of known solutions only made businesspeople more self-conscious of their role. Many became defensive, others sought new solutions.

All this seemed to come to a head when the eminent Milton Friedman took pen in hand to calm the fears of businesspeople by reminding them that the business of business is profit. By playing its role in a pure and efficient manner, he contended, business could produce the wherewithal for financing all the good things that individuals wanted, including more goods and services, help for the poor, better education, equal opportunity, and an end to racial discrimination. This sounded like a "trickle down" theory and immediately aroused the emotions of many, including businesspeople.

The retreat of business under this three-decade assault of criticism and lack of respect began to ebb when businesspeople succeeded in telling their story to the public, to workers, to consumers, and to shareholders, and became more involved in national policies. The role of business was being made visible. And so business gradually turned from defending its role to extolling its virtues.

Some of the messages were crude, some downright self-serving, but happily some were brilliant. Slowly, very slowly, the message began to get through to people. This paper will examine the essence of that message because economic news is big news. The media are allocating more and more time and space to business news. In order to participate in those discussions intelligently—in order to guide the business communications of the future—we must understand the American business system.

The Role of Business

We can start by noting that the role of business is to:
- Invest in productive facilities through innovation and risk-taking.
- Use funds to coordinate natural resources and people into a productive firm.
- Reward the suppliers of funds whether they be part-owners or simply creditors.

Consequently, we can say that the principal activity of business is *investing*; every other activity is a satellite of that major responsibility.

And yet, as we view the condition of business today, we find that its major failure is investment. The signs of failure are clear.

Productivity Is Deteriorating

The productivity of the nation has fallen considerably during the past few years. Productivity is a commonly used word among businesspeople and economists, but it is difficult to measure and generally misunderstood. One wise economics professor told me that the average man's definition of productivity is "a process whereby a fat capitalist in a big limousine steps out every so often to whip the blue-collar worker into higher output." This concept results from the expediency of defining productivity as *output per man-hour*. While this is a nice, easy measure of productivity, it does not describe the process of obtaining higher productivity—only the end result.

Another word for productivity is efficiency—producing more goods and services with ever smaller inputs of energy, man-hours, and human effort. Consequently, efficiency must be measured at all levels, from the chairman of the board to the maintenance man—it relates to all the factors that contribute to production including water, air, energy, capital, land use, mineral resources, and the contribution of government and its people. Statisticians try to capture all of this in that simple measure called output per man-hour, which is calculated by dividing the volume of output by the number of man-hours used to produce that volume.

Using the all-inclusive measure of productivity, we find a significant deterioration in all segments of the economy.

Farm productivity used to be our major success story. In the 1950s farm productivity increased an average of 4.9 percent a year; in the 1960s it was 5.1 percent and in the 1970s the rate of increase had fallen to 3.2 percent a year. But even this deteriorating performance is excellent when compared with the productivity gains in the nonfarm business sector.

This gain in farm productivity was accomplished in many ways. The economies of scale became apparent to the American farmer and acquisitions and mergers went on at a tremendous rate. The average size of farms in 1950 was 215 acres; by 1980 the average size of a farm doubled to 430 acres. More significantly, about half of our farm output comes from the 376,000 farms that are 500 acres or more. Investment in farm machinery has been going on at a terrific rate, and the average size of a farm tractor is now 60 horsepower, up from 27 horsepower in 1950. New tractors sold have more than 100 horsepower.

The number of farmers shrank from 10 million in 1950 to 3.8 million in 1980. Sixty years ago we were singing songs about how we were going to "keep them down on the farm after they had seen Paris"; this shift took care of the problem.

And this is the way I would like you to think of productivity—as a way to give people freedom and choice. After World War II, the boys did not want to stay on the farms and so no one bemoaned the farm productivity that displaced farmers. Our marvelous climate and vast land area joined with this productivity to make us the breadbasket of the world. That is an example of what productivity can do for an economy and an industry. Today, there seems to be a desire to return to small farms—a yearning on the part of some to get back to the land. For a small entrepreneur, this is a rough road. Mother Nature is not always helpful, but even here the opportunities will be available to those who reach out for them. Recently someone perfected a way to grow lettuce in water and is building a growing national enterprise on that know-how.

Increases in output per man-hour in nonfarm business averaged 2.1 percent in the 1950s; 2.7 percent in the 1960s; 1.5 percent in the 1970s; and from 1978-1982 the average gain was only 0.3 percent.

Consequences of Reduced Productivity

The failure of U.S. nonfarm productivity to show improvement in recent years had its effect in the many ways that all of us can easily recognize:

1. Reduced efficiency caused costs to rise which in turn were reflected in higher prices—and we eventually priced ourselves out of the markets in many goods, services, and countries.

2. The value of the dollar fell, in part because the economic performance of the United States, which is the ultimate indicator of the value of a nation's currency, was declining.

All during the 1960s, it was becoming clear that the U.S. dollar was overvalued, that is to say, the economic performance of the United States was worsening and sooner or later that loss of efficiency had to be reflected in the value of the dollar. This was particularly true in the dollar's relation to currencies like the Swiss franc, the German mark, and the Japanese yen, currencies of countries where efficiency was much better than in the United States. This pressure led President Nixon to let the dollar float in successive stages in 1971 and 1972 and it was no surprise to anyone that it floated down.

In 1972, when the agreements to let currencies seek their levels were made, it was clear that U.S. goods were overpriced in international markets and foreign goods were a bargain. We were importing more than we exported. If a country's currency operates in a free market, or at least in a freer market—as the U.S. dollar did after 1972—the excessive price of that country's goods is compensated for by a deterioration in its currency.

3. Productivity also affects decisions on imports. A devalued dollar

tends to discourage imports because the cost of imported goods rises since it takes more dollars to buy another nation's currency. This process, however, is disturbed when productivity or efficiency is impaired. The higher costs of production and prices in the United States that result from inefficiencies offset the cost disadvantage a foreign producer develops when the dollar weakens in relation to that foreign producer's currency.

Let me explain this disadvantage of decreasing efficiency in more detail. Theoretically, if the United States were a closed economy, its industry mix would reflect its available resources. Concern for security and balance would outweigh concern with worldwide competitiveness—and in a sense this is what guided U.S. investment policies for many decades. Participation in foreign markets came through investments in overseas plants as much as through exports. In part this was caused by nationalist policies that demanded investment to increase local employment. At times, these countries provided special incentives, such as low-cost loans. The only thing that matters in a closed economy is that the volume of goods and services produced be quickly translated into sales; i.e., the demand should equal the production over a fairly short period of time. In the closed economy, the relative efficiencies of different producers would be reflected in the average price of their products. But in an open economy where there are outside producers who operate under different rules and with different price structures, the discipline is different. If the United States imports from more efficient producers, then it must find equivalent U.S. efficiencies to export. An economy that is not mindful of this need will indeed experience loss of growth at first and ultimately loss of life. During the past ten years in particular, U.S. producers have permitted efficiencies to drop in many of the exportable goods sectors of production while they built up a services sector that, generally speaking, has less available for export.

These examples show that investment and increased productivity are the main responsibilities of business and yet business appears to have failed us in this all-important contribution.

The reason for this failure is the subject of much current debate and of current national economic policy. Indeed, if we want to find a source of the failure of economics in the past thirty years, it is in this important segment of the economy; namely, investment in terms of both its size and its quality. The economics of the future will therefore be the economics of investment, of capital formation, and of savings and productivity. Supply-side economics approaches this need but is incomplete in its approach.

Remembering that economics is not a science, but rather an evolving and ever-changing theory of value and behaviorism, we should view supply-side economics as a timid step in the next stages of economic theory and practice.

Post-war Economic Policies

During the past forty years, most industrial countries have been guided by using the economic foundation laid by Adam Smith as modified by Keynesian theories. Keynesianism differed from its predecessors by shifting concern from production (or supply) to demand. In a world where the major suppliers of finished goods were in the highly industrialized countries that had relatively free and easy access to raw materials, the shift in emphasis from production to demand was indeed sensible. As a matter of fact, it was so sensible and it worked so well for thirty years, it lulled many economists into thinking that economics at long last rested on a durable and unchanging foundation of theory. By the mid-1960s economists had become confident and arrogant and began to build forecasting models patterned after the theories of John Maynard Keynes. They used the system of national income accounting that was developed in the 1930s and implemented after World War II. The popular measure of national output called Real Gross National Product is part of this system. Also incorporated in this system are the measures known as Personal and Disposable (or after-tax) Income. This system of accounting not only permitted us to measure who was receiving income and how he or she was spending it, but it also gave us a quarterly measure of how well the overall economy was doing. In itself, national income accounting was quite an innovation.

National income accounting is almost entirely spending oriented and therefore is Keynesian in orientation because it is concerned with spending (or demand for goods and services) and only incidentally with output.

According to that accounting system, the sum total of everyone's spending in the nation equals the total output. Spending drives the accounting system—and it drives the analysis. Motivations are in relation to spending—not producing—and therein lies the problem.

When economists slip in their theories, that is significant only to other economists. But when national planners use incorrect theories as the basis for national policies, then that affects all of us.

It started in 1946 when Congress passed the Full Employment Act, which charged the president and the Council of Economic Advisers to the president with the responsibility of maintaining full-employment conditions in the United States. Remember that the Great Depression of the 1930s was still a vivid memory to many and that we came out of World War II with a strong feeling that the massive breakdowns in the system in the 1930s could and would reoccur. With succeeding chairmen, the Council of Economic Advisers became bolder and more significant in economic policy. By the mid-1960s the role of business in contributing to growth was dwarfed by national economic policies.

Monetary policy, which had been the historic means of attempts to control the business cycle, moved into a role secondary to fiscal policy.

Government spending, taxes, and federal deficits were used regularly to fine tune the economy. The theories of John Maynard Keynes—and the mathematical models based on those theories—provided the justification for more and more involvement by the federal government.

Soon the system began to show some disquieting symptoms, such as a tendency toward even higher unemployment rates and persistent inflation. Long before Arab producers learned to use their cartel powers to lift oil prices, the U.S. economy was showing signs of a steady upward creep in prices. Other disconcerting signs were beginning to appear in the strange routes followed by both savings and investments. In the 1970s we had become so convinced that government was the prime mover in the economy, that we began to escalate legislation to control all forms of decision making. Small business could not make it under these rules, but many faulted big business and not government. All this activity was expensive, but salaries of government workers were the least of the burden. Gross mismanagement by the government, along with onerous and poorly evaluated regulations, took a heavy toll on investment and efficiency. By the mid-1970s the message was clear to those with open minds and that message was that the system was not functioning properly.

In 1974, after President Ford's summit on inflation was over, a reporter from the *Wall Street Journal* interviewed the twenty-six or so economists who participated in the summit. Since I was one of the participating economists, he asked me what the summit had taught the world. My reply was simple and direct: "It has taught us that Keynesian theory is dead but we haven't got the nerve to bury it." Although he acknowledged that thought in his article, he did not seem to have the conviction to print it as strongly as I had stated.

Today, the demise is known as the Crisis in Economic Theory.

Well, there is a crisis and it is in theory.

Causes of Investment Lag

Our theorists are beginning to learn at long last that demand must include concern over investment demand. Prior to this, most theory was based upon the notion that consumer demand was the prime mover in the economy. Disturbances in the economy had to be corrected through measures that increased consumer demand; it was presumed that investment demand would follow. Now there is general recognition that investment itself needs attention. Why is this so?

Investment provides not only the facilities to produce the goods and services that individuals want now, but it provides also for future wants. This requires a lot of planning. Future wants of the public must be anticipated and the *present* earnings of business must incorporate the cost of research, innovation, and the building of plant and equipment to meet those future needs. This had been a neglected area.

If investment is the driving force in the system, why haven't we had enough to keep us competitive and efficient? Have businesspeople been lax or afraid of risk? Have we had too little savings? Are we running out of investment ideas? Are we losing confidence in the ability of the nation to produce and consume more in the future, hence the lack of aggressive investment?

The answers to these questions are varied, numerous, and contradictory.

One group is steeped in the notion that if a few controls failed in the past, it is because they were too few. More controls are needed and these should extend to investment. The Socialist government in France is addicted to the notion that government should allocate capital, labor, and physical resources to some basic industries and the beneficial effects of such pinpointed nationalization can spread out and indirectly benefit all segments of the economy. There are all kinds of variations of the notion that capitalism, i.e., the free-market allocation of capital, will simply not work.

A second group feels that the large and continuing U.S. government deficits experienced since 1960 have preempted the savings from investment in productive goods. The record on deficits in U.S. government finances is indeed clear: they have been persistent and growing. But what is not clear is the effect of these deficits on the availability of funds to businesspeople for investment. This theory, popularly known as *crowding out*, seems logical, but it is not always provable. It is true that if the government borrows year after year while it taxes heavily, it both shrinks capital markets and drains them. That certainly creates a shortage of capital for use by the private sector and thus the crowding out occurs. But what if savings are high enough to finance both government and business needs? Then the crowding out will not occur. Furthermore, what if business investments were low for other reasons, say for lack of confidence in the future of the business, or uncertainty over new business ventures? Then no amount of savings would increase investment. As a matter of fact, unduly high savings could induce a major recession if there is no confidence in the future. Investments do not automatically flow from savings: they flow from confidence in the future and from proper rewards.

A third group feels that investment during the past decade has been influenced and limited somewhat by a composite of disincentives consisting of high taxes, onerous and costly government regulations, national economic policies that lead to stagnation and inflation, and relatively low returns on some investment.

The evidence in support of this group's analysis of the relatively low levels of investment is quite strong. Government regulations relating to health, safety, and the physical environment drained billions of dollars from investment channels that would have increased efficiency and productivity. Some estimates have placed the cost at $100 billion a year, or 30 percent of total investment. Furthermore, not only was the more productive investment denied but the regulatory burden actually reduced the efficiencies in existing plants. Supply-side economics, which is now in its early stages of application, deals with these disincentives by permitting business to recover its investment more quickly and by forcing more efficiency in government regulatory activity. This type of program is not a quick fix for investment, but it is aimed at restoring confidence and increasing rewards over time.

Clearly, what we need today is a theory of investment that deals with the various dimensions of the investment decision, namely:
- Are rewards for risks and innovation correct?
- Is the national environment conducive to growth and investment?
- Will the availability and cost of financing new investment be a limiting factor?
- Does cash-flow analysis and management need to be adjusted?
- Will the changing role of financial intermediaries affect the financing of new investments?

This kind of analysis is needed. Failure to understand the multifaceted nature of investment will prevent attainment of the goal of efficiency or higher productivity. The questions are many and the market, imperfect as it is, nevertheless delivers the best answers to them. Does a firm that invests in overseas production facilities help, hurt, or simply not affect U.S. business? Should U.S. banks or other financial institutions lend money for such investments? Should individuals have access to credit markets to invest in massage parlors? Some, concerned over moral issues, would say no. But massage parlors do provide employment and services. Should U.S. Steel acquire Marathon Oil and should banks lend money to finance that acquisition? Imagine the enormous task of controlling investment and having to make all those decisions. The conflicts inherent in the system would quickly blow up the process.

In a market-oriented system such as ours, we leave the answers to those questions for individuals to decide. They often become bruised in the process. To some, the decisions made in the marketplace are fair and efficient; to others they are inefficient because there is no master plan. We pay a price for market-oriented capitalism. That is the first thing we must understand if we are to live comfortably with the idea of free markets. They are not perfect—they are simply the best that one can do. You might have ideas, judgments, and convictions, but you would really have no scientific basis for making that decision. But the market does.

If one company or industry overcompensates, it will be flooded with talent, in which case the rise in pay would end or the enterprise would price itself out of the market. There are checkpoints in the market system which eventually work. Eventually, however, it does not always satisfy everyone, and that is the source of well-meaning but generally harmful interference. It is the interference with these corrective mechanisms that causes the problems. We have had thirty years of increased interference.

We are attempting a slow but steady disengagement. That is the initial contribution of supply-side economics.

The Record of U.S. Investment

Having established that investment is the main responsibility of business, what remains is the need to determine whether business can meet this responsibility. There are two ways to approach this question. The first is a macroeconomic approach—to examine the investment performance over time for business as a whole. Here again we basically turn to the system of national accounting for some statistical history.

Investment in plant and equipment during the past three decades has averaged about 10 percent of gross national product. On the surface this would imply that the investment performance has been reasonable. But a more careful examination shows that the rapidly inflated costs of replacing worn-out equipment were taking an ever-rising share of total outlays for plant and equipment, leaving a diminishing proportion for new capacity. In the late 1960s, almost 65 percent of the investment for plant and equipment represented net new investment, that is, investment after replacements are deducted. In recent years that proportion has fallen below 50 percent.

Putting it another way, the stock of capital goods in use rose more slowly in the 1970s than in prior periods. This smaller allocation to new physical capital was compounded by the lagging trends in investment in research and development in the United States, resulting in a slower flow of new technology and efficiency-inducing projects. There is much statistical evidence to corroborate these facts.

Why did this happen? There is no doubt that public policies contributed to this erosion in the capital planning of the nation. Depreciation allowances by the Internal Revenue Service—that is, the permissible rate of capital recovery—were too slow and required acceleration long before the Economic Recovery Tax Act of 1981 permitted faster recovery of capital.

The combination of monetary and fiscal policies acted to destabilize the economy, with periods of low interest rates followed by periods of high rates and faster inflation. Gradually, this lack of stability impaired the long-term vision of company planners, particularly financial planners. Investment became more defensive and less aggressive.

By pampering the consumer side of the economy, succeeding administrations neglected the investment side. Over time the imbalance and its resulting inefficiencies became crystal clear.

Finally, profitability in many capital-intensive industries has been trending down in recent years and this may have contributed to the shortfall in capital investment. But whatever the reasons, one can see the fallout in several pressures on today's business decisions:
- Mergers are escalating.

- Foreign competition has intimidated many industries.
- Market aggressiveness seems to have diminished.
- Cost management has lacked creativity.
- Resource management has been hobbled by government regulations.
- Limits to economies of scale may have been reached.

These adjustments by individual companies were the natural outgrowth of the unhealthy investment climate that developed in the 1960s and 1970s.

Management

Our discussion would not be complete if we did not deal with microeconomics, or the quality of planning by individual companies—in a word, management.

Management science has been among the big growth industries during the past three decades. During the 1950s managerial concerns were mainly in organizational forms. How to structure the company to maximize results was the prime concern of more sophisticated managers. Forms of organization changed over the years and are still changing. changing.

Concurrently with changing structural forms came the growing importance of the financial department. This group became the center of control. Profits and cash flow, which were always the indications of success in the past, became the sole determinants of future investment. More-and-more scientific measures of cost management were being developed. And as the complexity of the organization itself increased, so did the financial controls.

As companies became multinational, the financial controls had to be extended to foreign operations, and the allocation of capital as well as its movements became dominated by international concerns. The efficiency of cash management by business has skyrocketed as a result of these trends.

Marketing also came of age in this period. The use of psychologists and behavioral scientists to help advertise and sell were early post-World War II trends. Subsequently, marketing activity stretched to include finding new markets for existing products as well as markets for new products. Techniques for regional and customer analysis began to appear.

Personnel management, always an important activity, also expanded to meet new needs. Wages and work practices were supplemented with fringe benefits, administration, and implementation. Government regulations needed to be studied and enforced. It is only recently that the more exciting aspects of personnel management have begun to appear— namely, motivational management.

And finally we get to technology and the tremendous promise it offers to increase efficiency. Advances in technology are not only related to investments in research and development, but also to that magnificent quality in a human being that fosters creativity, innovation, and the daring to do something different.

The highly structured enterprises that make up most of our current business structure will meet their most severe test in the 1980s. For all of us who perceive and value the role of the market in directing and controlling business decisions, this is a moment of truth. Can Adam Smith's invisible hand properly guide individual businesses as they perform their role in the future? Is the visible hand of government needed in the marketplace and, if so, where and how far? The answers will lie in a large measure in the quality and size of investments made by U.S. businesses and the productivity trends of the future U.S. economy. Profits will still be the measure of success and the prime mover in new enterprises, but businesspeople, as well as individuals, will have to learn how to live with the greater risks of a freer economy. Is our society ready for that challenge? The question is just being tested—the answer is in the future.

Our job, and yours in particular as you continue your studies of the workings of this marvelous system and move on to function actively and powerfully in it, is to see that the answer is right. That right answer incorporates a vision of a society that rewards its risk-takers, innovators, and achievers and still has the heart to understand and deal with the problems of the disadvantaged and helpless in its community.

SECTION IV
Challenges to Private Enterprise

While one may extol the virtues and power of the private enterprise system, one cannot deny the challenges that face that system and our nation. Indeed, certain challenges have been considered so serious and impervious to market solutions that massive government interventions have been seen as necessary and justified. In this section, five such challenges are discussed: retirement security, employment security, welfare, managing public lands, and the problems of the urban environment.

Colin Campbell discusses retirement security and points out that Social Security alone cannot be counted on to provide it. Do not put all your eggs in one basket, he suggests, even when the government is holding it.

Government intervention is counterproductive to the goal of employment security, according to James Bennett. He counsels that, in the long term, reliance on the marketplace is better than tinkering with it when optimizing employment.

Charles D. Hobbs maintains that in its efforts to provide welfare for the needy, the federal government has created a burgeoning industry devoted to its own goals, which are only marginally related to service for the poor. He finds that this industry crested in 1981, however, and makes suggestions to hasten its decline.

While there are sound reasons for public land ownership, explains John Baden, we would be far better served in economic and environmental terms if the marketplace were allowed to dictate the use of much land now controlled by the government.

Finally, James Rouse challenges the private sector to pick up the slack left by government's retreat from urban programs. He calls for inventiveness, for new relationships, and for companies to use their unique talents and resources to deal with social problems in ways consistent with good business. If this is accomplished, he predicts an exciting, creative future for private enterprise.

The problem of retirement security for individuals has been underlined by the financial problems of the Social Security system. COLIN CAMPBELL *deals with this problem and offers a perspective for Social Security reform.*

The short- and long-term problems of the Social Security system can no longer be corrected by simply raising payroll taxes, Campbell maintains. Using general revenues is also unacceptable. Consequently, system solutions must be found by cutting benefits in some way.

Campbell explains that changes in the way retirement benefits are indexed will provide some short-term relief. In the long term, however, he says that we must return to the realization that Social Security should provide a minimum income rather than replacement of working income. He advises individuals to recognize that there are risks associated with expectations of certain benefit levels. Campbell reminds us that it is unwise to "put all your eggs in one basket"—even when the federal government is carrying the basket.

15

Retirement Security: Perspective for Reform

COLIN D. CAMPBELL

To most people, retirement security is a subject of great importance. People want a source of income in their old age when they may no longer be able to work. This paper is primarily about old-age and survivors insurance (OASI), a major program in the Social Security system, and a program that has a predominant role in the retirement security plans of most persons. Beginning in 1974, there has been increasing public concern about the future of the Social Security system because it has encountered a series of unexpected financial problems.

Currently, the Social Security system is said to have both a short-run and a long-run financial problem. Each year from 1975 to 1981, annual expenditures for OASI have exceeded payroll tax receipts.[1] In both the 1980 and 1981 annual reports of the board of trustees of the Social Security trust funds, it was predicted that the small OASI trust fund would be depleted in 1981 or 1982.[2] In December 1981, legislation was passed by Congress to permit the shifting of revenues from the disability insurance (DI) trust fund to the OASI trust fund during the fiscal year 1982. It is hoped that this will provide sufficient revenue for the OASI trust fund to meet its commitments in 1982 and that Congress will take the necessary measures to restore financial balance to the system by 1983.

In addition to this short-run financial problem, forecasts made by the actuaries in the Social Security Administration show that the payroll tax rates scheduled in the law over the next seventy-five years are not high enough to cover the projected costs of the system. The Social Security system has been operating with a long-run (seventy-five year) actuarial deficit since 1973. The long-run cost projections indicate that payroll tax rates will have to be increased very sharply around the year 2031 in order to cover the cost of the system.

In the past, whenever the Social Security system's expenditures exceeded its revenues—whether short-run or long-run—the imbalance was corrected by raising payroll tax rates or by increasing the taxable wage base of the payroll tax. An important new development is that raising taxes is probably no longer a satisfactory solution to either the short-run or the long-run financial problems of the system. In the early years of the system when not many persons were eligible for benefits, payroll tax rates were so low that there was little objection to raising them. Now that 95 percent of all retired persons are receiving Social Security benefits, payroll tax rates have become so high that it is difficult to raise them further. The Reagan administration has announced that it will oppose any further increases in payroll tax rates. The Reagan administration has also announced that it is opposed to the use of general revenues—other taxes than the payroll taxes earmarked for Social Security—to finance part of the old-age, survivors, and disability insurance program (OASDI).

The most recent action taken by the federal government to solve the Social Security system's financial problems is the appointment in December 1981 of a fifteen-member bipartisan National Commission on Social Security Reform. The function of the commission is to recommend measures to restore "financial soundness" to the Social Security system. This is not the first commission of this type. In 1974 and again in 1975, Congress appointed a consultant panel to investigate the Social Security system's financial condition.[3] In addition, both the 1975 and 1979 Advisory Councils on Social Security reviewed these problems very thoroughly.[4] Also, two commissions were appointed by President Carter to study the financial problems of Social Security and private pensions.[5] The special function of the National Commission on Social Security Reform appears to be to determine how best to cut benefits. If solving the Social Security system's financial imbalance by raising taxes is ruled out, benefits must be cut in some way.

The first topic I will comment on is the causes of both the short-run and long-run financial problems of the Social Security system. Then, I will discuss the reasons why raising taxes is probably no longer a satisfactory solution to these problems and evaluate the effects of cutting back on the growth of Social Security benefits.

The Short-run Problem

Exhibit 1 shows that from 1970 to 1982, the payroll tax rate (employer and employee combined) for OASDI was increased from 8.4 percent to 10.8 percent; including hospital insurance (HI), the tax rate was increased from 9.6 percent to 13.4 percent. The taxable wage base was increased even more rapidly than the tax rate. Between 1970 and 1982, the maximum wage base of the payroll tax per worker went from $7,000 to $32,400—over four times the original amount. As a result of the large increases in the taxable wage base, the percentage of covered workers with their entire earnings taxed rose from about 64 percent in 1965 to 85 percent in 1977 and is expected to rise to more than 90 percent.[6] The upward trend in payroll taxes will continue during the rest of the 1980s. The payroll tax rate for OASDI is scheduled to increase to 12.4 percent in 1990; the tax rate for old age, survivors, disability, and hospital insurance (OASDHI) is scheduled to rise to 15.3 percent (see Exhibit 1). At the same time, the taxable wage base will increase in the future with

Exhibit 1: **Social Security tax rates for OASDHI, employee and employer combined, 1969-1990**

Year	Tax rate[a] (excluding HI)	Maximum wage base	Tax rate (including HI)
1969-1970	8.4 %	$ 7,800	9.6 %
1971	9.2	7,800	10.4
1972	9.2	9,000	10.4
1973	9.7	10,800	11.7
1974	9.9	13,200	11.7
1975	9.9	14,100[b]	11.7
1976	9.9	15,300[b]	11.7
1977	9.9	16,500[b]	11.7
1978	10.1	17,700[b]	12.1
1979	10.16	22,900	12.26
1980	10.16	25,900	12.26
1981	10.7	29,700	13.3
1982	10.8	32,400[b]	13.4
1983-1984	10.8	[b]	13.4
1985[c]	11.4	[b]	14.1
1986-1989[c]	11.4	[b]	14.3
1990[c]	12.4	[b]	15.3

Note: HI = hospital insurance.

[a] The OASDI payroll tax rate for the self-employed is approximately 75 percent of the combined employee-employer OASDI tax rate (or one and a half times the employee rate).

[b] From 1975 through 1978 and starting again in 1982, automatic increases in the maximum wage base were made each January. The amount of the increase is based on the rise in average wages between the first quarters of the two previous years, rounded to the nearest multiple of $300. The increases in the maximum wage base from 1979 through 1981 were legislated in 1977.

[c] As scheduled in the law.

Source: *Social Security Bulletin, Annual Statistical Supplement, 1977-79* (Washington, D.C.: Government Printing Office), 34.

the rise in average wages. Despite these tax increases, Social Security's current revenues will not be large enough to cover its costs.

The first annual report to recognize the system's short-run problem was in 1975. In this report, the board of trustees predicted that additional revenues would be needed to prevent the exhaustion of both the OASI and DI trust funds soon after 1979. An interesting aspect of the system's present difficulties is that in the early 1970s the board of trustees was not only unaware of any long-term deficit, but also its short-term (five-year) forecasts were very optimistic.[7] In the *1972 Annual Report*, the trustees expected that over the short run, payroll tax revenues would exceed expenditures by substantial amounts.

The Wage-Price Differential—The decline in the real-wage differential—the principal cause of the system's unexpected shortfall in current revenues—is shown in Exhibit 2. (This differential is the difference between the percentage increase in average wages in covered employment and the percentage increase in the consumer price index.) The average real-wage differential dropped from approximately two percentage points in the 1960s to 0.2 percent between 1970 and 1974, and then fell below zero for the rest of the 1970s and for 1980. In the 1960s, wages rose two percentage points faster than consumer prices; in the 1970s, wages rose at approximately the same rate as consumer prices. The smaller real-wage differential in the 1970s is the result of both slower

Exhibit 2: **Real wage differential, 1960-1980**

| | Average annual percentage increase | | |
Calendar year	Average wages in covered employment	Consumer price index	Real wage differential[a]
1960-1964	3.4%	1.3%	2.1%
1965-1969	5.4	3.4	2.0
1970-1974	6.3	6.1	0.2
1975-1979	7.8[p]	8.1	-0.3[p]
1980	8.5[p]	13.5	-5.0[p]

[p] Preliminary.

[a] The difference between the percentage increase in average annual wages in covered employment and the percentage increase in average annual consumer price index.

Source: *1981 Annual Report of the Board of Trustees of the Federal Old-Age and Survivors Insurance and Disability Insurance Trust Funds* (Washington, D.C.: Government Printing Office, 8 July 1981), 29.

increases in the productivity of labor and upward biases in the consumer price index.

If consumer prices rise faster than wages, the Social Security system is in trouble. Under such conditions, because the benefits of those already retired are indexed to consumer prices and revenues are obtained from payroll taxes on covered wages, Social Security expenditures rise faster than revenues. In a pay-as-you-go system, the payroll tax rate is very sensitive to changes in the ratio of average benefits to average covered wages. As shown by the formula in Exhibit 3, the payroll tax rate is equal to the ratio of the number of beneficiaries to the number of workers multiplied by the ratio of average benefits to average covered wages. The equation for the payroll tax rate shows that if the ratio of beneficiaries to workers is held constant, the payroll tax must rise if the ratio of average benefits to average covered wages increases.

Exhibit 3: **Derivation of formula for the payroll tax rate**

In a pay-as-you-go system:

Total payroll tax receipts = Total benefits

Total payroll tax receipts = The payroll tax rate (t) times the number of workers (N_w) times the average covered wage (W)

Total benefits = Number of beneficiaries (N_b) times the average benefit (B).

Therefore $t \cdot N_w \cdot W = N_b \cdot B$, and

$$t = \frac{N_b}{N_w} \cdot \frac{B}{W}$$

It is unusual for consumer prices to increase at approximately the same rate as wages, as they did in the 1970s. Throughout most of the history of the United States, wages have risen faster than prices because of increases in productivity. The reasons for the decline in productivity during the 1970s are varied and are still not well understood.[8] The chief causes of the slowdown are thought to be shifts in the age-sex composition of the labor force that have reduced the average productivity of labor, relatively low rates of saving and investment, and certain undesirable effects of inflation.

***Difficulties in Measuring Price Trends*—**In addition to the decline in the growth of productivity, there is an upward bias in the consumer price index that has affected the decline in the real-wage differential. This bias is significant because small changes in the consumer price index may have pronounced effects on the cost of the Social Security system.

There are several causes of this upward bias. When certain prices rise very rapidly, as did the price of oil in the 1970s, a *fixed-weight* index becomes overly affected by those items whose prices have risen rapidly, and the overall rate of inflation may be exaggerated. Also, the way the consumer price index treats skyrocketing prices of newly purchased homes has been criticized. It is said that housing prices should be treated differently than the prices of consumer goods and services because houses are not consumed or used in the month in which they are purchased. To correct this source of error, the Bureau of Labor Statistics announced in 1981 that over the next few years the price of housing in the consumer price index would be replaced by a measure of the rental equivalent of housing.

***Solving the Short-run Problem*—**The first efforts to solve the system's short-run financial problem were in 1977. To provide additional revenues, Congress sharply raised payroll taxes in the 1977 amendments to the Social Security Act. In the board of trustees' *1978 Annual Report*, the first following the 1977 amendments, the trustees state overoptimistically: "The Social Security Amendments of 1977 have restored the financial soundness of the cash benefit programs over the short-range and medium-range periods, beginning in 1981, and greatly improved the long-range actuarial status."[9] Only a few years later, it was realized that the system was still short of the revenues it needed to cover its current costs.

The reason the board of trustees in 1978 believed it had solved the short-run deficiency in revenues is that it did not expect prices to continue to rise as fast as wages. In the board's projections, it assumed that wages would rise at least one percentage point faster than consumer prices. Actually, average wages in covered employment rose 3.1 percent less than consumer prices in 1979, and 5.0 percent less in 1980.

The *1981 Annual Report* of the board of trustees still optimistically predicts that in the 1980s wages will rise faster than consumer prices. Supporters of the new Reagan economic program of reducing tax rates, lowering the rate of inflation, eliminating much government regulation, and lowering the ratio of taxes to income believe that these economic policies will restore the traditional relationship between the growth of wages and consumer prices. In the board of trustees' worst-case projection and in its pessimistic projection (Alternative III) made in 1981, wages are expected to rise faster than the consumer price index by 1984.[10] In the other three more optimistic forecasts, wages are assumed to rise faster than consumer prices by 1982, and to eventually level off at 1.5 percent to 2.5 percent above the percentage increase in consumer prices.[11]

The Long-run Problem

The board of trustees first recognized in 1974 that the Social Security system had a long-run financial problem related primarily to the decline in the birth rate. In 1974, the actuaries reduced their forecasts of fertility rates, and the predicted long-range actuarial deficit jumped from approximately zero to about 3 percent of taxable payroll. A deficit of this size meant that payroll tax rates scheduled in the law for future years were about 3 percent too low.

The birth rate in the United States rose from 19.4 per 1,000 of population in 1940 to 25.3 per 1,000 in 1957 and then declined to 15.3 per 1,000 of population in 1978.[12] Even though the decline in the birth rate started in 1957, the system's actuaries did not adjust their projections to the decline in the birth rate until 1974.[13] Some delay would be expected because when the birth rate started to decline, the actuaries did not know that it would fall further. What is astonishing is that they did not begin to revise their birth-rate projections until seventeen years after the decline started.

At the time of the 1977 amendments, Congress recognized that the tax increases legislated at that time were not sufficient to correct the long-run financial imbalance in the system caused by the decline in the birth rate. The 1977 amendments did correct a flaw in the automatic indexing formula for Social Security benefits that would have raised long-run costs very sharply.[14] Without this correction, the long-run deficit of the Social Security system would be much larger than it is.

The Amount of the Long-run Deficit—The most recent estimate of the long-run actuarial deficit is presented in the board of trustees' *1981 Annual Report*. According to the intermediate forecasts (Alternatives II-A and II-B), payroll tax rates scheduled for OASDI over the next seventy-five years are from .93 percent to 1.82 percent too low. The deficit will become especially serious after the year 2031. Although it is estimated that there will be a surplus in the OASDI accounts from 1981 to 2005, and a small deficit from 2006 to 2030, there will be a deficit of from 3.39 percent to 4.41 percent of payroll from 2031 to 2055.[15] If hospital insurance is included, the estimated deficit starting in the year 2031, based on intermediate assumptions, is much larger—between 8 percent and 9 percent of payroll.[16] This means that the scheduled payroll tax rate of 15.3 percent for 1990 and later may be 8 percent to 9 percent too low to cover the costs of the Social Security system in these future years.

Reasons for the Long-run Shortfall—The unexpected decline that has occurred in the birth rate will increase the cost of the Social Security system by increasing the ratio of the number of beneficiaries to the number of workers. The formula for the payroll tax rate in Exhibit 3 shows that if the ratio of average benefits to average covered wages is held constant, the payroll tax rate must rise if the ratio of beneficiaries to workers increases. At the present time, because the ratio of beneficiaries to workers is approximately 30 percent and the ratio of average benefits to average covered wages is 36 percent, a payroll tax rate of 10.8 percent (the OASDI rate in 1982) roughly balances receipts and expenditures. Fifty years from now, according to the intermediate cost projections, the ratio of beneficiaries to workers is expected to rise to 50 percent.[17] At that time, those persons born during the baby boom in the 1940s and 1950s will have retired, and the labor force will be relatively small because of the decline in the birth rate in the 1960s and 1970s. If the ratio of beneficiaries to workers rises, as predicted, to approximately 50 percent and the ratio of average benefits to average wages is held the same (at 36 percent), a payroll tax rate of 18 percent would be necessary.

Two additional reasons for expecting a rise in the ratio of beneficiaries to workers in future years are the decline in the mortality rate and the trend toward earlier retirement. The mortality rate dropped sharply during the 1970s. The number of years that an average person at age 60, for example, can expect to live increased more than one year between 1969-1971 and 1978 (for white males from 16.07 years to 17.2 years).[18] Also, the labor-force participation rate of men age 55 to 64 dropped from 83 percent in 1970 to 73 percent in 1979.[19] Although the labor force participation rate of men 65 years of age and older has been declining over the past eighty years, for men younger than age 65 this is a new development. Both the improvement in life expectancy and the trend toward earlier retirement will add to the cost of Social Security by increasing the ratio of beneficiaries to covered workers.

The Reluctance to Raise Taxes Further

The unusual aspect of both the short-run financial problem of the Social Security system and the expected long-run problem is that one of the obvious solutions—raising taxes—is a very unattractive option. The cause of the system's short-run deficits in 1975, 1979, and 1980—a more rapid rise in prices than in wages—also reduced the real income of wage earners. Under such conditions, one would expect workers to object to having to pay higher payroll taxes so as to maintain the real purchasing power of Social Security benefits. If prices rise at approximately the same rate as wages, as they did in 1970-74, 1977, and 1978, payroll taxes would still have to be raised. This is due to the fact that average benefits rise not only because they are indexed, but because each year retirees have built up more benefit credits. Under these conditions also, one would expect workers to object to having to pay higher payroll taxes when their own real incomes are not increasing.

Raising tax rates is also not an attractive solution to the long-run actuarial deficit. In a pay-as-you-go social insurance system, the future retirement benefits of those who are currently working must be financed by taxes paid by future generations. As a result, the tax burden must not become so heavy that future generations are not willing to pay it. Official projections indicate that the combined employer-employee payroll tax rate may have to be raised to over 20 percent by the year 2031. Although it is not known whether future generations would refuse to bear a tax burden of this size, the higher the tax burden, the greater the risk that the burden will not be politically acceptable to future generations of taxpayers.

Correcting the long-run actuarial deficit by increasing taxes also raises the same issue of intergenerational equity as did raising tax rates to solve the short-run financial problem. Adjusting the Social Security system to the decline in the birth rate by increasing payroll tax rates places the entire burden of such contingencies on wage earners.[20] The formula for the payroll tax rate in Exhibit 3 shows that if there is no reduction in the benefits of retirees (the ratio of benefits to wages is kept constant) and the ratio of beneficiaries to workers increases because of a decline in the birth rate, the entire burden would be on those who are still employed who would have to pay the higher payroll tax rates.

Another argument against raising taxes further is that income and payroll taxes are already so high that further increases may have disincentive effects and be somewhat counterproductive. Because higher tax rates may erode the tax base, the limits to raising taxes may be economic as well as political. The high income and payroll tax rates that now prevail already appear to be causing some people to work fewer hours a week, to take longer vacations, to retire at an early age, to take jobs where the conditions of employment are pleasant, or to move to attractive areas of the country where the climate is mild. Also, recent studies of the underground economy indicate that high tax rates are eroding the tax base by encouraging tax evasion. One of the reasons for the slowdown in the productivity of labor (which contributed to the system's short-run deficits) may be the current high tax rates on savings and investment. If so, raising payroll tax rates further would not be an effective way of correcting the system's financial imbalance.

Correcting the financial imbalance in the Social Security system by raising taxes also runs counter to the current political mood and to President Reagan's economic program of cutting tax rates and avoiding further increases in the percentage of income paid in taxes. In the 1970s, the rise in the cost of Social Security was a major factor contributing to the increase in federal taxes as a percentage of the net national product.[21] Because payroll tax collections for OASDHI amount to about 25 percent of total federal tax revenues, when the cost of Social Security rises, the federal tax burden also tends to rise. Even without further increases, the increases in payroll tax rates already scheduled for the 1980s will make it difficult to bring to a halt the upward trend in the federal tax burden.

The report of the National Commission on Social Security appointed by President Carter recommended a 2.5 percent surcharge added to the personal income tax to restore financial soundness to the Social Security system. These revenues would be used to finance one-half of the cost of the HI program and would release some payroll taxes for the OASDI program. While this proposal would make it possible not to increase payroll tax rates, it would increase income tax rates and still have the undesirable effect of raising tax burdens overall. Another objection to this recommendation is that many people are opposed to financing Social Security with general revenues because they view Social Security as a system of compulsory saving, and they believe that the benefits received by a person should be related to the taxes he or she has paid in.

Reducing Benefits

Although the principal reaction to the financial problems of the Social Security system was initially the increase in taxes legislated in 1977, there have also been numerous cuts in benefits. The extent of the cuts is remarkable, even though they have not been large enough to eliminate the deficits, and there are undoubtedly more cuts to come. Throughout most of the history of the Social Security system, benefits have been expanded rather than cut.

Benefits were cut both in the 1977 amendments to the Social Security Act and in the Omnibus Budget Reconciliation Act of 1981. The 1977 amendments froze the minimum benefit at $121 a month; eliminated the *monthly* earnings test that had made it possible for retired workers to receive their full pensions in months in which their earnings fell below a monthly limit, regardless of the amount of their annual earnings; and treated spouses who are entitled to a government pension based on their own employment by the federal government or a state or local government not covered by Social Security in the same way as spouses who have worked in employment covered by Social Security—they are not entitled to both the Social Security benefit for spouses equal to 50 percent of their husband's benefit and the government pension they have earned (they get only the larger of the two). The 1977 amendments also terminated the policy of giving Social Security coverage based on investment income to limited members of partnerships. The Omnibus Budget Reconciliation Act of 1981 eliminated completely the minimum benefit for future beneficiaries, phased out student benefits for persons age 19 and over, eliminated lump-sum death benefits for those without surviving spouses or dependents, eliminated child-care benefits for parents of children age 17 and 18, and established a disability Megacap limiting the sum of all benefits given to a person to no more than 80 percent of his or her average current earnings.

In addition to these cuts, in 1977 when Congress revised the benefit formula for calculating Social Security benefits, it also significantly reversed the upward trend of Social Security *replacement rates* that had occurred in the 1970s. (Social Security replacement rates are the ratio of the benefit paid to a worker in his or her first year of retirement to his or her earnings in the year before retirement and are an important measure of the size of pension benefits.) Exhibit 4 shows that from 1953 to 1970 replacement rates varied between 29 percent and 34 percent for a single worker retiring at age 65 with average earnings, but then rose very sharply to over 50 percent from 1971 to 1981. For married workers with both husband and wife age 65 or over, replacement rates are 50 percent larger than those shown in this table. Also, as Exhibit 4 shows, replacement rates vary with a person's earnings. This is because of the progressive tilt in the percentages allowed in the benefit formula.

Exhibit 5 shows that the target replacement rates for 1985 are significantly below those from 1976 to 1981. The replacement rate for a single worker with average earnings retiring at age 65 is scheduled to drop approximately 20 percent from a replacement rate of 50.8 percent to 40.6 percent. This reduction was made at the same time that the benefit formula was changed in the 1977 amendments to the Social Security Act. In these amendments, the old benefit formula was replaced with a new formula that corrects the flaw in the way benefits had been indexed for inflation. From 1979 to 1982, the benefits of those retiring could be calculated with either the old or the new formula. In 1983, the benefits of all persons retiring must be calculated with the less favorable new formula.

In addition to the cuts in benefits that have already been made, further cuts are being recommended. To solve the system's short-run financial problem, it has been proposed that instead of indexing the benefits of retired persons to consumer prices, benefits be indexed either to the increase in wages or in consumer prices, whichever is lower. An alternative suggestion made by Professor Martin Feldstein is to increase benefits by the excess of the rate of inflation over 2 percent—if, for example, the consumer price index rose 8 percent, benefits would rise by 6 percent.[22] A third suggestion is to attempt to lower the increase in benefits by tying benefits to some other type of index, such as the personal consumption expenditures deflator published by the Department of Commerce. In recent years, the personal consumption expenditures deflator has risen less rapidly than the consumer price index.

To solve the system's long-run financial problem, two major types of cuts have been recommended. Many persons have recommended raising the retirement age for full benefits from 65 to 68. The National Commission on Social Security appointed by President Carter recommended gradually increasing the retirement age from 65 to 68 over

Exhibit 4: **Replacement rates for single workers retiring at age 65, 1953-1981**

Year	Low earnings	Average earnings[a]	Maximum earnings
1953	53.5%	30.7%	28.3%
1954	51.9	29.3	28.3
1955	54.8	34.3	32.8
1956	53.8	33.5	29.6
1957	52.3	32.5	31.0
1958	50.8	31.9	31.0
1959	52.7	33.5	33.1
1960	51.8	32.8	29.8
1961	49.6	31.7	30.0
1962	48.8	31.3	30.2
1963	46.8	30.3[b]	30.5
1964	46.4	29.8[b]	30.8
1965	48.9	31.5[b]	32.9
1966	48.1	31.3[b]	33.2
1967	52.1	34.2	27.9
1968	49.7	32.4	28.4
1969	47.1	30.8	24.7
1970	52.2	34.3	29.2
1971	51.5	36.4	32.8
1972	52.3	34.9	33.2
1973	58.4	39.4	35.5
1974	56.3	38.3	30.5
1975	59.7	40.7	28.8
1976	60.6	42.4	31.0
1977	61.8	43.6	32.4
1978	62.1	44.4	33.4
1979	62.1	45.5	34.1
1980	64.2	47.1	29.9
1981	70.2	50.8	31.0

[a] The earnings record for persons with average earnings is the annualized average wage for all workers in the first quarter of each year. The earnings record for persons with low earnings is $3,200 for 1974; for other years, it is the same ratio to the earnings of persons with average earnings as prevailed in 1974 (39.8 percent).

[b] The lower replacement rates for persons with average earnings than for those with maximum earnings in 1963-66 result from the fact that, because the maximum taxable earnings base remained unchanged in 1959-65, the former had almost the same "final" earnings as the latter, but had significantly lower "career" earnings.

Source: Robert J. Myers, *Summary of the Provisions of the Old-Age, Survivors, and Disability Insurance System, The Hospital Insurance System, and the Supplementary Medical Insurance System*, SSA Program Circular No. 796 (Washington, D.C., Government Printing Office, July 1981), 28.

Exhibit 5: **Targets for Social Security replacement rates for 1985**[a] **(percent)**

	Replacement rate[b]	
Level of earnings	Single person	Couple
Federal minimum wage	53.5%	80.2%
Average	40.6	60.9
Maximum	24.5	36.7

[a] Replacement rates for subsequent years are similar to those in 1985.

[b] For persons 65 years at retirement.

Source: Robert J. Myers, Summary of the Provisions of the Old-Age, Survivors, and Disability Insurance System, The Hospital Insurance System, and the Supplementary Medical Insurance System, SSA Program Circular No. 796 (Washington, D.C: Government Printing Office, July 1981), 29.

the period 2000-2012. A principal argument in favor of raising the retirement age is that, because of improvements in longevity and health, it would be a logical policy. A second proposal is to gradually lower replacement rates below those targeted for 1985 and subsequent years shown in Exhibit 5. This could be done by making relatively minor changes in the way in which the benefit formula is indexed to rises in prices and wages.

Significance of Reducing the Growth of Benefits—If further cuts in Social Security benefits are made, the high replacement rates achieved in the 1970s will have been short-lived. This is significant because it would reflect a shift in the basic goals of the Social Security system—away from the goal of providing persons with a large enough income to permit them to maintain the same standard of living they had while working and toward the goal of providing persons with no more than a minimum floor of income.

It is not generally realized how ambitious the target replacement rates reached in the 1970s are. As shown in Exhibit 5, the 1985 target replacement rate for a worker age 65 with earnings at the federal minimum wage is 53.5 percent if single and 80.2 percent if married. Also, the 1985 target replacement rate for a worker age 65 with average earnings is 40.6 percent if single and 60.9 percent if married. According to most estimates, Social Security replacement rates between 65 percent and 80 percent are high enough to enable couples with low or average earnings to maintain their customary standard of living.[23] This is because retirees do not have to pay work-related expenses, are entitled to Medicare, and pay lower taxes because Social Security benefits are excluded from both income and payroll taxes. Because of the very heavy taxes on higher incomes, it has been estimated that persons with incomes as high as

$50,000 a year can maintain pre-retirement living standards with replacement rates of only 50 percent to 55 percent.

If replacement rates are cut back below the 1985 targets in Exhibit 5, retirees in the 1980s will have to supplement their Social Security benefits with other types of saving for retirement security. Replacement rates will be closer to their levels before the 1970s. Exhibit 4 shows that before 1970 replacement rates of persons with average earnings were only 30 percent for a single person and 45 percent for a married couple. Because of the lower replacement rates in the past, most retired persons supplemented their Social Security benefits very substantially. About 65 percent of persons age 65 and over, for example, own the home they live in.[24] Home ownership is an important type of retirement security because of the large portion of a person's income spent for housing. In addition to home ownership, 28 percent of the retired population age 65 and over receive benefits from an employee pension plan and, according to estimates made in 1977, the number of persons receiving federal, state, or local government retirement pensions was 3.8 million.[25] Also, most retired persons have supplemented their Social Security benefits with some income from savings deposits, stocks, bonds, or business real estate, and a few persons receive large amounts of income from these sources.

Diversification as Protection Against Risks—If Social Security benefits are subject to risks, a benefit policy of providing persons with a minimum floor of protection and expecting most persons to supplement their Social Security benefit with other types of saving may be better than a policy that sets replacement rates so high that people can expect to rely solely on their Social Security benefit. Social Security beneficiaries incur risks whenever the benefits they expected to receive are eliminated or the amount of their benefits is reduced below the amount that they anticipated. Both of these types of risk have been experienced by people receiving Social Security benefits in recent years. While the federal government has attempted to keep risks at a minimum, serious financial problems in a pay-as-you-go social insurance system are unavoidable if the growth of productivity declines or the birth rate drops sharply. Although persons have often assumed that Social Security was not subject to risk because it was a government system financed by taxation, recent experience shows that this is not true.

Summary

There is little doubt that important changes are ahead for the Social Security system. There are two major needs. To correct the short-run problem, there is a need to change the way retirement benefits are indexed so that the system does not run out of funds whenever consumer prices rise faster than wages. Although it is to be hoped that the productivity of labor will resume its normal growth trend, some type of permanent adjustment should be made so as to avoid in the future the kind of difficulties that are certain to occur whenever prices, for whatever reason, rise as fast as wages.

To correct the system's long-run problem, the system should be changed in some way so that unexpected increases in the ratio of the number of beneficiaries to the number of workers do not place too heavy a tax burden on the working generation. This could be achieved either by raising the eligibility age for full benefits or by lowering replacement rates. Although reducing the growth of benefits in these ways may seem to be impossible politically, during the 1970s Social Security replacement rates were raised far above those in previous decades. The system's long-run financial deficit could be corrected by returning to the levels of replacement rates that existed before the 1970s. Because these replacement rates did not provide large enough benefits to cover a person's entire retirement needs, persons had to supplement their Social Security benefits with other types of saving. However, if social insurance programs are subject to risk just as are other types of saving, retirees ought not to rely solely on Social Security for their retirement needs. The best retirement policy is one that is diversified, and the old saying, "Don't put all your eggs in one basket," still applies.

Endnotes

1. *1981 Annual Report of the Board of Trustees of the Federal Old-Age and Survivors Insurance and Disability Insurance Trust Funds* (Washington, D.C.: Government Printing Office), 47. (Hereafter, OASDI annual reports will be cited simply as "Annual Report.")

2. *1980 Annual Report*, 5, and *1981 Annual Report*, 3. The board of trustees is required by law to submit to Congress an annual report on the status of the OASDI trust funds. The members of the board are the Secretary of the Treasury, the Secretary of Labor, and the Secretary of Health and Human Services. The Commissioner of Social Security is the secretary of the board. The annual reports of the board include five-year estimates of income and outgo as well as estimates of OASDI expenditures as a percent of taxable payroll for the next 75 years.

3. For a summary of their findings, see *Report of the Panel on Social Security Financing to the Committee on Finance, United States Senate*, 94th Congress, 1st session, February 1975; and *Reports of the Consultant Panel on Social Security to the Congressional Research Service, Prepared for the Use of the Committee on Finance of the U.S. Senate and the Committee on Ways and Means of the U.S. House of Representatives*, Joint Committee Print, 94th Congress, 2nd session, August 1976.

4. See *Reports of the Quadrennial Advisory Council on Social Security*, House Document No. 94-75, 94th Congress, 1st session, March 10, 1975; and *Social Security Financing and Benefits, Report of the 1979 Advisory Council*

(Washington, D.C.: Department of Health, Education and Welfare, 7 December 1979).

5. See *Social Security in America's Future: Final Report of the National Commission on Social Security* (Washington, D.C., Government Printing Office, March 12, 1981); and President's Commission on Pension Policy, *Coming of Age: Toward a National Retirement Income Policy* (Washington, D.C.; Government Printing Office, 26 February 1981).

6. *Social Security Bulletin, Annual Statistical Supplement, 1977-79* (Washington, D.C.: Government Printing Office), 88.

7. *1972 Annual Report*, 18-21, 32.

8. See John W. Kendrick, "Productivity Trends and the Recent Slowdown: Historical Perspective, Causal Factors, and Policy Options," and Edward F. Denison, "Where Has Productivity Gone?" in *Contemporary Economic Problems*, ed. William Fellner (Washington, D.C.: American Enterprise Institute, 1979), 17-77.

9. *1978 Annual Report*, 53.

10. *1981 Annual Report*, 29. In 1981, the board of trustees presented a short-run "worst case" cost estimate and four long-range alternatives based on four different sets of demographic and economic assumptions. Alternative I is known as the optimistic set of assumptions; Alternatives II-A and II-B, the intermediate sets; and Alternative III, the pessimistic set. Alternatives II-A and II-B have the same demographic assumptions. Alternative II-A assumes a more rapid rate of growth, a lower rate of inflation, and a higher real-wage differential than Alternative II-B.

11. For a critical analysis of the projected rise in the real-wage differential, see Roland E. King and Clifford K. Powell, "A Critical Analysis of the Assumptions in the 1980 Social Security Trustees' Reports," *Society of Actuaries, Transactions*, vol. 33 (Chicago, Illinois: Society of Actuaries, 1981), 87-98.

12. U.S. Bureau of the Census, *Historical Statistics of the United States, Colonial Times to 1970* (Washington, D.C.: Government Printing Office), 60.

13. See Robert S. Kaplan, *Financial Crisis in the Social Security System* (Washington, D.C.: American Enterprise Institute, 1976), 5.

14. See Colin D. Campbell, *The 1977 Amendments to the Social Security Act* (Washington, D.C.: American Enterprise Institute, 1978), 11-14; *Financing Social Security*, ed. Colin D. Campbell (Washington, D.C.: American Enterprise Institute, 1979).

15. *1981 Annual Report*, 58-59.

16. See A. Haeworth Robertson, *The Coming Revolution in Social Security* (McLean, Virginia: Security Press, 1981), 90.

17. *1981 Annual Report*, 60-61.

18. *Vital Statistics of the United States, 1978*, vol. 2, sect. 5 (Washington, D.C.: Government Printing Office).

19. Robert L. Clark and David T. Barker, *Reversing the Trend Toward Early Retirement* (Washington, D.C.: American Enterprise Institute, 1981), 13.

20. Richard A. Musgrave, *Financing Social Security: A Reappraisal*, Discussion Paper No. 753 (Cambridge, Massachusetts: Institute of Economic Research, Harvard University, April 1980).

21. For an analysis of the rise in the federal tax burden, see Rudolph G. Penner, "The Future Growth of Government Budgets," in *Contemporary Economic Problems, 1980*, ed. William Fellner (Washington, D.C.: American Enterprise Institute, 1980), 103-33.

22. Martin Feldstein, "Slowing the Growth of Social Security," *Wall Street Journal*, 24 September 1981, 30.

23. See Alicia H. Munnell, "The Future of the U.S. Pension System," in *Financing Social Security*, ed. Colin D. Campbell (Washington, D.C.: American Enterprise Institute, 1979), 260.

24. Bureau of the Census, *Annual Housing Survey: 1979, Part A, General Housing Characteristics* (Washington, D.C.: Government Printing Office, August 1981), 6.

25. President's Commission on Pension Policy, *Coming of Age: Toward a National Retirement Income Policy* (Washington, D.C.: Government Printing Office, February 26, 1981), 21: *Social Security Bulletin, Annual Statistical Supplement, 1977-79* (Washington, D.C.: Government Printing Office), 67.

Pointing out that employment security is a paramount concern of all who work, JAMES BENNETT *finds that pursuit of such security through governmental intervention is counterproductive. Through analysis of specific legislation, he shows that both individual workers and society as a whole suffer harm.*

Among Bennett's conclusions: government intervention in the labor market produces outcomes vastly different from the stated intent of the legislation; is costly to society; is generally ineffective; and often harms the employment security of those whom it was supposed to help.

Despite its wide-ranging powers, Bennett maintains, even Congress cannot repeal the basic laws of supply and demand.

16

Employment Security: Government, Union, and Market Protection

JAMES T. BENNETT

In his classic work, *Of Human Bondage*, W. Somerset Maugham observed that "[T]here is nothing so degrading as the constant anxiety about one's means of livelihood...."[1] As in the past, employment security remains today a concern of paramount importance to all who work, regardless of the color of one's collar. Large-scale government intervention in the market for labor is a relatively new phenomenon, for prior to the onset of the Great Depression of the 1930s, the role of government in providing employment security for workers was minimal and limited to certain industries such as the railroads. For the most part, the market for labor was unfettered by public-sector intervention and individuals were free to choose the conditions of work and pay that most enhanced their well-being in accordance with their individual preferences and abilities.

The Great Depression, however, may be considered an important watershed for the labor market. The economic dislocations of the 1930s were not only very severe and prolonged but also were international in scope. Millions of Americans lost their jobs and could not find alternative employment—the unemployment rate has been estimated to have reached as high as 25 percent in 1933—incomes plummeted, and the economic and political fabric of society came under enormous stress. The nation, throughout its history, had experienced financial panics and recessions, but nothing as severe as that of the 1930s. Although it is interesting to speculate on the causes of this economic upheaval, our concern is solely with the ensuing consequences. Stated simply, the Great Depression was widely perceived as direct and incontestable evidence of *market failure*, i.e., the market mechanism could no longer be trusted to provide jobs for those who were willing to work or to provide adequate compensation for those who held jobs. Employment security and unregulated labor markets were, therefore, regarded as incompatible and, consequently, government regulation of the market for labor was widely accepted as the appropriate means of protecting the employment security of American workers.

Throughout the 1930s, Congress enacted laws that influenced the relationship between employers and employees: the Davis-Bacon Act (1930), the National Labor Relations Act (1935), and the Fair Labor Standards Act (1938)(FLSA). Note that the title of the FLSA implies that labor standards would somehow be *unfair* without the provisions of this law. The tradition of government regulation of labor markets has continued with the passage of such acts as the Occupational Safety and Health Act (1970), the Comprehensive Employment and Training Act (1973)(CETA), and even the Civil Rights Act of 1964. The key assumption behind all public policy initiatives in the labor market is that an individual worker is incapable of protecting and maintaining his or her own best interests in the world of work and that security and safety can only be achieved on a collective basis. Much labor legislation has centered on the encouragement of unionization and the promotion of collective bargaining for wages, hours, and working conditions. Collective bargaining was viewed as the major solution for the perceived imbalance of power in the marketplace between individual workers and "big" business.

Although market failure is frequently advanced as a justification for public or collective intervention, there is now a substantial and growing body of literature that clearly indicates that the inadequacy of market outcomes is only a necessary, but by no means a sufficient, condition for government intervention in the economy.[2] Before any government involvement is justified, the alleged failures of the market must be compared to the prospective failures of government in correcting them. Abundant examples exist of government intervention actually exacerbating problems caused by market inadequacies rather than curing them, e.g., urban renewal, poverty programs, and the regulation of the truck and airline industries. When politicians determine wages and conditions of work, the decisions made will depend on political perceptions of the personal benefits (votes, campaign contributions, and so forth) that accrue from alternative courses of action. Equity, however defined, is no more likely under political resource allocation than market allocation, and politics can produce greater inequities than the market.[3] Labor union leaders are also influenced by political considerations and can (and do) have objectives and goals very different from those of labor union members.[4]

The purpose of this discussion is to show that government intervention in the market for labor produces outcomes that are often not only vastly different from the stated intent of the legislation but are also very costly to society. In many cases, programs that are publicly promoted as aiding those workers whose employment security is most theatened actually favor special-interest groups at the expense of those who are purportedly protected. Public policy initiatives to repeal the laws of supply and demand in the market for labor or in the market for any other good or service are inevitably doomed to failure. Congress may just as well legislate a repeal of the law of gravity. Moreover, contrary to conventional wisdom, there is little convincing evidence that labor unions have enhanced the employment security of workers in general or of those workers in particular who are most disadvantaged in the labor market: the young, the unskilled, and the minorities. In the sections that follow, brief discussions are given of selected government attempts to regulate the market for labor, the results of these programs, and their cost to society.[5]

The Davis-Bacon Act

The Davis-Bacon Act became law on March 31, 1931, for the purpose of protecting local wage rates on federal construction from competition with lower-wage, nonlocal labor. The act requires that all workers on federal construction must be paid *prevailing* local wages. The prevailing wage rates, however, are not those rates set by competitive bidding in the marketplace, but are determined by the U.S. Department of Labor. As administered by the Labor Department, prevailing wage rates are union wages that, at times, are taken from labor contracts in distant areas. Though they are less well-known, the Labor Department also specifies construction techniques on federal projects by establishing work classifications which incorporate work rules of local labor organizations. For example, if unions have restrictions against spray guns for painting, the Labor Department will enforce this rule by refusing to certify wage rates for anyone to use them.

The Davis-Bacon Act produces costly distortions in the market for labor. One study has placed the cost at between $500 million and $1 billion per year.[6] This cost range is an estimate of the additional expense resulting from government wage regulation on federal projects and arises from a number of sources: (1) union labor is used on construction projects instead of lower-wage, nonunion labor that would otherwise have performed the work, $228 million to $513 million; (2) union labor is actually paid higher wages while working on federal projects than it normally receives, $69.6 million to $284.6 million; (3) administrative costs to contractors resulting from Davis-Bacon regulation, $190 million; and, (4) taxpayer dollars to support Department of Labor administration of Davis-Bacon, $12.4 million.

In simple terms, the Davis-Bacon Act is a costly means of transferring income to union members who work on federal construction projects and to government workers who administer its provisions at the expense of taxpayers. The ramifications of this regulation, however, are far more extensive. When wage rates in construction are mandated, the most significant cost component is controlled, competition among contractors is reduced, and large, multistate enterprises are favored over smaller and, notably, nonunion contractors. Thus, the economic benefits conferred on union labor are obtained in large degree at the expense of nonunion labor whose employment security is reduced by government interference in the market.

The Fair Labor Standards Act

One of the most important examples of government interference in the market for labor is the setting of minimum wages under the FLSA. The minimum wage undermines the employment security of literally millions of Americans and, indeed, precludes many from participating in any way in the labor market. At the outset, it should be recognized that the stated objective of the minimum wage provision of FLSA is laudable: to provide a subsistence income for those who work. Although such a goal is desirable, the actual outcome is far different from the intent of the law. A legislated minimum wage, if it is to have any effect whatever, must raise the price that employers pay for labor above that which prevails in the market. In a free market for labor, firms will hire workers at a wage equal to the value of the additional output they produce. Therefore, employees will be paid an amount equal to their individual contribution to the firm's profit. Competition among firms for workers will ensure that labor receives its fair share of the economic pie; no more and no less. If, on the other hand, a firm attempted to pay individuals a wage lower than their productivity, it would lose them to other firms that were willing to pay the appropriate wage. On the other hand, if a worker attempted to command a wage above the value of his or her productivity, other job seekers willing to work at the going wage would be hired instead.

Although Congress may possess the power to legislate wages for workers above the market wage, it is not possible to legislate an increase in productivity. If the established minimum wage exceeds the value of the output produced by a worker, the worker will not be able to find employment. Thus, although the minimum wage law was intended to aid lower-paid workers who are generally poorly educated, young, unskilled, and members of minority groups, the vast majority of economists are convinced that the law adversely affects precisely these workers. A mandated increase in wages results in employers raising quality standards and hiring better skilled and more productive workers.

Over time, Congress has increased both the hourly minimum and the number of workers covered; today about 65 percent of all nonagricultural workers are covered by minimum wage legislation.[7] As would be expected, research has shown that every increase in the minimum wage rate has resulted in increased unemployment, particularly in low-wage, labor-intensive industries. Teenage unemployment rates, especially for nonwhites, have soared: in 1979, the unemployment rate of nonwhites aged 16-19 exceeded 32 percent, more than twice the rate for white cohorts. It has been estimated that a 25 percent rise in the minimum wage would reduce the employment of low-skilled teenagers by 25 percent.[8] Unskilled adults also are displaced by minimum wage increases. Moreover, an important effect of minimum wages is to discourage workers from participating in the labor market. The number of persons who leave the labor market in despair of finding a job may be as high as three times the number who are counted as unemployed because of this regulation.[9]

The discussion above clearly indicates that government intervention in the labor market in the form of minimum wage rates has a severe impact on the employment opportunities of those who are less able to compete effectively because of a lack of skill and training. It is difficult, if not impossible, for a worker to climb the job ladder when government interference prohibits attainment of the bottom rung. Certainly, employment security of the individual cannot be enhanced if the worker cannot obtain a job of any sort.

Minimum wages have failed to alleviate poverty and to provide a better standard of living, but the regulation of this aspect of the labor market has served the interests of one group admirably: the private-sector unions. Unions lobby for and politically support increases in the minimum wage because as the cost of low-skilled workers rises these workers are less competitive with more highly paid union workers. Further, a higher minimum wage gives union leaders additional leverage for increasing the union wage scale. Empirical research has been presented to show that the average union member gained $435 as a result of the increase in the minimum rate from $1.60 to $2.00 per hour in 1974. Overall, total union wages rose by $435 billion. The benefits from minimum wages accrue to a narrowly focused special-interest group, labor unions, while the costs are borne by those least able to bear them and by consumers at large who must pay more for products produced by unionized firms. There is much more rhetoric than reality in the claim that the minimum wage law helps the disadvantaged. While it is impossible to quantify all the costs associated with minimum wages, one estimate has placed the burden on society at an amount in excess of $8 billion per year.[10]

Occupational Safety and Health

When the Occupational Safety and Health Act became law in 1971, the federal government established the principle of federal authority over practices in the workplace. Virtually every aspect of the work space (including the number and placement of toilet facilities) came under the control of the government. Although it is not widely understood or appreciated, the act has very significant implications for employment security. Occupational safety and health regulations contain extremely detailed restrictions on the work environment that have a significant impact on both industry costs and prices. Firms have had to undertake massive amounts of investment to comply with the act's regulations; in 1975, private industry spent about $4 billion on equipment for worker health and safety.[11] The incidence of these regulations fell primarily on five basic industries: chemicals, metals, wood products, paper, and automobile manufacturing. Research has demonstrated that prices in these industries have increased more than in others.[12] As prices rise, domestic goods become less competitive with nonregulated foreign products and, particularly in the case of autos and steel, tens of thousands of jobs have been lost as a result of foreign competition.

As prices rise and the quantity demanded is depressed in regulated industries, production and investment in those industries is replaced by that in the occupational safety equipment industries. It would appear that total output would remain unchanged, only its composition would be altered. However, there would still be some long-run substitution of safety equipment for capital investment which would reduce the growth of the gross national product (GNP) generated from capital. To the extent that this occurs, full capacity GNP will increase at a lower rate. One investigator has estimated that the opportunity costs of safety regulation would result in a level of GNP by the mid-1980s that is 5 percent lower than otherwise would exist. At 1979 prices, these opportunity costs would equal approximately $115 billion in forgone output.[13] Lower levels of output imply fewer jobs and employment security is, indeed, a hollow concept for an individual who cannot find work because jobs do not exist.

Clearly, occupational safety and health regulation is costly. Yet opposition to such constraints would be perceived as akin to condemnation of motherhood. Who can possibly advocate unsafe or unhealthy conditions for workers? The fact is, however, that despite the costs, there is strong evidence that these regulations have done nothing to improve the work environment. As one student of the Occupational Safety and Health Administration (OSHA) has put it,

> What is clear is that the agency's enforcement policies have not had any direct impact on job hazards. Moreover, even if these efforts were effective, their desirability would be doubtful since the preponderance of violations are not for dimly understood health hazards, but for readily monitorable safety hazards, the type which market forces are well-equipped to handle through compensating wage differentials. In short, policy-makers have paid too little attention both to the potential desirability of the present intervention

and to the economic mechanism through which the enforcement activities will exert their influence.[14]

Thus, although substantial direct and indirect costs are incurred in the name of government protection of the health and safety of workers, there is no convincing evidence that this goal is being achieved. Although OSHA regulations do not protect workers, they greatly benefit the government employees who make their living promulgating and enforcing them. Employment security is reduced for the worker who purportedly benefits from this government intervention in the market for labor, but the employment security of the bureaucrat is enhanced.

Federal Manpower Programs

Federal government efforts at employment programs can be traced back to the 1930s when the Works Progress Administration, the Public Works Administration, and the Civil Conservation Corps were instituted. These and other programs have focused on three basic issues: the direct creation of jobs, skill development, and job placement. The Great Society programs of the 1960s revived some of the long-dormant initiatives of the Great Depression with the Manpower Development and Training Act of 1962, the Job Corps, the neighborhood Youth Corps, and the various aspects of CETA. All of these programs have as their rationale the implied failure of the marketplace to provide adequate jobs or training for workers. In fiscal year 1979, about $13 billion was expended on CETA programs under various guises.

By any standard of assessment, federal efforts to provide jobs and employment security through manpower programs have been of highly dubious value. In part, the failure of CETA programs to achieve the stated objective can be attributed to what is known as *displacement effects*. The federal government has made grants to state and local governments to hire workers and the federal funds are used to replace state and local funding for jobs so that very few *new* positions are created. Very pessimistic assessments have been made of the permanent employment effects of the massive expenditures associated with such programs. Studies have shown that only between 6 percent and 9 percent of federal grant dollars actually end up in the wage bill.[15] If such assessments are accurate, the short-run employment impact of the federal expenditures of $13 billion in 1979 was the creation of about 448,500 new public-sector jobs at a cost of $28,986 per employee. The long-run employment effect was the provision of 97,500 permanent public-sector jobs at a cost of $133,330 *per worker*. In deriving these figures, it is assumed that the average participant in the jobs program was paid an annual salary of $10,000. Therefore, it is evident that vast sums were expended on program administration and that the primary beneficiaries of federal manpower programs were the government employees who administer them rather than participants for whom the initiatives were purportedly designed.

Employment and Earnings Discrimination

Title VII of the Civil Rights Act of 1964 is the foundation of federal regulatory policy regarding discrimination in employment. The act makes it illegal for an employer to discriminate against an individual on the basis of race, color, religion, sex, or national origin in any way that would deprive an individual of employment opportunity or equal pay for equal work. These provisions are administered by the Equal Employment Opportunity Commission (EEOC), which seeks to prevent employment discrimination by obtaining voluntary compliance of employers on a case-by-case basis with the commission's dictates and by pursuing court action on behalf of complainants. Though admirable in intent—who would advocate discrimination?—the actual outcomes of EEOC efforts have hardly lived up to expectations.

Only one research study has concluded that government attempts to end discrimination in labor markets have been successful;[16] other studies, however, have shown that the analysis in this work is seriously flawed.[17] Instead, a large (and expanding) body of literature exists that indicates that the efforts of the EEOC have not been effective in reducing discrimination and actually may have exacerbated the employment difficulties of minorities.[18] Employers may be reticent about offering jobs to individuals when so doing could lead to litigation in the courts and the associated expenses because of some administrative action by an agency of the federal government. The EEOC, despite its ineffectiveness, is not costless to society. In fiscal year 1979, the administrative costs for this agency were about $217 million; this figure does not include the tens of millions of dollars expended by private firms in filling out government forms and developing affirmative action plans, so the total cost is far higher.

An unregulated labor market is perfectly capable of dealing with discrimination. Most people believe that employer bias is the major cause of discrimination; however, it is pressure from the community, majority employees, or unions that most often leads to discriminatory practices. If employers can hire equally productive minority workers at lower wages than, say, white males, the profit motive creates a strong incentive to do so. If an employer continues to hire high-wage white workers when similar minority employees are available at lower wages, the costs of the firm will be higher than those of nondiscriminating competitors. Higher costs of production will obviously reduce profits; therefore, it does not pay to be a racist or sexist employer. Nondiscriminating employers will refuse to offer whites higher wage rates than they offer to equally productive minority workers. Whenever it is less costly to hire minority rather than majority employees, the unbiased employer will take advantage of the situation. An equal opportunity policy within the marketplace for labor will reduce relative costs and give nondiscriminating employers an advantage over a competitor who discriminates.[19] The relationship between costs of production and employer discrimination has been well articulated by Sowell:

> In general, job discrimination has a cost, not only to those discriminated against and to society, but also to the person who is discriminating. He must forgo hiring some employees he needs, or must interview more applicants in order to get the number of qualified workers required, or perhaps offer higher wages in order to attract a larger pool of applicants than necessary if hiring on merit alone. These costs do not necessarily eliminate discrimination, but discrimination—like everything else—tends to be more in demand at a low price than a higher price.[20]

EEOC regulations such as the *equal pay for equal work* rule actually lower the costs of discrimination in employment. If, for instance, an employer is forced to pay the same wage to men and women, discriminatory hiring practices become less expensive. An employer's profits are no longer lowered by passing over equally qualified women to hire men. If it becomes difficult for women or minorities to accept employment at lower wages, their ability to make employers absorb the costs of discrimination is reduced. Therefore, the strict enforcement of an equal-pay-for-equal-work regulation will, more likely, lead to more employment discrimination rather than to less.

Because equal-pay rules have probably caused more employment discrimination, the use of employment quotas has gained popularity among regulators. Under a system of quotas, employers who react to legally mandated higher wages for women and minorities by reducing their employment of such persons will be found guilty of employment discrimination. A policy of employment quotas in conjunction with equal-pay rules might reduce discrimination but the costs of such a program relative to the market solution are huge. Quotas do not make a distinction between workers with real productivity differences. If less-productive women and minorities replace more-qualified men, economic efficiency will decline, producing a general welfare loss to society. In addition, hiring quotas eliminate the link between employment and productivity by requiring firms to employ a certain percentage of minorities and females regardless of their performance or credentials. Workers hired under such a system will be less motivated to produce; a decline in total productivity thus occurs; and total output, income, and employment are therefore lower. It is impossible to guess the overall welfare loss of such a regulatory program, but it could easily fall into the billion dollar category.

Here again is yet another example of costly government involvement in the market for labor which obviously benefits the bureaucrats who administer the EEOC program but which may actually hinder the job security of those who supposedly benefit.

Occupational Licensing

It should not be assumed that all government involvement in labor markets occurs at the federal level, nor should it be assumed that all regulation is intended to benefit the poor, disadvantaged, or blue-collar workers. Occupational licensing restrictions are typically imposed by states and localities and often apply to the professions such as law and medicine. The licensing of various professions has generally been considered to be a necessary practice in order to protect persons from incompetent and dishonest service by businesspeople, professionals, and laborers. However, researchers and policy makers are beginning to realize that licensing restricts freedom of entry into various fields of work, thus creating occupational cartels that restrict employment security by denying some individuals the right to employment in a profession or trade.

Any government policy that restricts the supply of labor will eventually lead to increased incomes. Therefore, occupational licensing requirements, regardless of their intention, have the effect of reducing entry into a profession and limiting the labor supply. Although there are numerous studies of the impact of unions on the supply of labor and the determination of wages (unions are simply licensing institutions), very little research has been undertaken to document the effects of licensing in other areas. Most studies have concentrated on the legal and medical professions.[21] For example, it has been shown that there is little movement between states among dentists and lawyers due to licensing practices within states and the lack of reciprocity agreements. In addition, there is a significant relationship between licensing-exam failure rates and the average incomes in dentistry and law.[22]

Walter Williams has pointed out that occupational licensing is another form of labor market restriction that produces ill effects for minorities and other disadvantaged persons. As an example, he mentioned the taxicab business where there are low skill requirements and no major capital requirements for entry (only an automobile is needed). This profession could provide minorities and youth with self-employment and the potential for earning a lucrative income. However, because there are high-cost licensing requirements in most cities, many would-be entrants are prevented from participating. Williams indicated that some cities grant monopolies to a single taxicab company while others require the purchase of license medallions which are extremely expensive. Los Angeles awarded the Yellow Cab company an exclusive franchise to operate within its city limits. New York City issued medallions at a cost of $26,000 and $28,000 in 1975, and Chicago and Baltimore charged as much as $18,000 in the same year.[23] There is a large number of licensed occupations that have unjustified restrictions that reduce employment opportunities and, thus, employment security that would otherwise be available for minorities, youth, and other disadvantaged members of society.[24] The net effect of occupational licensing is to increase the incomes of those individuals who are licensed at the expense of consumers; the government employees who administer the licensing function also benefit.

Unions and Collective Bargaining

Conventional wisdom dictates that labor unions play a major role in protecting the employment security of workers. The federal government has, since the 1930s, fostered the unionization of employers through the provisions of the National Labor Relations Act. The relationship between employment security and unionization warrants close examination; however, labor unions attempt to provide collective security in employment for workers by monopolizing the supply of labor. Unions claim that individual workers need their protection against the greater economic power of employers in the marketplace for labor. There is little doubt that unionized workers, relative to their nonunion counterparts, receive higher pay. A variety of studies has shown that union wages relative to nonunion wages are from as little as 10 percent to as much as 50 percent higher.[25] But, what do such statistics really mean? As is often true, conventional wisdom may be incorrect. There are convincing arguments to suggest that unionized workers may not benefit measurably from the regulation of labor relations. The wage differential of union workers relative to nonunion workers is obtained at the expense of workers in the nonunion sector. To the extent that regulation encourages collective bargaining, a transfer of income from nonunion to union workers occurs. In 1976, approximately 25 percent of the nonagricultural work force was unionized—a small minority of workers. The regulation of labor relations, therefore, benefits a special minority interest group within the economy at the expense of others whenever an income transfer to unionized workers is produced because of government involvement in employer-employee relations. Although there have been increasingly vocal negative sentiments expressed which condemn special-interest groups that obtain benefits for a minority at the expense of the majority, labor unions have, for the most part, escaped widespread criticism. If for no other reason, the entire spectrum of labor relations regulation should be carefully examined because of the special-interest nature of the gains that accrue to the unionized sector at the expense of the majority of American workers.

Even though regulation may benefit unionized employees *as a group*, it does not by any means follow that all individual union members are better off because of the transfer of income from the nonunion to the union sector, for important income transfers occur within the unionized sector itself. A central tenent of unionism has always been the standardization of wage rates for all workers; such a system permits little differentiation among workers on the basis of performance or productivity. Without standardization of wages, economic theory indicates that employers would pay more to attract and retain highly productive workers. When all workers are paid at the same rate, a more productive worker must forgo a higher wage; in essence, an income transfer occurs in which less-capable employees are subsidized by more-capable workers. Stated simply, an efficient worker can be penalized by the standardization of wages even if the average wage paid to all workers in an organization is higher. There are no estimates of the size of the transfers within the union sector from more- to less-productive employees, but a reasonable guess would indicate that the potential magnitude is enormous. If one assumes that performance among workers is approximately normally distributed, that is, about one-half of the unionized workers are more efficient than the average worker and the other half are less efficient, then approximately one-half the unionized work force is paid less than would be the case without the standardization of wage rates while the other half is paid more.

A second reason that regulations that encourage collective bargaining may not benefit the unionized worker may be found in recent research indicating that the higher average wages paid to the union sector may not be due to unionization at all.[26] The logic of this statement is based upon the notion of cause and effect: Are the wages of unionized workers higher because of the presence of unions or do unions simply have greater success in organizing high-wage industries (or, alternatively, do unions simply choose as a matter of strategy to concentrate their organizing efforts upon high-wage industries)? A survey of this literature which raises serious doubt about the efficacy of unions in increasing wage rates concluded that

> ... it appears that wages affect unionization to a greater degree than unionism influences wages, but paradoxically workers presumably become union members because they believe that the latter causal direction predominates.[27]

One point, however, should be stressed: All studies of the union wage effect overstate the union-nonunion wage differential because all assume that the differential is obtained at zero cost. As every union member is all too well aware, unions collect dues, fines, fees, and assessments from their members that, in total, amount to billions of dollars each year. If these costs alone were taken into account, the union-wage differential would unquestionably be smaller. The differential would be reduced still further if research was conducted on employee income rather than on wage rates. At the very least, strikes have a negative effect on employee income while leaving the wage rates unchanged. Of what value is an artificially inflated wage rate if, in order to obtain it, the employee through his or her union, was on strike for such a long period of time that his or her income remained at or near the pre-raise level over the life of the contract?[28]

Even if unionization does produce higher wages, there is a third reason why at least some individual workers will suffer. The employer's response to higher wages is both predictable and immediate: The employer responds to higher wages by reducing the size of the work force. Those employees who lost jobs and are displaced receive none of the benefits. The notion of employment security through unionization is a hollow concept for the union member without a job or prospects of returning to work. Witness the plight of the hundreds of thousands of steel and auto workers now on indefinite layoff with little or no prospect of ever returning to their jobs.

There is increasing evidence that workers in the private sector are questioning the benefits of membership in unions and, by implication, the government regulations that foster collective bargaining. Private-sector unions are experiencing a secular decline in membership and the origins of this decline can be traced back at least as far as the 1950s. In the private sector, union membership has fallen as a percentage of the number in the nonagricultural labor force, i.e., in relative terms, as well as in absolute numbers. As a percentage of nonfarm employment, total union membership declined from about one worker in three in 1955 to about one in four in 1976. Because total membership data include the flourishing public-sector membership (which increased by 75 percent between 1968 and 1974), it is clear that membership in the private sector has declined dramatically.

Membership has declined because labor unions are failing to attract new members and to retain old members. Data from the *Annual Report* of the National Labor Relations Board indicate that unions are now winning a smaller proportion of certification elections and are losing a larger proportion of the decertification elections than previously. In 1956, unions won almost two-thirds (65.3 percent) of all certification elections; by 1966, however, the victory rate had diminished to 60 percent and, by 1976, less than half (48.2 percent) of the certification elections produced a union victory. A similar trend is also apparent in the data on decertification elections. By 1977, labor unions were losing three-fourths of all decertification elections—the highest loss percentage ever reported. To make matters worse for the unions, the number of decertification elections has also increased substantially. Between 1977 and 1979, a total of 2,433 decertification elections were held; between 1967 and 1969, only 766 were conducted. More decertification elections were lost by unions in the three-year period 1977-1979 (a total of 1,822) than in the entire decade 1960-1969, when only 1,628 union defeats were recorded. The record shows that employees are much less inclined to join unions or to remain unionized now than only a few years earlier.

Stated simply, it is reasonable to question the continuation of regulations that, directly or indirectly, encourage the continuation of collective bargaining when the American worker (who, by conventional wisdom, is the prime beneficiary of collective bargaining) has, over a long period of time, shown increasing disenchantment with unionization in the private sector. It is questionable for union officials, bureaucrats, and politicians to insist that the regulation of employer-employee relations in general, and collective bargaining in particular, is in the best interest of the worker when workers have clearly demonstrated by their actions in rejecting unionization that they think otherwise.

Conclusions

This discussion of government intervention in the market for labor in order to provide employment security has amply illustrated that these initiatives are costly to society, generally ineffective, and may harm rather than help the employment security of those workers who purportedly benefit. The principal beneficiaries are the government employees who administer the programs, politicians who seek votes through public spending, and labor union leaders. There is no evidence that market failure has occurred with regard to labor, but there is convincing evidence of the failures of government involvement in this market. Despite its wide-ranging powers, even Congress cannot repeal the basic laws of supply and demand.

Endnotes

1. W. Somerset Maugham, *Of Human Bondage* (New York: Doubleday, 1942).

2. See Charles Wolf, Jr., "A Theory of Nonmarket Failure: Framework for Implementation Analysis," *Journal of Law and Economics* (April 1979): 107-139. 139.

3. A classical example is federal urban renewal programs which have demolished about twice as many housing units as they have replaced, and a large percentage of those replaced have been for middle- and upper-income individuals. Wealthier individuals are not only better off competing in the marketplace than less wealthy individuals, but are also more influential politically.

4. See James T. Bennett and Manuel H. Johnson, "The Impact of Right-to-Work Laws on the Economic Behavior of Local Unions: A Property Rights Perspective," *Journal of Labor Research* (Spring 1980): 1-27.

5. A more detailed and comprehensive analysis of these topics appears in Dan C. Heldman, James T. Bennett, and Manuel H. Johnson, *Deregulating Labor Relations* (Dallas: The Fisher Institute, 1981).

6. John P. Gould and George Bittlingmayer, *The Economics of the Davis-Bacon Act: An Analysis of Prevailing Wage Laws* (Washington, D.C.: American Enterprise Institute for Public Policy Research, 1980). See especially 68.

7. Neil W. Chamberlain, Donald E. Cullen, and David Lewin, *The Labor Sector*, 3rd ed. (New York: McGraw-Hill, 1977), 507.

8. Edward Gramlich, "The Impact of Minimum Wages on Other Wages, Employment and Family Incomes," *Brookings Papers on Economic Activity* (Washington, D.C.: Brookings Institution, 1976), 409-451.

9. Jacob Mincer, "Unemployment Effects of Minimum Wages," *Journal of Political Economy*, part 2 (August 1976), 87-104.

10. Heldman, *Deregulating Labor*, 97.

11. See *5th Annual McGraw-Hill Survey of Investment in Employee Safety and Health*, (New York: McGraw-Hill Publications Company, Economics Department, May 1977).

12. Paul W. McAvoy, *The Regulated Industries and the Economy* (New York: W.W. Norton, 1979) 89; 139, n.9.

13. Edward Denison, "Effects of Selected Changes in the Institutional and Human Environment upon Output per Unit of Impact," *Survey of Current Business* (January 1978): 24-44.

14. W. Kip Viscusi, "The Impact of Occupational Health and Safety Regulation," *Bell Journal of Economics* (Spring 1979): 136.

15. See George E. Johnson and James D. Tomola, *An Impact Evaluation of the Public Employment Program*, Technical Analysis Paper No. 17 (Washington, D.C.: U.S. Department of Labor, Office of the Assistant Secretary for Policy Evaluation and Research, Office of Evaluation (April 1974), 8, ff; Orley Ashenfelter and Ronald Ehrenberg, "The Demand for Labor in the Public Sector," in *Labor in the Public and Non-Profit Sectors*, ed. Daniel S. Hamermesh (Princeton: Princeton University Press, 1976).

16. Richard B. Freeman, "Changes in the Labor Maket for Black Americans, 1948-72," *Brookings Papers on Economic Activity* (Washington, D.C.: Brookings Institution, 1973), 67-120.

17. Robert J. Flanagan, "Actual Versus Potential Impact of Government Antidiscrimination Programs," *Industrial and Labor Relations Review* (July 1976): 486-507. See, also, Richard Butler and James J. Heckman, "The Government's Impact on the Labor Market Status of Black Americans: A Critical Review," in *Equal Rights and Industrial Relations*, ed. Leonard Housman, *et al.* (Madison, Wisconsin: Industrial Relations Research Association, 1977), 255-256.

18. For example, see Arvil V. Adams, *Toward Fair Employment and the EEOC: A Study of Compliance Under Title VII of the Civil Rights Act of 1974* (Washington, D.C., Equal Opportunity Commission, August 1972); Benjamin W. Wolkinson, *Blacks, Unions and the EEOC* (Lexington, Massachusetts: D.C. Heath, Inc., 1973); Alice Kidder, "Federal Compliance Efforts in the Carolina Textile Industry; A Summary Report," *Proceedings of the Twenty-fifth Annual Meeting of the Industrial Relations Research Association* (Madison, Wisconsin, 1973), 353-361; and, Andrea Beller, "The Effects of Title VII of the Civil Rights Act of 1964 on the Economic Position of Minorities," Ph.D. dissertation, Columbia University, New York, 1974.

19. James D. Gwartney and Richard Stroup, *Economics: Private and Public Choice*, 2nd ed. (New York: Academic Press, Inc., 1980), 637.

20. Thomas Sowell, *Race and Economics* (New York: David McKay, 1975), 168.

21. Selected studies of interest which cover several occupations and deal with theoretical issues include Milton Friedman and Simon Kuznets, *Income from Independent Professional Practice* (New York: National Bureau of Economic Research, 1954); Simon Rottenberg, "The Economics of Occupational Licensing," in *Aspects of Labor Economics*, ed. H. Gregg Lewis (Princeton, New Jersey: Princeton University Press, 1962), 3-30; Thomas Moore, "The Purpose of Licensing," *Journal of Law and Economics* (October 1961): 93-104; Benjamin Shimberg, et al., *Occupational Licensing: Practicing and Policies* (Washington, D.C.: Public Affairs Press, 1973); U.S. Department of Labor, Manpower Adminis-Administration, *Occupational Licensing and the Supply of Nonprofessional Manpower*, Monograph No. 11 (Washington, D.C.: Government Printing Office, 1969).

22. Arlene Holen, "Effects of Professional Arrangements on Interstate Labor Mobility and Resource Allocation," *Journal of Political Economy* (October 1965): 492-498.

23. Walter Williams, *Youth and Minority Unemployment* (Stanford, California: Hoover Institution Press, 1977), 25-26.

24. See Stuart Dorsey, "The Occupational Licensing Queue," *Journal of Human Resources* (Summer 1980): 424-433.

25. For a survey of this literature, see Heldman, *Deregulating Labor*, 112-114.

26. This literature is surveyed briefly in James T. Bennett and Manuel H. Johnson, "Free Riders in U.S. Labour Unions: Artifice or Affliction?" *British Journal of Industrial Relations* (July 1979): 158-172.

27. C.J. Parsley, "Labor Unions and Wages: A Survey," *Journal of Economic Literature* (March 1980): 29.

28. Consider an employee whose wage rate is $10 per hour: Over a forty-hour week his pay is $400 per week. Suppose, to win a wage rate hike to $12.50 per hour, his union went on strike for six weeks. Aside from such offsetting income as, for example, unemployment compensation and food stamps (which unions have pushed for precisely because they have the effect of mitigating the impact of strikes), this employee would have to work twenty-four weeks at the higher rate before he merely made up the income loss from the strike. On the impact of welfare payments, see Armand Thieblot and Ronald Cowin, *Welfare and Strikers: The Use of Public Funds to Support Strikes* (Philadelphia: University of Pennsylvania, Wharton School, 1972).

Taking both economic and environmental considerations into account, and admitting sound economic justifications for some public land ownership JOHN BADEN *finds the amount of land currently held by federal agencies to be grossly excessive. Entrepreneurs, operating in competitive marketplaces, are more desirable agents for the achievement of economic and environmental goals than is the federal government.*

Baden calls for institutional reform of public land ownership and management. When we rely on the public sector to make decisions, authority is separated from responsibility and social loss is inevitable. The social loss comes from systematically reduced environmental quality and economic efficiency, produced by ill-conceived programs and premature development generated by government bureaucrats. Returning land and resource management to a system composed of property rights and free markets, Baden contends, will move resources to their highest uses.

17

Public Lands Policy: What Legacy for the Future?

JOHN BADEN

On June 20, 1970, the Public Land Law Review Commission submitted its report, *One Third of the Nation's Land*, to President Nixon. The first sentence of the 342-page report reads: "Feeling the pressures of an enlarging population, burgeoning growth, and expanding demand for land and natural resources, the American people today have an almost desperate need to determine the best purposes to which their public lands and the wealth and opportunities of these lands should be dedicated."[1] Now, a decade later, individuals are responding to this challenge in ways that would startle and amaze the report's authors.

Since 1970, we have witnessed an energy crisis, timber crises, environmental and economic problems with predator control, the maturation of environmental interest groups, the mumblings of a strategic mineral crisis, and the spectre of massive water-allocation problems. Many have argued that the various systems of federal land management should be fine-tuned and reformed and that we need to develop even more sophisticated analytic techniques. At the same time, the Sagebrush Rebellion has indicated that the citizenry is undergoing a significant intellectual change regarding the management of the public lands.

Perhaps of greater interest is the number of prominent resource economists in the private, the nonprofit, and the public sectors who have advocated the divestiture of many federal lands to the private sector. It may surprise some that their arguments are based on both economic efficiency and environmental quality.

Most analysts will agree that the private sector, with its reliance on property rights and the rule of willing consent, is superior in terms of narrow economic efficiency. To some, however, it is surprising that equally powerful arguments can be made in terms of environmental quality. Forestry professors, like Barney Dowdle at the University of Washington and William Hyde at Duke University, have presented data showing that the U.S. Forest Service is systematically subsidizing reductions in the environmental quality of the nation's forests while engaging in inefficient forestry management programs. Marion Clawson, the dean of natural resource economics and former director of the Bureau of Land Management, is currently focusing his considerable energies on whether significant portions of the federal lands should be transferred to private ownership.

Clearly, this represents a real departure from the orientation that dominated the past decade. The intellectual center of this new development in policy analysis is a group working out of Bozeman, Montana. With six active researchers and an excellent staff, we have assaulted the traditional assumptions underlying public land policy. This paper offers an overview of this work, with an emphasis on the national forests.

The Public Lands

Originally, the political and economic organization of the United States assumed that the overwhelming majority of the nation's productive assets would be privately held and managed. While this is generally true, one-third of the nation's lands—that is, 770 million acres—is still owned and managed by the federal government.

In some states, the percentage of public land is negligible. Only 3 percent of the land in Connecticut, Delaware, Maryland, New Jersey, and Alabama and roughly 2 percent in Indiana, Massachusetts, Pennsylvania, and Illinois are federally owned. But the situation changes dramatically when one moves west: 46 percent of California, 44 percent of Arizona, 63 percent of Idaho, 86 percent of Nevada, 52 percent of Oregon, and 63 percent of Utah are owned and managed by the federal government. More than twenty federal agencies administer this land. Two agencies, however, have control over 85 percent of the land: the Bureau of Land Management (BLM) in the Department of Interior, and the U.S. Forest Service in the Department of Agriculture.

The thrust of my argument is relatively simple. While there may be sound, economic justifications for some public ownership, the amount currently held by federal agencies is grossly in excess of the optimum. This statement is supported by both economic and environmental considerations.

The Political Economy of Land Management

Land and its associated resources are valuable assets. Commodities such as timber, forage, energy, minerals, and environmental amenities are all important. When measured in terms of social welfare, our goal is presumably to optimize the net values that flow from these resources. Clearly, different institutions will influence to what degree we will attain this optimum.

Knowledgeable observers will agree that the current system of federal management is woefully deficient. Thus, fundamental institutional reform seems highly appropriate. In designing this reform, it is useful to recall that the United States began as a social experiment. Let us review the experiment and consider the data as our first step in dealing with reform.

In 1989 we will mark the 200th anniversary of the U.S. Constitution. Most observers will agree that our Constitution is the most successful social experiment ever conducted. The Constitution made it difficult and expensive to use the government as a mechanism to transfer resources from one group to another.[2] Under the Constitution, people are made better off if they produce more wealth and refrain from investing in transfer activities. In other words, entrepreneurship should be rewarded.

Entrepreneurial activities are probably the most socially valuable and most underappreciated actions in American society. In terms of improving general social welfare, entrepreneurs are the most useful citizens in society—when they are operating in the private sector. This brings us to a basic rule of economics.

Most economists will tell you that there is no such thing as a free lunch. Every action has an opportunity cost; that is, something of value must be given up to obtain something else of value. In general, these economists are right. There is, however, an important exception. If higher-valued outputs can be generated from the same inputs, then we have the equivalent of a free lunch. If the same outputs are produced for less inputs, society again gains a free lunch. This, of course, demonstrates the magic of the market. Self-interested individuals are made to act as though they care about general social welfare.

Just what is an entrepreneur? Entrepreneurship may be largely composed of a magic elixir; but for the purposes of this paper, we can attempt a loose definition. An entrepreneur is one who is alert to and acts on the potential rearrangements of factor inputs and the opportunities for marketing the resulting outputs. In other words, the entrepreneur moves resources to their most highly valued uses in order to make a profit. Entrepreneurs, like others, are motivated by self-interest and the interests of those for whom they care.

Again, when operating in the private sector, entrepreneurs advance their interests by moving resources to more highly valued uses. For example, particle board, a highly useful building material, is made from by-products that formerly had a disposal cost. Someone with entrepreneurial vision converted a material with a negative value to a highly valued, socially useful commodity. Cottonseed cake, now used as a nutritious livestock supplement, provides another example of waste being turned into a valuable product.

In such cases, the entrepreneurs must risk their resources and those of their backers on their entrepreneurial vision. The reality checks underlying this risk impose a powerful discipline. The entrepreneur's actions are subject to the preferences of others as expressed in the market, giving him or her an immediate indication of the value of a product. By contrast, the coercive power of government can be used to force us to buy MX missiles, Teton and Tellico dams, outrageously destructive BLM and Forest Service land management practices, and welfare programs that enrich bureaucrats while destroying the social fabric of poor families and reducing their chances for personal advancement.[3]

Bureaucratic Entrepreneurship and the Environment

As just indicated, entrepreneurs have the vision and control the resources necessary to rearrange inputs and to produce alternative outputs. Private sector entrepreneurs advance their interests by moving resources to more highly valued uses. The contrast with the public sector entrepreneur is as dramatic as it is depressing.

Public sector bureaucrats, just like real people, are primarily self-interested. The bureaucrat's welfare is largely a function of his discretionary budget and his GS rating. Thus, he seeks larger budgets, more employees, and enhanced power. He obtains his objectives by developing linkages among special-interest groups, congressional committees, and bureaucratic agencies. In this way, the coercive power of government is used to exploit the many for the benefit of the few.

Western water projects provide a good example of this process. The Central Utah Project, the Central Arizona Project, and the Garrison Diversion are classic cases. The results of these projects are monuments to the folly of the transfer society. We can expect the average citizen to remain rationally ignorant of the details of such projects. As a result, governmental bureaucrats are then in a position to exploit the public treasury.

From the perspective of bureaucrats and special-interest groups, the federal treasury is a common pool resource. The logic of common property resources is well-developed in economics, but that logic has only recently been expanded to include the federal treasury.[4]

Perhaps more important are the negative environmental consequences of bureaucratic governance. Two of our publications, *Earth Day Reconsidered* and *Bureaucracy vs. Environment*, detail the environmental impacts of this system.[5] While this point should be emphasized, the evidence has already been studied and the case made. The emphasis in this paper, therefore, will be on institutional reform.

Disenchantment with Federal Policy

The 1970s were christened the environmental decade. The 1980s may become the decade of the Sagebrush Rebellion. Former Secretary of Interior James Watt sought to defuse the Sagebrush Rebellion bomb, but the conditions that prompted the rebellion will remain. The problem is not one of bad people, and the solution will not be to select their replacements. Institutional reform is required before optimal management practices can be expected.

There is clear and compelling evidence that American citizens are becoming disenchanted with both the scope and the quality of governmental management in nearly all sectors of society. In no region is this more pronounced than in the West. The reason is obvious: In no other region is the federal government so dominant a force. The most obvious manifestation of this feeling can be found in the Sagebrush Rebellion.

Mentioning the Sagebrush Rebellion is likely to evoke an emotional response. Ranchers, farmers, miners, sportsmen, and environmentalists (certainly not mutually exclusive categories) are likely to have strong feelings about the issue. The intensity of the reaction is closely related to individual experience and expectations. Unfortunately, high emotions are often incompatible with careful reasoning.

The Sagebrush Rebellion is a complex phenomenon with many interrelated features. It is important to remember that any time policy changes, there are both winners and losers. In evaluating such a change from the perspective of general social welfare, the critical question becomes, "How do the net expected benefits compare with the net expected costs?"

Although it is easy to build a case that both efficiency and productivity will be significantly improved by the divestiture of federal lands, the environmental consequences are less obvious. They are also more emotional. To understand this issue, it is useful to consider how concern with resource management has evolved.

During the 1970s, environmental activists overwhelmingly favored increased governmental control of natural resources. They believed that if decisions could be made by articulate and idealistic people with the appropriate philosophy, and bills could be paid by the capitalists who had abused Mother Earth, then real progress could be made. If social concern could replace greed, then harmony and tranquility would reign. The general public would be better served, they thought, if environmentally aware and socially concerned leaders could use the coercive powers of government to stifle the self-interested, venal behavior of the private sector.

Throughout the 1970s, however, a small group of academics ran a fundamentally different line. They believed in a natural coalition that could bring ecologically sensitive conservationists and fiscal conservatives together with individuals who place a high value on freedom. Those of us who love our country but fear the growth of our government see evidence that there is a better alternative to increased bureaucratic control over natural resources. The results of the 1980 election suggest that this coalition has promise.

Most professional preservationists and environmentalists view the election of Ronald Reagan and his subsequent appointments as unmitigated disasters—a rejection of all the environmental decade stood for. But this is an overly pessimistic view. If ends count rather than means, there is reason to hope.

As suggested previously, natural resource systems in the public sector have been managed as transfer systems. Although American society was originally organized to foster productivity, it has increasingly become oriented toward the political transfer of wealth. The negative implications of this development for natural resource management are profound.

Organized preservationists and members of environmental interest groups tend to be relatively wealthy and well-educated. These individuals hold a comparative advantage in their dealings with the political system. Although money and political power are always positively related, in a democratic context the conjunction of education and access to wealth is especially powerful. By capturing the intellectual game and defining what is good and what is bad, these individuals are able to dramatically increase their influence.

Preservationists use the coercive power of government to gain subsidies for themselves—and for others—in the form of enhanced amenities. For example, they obtain subsidized recreation and the preservation of low-density amenities. One strategy ignores or downplays the opportunity costs of forgone development. This is obvious in the constraints imposed on housing developments and on mineral and timber developments on federal lands administered by the BLM and the U.S. Forest Service.

This is not to suggest that environmentalists have a monopoly on self-interest. Developers confronting increased energy and housing prices seek subsidies for their activities in these areas. The push for subsidized development of synfuels is a case in point. Less obvious and perhaps more important are the implicit political subsidies that allow developers to ignore the spillover effects (externalities) imposed on others by development practices. An important example of this kind of subsidy is the Price-Anderson Act, which limits the liability for damages associated with accidents at nuclear plants.

Both environmentalists and developers are motivated by self-interest. Neither party has a monopoly on virtue. While both speak for the so-called public interest, neither has a comprehensive view of what that interest is. When we rely on the public sector rather than property rights and market exchange for the allocation of resources, authority to make decisions can be separated from responsibility for those decisions, and social loss is inevitable.

Bureaucratic entrepreneurs have gained substantial power and authority during the past decade. These public sector adventurers have effectively utilized recurrent crises in energy, minerals, water, and so forth to generate large budgets and to increase their discretionary control over natural resources. As a result, they have systematically—though unintentionally—reduced environmental quality through ill-conceived and premature development. Given that decisions made in the public sector are primarily determined by using political rather than economic criteria, the developments these bureaucrats have fostered have tended to be inefficient and prodigal of resource utilization.

The problem is not one of bad people. Be they environmental preservationists, myopic developers, or competent and well-intended public servants, when an opportunity is surveyed it is viewed from a personal perspective. Options that decrease the decision maker's welfare are unlikely to be supported. From the standpoint of social welfare, the system of public management is often inherently perverse.

The managers of the Department of Interior's BLM and Fish and Wildlife Service and the Department of Agriculture's Forest Service tend to be technically competent and well-intended. This conjunction, however, by no means guarantees that they will produce socially optimal results. Individuals operating within a bureaucratic context are effectively buffered from the social consequences of their actions. Neither opportunities forgone nor poor investments reduce the wealth of governmental decision makers. By contrast, a system of private and transferable property rights encourages efficient resource utilization. It is exactly this advantage that public sector managers lack.

Reform generated by the Sagebrush Rebellion can lead to the development of a responsible resource management system that is relatively free of the distortions that accompany political management. By designing and fostering a management system based on property rights and free exchange among consenting parties, we can systematically encourage the movement of resources to more highly valued uses.

It is important to recognize that statutory wilderness areas and environmental amenities have a positive value. In many areas, the most highly valued use of public land is for wildlife, recreation, and grazing. If the value of the amenities is higher than the value of development, then it is clear that society is ahead if the amenity is preserved. But in those few locations where valuable minerals are economically available, society suffers if mining is not allowed.

If ownership of federally owned wild and scenic areas were transferred to those in the private sector who value it most highly—that is, established environmental groups—social welfare would almost surely be enhanced. Should a valuable mineral be discovered on such lands, the owners would have to confront the consequences of failing to develop it. If the land was developed under their control, they could take the value of the mineral, net of development costs, and purchase land or easements to additional amenity areas. Under this system, the areas developed would be handled with prudence and sensitivity. Rather than confronting binary choices, decision makers could consider a range of potential development strategies and have every incentive to display a sensitivity to the opportunity cost of their actions.

Obviously, even more possibilities exist in the area of rangeland management. There is no economic, moral, or ecological reason why federal agencies should manage western grazing lands. The absence of property rights to this forage leads to overgrazing, ineffective and nonexistent grazing development, and subsidized and socially irrational management practices. These practices often result in ecological and economic costs that far exceed their value. It is extremely difficult for bureaucracies to be time- and place-specific in their management. Thus, environmental and economic errors are common.

In general, we have found the political decisions made on natural resource systems to be inconsistent with ecological quality, efficient resource management, and basic standards of equity. As resources grow increasingly scarce, it becomes more difficult to justify the continuation of management systems that either subsidize development and destroy environmental quality or refuse to recognize the opportunity costs of nondevelopment. By establishing a system where responsibility and authority are clearly linked, a system based on property rights and willing exchange, we can most successfully cope with scarcity.

Although the Sagebrush Rebellion may now be primarily of historical interest, it did set the stage for serious considerations of reform. In terms of social welfare, the Sagebrush Rebellion's goal of turning federal lands over to the states may or may not have led to an improvement. It is likely that state governments would respond to interests not held by the federal government. But this is merely to speculate on the consequences of replacing one public bureaucracy with another. Such a shift represents a clear case of a transfer activity, and it fails to address the real issues. In my view, privatization is preferable on grounds of both economic efficiency and environmental quality.

Smokey the Bandit

The U.S. Forest Service manages a quarter of the nation's timberland and 50 percent of its softwood inventory. In total, 91,189,000 acres of productive timberland are assigned to Forest Service management. Millions of additional acres are managed by the BLM, the Bureau of Indian Affairs, other federal agencies and departments, and state governments.

Public timber management in the United States is predicated on the erroneous assumption that a market economy operated by private decision makers is unable to effectively manage this valuable resource. Holding to this assumption has caused a great deal of mischief, and it is becoming more and more burdensome and expensive. Yet, it is understandable.

Nearly everyone will agree that the amount of forested land—and thus the amount of timber inventory—in what is now America was excessive when the pilgrims landed on Plymouth Rock. Until recently, timber was so plentiful in the United States that its value was not significantly greater than zero. As recently as 1970, millions of board feet of timber were sold in the West for less than ten dollars per thousand board feet. With 10,000 board feet, you could build a fairly extensive house, and the value of timber in that house could be less than $100. Remember, this was in 1970, not 1870.

Under these conditions, it simply did not make sense—socially or privately—to divert resources to grow additional timber. Thus, harvested forests were not often regenerated. During the late nineteenth century, it was widely believed that the market would not adjust to a scarcity of timber and that on July 7, 1911, the very last tree in America would be harvested. Obviously, Gifford Pinchot and his friends failed to credit speculators with sufficient greed. Can you imagine what the last few hundred billion board feet of timber would be worth?

As a result of some faulty analysis imported from European schools of forestry, Americans are now suffering the consequences of public sector timber management. Perhaps we could have afforded the luxury of inefficient management when timber was plentiful and cheap; but as resources become increasingly scarce, it is crucial that they be managed with the efficiency that only markets can provide.

Not only is timber becoming scarce, but amenities are also becoming more valuable. How do our public sector managers respond to this scarcity? The Forest Service is systematically squandering our timber resources, failing to capture billions of dollars of revenue, and subsidizing the destruction of environmental quality. This is neither a casual nor a radical condemnation but, rather, represents a near consensus among forest economists.

Marion Clawson, in his 1976 *Science* article, examined the basis for the growing criticism of public management of natural resources.[6] Recent work by Baden and Stroup and William Hyde has been published by distinguished university presses.[7] Journal articles, such as Hyde's "National Forest Logs Red Ink for Treasury" and Thomas Lenard's "Wasting Our National Forests: How to Get Less Timber and Less Wilderness at the Same Time,"[8] are becoming more common. All of these publications focus on a similar theme. Under current U.S. Forest Service management we produce less timber at a higher cost than is necessary. At the same time, by logging ecologically fragile areas we despoil millions of acres of prime recreational land.

Under efficient mangement, we can dramatically increase timber production and still expand opportunities to achieve environmental and recreation values. As William Hyde states:

> The private sector is moving toward efficient rates to guide silvicultural management, and market incentives are likely to reinforce this trend. The public, an important sector of the timber

> The private sector is moving toward efficient rates to guide silvicultural management, and market incentives are likely to reinforce this trend. The public, an important sector of the timber industry, owning as it does one-quarter of national production and one-third of Douglas-fir regional production, remains reluctant to embrace this trend....
>
> There is some doubt that the public sector will ever be efficient in the usual economic sense. It has little incentive. Nevertheless, efficiency is a useful benchmark against which to judge public sector performance. Efficiency results can be compared to those obtained under current management criteria. The difference between the two represents the public costs of the latter.[9]

As Hyde suggests, we should not expect efficiency from the public sector. Fortunately, most American citizens are no longer so naive that they believe this can ever happen.

If the public forests are to make their best contribution to social welfare, public managers must discover and produce a changing mix of products. One basic rule of government must be considered, however: It is exceedingly difficult for bureaucracies to be time and place specific. Unlike organizations in the private sector, public bureaucracies do not often respond to changes in relative scarcities or in citizens' preferences.

It is obvious that management strategy should change as the demand for forest products changes. If each product were marketed, managers could respond efficiently to these changes. But in the absence of the information generated by prices, the manager's task is virtually impossible. Decisions are based on information and incentives that are generated by a perverse institutional framework. As a result, we cannot expect socially optimal decisions. The solution to poor management lies in institutional reform, not in firing bad people or in hiring better ones.

When all forestry goods carry prices that correctly state their opportunity costs, individuals in a market based on property rights and the rule of willing consent will systematically move resources to their highest uses. The market system is best understood as an information system. Prices provide condensed information on relative values. These values are in turn strongly linked to incentives to act on that information. When relevant facts are distributed, prices foster the coordination of vast numbers of individuals. In brief, prices minimize the amount of information necessary to make an intelligent decision.

By contrast, centralized bureaucracies maximize information requirements. Because the bureaucrat does not own the resources he manages, he does not have to face the reality checks imposed by losses or gains in personal wealth. As a result, we simply cannot trust a Forest Service manager, for example, to make the right decisions. In the political sector, therefore, myriad checks and balances—that is, red tape—are imposed on the decision maker.

The Forest Service has responded to the managerial challenge of the 1970s by asking for more money. Even though Forest Service bureaucrats waste billions of dollars every year on inefficient practices, they are uninhibited in their enthusiastic demand for greater control over resources. By demanding more highly skilled foresters, biologists, computer analysts, engineers, archeologists, landscape architects, wildlife managers, hydrologists, and other experts, they hope to solve their problems. Unfortunately, there is little evidence that they understand what their problems are.

There is simply no way that these experts can duplicate the coordination provided by the price signals in a market context. When each resource user surveys the available options and bids for their use, the controlling bids convey condensed information on desires, options, and opportunities. Winning bids in the market replace armies of experts, public speakers, and litigants.

There are, of course, well-known flaws in the market. Externalities and public goods exist, and they are very important. But compared to the information problem and the distortions generated by the political process, market problems are often easy to handle. Many supposed market problems are either solved by entrepreneurs or by governmental regulation.

A Modest Proposal for Reform

Again, let me emphasize that these problems cannot be attributed to either the incompetence or the moral failings of professional planners, scientists, or managers. Rather, they are the predictable consequence of existing institutional arrangements. A lack of good data is inherent to systems that fail to price outputs as well as inputs and that do not recognize the opportunity costs of capital. Further, political pressures always exist when decision makers are responsible only through the political system. I marvel not at the size of the problem, but rather that the national forests are managed as well as they are, given the perversity of the system.

The reform I propose here is both modest and simple. Privatize the commercial timber land of the national forests. While the land involved could be expanded to include recreational lands, the benefits from reform will be greatest on commercial timberland. Not everything can be accomplished at once. If this plan was adopted, many of the obstacles to good management would be overcome. Decision makers would automatically select the optimal amount of validated information, and political obstacles to efficient management would be substantially diminished. Equally important, environmentalists, timber producers, miners, recreationists, and others who make demands on the forests would quickly move toward positive, constructive accommodation. Different systems lead to different behavior.

Let me give you an example of how this plan would work. The National Audubon Society is noted for believing that environmental protection should be given priority on public lands and no sacrifice is too great when considering this goal. But on the seventy tracts of land owned by the Audubon Society, a more conciliatory position dominates. For example, oil and gas companies find it easier to deal with the Audubon Society when developing its own land is the issue than when the land is owned by the federal government.

Long ago, National Audubon Society executives recognized that if a careful and ecologically sensitive plan was developed for producing oil and gas, then the subsequent revenues could be used to improve existing preserves and to acquire rights to new ones. Likewise, the oil and gas companies found it profitable to find ways to innovatively operate on Audubon lands at an extremely low cost (and sometimes at a benefit) to environmental values.

When acting in the market, the Audubon Society continually explores the purchase of land or easements to protect wildlife. In this situation, it faces strong incentives to minimize the impact of its demand on other resources valued by society. Only by doing so can the society minimize the cost of what it obtains. In much the same way, the owner or developer of a forest faces strong incentives to find ways to sell easements or environmentally important portions of the land to environmental groups whenever the sale can be made at a low opportunity cost. Environmental groups, such as the Nature Conservancy, currently own title, easements, or covenants for several million acres of land.

Whenever someone owns a piece of land, those with a potential interest in it begin to act as if they cared about the preferences of others. Each party's goal can best be reached through close, constructive, and imaginative cooperation with the others. For example, thousands of farms and ranches provide fee hunting and fishing. When exchange is made in accordance with the rule of willing consent, such trades must be mutually beneficial or they will not take place.

The contrast with the sharp and acrimonious debate over public land policy is stark indeed. In the political sector, an effective strategy is to discredit the other side and reject compromise unless defeat is inescapable. When the price to the user is zero, each side wants it all.

Of course, there are some who will object to this proposal. At least someone will raise the spectre of Weyerhauser, Boise-Cascade, International Paper, Champion International, or the 200 largest timber companies getting together to monopolize the land. Although this would certainly *not* occur, even this worst possible scenario would be preferable to the current Forest Service monopoly. The timber companies would want only that land that would yield a profit. A large proportion of the timber currently being logged under Forest Service management has negative value as timber. It is primarily valuable because of its recreational, grazing, and watershed production. Millions of acres of uneconomical land are logged only because the Forest Service taps the common pool of the federal treasury and cross-subsidizes uneconomical sites with economical sites.

Private firms are not in the business of losing money. Those that do are called bankrupt, and they control ever fewer resources. While the Forest Service can harvest stands of timber at a loss and not feel the consequences, no private firm could survive such an attitude. There is no analogous mechanism for Smokey the Bear and his helpers.

Fortunately, the conflict between timber and recreational values is often overstated and would substantially diminish with private ownership. The most attractive recreational sites and those areas that produce more amenity values usually have low timber-growing potential. With few exceptions, prime timberland normally does not coincide with prime recreational land.

The basic rules of policy analysis state that (1) not all good things go together and (2) there are no cost-free solutions. In the case of natural resources, however, many good things do go together. The analysts must identify and describe those systems that foster this cooperation. The present system is hopelessly flawed, and its costs are unacceptable on both environmental and economic grounds. Any successful reform must connect authority with responsibility while providing good information. A market system based on property rights and the rule of willing consent meets these criteria much better than any other.

Endnotes

1. Public Land Law Review, *One Third of the Nation's Land* (Washington, D.C.: Government Printing Office, 1970), 1.

2. Terry Anderson and P.J. Hill, *The Birth of a Transfer Society* (Stanford, California: Hoover Institution, 1980).

3. George Gilder, *Wealth and Poverty* (New York: Basic Books, 1981).

4. Rodney D. Fort and John Baden, "The Federal Treasury as a Common Pool Resource and the Development of a Predatory Bureaucracy," in *Bureaucracy vs. Environment*, ed. John Baden and Richard Stroup (Ann Arbor: University of Michigan Press, 1981), 9-21.

5. *Earth Day Reconsidered*, ed. John Baden (Washington, D.C.: Heritage Foundation, 1980).

6. Marion Clawson, "The National Forests," *Science* 191 (1976): 762-67.

7. Baden and Stroup, *Bureaucracy vs. Environment*; William F. Hyde, *Timber Supply, Land Allocation, and Economic Efficiency* (Baltimore: Johns Hopkins University Press, 1980).

8. William F. Hyde, "National Forest Logs Red Ink for Treasury," *Wharton Magazine* (Fall 1981): 66-71; Thomas Lenard, "Wasting Our National Forests: How to Get Less Timber and Less Wilderness at the Same Time," *Regulation* (July-August 1981): 29-36.

9. Hyde, *Timber Supply*, 169-70.

Welfare is an industry, says CHARLES D. HOBBS. *Composed of 8 million workers distributing payments and services to 60 million beneficiaries, the industry is dominated by the federal government which establishes its goals. According to Hobbs, these goals include producing continuous growth of welfare expenditures at a pace greater than national economic growth; centralizing control and administration of welfare programs at the federal level; increasing the complexity of the welfare system; and creating jobs for people in the welfare industry.*

The welfare industry, founded in the 1930s, has achieved these goals to a remarkable degree, Hobbs admits, but as of 1981 the industry peaked out and now is declining. This is an extremely positive development, he maintains, and he makes several recommendations to hasten the welfare industry's fall.

18

The Decline and Fall of the Welfare Industry

CHARLES D. HOBBS

It is a remarkable coincidence of history that the first volume of Edward Gibbon's *Decline and Fall of the Roman Empire* was published in the same year as America's Declaration of Independence. Gibbon was thirty-nine, Thomas Jefferson only thirty-three, and I have often wondered which of these two young authors King George III—himself only thirty-eight—found the more disturbing.

I suspect it was Gibbon. It would be another century, after all, before Lord Acton would point out the worldwide impact of Jefferson's idea that governments derived "their just powers from the consent of the governed." I doubt whether King George III paid much attention to those words in 1776; Jefferson was still an obscure revolutionary in the colonies.

But the sardonic and scholarly Gibbon was a charter member of the king's political world: scion of a wealthy London family, member of Parliament, a commissioner of trade and plantations. His history of the latter days of Roman civilization was instantly acclaimed a masterpiece, although George's reaction to it may have been somewhat less enthusiastic. He is said to have paid an unexpected visit to Gibbon at a time when the historian was laboriously rewriting, from notes and memory, the *Decline and Fall* manuscript, the original having been inadvertently destroyed by his housekeeper. The king looked in and muttered, somewhat distractedly, "Always scribble scribble, eh, Mr. Gibbon?" So much for royal magnanimity!

But George was an intelligent and dedicated monarch, and he may well have seen in Gibbon's cataloging of the internal decay of Roman civilization the disturbing possibility that the British Empire would eventually suffer the same fate. Judged by our standards, Gibbon may have given too little weight to the economic and social factors behind Rome's downfall, but he certainly understood how bureaucratic processes perverted and rotted out Rome's noble institutions—the army, the traditional religion, and the government—leaving a hollow shell to be easily shattered by the barbarians.

There is a point to all this history. I chose the title and theme of this paper because of what I see as the astonishing parallel between the lesson Gibbon and Jefferson were teaching the English about bureaucracy and tyranny and the lesson we are currently struggling to learn about the tyranny of our own bureaucracies. Santayana wrote that "Those who do not remember the past are condemned to relive it." As we stand at what may well be a critical turning point in our national political history, it is as important to remember what Gibbon had to say about the death of Rome as it is to remember what Jefferson had to say about the birth of America.

I am going to address the welfare system and the welfare industry. The first is a familiar concept; the second, perhaps not so familiar. My thesis is that the United States has reached and passed its zenith as a welfare state. The zenith was Jimmy Carter's 1981 budget, and the turning point was Ronald Reagan's revision of that budget, followed by his success in achieving adoption of his own 1982 budget. The stage is now set for the total overhaul of the welfare system and the dismantling of the bloated and oppressive bureaucracy that I call the welfare industry.

Most of us know something about the welfare system, some of us think that we know a lot about it, but in truth the system is so massive and complex that no one can comprehend it in its entirety. We are all like the group of blind men, each trying to define an elephant by touching different parts of it.

The Conception of Welfare

The national welfare system, America's attempt to combat individual poverty on a national scale, is half a century old. It had its genesis in federal programs created to alleviate the severe, but supposedly temporary, poverty of the Great Depression. Conceived in crisis, these programs gave the federal government crisis powers to redistribute income. Those who had jobs were taxed to provide welfare to those in need because they had lost their jobs or pensions.

Initially *need* was defined as bare subsistence: benefits were small, in cash, and were intended to be temporary. A principal goal of the program was to restore the needy to self-sufficiency and thus to reduce future dependence on public assistance.

World War II ended the depression but the programs continued. Their crisis powers, with the crisis at an end, became tools of expansion. As the nation entered its long period of post-World War II prosperity, welfare managers found that by defining higher levels of need they could uncover more poverty, necessitating more welfare. Congress endorsed expansion proposals, reflecting the national mood that everyone should participate in prosperity. The original cash assistance programs grew and were augmented by new programs to meet more specific needs: for food, housing, job training, and health care. Each program begot its own bureaucracy, and as the bureaucracies competed and cooperated, they gradually took on the attributes of an industry, with product lines of welfare benefits, a market of the nation's needy, and a labor force of public and private welfare providers.

The goal of restoring self-sufficiency and reducing dependency on government aid was dropped, except as a public relations slogan. The bureaucrats and politicians who became leaders of the welfare industry realized that their self-interest was better served by more people becoming more dependent on government. They developed goals to benefit the industry rather than the poor, goals related to financial growth, system control, and organizational power. Financial growth could be achieved by regularly raising the levels and expanding the types of needs so that welfare expenditures could increase at a pace faster than general economic growth. System control could be achieved through centralization of policy development and administration and by making the programs so complex that only the industry could understand and interpret them. Organizational power could be achieved by substituting industry-provided services for cash assistance, which would require a larger and broader-based industry labor force.

In the early sixties these goals were sanctioned dramatically by Lyndon Johnson's declaration of a national war on poverty, a reaction to the growing social unrest that, in retrospect, was probably as much the product of despair at the dehumanizing aspects of the welfare system as it was an indicator of the need for more welfare. But war was war and the enemy—poverty—was engaged in the traditional manner: with more spending, more centralization, more complexity, and a larger army of social workers.

Since then welfare has grown at an alarming pace. In fiscal year 1981 welfare expenditures totaled $370 billion, up from less than $4 billion fifty years ago, and only $100 billion ten years ago. The welfare system and the industry it supports now consume 55 percent of the federal budget; 29 percent of all federal, state, and local government expenditures; and more than 12 percent of the gross national product (GNP). One of every four Americans currently receives some form of welfare, and 8 million Americans earn either all or part of their livelihood providing welfare benefits. In the past ten years, welfare spending has grown 1.27 times as fast as the GNP, 1.57 times as fast as the cost of living, and 1.89 times as fast as average wages. Uncontrolled growth in welfare spending, particularly in the last decade, has been the principal cause of federal budget deficits, which in turn have fueled increasing rates of inflation. Worst of all, growing numbers of American workers now find themselves subsidizing welfare recipients at higher standards of living than their own, while their own standards of living decline.

Control of the national welfare system is concentrated in the federal government. There are forty-seven major welfare programs; all but two are federal programs, and federal expenditures constitute 80 percent of total expenditures.

The ten most expensive welfare programs are:

Social Security (OASI)	$ 124.0 billion
Medicaid	$ 30.1 billion
Unemployment compensation	$ 28.1 billion
Medicare (hospital)	$ 27.1 billion
Veteran's benefits	$ 24.6 billion
Social Security (disability insurance)	$ 17.7 billion
Public Assistance Grants (AFDC)	$ 14.2 billion
Worker's compensation	$ 13.6 billion
Food Stamps	$ 11.6 billion
Supplemental Security Income (SSI)	$ 9.3 billion

Total expenditures for these ten programs in 1981 were $282.6 billion: 76 percent of total welfare expenditures.

Two decades—the thirties and the sixties—produced the bulk of the nation's welfare programs. Ten were enacted in the thirties and twenty more were enacted in the sixties. Only four were enacted before 1930, five between 1940 and 1960, and seven since 1970.

In recent years, however, legislation of welfare policies and programs has been accomplished principally through amendments to existing acts. Twenty-six of the forty-seven programs, including all of the ten most expensive, have been significantly expanded in the last ten years through amendments.

There is, as might be expected, a strong correlation between the age of a welfare program and the size of its expenditures. Eight of the ten most expensive programs were enacted before 1960.

There is also an interesting correlation between types of benefits and ages of the programs. A wide variety of different welfare programs may be summarized as cash-only, where the benefits are provided directly to the recipient as cash or other negotiable items such as food stamps, or as service-only, where the benefits are provided through the services of the government or a third party reimbursed by the government. Of the thirteen cash-only programs, seven were enacted prior to 1960, whereas eighteen of the twenty-three service-only programs have been enacted since 1960.

In summary, the programs making up the national welfare system are characterized by extremely high expenditure growth rates and rapid expansion of benefits and beneficiaries. The older the program, the more likely it is to be one of the most expensive; and the younger the program, the more likely it is to provide service instead of cash. Control of the programs and thus of the welfare system is almost totally in the hands of the federal government, centered mainly in the Department of Health and Human Services (HHS) and a few other departments. The welfare system can therefore be characterized as expansionary, complex, centralized, and tending toward the provision of services instead of cash.

A Welfare Industry

Coincident with the extraordinary growth of welfare expenditures has been the development of a national welfare industry, now composed of 8 million public and private workers distributing payments and services to 60 million beneficiares. The federal government, with its taxing power and authority to regulate the states, has provided the focus of control for this industry since the 1930s, establishing industry goals and imposing them on the development of the welfare system.

The first of these goals is to make welfare a growth industry; that is, to produce a continuous growth of welfare expenditures at a pace greater than national economic growth. The industry has rationalized this goal by defining poverty as need, and has met the goal by periodically escalating the levels of need defined in welfare law and regulation. Defining a higher level of need automatically makes more people eligible for welfare and, at the same time, creates pressures to raise benefits for those already eligible. In effect, need in the welfare industry has been made synonymous with demand, and control of how need is defined is control of production and industry growth.

The inherent subjectivity of any definition of need, and the industry's recognition that the definition could best be controlled for growth if it issued from a godhead, led to the second goal of centralizing control and administration of welfare programs at the federal level. This goal has been rationalized on the basis that there should be nationwide uniformity in welfare policies and benefits, and that the states cannot provide such uniformity. For years the national *oracle* for determining nationwide need has been housed in HHS, which used to be the Department of Health, Education, and Welfare (HEW), and every major revision of welfare law has used federally defined need as a rationale for increasing federal control of policy and administration.

The third goal of the welfare industry is to make the welfare system increasingly complex, for complexity eases the task of system control and expansion in the face of fluctuating political pressures. With federal laws governing forty-six of the forty-seven welfare programs, the only potential deterrent to excessive growth is an informed Congress responding to public dissatisfaction with welfare costs. By complicating the design of welfare programs the industry has made the system extremely difficult for Congress to understand. Moreover, most members of Congress have been reluctant to become experts on welfare because of the political unpopularity of welfare in the public eye. As a result, Congress has come to rely on industry experts to draft welfare legislation, and the experts have furthered their own and the industry's interests by fostering complexity.

The fourth goal of the welfare industry is to create jobs for people in the industry. Emphasis on this goal in the past fifteen years has resulted in an explosive increase in service programs as compared to programs providing cash assistance. The rationalization for service instead of cash is that poor people do not spend money intelligently and that it is better for society if the government spends it for them. By promoting service programs, the industry has taken direct control of a greater proportion of welfare expenditures, has increased industry job opportunities, and has made itself the principal market for a number of service trades.

These four industry goals have been met to a remarkable degree: expenditures have consistently grown faster than the pace of the economy; all but two of the forty-seven programs are controlled by the federal government; interactions between these programs are so complex that no one—not even the industry itself—can calculate their interrelated effects; and industry employment has expanded to the point where the government is a monopsony to several welfare-related service trades, particularly those providing health care.

These four industry goals have been met to a remarkable degree: expenditures have consistently grown faster than the pace of the economy; all but two of the forty-seven programs are controlled by the federal government; interactions between these programs are so complex that no one—not even the industry itself—can calculate their interrelated effects; and industry employment has expanded to the point where the government is a monopsony to several welfare-related service trades, particularly those providing health care.

Yet these trends have not been popular. Public dissatisfaction with welfare policies and the size and cost of the programs has made reform of the welfare mess a perennial political issue. Opinion surveys indicate public desire for reforms to eliminate cheaters, cut costs, provide adequate aid to those who cannot work, require work of those who can, and simplify the distribution of benefits. Yet every attempt at national reform either has not been enacted or has resulted in even faster growth and higher costs, because the welfare industry, controlling the program design and evaluation process through the federal bureaucracy, has altered reform concepts to meet its own expansionary goals.

Seeking a National Guaranteed Income

For the past fifteen years the welfare industry has actively sought enactment of a national guaranteed-income policy. Although in practice the system provides benefits to anyone "in need," the federal government has never had the authority to set system-wide, uniform benefit levels. Assignment of this authority to federal agencies would essentially complete the industry's goal of centralization of the welfare system.

Two concepts have been developed to implement a guaranteed income policy. The first is the concept of family allowances—payments based only on family size and not determined by need. Family allowances were first conceived as a stimulant to population growth by France in 1932, and currently Canada and most European nations have family allowance plans. The foremost American proponent of this concept is Daniel Moynihan. As a means of implementing a guaranteed income policy, the concept of family allowances is simple and efficient. But as a means of redistributing wealth, the concept has proven politically unacceptable since it pays the same amounts to rich and poor alike.

The second concept is the negative income tax, originally proposed by economist Milton Friedman in the 1940s. In this concept the government takes taxes from people with incomes above a certain level, just as it does now, but pays subsidies as negative taxes to people with incomes below that level.

Let me illustrate this concept, since I believe that, despite a certain amount of publicity, it has not yet achieved wide understanding.

Assume a family has income tax exemptions and deductions totaling $10,000. If that family has a gross income of $10,000, its exemptions and deductions just offset its income. It has a zero taxable income and therefore pays no income tax. If its gross income is greater than $10,000, it pays income tax on a graduated scale—the higher the income, the higher the percentage of income represented by the tax. If its income is less than $10,000, it has what Friedman calls a *negative income*, which is currently disregarded by the tax system. That is the way things now work.

Under Friedman's negative income tax scheme, the family with $10,000 in allowable exemptions and deductions, but less than $10,000 in gross income, would be paid a part of the difference by the government. If gross income were $5,000, and the negative tax rate were 50 percent, the government would pay the family $2,500, bringing its total spendable income to $7,500. If the family had no income, the government would pay $5,000, which would represent a guaranteed minimum income.

Friedman stressed the difference between the break-even income, in this case $10,000, at which the family neither pays taxes nor receives a subsidy and the minimum guaranteed income, in this case half that amount, or $5,000. He felt it essential to retain a difference between these two in order to preserve an incentive for low-income families to earn additional income.

Friedman envisioned the replacement of all existing welfare programs by the negative income tax. He also proposed transferring the administration of the negative income, tax-based welfare system to the Internal Revenue Service (IRS), a move calculated to destroy existing federal and state welfare bureaucracies.

In assessing these two concepts the welfare industry was faced with a Hobson's choice: a family allowance program would greatly expand industry scope and power but was politically untenable, while a politically appealing negative income tax system would reduce the industry itself to a handful of tax accountants.

The dilemma was solved by publicly endorsing the negative income tax concept and then altering it severely to conform to industry goals, in an impressive application of the industry-controlled program-design process. The process produced a series of conceptually identical reform proposals: the first, a guaranteed-income proposal prepared for and rejected by the Johnson administration; the second, the Nixon-Ford Family Assistance Plan; and, finally, the Carter Welfare Reform Plan in its several versions.

Friedman's original conception of the negative income tax was in consonance with only one of the industry's goals—system expansion—and partially supported another—centralization—although centralizing welfare administration in the IRS was hardly the industry's idea of heaven. The industry's program designers adapted Friedman's concept for the Johnson administration by restoring administrative control to HEW—thus preserving the welfare bureaucracy—and by limiting application of the negative income tax concept to only two welfare programs—Aid to Families with Dependent Children (AFDC) and what is now Supplemental Security Income (SSI)—leaving all of the other programs intact and thus salvaging the goals of system complexity and industry employment.

When the Johnson administration rejected the proposal, the industry added job-training and child-care provisions—to increase industry employment—and sold it to the Nixon administration, where it became the Nixon Family Assistance Plan. Although this plan twice failed to pass Congress, the industry further embellished it with earned income credits—to further expand the welfare population—and with guarantees of federal jobs for welfare recipients—to further increase industry employment. It then reappeared as the Carter Welfare Reform Plan.

Despite the reform rhetoric in which these plans were wrapped, neither was original and neither met the reform desires of the public. Moreover, both are essentially the same plan, a plan contrived by the welfare industry to make the negative income tax concept fit its goals.

Welfare costs cannot be controlled by reform of one or a few programs, even if the industry can be kept from influencing design of the reform, because of the way welfare programs overlap and provide duplicative benefits. Adding new recipients to one program usually does not affect their eligibility for others. Moreover, what might seem to be a reasonably modest benefit from a single program becomes part of an unexpectedly generous, and costly, benefit package when the combined effects of all programs are calculated.

For example, a single-parent family with two children, defined by the government as poor, is theoretically eligible for twenty-five national welfare programs, and selective participation in a dozen or so of them can raise the value of welfare benefits to four or five times the value of the AFDC cash payments that are usually thought of as welfare. Among the programs for which such a family would be eligible are Medicaid; food stamps; free nutritional supplements for mothers and infants; free school and summer meals for school-aged children; low-rent housing; free child care; family planning and other social services; legal aid; job training and placement; earned income tax credits; and low-income energy assistance. If the parent gets a job, chances are the family will remain eligible for all of these programs, including AFDC payments. Taking away the family's AFDC payments will not affect its eligibility for the other programs and in some cases will actually increase the benefits from them.

Compounding of benefits through overlapping programs is the major cause of the high welfare cost growth rate. Many welfare families are better off financially by their participation in several programs than are the families of workers whose taxes pay for the welfare.

As long ago as 1969 the Congressional Research Service demonstrated that a welfare family in Portland, Oregon, consisting of a mother and four children, could theoretically compound $2,808 in AFDC cash payments with benefits of fourteen other programs for a total untaxed income of $13,799, equal to a worker's before-tax income of $16,500. Given the growth of welfare benefits since 1969, current benefits to the same family would be twice as high. In terms of programs, a low-income family consisting of a mother and two children, one an infant and the other in school, is theoretically eligible, as I have said, for twenty-five welfare programs. Adding a father to the family raises the number of programs to twenty-eight. Then, adding a teen-aged child and a grandfather, the family becomes theoretically eligible for thirty-eight programs.

Beyond a certain point such theoretical calculations only serve to point up the absurd complexities of the welfare system. Here, for example, is a family of nine that could theoretically qualify for forty-two programs. It consists of an alcoholic Indian veteran, simultaneously in job training and going to college, who lives in New York City with his 75-year-old retired father, his 60-year-old work-disabled mother, his disabled coal-miner brother (now on sick leave from a railroad job), his recently unemployed sister-in-law, and his mentally retarded Cuban refugee wife and their three children, one an infant hemophiliac, one a ten-year-old junkie, and the third a teen-aged school dropout. How's that for social engineering!

While my example is absurd, it is not absurd to envision two-generation families benefiting simultaneously from fifteen or more programs and three-generation families benefiting from twenty or more programs. Given the growth rates of total welfare expenditures as compared with the relatively much smaller increases in welfare population, we can only conclude that this degree of overlap is, in fact, more the rule than the exception. Unfortunately, it has not been measured, because the industry—the source of all the data—does not want to measure it.

Forcing workers to subsidize welfare recipients at higher standards of living than their own is the fatal paradox and ultimate absurdity of the wealth redistribution theory. The paradox cannot be solved by adding welfare to the incomes of more workers, as Nixon and Carter proposed, because as long as welfare costs grow faster than wages, the welfare burden on all workers, including those receiving welfare, will increase.

Reagan: Industry Critic

The costs and inequities of the welfare system are products of the policies and programs of the welfare industry. Ronald Reagan's election to the presidency and a conservative shift in the Congress, both due in large measure to public dissatisfaction with government size and growth, have set the stage for the first major challenge to the aspirations of the industry. Among national political leaders, Reagan has been the most consistent and severe critic of federalized welfare. As governor of California he was able, in the early seventies, actually to retard welfare growth for a few years in that state, despite the intense, but somewhat disjointed, opposition of a surprised welfare industry. His California reform program was a blend of budget limitations, benefit increases for the truly needy, eligibility and benefit restrictions on the not-so-needy, and administrative controls on system operations, bolstered to a generally unrecognized degree by his personal campaign to convince people that welfare was an unsatisfactory substitute for a productive life.

As president, Reagan has adopted a similar approach to constraining welfare growth, but up to now he has only scratched the surface of what can be done to reduce wasteful welfare spending and unnecessary dependency. True welfare reform must encompass the entire system, and must start with a restructuring of the industry to remove the incentives for growth, complexity, and centralization that have operated in the past.

The principles for reform may be stated most simply as the reverse of the industry's own goals:

1. *Reverse the pattern of welfare expenditure growth.* The most important goal of welfare reform must be to restore the original objective of welfare—to reduce dependency on government. Given the ridiculous current welfare spending levels—$8,000 per year for every man, woman, and child defined as poor by industry statisticians—the first step to reducing dependency is eliminating unnecessary spending. This can be

accomplished by identifying and then eliminating the rampant duplications of benefits among the welfare programs. I estimate that these duplications represent at least 20 percent, and perhaps as much as 50 percent, of all welfare spending. A smaller but significant portion of welfare expenditures—I estimate 5 percent to 15 percent—goes to those who are not needy in any commonly accepted sense of that term. Thus it is feasible to cut at least 50 percent of current government welfare expenditures without reducing benefits to below the levels of need set by federal and state governments.

2. *Reduce the number of welfare workers.* By encouraging dependency, the welfare system discourages productivity. Thus, the efforts of most welfare industry workers actually decrease national productivity. In recent years the growth of welfare industry employment has been due mainly to the expansion of service programs, in which either government employees or government-paid tradesmen provide services to welfare recipients. An effective way to reduce industry employment is to cash out all service programs, paying the money for the services directly to the recipients and letting them choose and pay for, or provide for themselves, the services they desire. There is ample evidence that welfare recipients, as individuals, spend money at least as wisely as other people; and there is also evidence that organizations paid by the government to serve welfare recipients are often wasteful and corrupt. The cashing out of service programs would put more money and more responsibility for choice in the hands of the welfare recipients, making the extent of welfare benefits clearer to the public. It would also substantially reduce the buying power of the welfare industry, and thus its monopsonistic influence over health care and other welfare-related service trades.

3. *Simplify the welfare system.* The complexity of the welfare system contributes heavily to its unnecessary costs and inequities. Complexity also supports industry control, because no one can understand the system well enough to criticize it effectively. The cashing out of all service programs would be the first step to simplification. The next step would be the amalgamation of all welfare programs into one that is based on need and incorporates a financial work incentive. Friedman's original negative income tax is the simplest and most logical concept for such a program, but the design for its implementation must be kept away from the industry. Simplification through a negative income tax program would eliminate the proliferation of overlapping benefits and make welfare administration a relatively inexpensive and routine task. Friedman himself has best summarized the advantages of a pure negative income tax welfare system:

> 1. It would help the poor in the most direct way possible.
> 2. It would treat them as responsible individuals, not as incompetent wards of the state.

3. It would give them an incentive to help themselves.
4. It would cost less than present programs yet help the poor more.
5. It would eliminate almost entirely the cumbrous welfare bureaucracy running the present programs.
6. It could not be used as a political slush fund, as so many current programs—notably in the "war on poverty"—can be and have been used.

4. *Decentralize control of the welfare system.* This is the most important and difficult step. As long as welfare is centrally controlled within the federal government, the system will be designed and operated to benefit the welfare industry. Decentralization of control and administration, under only the most general guidelines established only by Congress, is essential to welfare reform. Decentralization can be accomplished by the transfer of taxing authority for welfare payments to the states, with federal encouragement to the states to further decentralize administration to the local level, so that the industry will be prevented from rebuilding the existing system through federal and state bureaucracies. One way to decentralize the welfare system would be through private, cooperative welfare assistance corporations, a concept I developed a dozen years ago. The welfare assistance corporations would be profit-making, community-based enterprises with the legal requirement and proprietary right to provide, on behalf of the government, for the welfare needs of its member-stockholders who are welfare recipients. As welfare providers, the corporations would adopt the payment and service schedules of the government, but subject to modification upon vote of the welfare recipient member-stockholders. They would receive from the government the standard grant and proportionate share of administrative and service funds for each eligible recipient-member, plus a profit bonus for each member who becomes ineligible by taking and holding a job. In all other respects, they would operate as normal corporations under the laws of the states in which they were formed. One of the principal objectives of the welfare assistance corporations would be to place their member-stockholders in permanent jobs by a combination of outside job placement and inside job creation. The second principal objective would be to create sources of capital income for their member-stockholders through dividends and stock-value increases. Profits could be made both from successful product and business development and from short-term investment of welfare funds, prior to their distribution as individual grants. The concept is simple; but implementing it will be difficult, especially since it contradicts the paternalistic welfare philosophy and practice of the past fifty years.

I hope I have given you some insight into why and how the welfare industry must be dismantled, as well as expressing my optimistic belief that it will indeed decline and fall. The welfare system has failed those who need it and those who pay for it. Some observers, myself among them, believe that much of our nation's violence can be attributed to the inherent inequities and unmet expectations associated with massive wealth redistribution. Big government is a vindictive tax collector, an oppressive benefactor, and never a friend.

The only real beneficiary of the welfare system has been the welfare industry. And it is the industry that must be dissolved if welfare is ever to be refocused on its true purpose: to encourage those who can to help themselves, and to help those, and only those, who cannot.

How do we assure that the future of private enterprise will be a good one? That is the question posed by JAMES ROUSE, *and he deals with it specifically in relation to the problems of the urban environment. To provide decent housing, jobs, and health care for the poor in an era when government is pulling back, we need new processes and institutions, and new attitudes of inventiveness, creativity, and resolve.*

Rouse points to several examples of people coming together to creatively combat urban problems outside the realm of government. He calls for increased corporate giving, at least to the 5-percent-of-profits level traditionally allowed as a tax deduction. He also singles out Aetna Life and Casualty, Control Data Corporation, and Chicago's South Shore Bank as examples of companies using their unique capacities to solve social problems in ways consistent with good business.

The exciting, creative future of private enterprise, Rouse maintains, lies in using money, management, and manpower to make our society work better.

19

New Initiatives for the Urban Environment

JAMES W. ROUSE

The title of this volume is impressive: *The Future of Private Enterprise*. It raises a question about whether that future is threatened, as it is in France or Sweden; or has disappeared, as it has in much of the world; or is held in absolute derision, as it is in the developing nations. The more I travel through the world, the more I see that private enterprise is a tiny island and the United States is the biggest part of that tiny island.

It would not be out of order to raise the issue as another question: How do we assure that the future of private enterprise will be a good one? Or perhaps the real question is: Can private enterprise play a new and expanding role in fulfilling the hopes of our society and in advancing our civilization?

The sharp change in government responsibilities for meeting the needs of our society has come on us so suddenly and so surprisingly that we really stand shaken as a society today. I would hope that private enterprise will not only take up the slack that is left by government withdrawal from many programs, but that it will produce new creative initiatives beyond anything we have known in our society in the past.

Although the changed role of government has its most dramatic expression in what we have seen since President Reagan took office, it really did not begin there. For me, the landmark event was the passage of Proposition 13 in California (that was surprising to most people, I think) followed by a wave of tax and spending limitation legislation all across the country, in legislatures and city and county governments. It amounts to a statement that we have made as a society: We no longer are willing to accept government in the role that it has performed to an increasing degree over the past fifty years.

We have been made aware of the cutbacks in programs of enormous importance to people in cities, counties, and states; layoffs in jobs of all kinds; reductions and elimination of the programs of voluntary agencies. We have only seen the beginning of it. There are going to be cutbacks of programs that have lived substantially with government support in health, education, culture, and human needs. It is severe; it is painful. But it seems perfectly clear that it is what our society says is necessary.

I should confess where I stand in this. My political and ideological commitment was on the other side in the last election, and is very much on the other side of what is happening now in government. I am persuaded now, however, that we have become too dependent on government, too accustomed to saying, "Let George do it." George is always government—federal, state, or local. Bit by bit, we have accumulated this enormous bureaucracy, waste, and fluff in government.

The time had clearly come for a pruning and a cleansing of government. We simply could not go on this way. We had to find new ways, although it has taken a more painful pruning than we would have liked to have seen. There is no doubt that some cuts will be too deep, that programs will be eliminated that we will regret. But we had to do it. There was no other way of getting back to where we have to start from.

Enormous compassion is needed while we are in this process. But we also need an awakening, too. Private enterprise, not simply business but individuals and voluntary agencies, is being shocked and awakened—I hope for a new purpose.

I compare this situation with the riots of 1968. They were cruel, unjust, irrational, and in many respects stupid. But they were the most creative force that has ever hit the American city. The riots awakened business, politicians, individuals like you and me to the frustration, the oppression, the furor of the people who lived in the jungles of our cities without hope and without the possibility of participating in the American system in a way that they had a right to expect.

The riots did not die. They have had a cumulative and continuing impact in corporate board rooms, in political caucuses, in the attitudes of individuals. The riots transformed—although not adequately—the attitude toward black people in this country. It was a major transformation. We hope now that this abrupt and sudden reversal of the role of government expresses a new determination of people to deal with the situation we face with new creativity, new energy, and a new commitment—not simply by contributing a little more money.

It cannot be in America that we have decided to settle for a second-class civilization. It cannot be that we are opting for less support for health care, less concern for the poor, less support for the arts.

We have to believe that this is a great civilization, a growing civilization, and that, within the total resources of this country in wealth and in manpower, we have the capacity to move forward to greater heights and to a greater sense of serving human needs.

To do this, we must explore our resources in new ways; invent new processes; create new institutions; and find new ways to serve as individuals, as voluntary agencies, and particularly as businesses. We need a new attitude of inventiveness, creativity, and resolve. This can be an exhilarating period as we dig into ourselves, discovering self-reliance and new capacities as businesses and as individuals.

The spirit it calls for will be unique. We are accustomed to dealing with problems by analyzing them, defining them, developing programs, appropriating money, hiring people, and creating organizations. That is all gone. Now what is called for are personal, small-scale responses of the kind we have not been accustomed to giving.

Let me illustrate with several examples. One day on the "Today Show," Governor James Hunt of North Carolina explained how, every Monday morning, he volunteers for one hour as a tutor in a public school.

In Lynchburg, Virginia, the churches created a program in which real-estate agents, architects, merchants, and bankers every Saturday chop up trees for firewood and deliver it to the homes of 250 poor families for heating and cooking. Think of what happens when a banker has sawed up wood and delivered it to a poor family. Think of the relationship it establishes, the knowledge the banker develops of what is happening in that family.

In Washington, a little church set out to do something about housing for the poor. They asked me at that time what they ought to do and I said, "You can't do anything about it. It's too big and you're too small. There's no way you can deal rationally with it." Thank goodness they ignored that wisdom and went ahead anyway. They acquired two buildings that were once very fine apartments in the Adams-Morgan area of Washington—the Ritz and the Mozart—one had sixty units, the other, thirty.

These were not professional people or social workers. They did not know about housing, they only knew about caring for the poor. They arranged to get the money to buy the two buildings, then called for volunteers to help rehabilitate them. The day the group acquired the buildings, they were given notice of 942 violations of the Washington, D.C., housing code. The buildings had no front doors, mailboxes were ripped out of the wall, and the stench was so dreadful that I gagged when I walked in. The stench was from the elevator shafts, where the tenants had thrown the garbage, frustrated because the elevators did not work.

Three years and 50,000 volunteer-hours later, there was not a smell in those buildings. They were fit, livable, and decent. Jubilee Housing, as it came to be known, then acquired a third building, the Sorento, with thirty-two units, where the landlord had provided no heat for two years. Then Jubilee acquired a fourth, fifth, and sixth apartment building.

The volunteers kept working with these people, then the tenants began to work. Now, in order to stay, tenants have to work five hours a week on the building. Tenants handle the management and maintenance, vote on who lives in the buildings, and are now taking over ownership. No matter how bad the housing, the greatest fear of the poor is eviction, for they think, "Where in the world am I going to go?" Now that fear has been removed.

Jubilee Housing gradually developed support from businesses and professions in Washington. Price Waterhouse does the auditing; Jim Clark, president of the Hyman Construction Co., supervises the rehabilitation work. Businesses participate in a Committee of Support.

Jubilee has created Columbia Road Health Services to work with these people. It created the Committee of Compassion where nine of these poor people and one staff person listen to the individual needs of the tenants.

Jubilee has developed a group of supporters. As a supporter, you agree to pay $2 to $10 a week in response to a call, and you will not get a call more than once a week. But if you agree to $10 a week, you cannot just give $520 at once. You've got to give it each time one of those requests comes in. They now have over one hundred supporters giving more than $3,000 a month that the poor distribute to meet their needs.

Now these volunteers have started Jubilee Jobs. They did not know what they were doing at first, but began calling people about jobs. In four weeks, they placed thirty-one people in jobs in Washington.

I said, "How can this be? Why haven't these people gotten jobs earlier?" The answer was, "Nobody is interested in working on the employment of someone whose income is $10,000 a year or less. All that happens to these unemployed people is that they go in and are told to fill out an application. They have filled out applications so many times, they have stopped looking. They do not know where to go."

There are enormous opportunities for business, for individuals, for all of us to work in new ways to deal with these acute social problems.

In Baltimore, Mayor William Donald Schaefer started Blue Chip-in when the city lost over $3 million. Bernard C. Trueschler, chairman of the Baltimore Gas and Electric Company, and George McGowan, president, and other businesspeople in Baltimore stepped in and have taken over individual programs, making up for a half million dollars. That is just the tip. We have got to multiply that twenty times before we are through.

These illustrations are only an example of what has to be legitimately expected and performed by private enterprise if our society and our civilization are to move forward. Almost any illustration I could give of business response would be from local companies—a utility company, a merchant, a bank, a small business. By and large, the big national corporations do not understand the American city or the people who live in it; they are indifferent to their needs. Our corporations separate their top management from any real understanding or empathy with the people who live in our cities. This is systematic rather than an act of personal perversity on the part of American corporate leaders. Business in America is run for profits, for growth stock; you've got to increase the earnings. Managers are there for five or six years and then move on. Our major business corporations are unready for the challenge and response America calls for.

Look at corporate giving. The government permits any business corporation to give 5 percent of its net earnings to charity and deduct it as an expense. As a result, if a company gives $100,000 the federal government pays 50 percent of it and business pays 50 percent. Government thus holds out to the American business corporation the most remarkable challenge grant in our society. It says, "Give whatever you want, to any charity you want, and we'll match it." That's an extraordinary challenge grant. What's the result? American corporations give not 5 percent but less than 0.8 percent to charity.

When Lyndon B. Johnson was president, he appeared in Minneapolis at a fund raiser when the city was forming a Five Percent Club. What he said there was the truth: "It's obvious that you men in business have greater confidence in the government's ability to run these things than to run them yourselves, because if you didn't, you would take advantage of this challenge grant and contribute the full 5 percent. You give less than 0.8 percent, and it may be much less."

Some cities—Minneapolis, Louisville, and most recently, Baltimore—have formed Five Percent Clubs; that's an important illustration of what needs to occur.

In Baltimore, there are now twenty-three member companies of the Five Percent Club; in Minneapolis, forty-five; and in Louisville, just under forty. Very few of these companies are public corporations—probably only two in Baltimore, and maybe three in Minneapolis. They are privately owned companies where the owner, manager, and president do not have to reckon with an increase in earnings, or with growth stock, or with a structure that corporate managers think makes it difficult to contribute as much as 5 percent. There are public corporations that do not give their quota. The Dayton-Hudson Co., one of the great retailers in America, for thirty-five years has contributed 5 percent of earnings before taxes to charity. Its profits grow; it is one of the most successful retailers in America. If it can do it, there is no reason why every other major retailer cannot do it.

In New York there is a remarkable 75-year-old lawyer who started a personal campaign four years ago by filing proxy statements before annual meetings of public corporations, calling for a commitment to give 5 percent of earnings to charity.

When he got more than 3 percent of the stockholders to vote for it, then he could put the proxy back on the ballot the following year. In 90 percent of the cases where it has gone to a vote, he has gotten more than 3 percent of the shareholders.

He also sat down with management and attempted to negotiate an increase in annual giving. I went to see him one day in New York. I read all of his reports. The companies he's visited gave $1.9 million one year, $2.6 million the next year. I said, "Larry, it looks to me like you have personally increased corporate giving in America by about $500 million in the last two or three years."

He said, "No, it's not quite that big, but I do think it's over $350 million."

That is one man.

What we need in America now is a national campaign to increase corporate giving, to make it so fashionable, so important, so much of a part of belonging in the corporate system that you would be ashamed to be the head of a corporation that is not giving 2, 3, and then 5 percent of net earnings before taxes. If the business corporations in America gave what they have a right to give, charitable giving would increase by $9 billion a year.

In the last session of the Senate, when they were reducing taxes and going through a list of bounties to corporations, they increased that 5 percent to 10 percent. It seemed an odd thing to do when the total giving is only 0.8 percent, but maybe it was to call attention to this.

Business has a much larger role; it has to find out how to relate its capacity to public need.

The Jubilee Housing support group is an illustration of businesses and professions in Washington using their capacity to meet public need. The Aetna Life and Casualty Co., under John H. Filer, has used its lending power in remarkable ways for social purposes in America.

I recently sat beside William Norris, the head of Control Data, in a meeting of the American Enterprise Institute. Control Data is engaged in creative enterprises across this country to use its capacity for the public interest: for education programs for small farmers, on Indian reservations, for small tribes in Alaska. They are creatively using the strength and technical capacity of Control Data to affect the American system.

A remarkable man named Ron Gryzwinski, chairman of the South Shore Bank in Chicago, was an IBM salesman who went to work for a bank and became its general manager. He finally took a year off to go to the University of Chicago to study how a bank could really work in a community. He raised $4 million and looked for a bank that was losing deposits and was in a neighborhood going from white to black. He found both in the South Shore, an area with a population of 80,000, which had gone from 90 percent white to 90 percent black with a bank whose deposits had fallen from $80 million to $42 million. He bought it and now it has $92 million in deposits and a system of community development loans that are helping the neighborhood.

Banks can find new roles if they recognize this responsibility in our society. "George" is not going to do anymore. If we are going to get the government off our back, we have got to take on responsibilities ourselves.

In addition to increasing its charitable contributions, business needs to bring its management capability, its people, and its resources to serve public needs. The business corporation does not exist in America by some arrogant right. The business corporation exists because society licensed it to exist to meet social needs.

Profit is not properly understood as the purpose of business. Profit is the reward business receives for rendering an important service; the bottom line belongs at the bottom. When it becomes the top line, that business gets off the track.

The way to find new opportunities in business is to discover the needs and yearnings of people. The way to prosper in business is to do that extremely well. That is when the business system functions as a part of the American democratic system and as a part of a free society.

Baltimore's mayor has sparked an important beginning with his Blue Chip-in. Businesses need to multiply that, not to feel heroic about what they have done, but to get a taste of what their future responsibility is. Business needs to become involved in education, in crime prevention, in counseling, in transportation, in health, and with the poor. This is an exciting, creative future for the free enterprise system in our society. We need to find ways to give the resources—in money, organization, manpower, and management—to make our society work better.

Two years ago, my wife and I were part of a five-member bilateral commission to Russia. Most people who make trips to Russia come back with dreadful experiences; that is understandable because it is not much of a country.

But we had a marvelous experience because we were with three Russians in a small group. One of our group was the former mayor of Wilmington, Delaware, who arrived in New York to get on the plane with a ukelele under his arm. On those long trips in a small bus, Tom Maloney would take out his ukelele and sing. He was an energetic and colorful Irishman, and he had the Russians singing, "Yankee Doodle Dandy" and "God Bless America."

We had a marvelous trip. We came to know each other well during our ten days together. We got to the point where we could talk freely about our systems. Two of the Russians were members of the Communist Party. We had looked at Communist projects on the trip. They were poorly planned, poorly built, and poorly managed. Everywhere we went in Russia there was an indifference, a lack of initiative, a lack of creativity, a lack of service, a dumbness about the country.

They realized this, too. One of them said, "The problem with our country is that every Russian is born with a silver spoon in his mouth. He knows that he is going to have a job. He knows he is going to be educated. He knows his health is going to be cared for. He knows he is going to have housing and he knows he is going to be taken care of in his old age. There are no incentives in our system."

This was a very remarkable statement. Then he said, "But we do not have your poverty. We are willing to trade the freedom, and the better life that we might have had in exchange for that."

We would not be willing to do that. I think it is a bad trade. But his words left me asking, "Can it be that the strength, the energy, the creativity, and the potential of the free enterprise system cannot match what the Communist system does? Isn't it possible to shape and organize the resources and manpower and capability we have in this country to meet these needs instead of accepting them as an eternal part of the way we live?"

I think we are launched on a new era of performance by individuals, by small voluntary agencies, by little businesses, by big businesses. It can be an enormous turning point in the history of the world if we are able to do it. We have already seen an enormous turning point in our times. We have seen the Communist revolution in China—through tyranny—create the most gigantic social revolution in twenty-five years. It ought to be easier for us to turn this country around through our government, to reorganize what we can do in such a way that we make this free enterprise system effective.

I do not believe in threats. But it is not unreasonable to look at the other side. If we fail to respond, if we allow these human needs to drift through the grate, if we allow ourselves to become a second-class society, business will have thrown out the free enterprise system. There will be no confidence left in the profit system, the market system, or the business system. I do not believe it is true that there is enormous confidence today in business. I do not think most people understand profits. People have developed a skepticism, a disbelief, a disinterest. This can be turned around; the business community can generate confidence and belief in the business system, which is an absolutely essential part of democratic society. No place matches the marketplace to demonstrate the operation of a democratic society. In the marketplace, the ballot is cast every minute of every day, every time that cash register rings. People are saying what they are willing to buy; what they do not want, they reject.

We would lose enormously in this country if we ever let private enterprise fade away. I do not think we will, but I think we ought to recognize the stakes that we are dealing with in this country today as we call for new creativity, new initiatives, new spirit, new commitment, new sacrifice on the part of businesspeople and their corporations, big and small, to respond to this dramatic need.

SECTION V
Solutions to Problems of Private Enterprise

It is, perhaps, overly optimistic to speak of solutions in relation to private enterprise. Solutions suggest a certain finality and concreteness not really to be found in the dynamic environment promoted by private enterprise and democracy.

Still, it is appropriate to speak of overcoming the ills that have beset private enterprise in recent years and of effectively dealing with our society's specific problem areas. This task is undertaken by the authors of this book's final section.

Herbert Stein points the way toward "Balancing Economic Growth and Income Distribution." Our society demands both improvement in the overall standard of living and compassion for those who cannot share in general prosperity. These goals are not incompatible, Stein maintains, if we will maintain greater economic stability, reduce federal deficits, remove regulations that interfere with productivity, and return more responsibility to the local level.

Karl Bays deals with the specific problem of health-care costs. While underlining the tremendous success enjoyed by America's health-care system, he asks: Can we continue to afford such success? We can, he concludes, if competition is allowed to do battle with health-care costs.

The broad area of social problems is addressed by William J. Baroody. In this area, he maintains, solutions can be found not by finding new funding sources for old social programs, but by inventing new ways to provide social services. The solutions lie in our heritage of people helping people.

Finally, Paul McCracken offers means for "Restoring Our Prosperity." He assesses the Reagan administration's efforts in this regard against a prosperity standard of 5 percent unemployment, 2 percent inflation, and growth in real income of 25 to 30 percent per decade. McCracken finds we have the best chance in a decade of meeting these measures.

The relationship between economic growth and income redistribution has always been a fundamental consideration of economics but has special relevance at this historical juncture. HERBERT STEIN *suggests that while these objectives are not wholly incompatible, priorities are in need of reassessment. With the standard of living at historical highs and the percentage of the American population in economic poverty at a historic low, Stein suggests it is appropriate to avoid retrogression in the fight against poverty and to seek efficiency in government programs devoted to the plight of the poor.*

Since economic growth has deteriorated over the past decade, however, Stein maintains that progress in this dimension must be elevated in terms of its national priority. The resources to stimulate growth need not come from the poor, however, but from the vast reservoir of resources devoted to consumption by the nonpoor.

The solutions, according to Stein, have to do with greater economic stability related to inflation and unemployment, reduction of budget deficits, and removal of regulations that interfere with productivity and impinge on the poor. He also advocates a return of more responsibility to the community from the federal government, and changes in popular attitudes toward fundamental issues like work and efficiency. The failure of government programs has shown that results are best achieved privately and individually.

20

Balancing Economic Growth and Income Distribution

HERBERT STEIN

The relation between income redistribution and growth is an eternal subject in economics and social policy and is of unusual relevance at this particular moment. The period from 1929 through 1973 was one in which economic growth, the increase in the economy's capacity to produce, was more or less taken for granted. During that period, economists were preoccupied with the question: How might our country's capacity to produce be used? We took for granted that the capacity to produce would rise at an entirely satisfactory rate. By the 1960s, economists and government officials seemed to think that we had licked the problem of bringing the economy to operate at its full potential.

Economists looked around for new worlds to conquer. Walter Heller, chairman of the Council of Economic Advisers during the Kennedy and Johnson administration, reports that after they got their famous tax cuts through Congress, the Kennedy-Johnson economists thought they had solved the problem of economic stabilization, and they wanted to move on to something else. They decided they would concentrate on the problem of eliminating poverty. Had they succeeded, there would have been little left for the rest of us to do. But we are now at a turning point.

Usually, I am very suspicious of the constant identification of turning points. Every time we elect a new president we seem to think we have reached one of the great turning points of history. These turning points end up being only wiggles. At this moment, I believe, there is a tendency to think that the growth problem has been underestimated and that we need to turn our attention from the problem of income redistribution to the problem of growth, and do this in a quite radical and wholehearted way. There seems to be some feeling that we can now disregard the problem of income redistribution, by whatever definition, and emphasize overwhelmingly the problem of speeding up the growth of the economy. As I will indicate later in this paper, I think such a position is neither satisfactory nor sufficient. It is not sufficient because we conservatives need to find a new, reasonable balance between these objectives. Finding that balance will be important for the country, it will be important for the Reagan administration, and it will be important for the conservative movement.

If the problem is as simple as the question, Are income redistribution and growth compatible? I can answer that in a word: Yes! Of course, you can phrase the question differently; you can ask whether maximum income redistribution and maximum economic growth are compatible. The answer to that is no, if by maximum income redistribution you mean redistributing income to a condition in which everyone's income is equal—that is not compatible with maximum growth of the economy. But if you ask whether it is possible both to affect the distribution of income in a way that will make it more equal than it would otherwise be in a free market, and at the same time to have a fairly substantial rate of economic growth—the answer is yes, both analytically and historically. After all, we have been through a period of very rapid economic growth. Certainly up to 1973 one would have said that economic growth in the United States was proceeding at a quite satisfactory rate—and that was a post-New Deal, post-World War II era. It was a period in which we had—up to that time—an unprecedented amount of public policy devoted to affecting the distribution of income. Historically speaking there is no question that you can have some redistribution of income simultaneously with some economic growth. The questions are: How much should we value each of these objectives? How much should we value income redistribution? How much should we value economic growth? What is the magnitude of the trade-off, if any, between them? And what are the ways by which we can try to achieve both of these with as little sacrifice as possible of the other? This whole subject is not one that lends itself to precise, quantitative, scientific, and objective answers. As far as the analytical or empirical questions are concerned, we just do not know enough about the distribution of income, what it is, or what can change it. Similarly, we do not know what establishes the rate of growth, what it is, and what policies can change it. We do not know enough about these things even to state the questions in a quantitative way. Even if we did know those things we would not know what valuation to place on growth and income redistribution. These are subjective matters to which there is no possible scientific or objective answer. What I am going to give you in this paper is a personal and subjective view of what I think the state of our knowledge is, and what my estimation is of the relative importance of these objectives.

This whole subject can only be treated in a rather fuzzy way, at least by me. I am often reminded of an occasion when the distinguished economist Kenneth Boulding addressed a group of other economists in

Washington. I do not remember what he talked about or what he said, but I do remember that after his speech was over, a young man in the audience said, "Well, Professor Boulding, it seems to me that you have fudged this issue." Professor Boulding looked at him and said, "Young man, you will learn that the world is made of nothing but fudge." Consequently, when I fudge this issue, I am being very realistic about it.

First we will deal with the question of emphasis between these objectives and how much emphasis should be placed on the objective of economic growth. But first I must ask: Is income redistribution a legitimate objective of government policy at all? This question is raised often. Anyone can find lots of current writing that huffs and puffs and rejects the notion that the proper function of government is to try to change the distribution of income from what it would be in the absence of any government measure. This questioning, it seems to me, proceeds generally on rather extremist grounds. There is one line of argument that says it is just impossible to achieve complete income equality. Even if we could give everyone the same dollar income, people's capacity for being happy is obviously very unequally distributed, and people will not be equally happy if they all have equal income. Thus, they will be unequal in many respects other than their incomes. Some will be taller than others, some will be more talented than others, some will be prettier than others, and so on. So it is said the equalization of income is a meaningless and unachievable objective in any relevant sense.

The problem with that conclusion is that the issue in this discussion is not whether we favor achieving total equality of income. We are asking whether it is desirable in some degree, probably some limited degree, to change the distribution of income. It seems to me that this is quite a different question. This question is not answered by saying that some people will still be taller than others.

Another ground for questioning the validity or legitimacy of the income redistribution objective is the claim that the attempt to redistribute income is inconsistent with freedom. One can claim that taxing some people's income to hand it out to other people deprives the taxpayer of the freedom to spend money as he or she likes. If you consider that an intolerable invasion of freedom, then the ballgame is over and there is not much to question. But it seems to me that if the proposition is stated in a more reasonable and moderate way, it becomes very difficult to deny the legitimacy of societal concern with the distribution of income or the legitimacy of social policy in changing the distribution of income. It seems to me that we would all agree in general that a democratic society may legitimately choose to correct extremes of inequality that it finds offensive, just as it may try to correct other conditions that it finds offensive. It seems to me somewhat ironic that the same people who find pornography offensive and inconsistent with the moral conscience of America, and therefore feel that the government is entitled to prohibit pornography, feel that it is illegitimate for the government to try to change some aspects of the income distribution that many people in this society find offensive, and that some, in a use of a word that I detest, call "obscene."

We have a variety of objectives in this country. Freedom is one, and growth is one, and there is no reason for us to preclude ourselves from accepting some effort to bring the distribution of income into conformity with the national conscience. This problem is sometimes handled by saying: Well, yes, it is legitimate for the government to try to bring about equality of opportunity, or at least more equality of income. But this seems to me an unsustainable distinction although it is made by people whose opinions I respect very much.

I want to be clear that I am not making a case for trying to make the distribution of income equal. I am just saying that it is a legitimate function of government to do something about the distribution of income. It seems to me that the important point to discover is the degree of inequality and the aspects of inequality that really do offend society's conscience; what the costs of correcting that would be; and what methods of correction could be found that do not cost too much.

At this point it seems necessary to me to distinguish between two aspects of the reduction of inequality. One is the reduction of extreme wealth and the other is the reduction of extreme poverty. I would not in principle reject the reduction of extreme wealth as an objective of policy. I was brought up as an economist by Professor Henry Simons at the University of Chicago, who had unimpeachable credentials as a conservative, and liberal in the old-fashioned sense. He was in favor of progressive income tax. He favored methods of taxation that would set some limits on the income of the wealthy, essentially because he found levels of wealth that are extremely above those of the average people in the society unlovely. That was his word, "unlovely." It reflects an aesthetic judgment. He did not say that it was uneconomic or bad for the economy, or that it would produce too much saving. He just said that he and a lot of other people in the country did not like it, and that the country is entitled to create conditions that conform to the conscience of the society. Having said that, I must hasten to say that I do not now think that reduction of extremes of wealth in this country is a problem or that it is a subject we should address. One's opinion about this depends very much on what one thinks the extent of inequality is. I have been impressed by some estimates recently made by Professor Allen Blinder of Princeton, who found that the families in the United States who are in the top 20 percent of income have incomes that are eight times as high as the families with the lowest 20 percent of incomes. You can ask yourselves whether you think this ratio of eight to one is too large and requires correction, and whether you find it offensive. But then he goes on to point out that the families in the top 20 percent of income are bigger families. They have more workers per person and the workers in each family do more work per year. So if you ask yourselves what is the income per week of work of a family in the top 20 percent of income, it is not eight times as much as the income of a family in the lowest 20 percent income, but twice as much. And that, I think, gives us a quite different picture. This does not look to me like a shockingly large gap in the distribution of income.

One aspect of the problem of extreme wealth that has always been prominent in this discussion in the past is that some people believe wealth represents unfairness. They not only think that the wealth of the wealthiest people is very great but also that it had been achieved in some unfair way. But, as I observe the attitudes in this country, that viewpoint seems to have diminished a great deal since I was young. This is due in part to who it is who constitutes the wealthy now—for example, baseball players, rock stars, television commentators, movie stars, and so on. People are not inclined to think there is anything unfair about David Winfield getting a million dollars a year, even if he only got one hit in the World Series. This puts a different view on distribution of income than when our model of a very rich person was J.P. Morgan. The power of the wealthy also used to be an issue. It is clear that is not the case in the United States now. Very rich individuals are not necessarily very powerful. There is probably no very rich person in the United states, say in the past decade, who has been as powerful as Walter Cronkite was when he anchored the "CBS Evening News." Walter Cronkite, of course, is rich. But while there are many richer people, there are few who have enjoyed Cronkite's power. Power now lies in access to communications, organizations, large corporations, large trade unions, and associations of other kinds. Having a lot of money does not generate power that is particularly useful, especially since the passage of the election reform laws. As I look at our current situation I see no particular reason to be concerned with the upper end of the income scales.

The problem is at the lower end of the income scale. The main issue is the problem of balancing the reduction of poverty against the stimulation of growth. Here, too, we need to be aware of the figures, as measured by the conventional definition of poverty. The number of people in the United States who are in a condition of poverty has fallen very low. In 1929 something like 40 percent of the American people were in what we now consider poverty by the official definition. Today the percentage is somewhere around 5 percent, and if you ask what proportion of the population is in poverty over the course of several years, not just in one year, the number would be even smaller. Many people have concluded, and I think with some justification, that poverty as conventionally measured has been reduced to very low proportions in the United States. This conclusion may be valid in one sense, but there is another factor here to bear in mind. The present low degree of poverty is accompanied by enormous outlays. The government is spending enormous amounts of money in the name of reducing poverty. The federal government alone spends over $200 billion a year in transfer payments in the form of money, food stamps, rent subsidies, and so forth. Most of that has been popularly justified as doing something about poor people. But the question remains whether these expenditures are efficient. Do we need to spend in excess of $200 billion in order to reduce poverty? Can poverty be kept low less expensively?

My conclusion on income distribution is that we still need to be concerned with the poverty problem, although not as much as before because of the progress we have made, and not in the same ways.

Let us now turn to the other half of the question: Is economic growth a legitimate objective of national policy? Some conservatives may immediately answer yes, because economic growth has always been a tenet of the conservative movement. However, it is possible to give a negative answer, also on strictly conservative or libertarian grounds. One can say that national economic growth is simply the aggregate growth of all the individuals, families, and enterprises, each reflecting its own priorities. Individuals and families make decisions about saving, they make decisions about educating their children, they make decisions about moving from low-income occupations to higher-income occupations, and the sum of all those decisions is the rate of economic growth in the country. A perfectly conservative or libertarian view would say that the proper rate of economic growth for the country is the rate that emerges from all these individual decisions and that the government has no business setting targets for economic growth or trying to make economic growth higher than would emerge from all of these private decisions. The government, of course, does make a lot of decisions that affect growth. It makes decisions about education, about research, and on and on. But you can say that these decisions should be made with reference to their own particular objectives and that private parties should react to them, if they choose, in the light of their own objectives.

For a long time, I made this argument. But now I am less sure of this approach. For one thing, this approach never left me with any satisfactory way to determine the proper size of government surplus, although government surplus does have an effect on growth. For example. it has an effect on the availability of savings to finance productive investments. And if I do not know whether I care about growth or not, then I do not know how to decide the size of the government surplus. This is probably an extreme example of the decisions the government makes that are difficult to evaluate in their own terms and that require some position related to growth. Also, people do seem to have an interest in national economic growth. They find that living in a growing economy has benefits that they cannot achieve by their own actions. There are advantages to living in a society that is growing rapidly: you are the beneficiary of everyone's efforts to make the economy grow, but you have no way to influence everyone else's actions. An economist might call these advantages an externality. So within limits, it seems, society is entitled to choose to lean toward the higher rather than the lower rate of growth. But that still leaves the question: Should it do so?

The main thing that has moved me from neutrality about economic growth is the fact that economic growth has slowed down. When we were sure that we were going to continue to have a percent increase in output per worker per hour in the United States we were not concerned about it. Although the rise of output per worker per hour in the United States was 3 percent per year from 1947 to 1973, it has only been 0.7 percent per year 1973-1982, and only 0.3 percent per year 1977-1982. This makes a tremendous difference. If you ask how long it takes to double real income per worker per hour, when it was 3 percent income it would double in twenty-four years. At 0.7 percent it would take one hundred years. That makes a big difference in one's attitude toward the future in a variety of ways. It is not a matter of being poor or getting poorer. It is not a matter of having entered a new era of austerity or of being unable to meet our critical national needs, including our national-security needs. It is a matter of whether we should now adapt to a rather different way of thinking about the future. It is interesting that the no-growth movement disappeared in this country when the rate of growth actually did slow down. People were carrying banners in favor of no growth as long as it seemed assured that we were going to have plenty of growth, but once that became doubtful, those banners disappeared.

I believe that we should put more emphasis on growth than in the past, mainly because we have been getting less growth. But this does not mean that we should make an all-out effort to promote growth to the sacrifice of other objectives. With respect to poverty, there is not an urgent need to do much more against poverty in the conventional sense. In that sense, the objective has declined on the scale of priorities. But it is desirable to avoid retrogression. I think that it is important to make this statement as we look for ways to eliminate the prospective $160 billion deficit in the 1984 federal budget. We cannot say that we licked the problem of poverty and now we can eliminate poverty programs, because one way we licked the problem is with those programs. It is desirable to avoid retrogression, to try to achieve results more efficiently, and to improve conditions of life that do not seem to be dependent strictly on income.

It is difficult to both accelerate the rate of growth and to maintain or improve or progress against poverty. The difficulty is not in the conflict between them. The thing that will keep us from making progress against poverty is not that we also want to make progress on growth, or vice versa. Although both objectives draw on the same resources, the poverty problem is not heavily dependent on devoting more resources to it. That is not the problem. And while more resources could be devoted to growth, mainly in the form of more investment, those resources do not have to come from the poor. The consumption of the nonpoor is an enormous reservoir of resources from which to contribute to economic growth.

A basic fact about the American economy is that the great mass of the people above the poverty line are living very well, living better than almost anyone has ever lived in all history. There is a lot of room there for abstracting resources both now and in the future, to promote growth—if that is what we want, if there is a will to do it, and if we can figure how to do it.

I want to make a slight detour here and say a word about the popular notion that there is an easy solution to both the growth problem and the poverty problem—supply-side economics—that draws on some notions that are as old as economics, and are sound, but which has carried these notions to bizarre and unrealistic extremes. Supply-side economists believe that all we have to do is cut tax rates and the economy will immediately skyrocket. Further, this skyrocketing will have a major effect on poverty on the principle that "the rising tide lifts all boats." (Characteristically these people rely on quotations from John F. Kennedy.)

Now there are two problems with this line of argument. In the first place, growth on the scale promised is exceedingly unlikely. Granted, there is evidence in economic theory and investigation to suggest that cutting tax rates has a positive effect on the rate of growth. However, there is nothing to suggest that the effects are anything like the magnitude that has been promised by the extreme supply-siders. Moreover, if these tax rate reductions are accompanied by increased deficits, as may very well be the case, then the net effect may not be positive but negative as far as economic growth is concerned because of the adverse effect of the deficit on the supply of funds available for private investment. The second proposition is not true in spite of what John F. Kennedy said. As I once put it, "The rising tide does not lift the boats that are underwater."

Let me way a word about why increasing the growth rate is difficult. There are two approaches to increasing the growth rate. One is to increase the resources devoted to growth, that is, the investment in productive capital, the investment in education, the investment in research, and so on. The other is to increase the effectiveness of the resources devoted to economic growth. Now, to rely only on increasing the resources as a way of stepping up the economic growth requires an enormous shift. One of the few quantitative things I ever learned came from work I did with Edward F. Denison, who is probably the leading student of economic growth in the United States. What I learned is that the difference between a 2 percent growth rate and a 3 percent growth rate is not 1 percent, it is 50 percent. You then must ask what it will take in the way of increased resources to increase the growth rate by 50 percent.

The other way to approach this problem is to increase the effectiveness with which resources are used, and that is something that we just do not know how to do. There are a lot of people who think that if they can get the workers to sing Japanese songs the first thing in the morning they will be enormously more efficient, but that seems to be true only of

Japanese workers. What we have to do to make the U.S. workers more efficient is probably something different. Again we come to a problem of ignorance. Maybe it is because I am a professor that I think so many problems are due to ignorance.

Now let me turn to the other half of this aspect: Why is reducing poverty so difficult? It is difficult because it is not primarily a question of the amount of money devoted to the task. We are spending in the name of the poor more than enough to raise all of the poor out of poverty, as it is conventionally defined. The problems are threefold. First, most of the money that we spend in the name of poverty does not go to poor people, it goes to middle-income people. That is difficult to handle for two reasons; one is political. There are more people who are not poor than are poor, and therefore when you start a program aimed at the poor, the nonpoor make sure that they become its principal beneficiaries. A second problem is an economic one. If you try to make cutoffs and say we will provide this income, these food stamps, this kind of benefit to families whose income is up to $6,000, but not anyone whose income is above $6,000, then you create a tremendous disincentive for people to raise their incomes from $5,999 to $6,001. If you try to confine the benefits to people who are very poor, you create a strong disincentive against becoming independently nonpoor.

Another problem is that these transfer payments of welfare, food stamps, and so on create some of the problems that they are supposed to correct. They create the condition of dependency, they increase the disincentive to work, and they have been alleged to be the cause of the breakup of families. So they undo some of the good that they are intended to do.

The third problem is that transfers do not by themselves cure many of the undesirable conditions that we associate with poverty.

I think we need to do much better with stabilization policy in the future than we have done in the past. Inflation and unemployment are harmful both to economic growth and to poor people. We need to do better in restraining inflation and preventing unemployment, and we can do better if we are more foresighted about it. I think we have gotten ourselves into a very difficult condition in the United States by being shortsighted, by perpetually emphasizing the effort to get the unemployment rate down without sufficient consideration of the longer run consequences of inflation, and we have wound up with an inflation rate greater than we have had since the depression. This is unsatisfactory, but I think we know how to do much better. A second thing that can be done is to reduce the average size of budget deficits in this country relative to the GNP, because we have been absorbing too much of the national savings in financing deficits and this has had a negative effect on economic growth. To get the budget deficits down, I think we need to reduce some of the government expenditures that do not go to poor people. We can reduce some of the programs that go to middle-income people, and look for sources of additional revenue that will not disturb incentives to work, save, and invest. Also we can correct or remove regulations that interfere with productivity and impinge on the poor. Most obvious among these are import duties. Import duties reduce the efficiency of our economy and increase costs that are paid by poor people and are particularly burdensome on poor people.

We have similar problems with respect to agricultural policy, the net effect of which is to increase the cost of food to the poor and do little for the very poor farmer. If benefits have accrued to agriculture at all, they have accrued mainly to landowners. We have a number of things affecting labor, one of which is the Davis-Bacon Act. We have environmental and safety regulations, which while justifiable in principle, have been carried to an extent where costs do not justify benefits. Beyond that, we get into more difficult areas. I think that there is room for better administration of the poverty programs on the state level. We need to return more responsibility to the local community and not expect the federal government to solve all of these problems.

The federal government is good at dishing out money. But if we have problems that do not depend on dishing out money, we must find other sources of decision making, and other sources of leadership. One of the terrible things that has happened in this country is that the notion of leadership in the United States has become almost exclusively identified with the federal government and with the president of the United States. However much I respect the president, I think it is a dangerous condition if he is the only leader who commands any confidence. Perhaps I am nostalgic about the past, but I think there was a time, not so long ago— thirty years ago—when there were people in the country who took responsibility with respect to local and national problems. This is particularly true with respect to the people whose problems are not being adequately solved by a transfusion of money but who need a new injection of morale, optimism, and self-assurance. And finally, I think we need, and I think we are getting, revision of popular attitudes on a lot of questions including the question of work and the question of efficiency. For instance, in the business community we are beginning to see more awareness that businesses have been missing the boat on many possibilities and that they must accept responsibility for their future. I think an essential and inescapable lesson we learned from the failure of many government programs to deliver what was expected of them was not that we cannot achieve results but that the results have to be achieved privately and individually. We need to accept the notion that Washington is not going to bail us out. We have enormous opportunities. All of us, individually, have to address ourselves to our problems, and this will be the way in which social concerns are satisfied. I have a feeling that we are moving in this direction and that we are returning to a more traditional set of values, which will tend to give us more traditional and satisfactory results.

There is no single solution to social problems, says WILLIAM J. BAROODY. *Rather, finding solutions to these problems requires a concerted effort by all elements of the private sector and all levels of government.*

Efforts to deal with social problems for the past half century have been based on Franklin Roosevelt's belief: "Government has the definite duty to meet new social problems with new social controls."

While government has initiated massive action in response to Roosevelt's vision, it has not succeeded in solving many social problems. Still, Baroody maintains, the problems are real and cannot be met by merely writing checks to charities. There is a real difference, he points out, between finding a new way of funding social programs and finding different ways of providing social services. These new ways will come from a return to Americans' common heritage of people helping people through private, value-generating institutions.

21

Human Resources: What's the Solution?

WILLIAM J. BAROODY

My subject is "Human Resources: What's the Solution?" I believe my first duty when dealing with such a subject is to say that there is no single solution to the social problems of this nation, no single step that can allow us to meet all the social needs of our people. Gerald R. Ford, the Distinguished Fellow of the American Enterprise Institute (AEI) has addressed many seminars sponsored by AEI, and is frequently asked what his greatest disappointment was in the White House.

"The most frustrating thing of all," he says, "the thing that discouraged me the most, was that I could not turn some switch—I couldn't make one big decision that would solve the nation's problems and get our economy on the right track."

So, even the president of the United States, considered the most powerful man in the world, a man who some believe can push a button to destroy much of the earth, is not capable of pushing a button to solve the problems of one small piece of that earth.

That brings to mind a story. It seems there was a massive power failure at a major power plant that controlled much of the electricity for a heavily populated metropolitan area. All kinds of experts were brought in, all to no avail. As the blackout dragged on, the mayor became more frantic for a solution.

Finally, an old-timer was called in, a fellow who had worked on hundreds of power plants across the country and was considered tops in his field. The old gentleman approached the huge generator slowly, carefully considering it from many different angles. Finally, he took a hammer from his tool box, stepped up to the machine, and gave it a smart thwack. In a split second, the huge generator roared to life, and power was restored to the city.

A few days later, the mayor received a bill from the oldtimer for $1,000.11. Thinking there must be some mistake, the mayor returned the bill and asked for an itemized breakdown of charges. Well, the bill came back in a few more days, and it was still for $1,000.11, broken down as follows: "Eleven cents—for time and labor in thwacking the machine, one-thousand dollars—for knowing where to thwack it."

So there are some areas where a single stroke will do the trick, if you know where to apply it.

But, of course, it's going to take more than one smart thwack to get our economy going again and to meet the needs of the American people in the eighties. It's going to take a concerted effort by all the elements of the private sector and all levels of government. But it can be done; it's been done before.

Whether one agrees or disagrees with the Reagan agenda, it is hard to dispute that a part of that agenda involves a new role for all elements of the private sector, and for all levels of government under the rubric of the "New Federalism."

I believe a strong case can be made that restoring a more balanced relationship among the components of our society—government at all levels, business, labor, and private institutions such as family, church, and neighborhood associations—need not prove harmful to any part of our system.

Many in our society have come to assume that government must play the major role in providing social services. The irony here is that most Americans believe the government to be inefficient and unresponsive in meeting the needs of the people. That's the finding of a nationwide opinion survey commissioned by the AEI through our new Center for the Study of Private Initiative. This poll, conducted by the Roper Organization, found that:

- seven in 10 Americans think tax money used for human services is not used well;
- two out of three people say that government programs discourage many competent people from helping themselves; and
- an overwhelming majority of Americans regard family, church, and neighborhood as important in their lives, but also believe the role of these institutions has been weakened in recent years.

At the same time, however, the survey showed that Americans still want government to play a major role in higher education, to provide services to the needy—especially health care, employment, and economic development—and to protect the environment and assure civil rights. These contradictory tendencies in public opinion have become more and more pronounced over the past two decades, as government has assumed an ever greater role in the lives of the American people.

Government dominance of social services has obscured a crucial fact: private sector initiatives can be just as effective as government programs, and sometimes more so, because they emanate from the people themselves and thus more fully reflect their needs and desires. I firmly believe that corporations, churches, local organizations, and the general public know best how to provide social services. This has been true ever since Alexis de Tocqueville, visiting America almost 150 years ago, expressed awe at the effectiveness of our volunteer sector.

In *Democracy in America*, a book that de Tocqueville wrote in the 1830s, which is still discussed extensively in history and political science courses of the 1980s and is also quoted frequently by our current president, de Tocqueville marveled at the effectiveness and the numbers of private, voluntary associations in this country. He wrote that these private efforts achieved far more than any central government could ever hope to. And a major benefit of this private sector initiative, he wrote, was the spirit it instilled among those who gave of themselves and their resources; they benefited as much as those who received the help.

In fact, this has been a tradition of American society for 90 percent of our existence—all but the past two decades. The balance in our society has actually been eroding for more than four decades. Public policy during that time has been dominated by the public philosophy spawned by President Roosevelt. It was based on a single premise articulated by FDR in an address to Congress in 1938:

> As new conditions and problems arise beyond the power of men and women to meet as individuals (he said), it becomes the duty of the government itself to find new remedies with which to meet them.... Government has the definite duty to meet new social *problems with new social controls.*

Both Democrats and Republicans, wittingly or unwittingly, with all good intentions, accepted that premise and acted upon it for more than forty years. It is fair to say that the Great Society was the legislative result of Roosevelt's intellectual revolution.

Political debate through the years revolved primarily around the question of whether those new remedies mentioned by FDR should be applied through a centralized bureaucracy in Washington managing 550 categorical grant-in-aid programs, or through a decentralized government bureaucracy at the state and local level managing revenue-sharing funds and block grants.

Note the subtle, implicit assumption in either case that it should be government—either national or local—that deals with social problems.

That assumption, and the evolution of massive government programs that resulted from it, has distorted the function of government and other components of society. The basic function of government is to maintain the conditions necessary for people to enjoy the good life. It is not the role of government to define the good life.

In the course of arrogating to itself the responsibility for meeting all social help—or interference—of government, let me cite just a few examples.

The Honeywell Corp. has made Minneapolis a center for one new way of giving. Through the Honeywell Retiree Volunteer Project (HRVP), more than 350 retired Honeywell employees contribute one or two days a week to community work. Many of the jobs they do through this program—which include retrofitting typewriters for the handicapped, training young tool-and-die makers, and modernizing a hospital's heating and cooling systems—allow them to keep up the skills they developed over twenty, thirty, or forty years with Honeywell. The annual cost to the company is about $35,000.

The benefits of the HRVP are widespread. The community gets the services of high-skilled workers who have the ability and the desire to help the needy, Honeywell receives recognition within the community, and the retirees are able to go on practicing their skills. These volunteers contribute more than 86,000 hours a year to community work and the dropout rate is only 6 percent. There are hundreds of similar ways in which the elderly could contribute to efforts organized by their former employers. Such programs might also reduce to some degree the need for programs for the elderly.

Another striking case comes from Cincinnati, where some twenty-four major corporations and professional firms have formed the Cincinnati Business Committee (CBC) to provide technical assistance and management advice to the city government and school system. Through the CBC, these companies are also taking an active part in the formulation of a plan for downtown development.

Procter & Gamble (P&G) was instrumental in the CBC's foundation. P&G executive Thomas Collins was given leave for fifteen months to help organize the CBC; and Edward G. Harness, then chairman of P&G, and Ralph Lazarus, then chairman of Federated Department Stores, were the original co-chairmen of the CBC when it was formed in 1977. Both still serve on the CBC although they have stepped down as chief executive officer (CEO) of their respective companies. And Mr. Collins later took another twelve-month leave to work with the CBC on a school-related project.

In Philadelphia, a more broad-based organization, the Greater Philadelphia Partnership (GPP), appears to be achieving similar results. This organization includes the CEOs of major corporations—such as Sun Co., Hunt Manufacturing, INA, Pennwalt Corp., and others—together with heads of most of Philadelphia's major banks, along with community and academic leaders.

Since its initiation, the GPP has been involved in a variety of programs in housing, education, and economic development. It has a program known as the Philadelphia Mortgage Plan, through which it works with banks in developing new criteria for mortgages for inner-city residents. The GPP claims responsibility for seeing that more than $70 million in mortgages has been issued to inner-city residents, with the average loan totaling $11,000.

One community organization actively involved with the Greater Philadelphia Partnership is the House of Umoja, a grassroots group that is fast becoming a symbol of achievement in the inner city.

Ten years ago, Philadelphia was known as the "Street Gang Capital of America." More than forty deaths a year were attributed to street gang violence. Economic activity in the neighborhoods of West Philadelphia and other sections of the city was declining steadily.

When David and Falaka Fattah learned that one of their six sons had joined a street gang, they became very concerned; they sought to find out what attracted their son to the gang, and how they could keep him from ending up in jail. They determined that joining a gang was tied to a need for close-knit, family-type relationships. They decided to invite sixteen members of their son's gang to join their family, to move into their home in West Philadelphia. Thus was founded the House of Umoja, which is Swahili for "unity."

The Fattahs worked with these gang members to reach other gangs throughout the city. They were instrumental in convening a citywide gang conference that resulted in peace pacts among the gangs.

Equally important, they worked hard to instill in the youngsters a sense of responsibility for their actions, and a desire to support themselves, to be productive members of society rather than a drain on the system. They did this with little professional training or government assistance.

The results have been astounding. Gang-related deaths have been reduced from more than forty a year to about one per year over the past three years. More than 500 youths have lived in the House of Umoja over the past decade and many have gone on to take responsible jobs and in some cases have enrolled in college.

The House of Umoja has moved on to attempt economic development efforts as well. The group already has a thriving security company, which has contracts with a number of stores and a small shopping center. It has established a construction company with which it is building a Boys Town in West Philadelphia. It is also working on development of a mini-mall with a variety of small businesses to be operated by the House of Umoja.

The House of Umoja has established an advisory board composed of local business representatives from corporations such as SmithKline, Bell of Pennsylvania, Sears, and several major banks. These companies have given technical assistance, executive time, and technical aid with bookkeeping, marketing, and business planning.

Allow me to cite one other example. In St. Louis, a group known as Jeff-Vander-Lou collaborated with Brown Shoe Company to build a factory in its neighborhood. Jeff-Vander-Lou donated the land for the factory and trained local residents in leather work and shoemaking. Using a large percentage of employees from the local area, that factory ranks in the top five among Brown Shoe Company's twenty-seven factories in productivity.

It is important to note that these private sector efforts do not have to be simple cases of charity by businesses or individuals. Certainly, Brown Shoe Company is receiving dividends from its investment in that St. Louis neighborhood. Another company has been receiving national recognition for its success with inner city factories—Control Data Corporation.

Under the leadership of Bill Norris, the chairman of Control Data, the company has placed seven plants in poor urban areas and they have been productive operations. Admittedly, Control Data has had to do extra work with the local residents to get them accustomed to regular work habits, but the effort has paid off.

Mr. Reagan has appointed a Presidential Task Force on Private Sector Initiatives, which is chaired by William Verity, chairman of Armco Steel, and on which I am honored to serve. There are five key missions of the task force:

(1) To identify existing examples of successful or promising private initiatives and private/public partnerships and to give these models national recognition.

(2) To encourage more creative and effective use of the resources of mediating structures, corporations, and philanthropic organizations.

(3) To encourage partnerships to identify needs, choose priorities, and marshal resources.

(4) To identify government obstacles to private initiatives and make recommendations for their removal; also to recommend reasonable incentives to foster private initiatives.

(5) To contribute to the development of public policy by proposing practical options to the administration based on our findings.

Mr. Verity has appointed ten committees to pursue the various objectives outlined in those missions. He asked me to chair the committee on models of private initiatives, an area in which AEI has already done substantial work.

The late English writer G.K. Chesterton made an important point: "It is the first principle of democracy," he said, "that the essential things in men are the things they hold in common, not the things they hold separately."

And one thing we Americans hold in common is a heritage of people helping people through private, value-generating institutions. Let's understand that the private sector about which cynics scoff today has been debilitated by years and years of government programs, regulations, and disincentives that made it more difficult for private initiatives. That is not the private sector my father knew; it is not the private sector about which de Tocqueville wrote so glowingly in the early days of this nation.

The challenge facing all of us—not just Mr. Reagan and not just the government, but all of us—is to work out the best way in which the federal, state, and local governments; the business community; private institutions; and individuals can work together to solve the basic human problems facing this country.

We all have heard the cynics telling us what we can't do. What we need is a coherent vision of what we can do. We need to broaden our vision of America, open our eyes to the vast resources we have here, and take an active part in the evolution of this new public philosophy.

I began with the assertion that there are no easy answers to our social problems. But there are many human resources at our disposal, along with vast physical and moral resources, that can be focused upon those problems.

We recently celebrated the centenary of Franklin Delano Roosevelt, one of the most formidable leaders of our time. There are many of us who took exception to parts of the FDR philosophy, as I mentioned earlier, but there was no question about his extraordinary ability to inspire the American people.

One thing he wrote seems particularly inspiring when we speak about the potential of private human resources in this country. In the last speech he ever wrote, one he was scheduled to deliver the day after he died on April 12, 1945, Mr. Roosevelt wrote that "the only limit to our realization of tomorrow will be our doubts of today. Let me move forward with strong and active faith."

I can only add, "Amen."

Can marketplace dynamics do for health care what regulation and mandated cost controls have failed to do? Recounting the tremendous success of America's health-care system, KARL BAYS *points out that the system is a victim of its own success. Better health care for more people has resulted in certain inefficiencies and spiraling costs. Bays asks: Can we continue to afford success?*

Unless there are changes in the incentives under which our health system works, Bays says, we will continue to see dramatic increases in health-care costs. In this regard, competition may succeed where regulation has failed. Still, he warns, health care is one field where new concepts about things like competition will have to work with some older ideas, such as care and compassion.

22

Health-care Costs: The Competition Prescription

KARL D. BAYS

My topic is health care. That is an appropriate subject as we consider the future of private enterprise because health care in recent years has been one of the most successful enterprises in our country.

Health care as an American enterprise has succeeded in providing a better product—that is, better medicine and medical technology. Health care also has succeeded in providing that product to more people. More than a million Americans will wake up in hospitals tomorrow. A million and a half more will visit doctors.[1]

In economic terms as well, we can say that health care has succeeded. National expenditures of $284 billion last year alone were applied to everything from a schoolchild's immunization to a hospital's new cancer center.[2] The U.S. health-care industry today employs more people than the construction, trucking, automobile, or electronics industries. It employs more people than the federal government, including the armed services.[3]

But as health care has become a large enterprise, the cost of health care has become just as large an issue. That fact is part of what's behind my title, "Health-care Costs: The Competition Prescription."

There are various programs under discussion in Washington and elsewhere today that would seek to control health-care delivery, and its costs, by injecting more competition into the health-care system. Those programs are part of what I will cover. But before you start thinking about prescriptions, it's always wise to make a diagnosis. And, as I see it, the diagnosis for U.S. health care today is that this enterprise stands at a turning point. While discussing measures to control health-care costs, we must also discuss larger issues—issues that have to do with the quality of health care and its availability to people in this country. While discussing some new concepts about competition in health care, we must not forget some older ideas, and values, such as compassion in health care.

Out of the debate that is underway regarding U.S. health care today, we may reach decisions that significantly affect the future of this enterprise. Those same decisions could affect how health care is delivered to you and your family. So it is vital that all of us—as consumers, and as cititzens—understand the issues under examination now. If I could borrow just one other medical term, I think a case history of sorts would contribute to our understanding.

So many of the current reports about health care in our country imply, or say, that health care is a problem, or at least a serious concern. I agree that it is a concern—a vital one. But some history seems to show that many of the *problems* in health care today really are the fruits of the spectacular success that the U.S. health-care system has achieved.

To begin, we have developed new technology. It ranges from the antibiotics to polio vaccine. There are new diagnostic tests and new frontiers in genetic engineering. We have developed neurosurgical techniques and methods for intravenous nutrition. Those are just a few of the many strides that have been made just since World War II, and most of the breakthroughs I mentioned have been made just in the past ten years.

Perhaps the most amazing aspect of medical progress in this country is how routine it has become in recent years. Pneumonia, diphtheria, influenza—diseases that were among the leading causes of death very few years ago—are history, not a threat anymore. Procedures such as open-heart surgery are no longer a dream. They are commonplace. And it has all happened so fast.

At the same time we were developing new medical technology, we were making investments—huge investments—in the physical resources and the human resources needed to carry that technology to people. The physical resources include hospitals, laboratories, clinics, and other facilities. And one large government program, the Hill-Burton Act passed in 1946, provides an example of the investments we made. Hill-Burton was to provide federal assistance in building new hospitals. And, over a period of about thirty years, it resulted in the opening of 340,000 new hospital beds. For perspective, that's about one-third of all the community hospital beds in this country today.[4]

What about human resources? We invested there, too, and our investments included educational assistance for doctors, nurses, and other health professionals.

In 1950, we had fourteen physicians for every 10,000 Americans. Today, there are twenty-four. Furthermore, expanded medical education has brought us not just more doctors, but more highly specialized doctors in cardiovascular medicine, surgery, diagnostics, and many other fields.[5]

So the nation created new technology. We improved and expanded our system for delivering it. Those were two tangible results of a commitment this country made to more and better health care, in particular during the years after World War II. At the same time, however (and this is the key), we radically altered the way health care is paid for in this country. It is easy to forget that, as recently as 1940, only nine out of every 100 Americans had hospitalization insurance.[6] By and large, people who went to the hospital then paid out of pocket for their care. Only ten years later, however, about half of all Americans had hospitalization insurance. Much of that coverage was provided by employers, as an employee benefit. And that benefit expanded in the succeeding years. By 1965, a large majority (approximately 70 percent) of all Americans were insured against hospital costs.

It was in that same year, 1965, that we also made a national decision that has had huge ramifications for the economics of U.S. health care. Our decision was that we could do even better at providing care to people, and at helping them pay for it. We decided that, in our country, health care is a national as well as personal priority—that it's something people have a right to. In short, our decision was called Medicare and Medicaid. Under President Johnson, Congress passed a total of about forty health-care bills.[7] Among them, Medicare and Medicaid were, by far, the largest in both size and purpose. Medicare, a federally funded program, was to provide insurance coverage for the elderly and disabled. Medicaid was designed as a joint, state-federal program to cover the poor.

It is not an overstatement to say that, together, Medicare and Medicaid constituted a landmark—not just for health care, but for social policy in this country. At the very least, the history since 1965 shows that those programs were a resounding success—if what you are counting is health-care coverage for people who might not otherwise have had such coverage. In 1980, fifteen years after it was enacted, Medicare provided health services for 28 million elderly Americans. Medicaid in that year served 23 million poor people.[8]

So, our case history includes new medical capabilities, developed at a rapid rate. We expanded our system for bringing those capabilities to people. And we insured the vast majority of Americans, including the elderly, the disabled, and the poor, against worries about the cost of using that system.

If that history, by itself, does not necessarily add up to success, some other indicators show that a national commitment to excellent health care for all Americans has, indeed, paid off. Again, please do not take my word for it. Decide for yourself.

Life expectancy is one indicator of success in health care. And life expectancy went up three years during the 1970s alone. For elderly people, the people covered by Medicare, life expectancy is up two years since 1965. For all Americans it's up a full ten years since 1940.[9] The death rate from strokes is another indicator. It went down almost 40 percent in the 1970s, largely thanks to new pharmaceuticals. For heart disease, the death rate was down almost 20 percent at the same time.[10] While death rates have gone down, other indicators have gone up. In the urban setting, for example, an indicator might be the number of doctors available to poor people, including minorities, and the number of visits those people are making to those doctors. The number of doctor visits made each year by poor children increased 26 percent from 1964 through 1979.[11]

Figures like those are just one statement of the social benefits of a program such as Medicaid. More generally, increased life expectancy and new medical capabilities serve to summarize the benefits of a national commitment to better health care. And frankly I doubt whether any of us would be willing to attach a dollar figure to the value of a life saved or a life improved by better health care.

But there is another way—a quantitative way—to summarize our case history: As recently as 1965, U.S. health care accounted for about 5.9 percent of gross national product. Last year, it was 9.6 percent.[12] Considering those figures, the issue now becomes a simple question of whether we can afford to continue being so successful in health care. A related question is whether this nation can continue to let health-care costs grow faster than overall inflation, as they have for several years. That question is being asked throughout our health-care system today.

I can tell you, for example, that hospitals across the country have turned major attention toward finding ways to work more efficiently. They see the coming years as a time of growing demand for health services. But they also see the future as a time of growing pressure on the cost of those services.

The American public is voicing concern about health-care costs, too. A survey late last year showed that a large majority, 80 percent, of Americans are happy with the quality of their medical care, and with the availability of insurance to pay for that care.[13]

But just over half, some 54 percent, said they were dissatisfied with the cost of their medical care. That is not a landslide. Nor do the polls show any increase in dissatisfaction over the past couple of years. And my experience is that, when it comes to health care, people want to be sure, first and foremost, that it is there—for them and their families. Questions about the cost come second. Of course, that is not to say that this nation can afford to ignore the question of health-care costs. The issue is a serious one, and Washington is another place where it is being raised—with growing frequency. Considering some of the history we have covered, that should come as no surprise.

Medicare, Medicaid, and other health programs have grown since 1965 to account for a full 10 percent of the federal budget.[14] That is far more than the people who enacted those programs ever envisioned. A wider reading of government involvement in health care shows federal, state, and local programs today paying just over 40 percent of total health costs. They pay an even larger percentage of hospital costs.[15]

It is natural, and right, that government should be reacting to rapid increases in health costs, especially at a time of heavy concern about the overall economy.

On one front, the administration in Washington has proposed a budget that includes continuing growth in health spending, but at a sharply limited level. At the state level, we are seeing similar proposals for reduced growth in programs such as Medicaid. And, on other government fronts, the debate is about measures designed to create more competition in the health-care system, as a way to control costs.

I mentioned earlier that the changes that have been made in payment mechanisms for health care over the past forty years are key to much of what is happening in health care today. They are also key to the debate about increasing competition in this field.

What has happened, as a result of the proliferation of private and government insurance programs, is that some two-thirds of all doctor bills are paid through insurance. For hospital bills, it's about 90 percent. And that's a reversal of what the situation was forty years ago. At that time, almost 90 percent of a typical hospital bill was paid for out of the patient's pocket.[16]

What does that change mean? It means that many of the people—the great majority of the people, in fact—who use health care are insulated from worries about the cost of health care. Perhaps even more important, those who provide health care—the hospitals and doctors—tend to worry less about its cost, simply because "the insurance will cover it"

In other words, it is a question of incentives. Consumers are encouraged to use health care. They are encouraged by insurance programs that pay for it, or a large part of it, virtually automatically. The providers, by the same token, are encouraged to provide the care, including some of the most expensive kinds of care. The bill just goes to Blue Cross/Blue Shield, or Medicare, or Medicaid, or elsewhere. It is those incentives that the various competition proposals seek to change.

The competition prescription under debate today takes the form of several bills that have been introduced in Congress, and one that the administration plans to introduce. They vary in some particulars. But, overall, their intent is to create more involvement by consumers in choosing where they get their health care and how they pay for it.

Some proposals would use tax incentives to encourage people to choose lower-cost insurance, with higher deductibles or with a greater percentage of a doctor's bill or hospital bill paid by the patient. Others would put a limit on the amount of health insurance that a company could provide, tax free, to its employees.

The thought behind the proposed programs is that consumers would shop more carefully for insurance. Both consumers and insurers also would look more carefully at the size of the bills they receive from doctors and hospitals. The reasoning is that people would tend to go to the most efficient providers for care. Hospitals and other providers would therefore be competing based on their efficiency as well as on the quality of care they provide.

Some other proposals that you are likely to be hearing more about also would serve to change the incentives under which hospitals, in particular, operate. They would change the current system, under which a hospital receives reimbursement for its service *after* that service is provided.

Instead, the hospital would agree on a budget from Medicare and Medicaid, say, for the services it expects to provide under those programs for the coming year. It is called *prospective reimbursement*. And what it means is that the hospital would be encouraged to work as efficiently as possible. If it went over the established budget, it would have to make up the difference. If it did better than the budget, it would get to keep the remaining funds.

Under a prospective reimbursement program, therefore, hospitals would be in competition not just against other hospitals to see which is the most efficient, but also against their own budgets.

In general, competition along lines like those has been forwarded as an alternative to a regulatory approach to controlling health-care costs. Regulation in various forms has been tried. And, quite frankly, it might be tried again—in the form of a government cap on increases in hospital costs.

But regulation has not succeeded to date in providing an effective control. And I am one observer who does not see how it could succeed. It's an artificial restraint that doesn't speak to the basic dynamics behind increasing health-care costs.

Competition, on the other hand, has several things going for it. As one health-care analyst puts it, "Competition resonates well with certain basic American values, such as free enterprise and entrepreneurship."

But can it work in health care? Can marketplace dynamics do what regulation and mandated cost controls have failed to do? The fact is that competition is already working in several ways in this field.

The investor-owned, or for-profit, hospitals are one example. They are a phenomenon that came on the scene little more than fifteen years ago. Today, they represent about 20 percent of the hospitals in this country.[17] And, in many cities they represent real competition for the traditional, voluntary hospital. Other forms of competition include health maintenance organizations (HMOs) established to provide health services for a set fee. In some cities, like Minneapolis, HMOs have enrolled as members up to one-third of all eligible people, and expect to grow further.[18]

Hospitals of all sorts, meanwhile, are also working in more competitive ways. They are marketing health services such as health-promotion programs to local business. Other hospitals are competing by reorganizing to provide not just inpatient care but also ambulatory care and a wide range of other services.

I intentionally have covered a lot of ground in this paper. The purpose is to demonstrate the diagnosis I mentioned earlier—that we are, indeed, at a turning point in U.S. health care.

Of course, being at a turning point does not necessarily mean that we *will* turn. But what we as a nation and as consumers of health care need to understand is that unless the incentives under which our health system works do change we are all but certain to continue to see the kinds of increases in health-care costs that we have seen in recent years.

In fact, several trends indicate even faster increases in demand for health care during the years ahead. We are seeing an increase, for example, in the average age of the population. And, at least in part, that is attributable to better health care. But the aging trend means greater needs for health care. People over 65, for example, are the fastest growing age group in our population—and they are also the group whose health-care needs are the greatest. They use three times the amount of hospital care used by those in younger age groups.[19]

So, there is ample reason for considering methods to create more efficiency in health care. We need to be concerned about growing costs. We also need to be concerned about growing needs for health services.

But there are some important questions that we, as a nation, should keep in mind as we consider health care, its cost, and the possible benefits of increasing competition in this field. They are questions that we as citizens should be considering seriously at this turning point in health care. They also summarize much of what I have covered.

The first question has to do with what percentage of its resources a major industrialized country *should* devote to health care, compared to other essential needs. Some recent reports have expressed alarm about the fact that health spending is likely to pass 10 percent of GNP in the near future. But I wonder. Is 10 percent too much? Or is it not enough? Is health care a cost? Or is it an investment in a vital social service to which people really do have a right?

Other reports have focused solely on the increase in health expenditures. And the figures do show those expenditures growing at 12.6 percent a year over the past ten years. At the same time, however, it is interesting to note that expenditures for repairing, greasing, washing, parking, and renting automobiles have increased 12.9 percent a year.[20]

It becomes a simple question of priorities. Is it health care we will devote X percent of our resources to? Or is it cars, or education, or agriculture, or defense? What is the right balance? It is not just health-care costs we are considering, after all. It is really health care as a national priority. To bring it down to a very personal level, annual spending for health care ranks fifth among the expenditures made by a middle-income American family, according to government figures. Your family is likely to spend more for food, housing, transportation, and clothing.[21] The question becomes one of where health care *should* be placed as a priority for Americans and their families.

The next question is how we will work to ensure that our investments in health care—at whatever level—are the most productive possible investments. How can we ensure that a dollar, or a billion dollars, invested in health care will, in fact, lead to better health for an individual patient, or a nation of people?

The cost of health care *is* an issue. But it is really only part of a larger issue—the issue of continuing progress in health care, and of the availability of that progress to all Americans. The discipline of competition *is* an answer to questions about the productivity and cost-effectiveness of U.S. health care. But it is only one possible answer to the wider question about changing incentives in health care.

We are where we are in this field because the health system has done, quite simply, what the nation asked it to do. It provided more care and better care. It provided the care through a system of third-party payment that tends to insulate both doctors and patients from worries about the size of the ultimate bill.

Through public and private insurance programs and through the billions we have invested in this enterprise, we have structured incentives that encourage high-priced, high-technology health care, widely available to people. And the system has delivered just that. If we want to change those incentives now, we can do that. And I am one who believes in the values that a good, competitive system can provide.

Hospitals *should* be willing to compete—and not just with the hospital or clinic down the street, but against their own past record of both quality and efficiency. And, I can tell you for a fact that companies that serve hospitals *must* be willing to compete. American Hospital Supply Corporation is one of those companies. And, in our plans for continuing growth, competitiveness is our primary objectives. By that, we do not just mean selling more. We mean higher quality and efficiency—and effectively controlled costs—in providing products for hospitals and health care.

But I have a caution to offer about the competition prescription in health care, and about its promise for both the system and consumers. My caution is that competition will not be a cure-all. Health care is one field where new concepts about things like competition will have to work with some older ideas, things like care and compassion. That thought is one that may not fit easily with an analysis of health-care economics. But the need for compassion as well as competition is something that a hospital patient—or a nurse—readily understands.

I have said before that health care is one enterprise that exists not for the survival of the fittest, but for the care of the least fit. That is a tradition that we should not allow to be harmed by any changes we make in our health policy. Health care is also a field where ideals and higher motivations need to fit with national priorities and goals. The question is not just the government budget for Medicare and Medicaid. It is really a question of how we will continue our commitment to meeting the needs of the elderly and the disadvantaged. We cannot, and we should not, let competition and compassion work against each other. Health care, finally, is a field where a past record of success is never enough.

Yes, 90 percent of Americans have health insurance today. But that means 10 percent do not.[22] Yes, there are twenty-four doctors for every 10,000 Americans. But think about the urban setting, such as the West Englewood neighborhood of Chicago. The local health agency reports that, in that neighborhood, there is not a single primary-care physician for 60,000 Americans.[23] And, yes, we have succeeded in developing new technology. But the progress we have yet to make is described by every heart attack, every stroke, and every case of childhood disease in this country.

We can look, with a measure of pride, at how far health care has come in this country. We can look, with some optimism, at the promise that competition holds for health care in the 1980s and beyond. But, as we do that, I say we should not forget to look, with real compassion and firm dedication to further progress, at the future of U.S health care.

Endnotes

1. Jeff C. Goldsmith *Can Hospitals Survive: The New Competitive Health Care Market* (Homewood, Illinois: Dow Jones/Irwin 1981).

2. Preliminary figures from the Health Care Financing Administration (HCFA), U.S. Department of Health and Human Services, show U.S. health-care expenditures of $284 billion in 1981. Unpublished HCFA projections show expenditures of $320 billion in 1982.

3. U.S. Bureau of Labor Statistics for employees on nonagricultural payrolls by industry (November 1981), (Washington, D.C.: Government Printing Office).

Health services	5,631,800
Construction	4,369,000
Trucking and warehousing	1,251,500
Transportation equipment	1,803,000
Electronic equipment	2,131,300
Federal government	2,729,000
Armed services	2,159,000
Retail trade	15,769,000

4. *Can Hospitals Survive*, 10-11.

5. *The Health Care System: Can the Third Biggest Business Take Care of the Medically Indigent*, a paper by Joseph A. Califano, Jr., delivered to the Duke University Medical Center, March 14, 1982.

6. Figures on private insurance coverage are from *The Financing of Health Care—An Historical Overview*, a paper by J. Alexander McMahon, delivered to the Duke University Medical Center, March 23, 1981.

7. Califano, 7.

8. Califano, 2-3.

9. James Michael McGinnis, "Recent Health Gains for Adults," *New England Journal of Medicine* (18 March 1982): 671.

10 Ibid.

11. Califano, 3.

12. Health Care Financing Administration figures.

13. Public opinion figures are from nationwide surveys conducted by The Cambridge Reports in the third quarter of 1981 and the first quarter of 1979.

14. In 1982, an estimated 10.1 percent of federal expenditures will be made on health care. U.S. Office of Management and Budget figures, reported in *U.S. News and World Report*, 15 February 1982.

15. Health Care Financing Administration figures.

16. Califano, 4.

17. Of 6,965 U.S. community hospitals, 1,351 or 19.4 percent are investor owned. Federation of American Hospitals figures.

18. U.S. Department of Health and Human Services figures, reported in the *Chicago Tribune*, 9 March 1982.

19. U.S. Census Bureau and Department of Health and Human Services figures, reported in *Environmental Update*, January 1982, American Hospital Supply Corporation.

20. Figures prepared by Uwe Reinhardt, Princeton University, March 1982.

21. Figures from the *Handbook of Labor Statistics*, U.S. Department of Labor, 1980 (Washington, D.C.: Government Printing Office).

22. In 1978 it was estimated that from 5 percent to 11 percent of the U.S. population lacked health insurance. McMahon, 7.

23. Data from the Chicago Health Systems agency, reported in the *Chicago Tribune*, 11 January 1981.

While the United States faces some very difficult-to-correct economic maladjustments, PAUL W. MCCRACKEN *feels that we are on our way to restoring our prosperity. Assessing the Reagan program, he finds that its problems have more to do with people's expectations than with fundamental policies. Extraordinary progress, he points out, has been made against inflation, particularly in relation to labor costs.*

McCracken's conclusions are optimistic. We have the best chance in a decade to return the U.S. economy to levels of performance enjoyed during the first two-thirds of the twentieth century—5-percent unemployment; 2-percent yearly inflation; and gains in real income of 25 percent to 30 percent per decade.

23

Restoring Our Prosperity

PAUL W. McCRACKEN

I am an economist. There was a time when that was considered to be an honorable profession. I am not sure that is true anymore.

Occasionally you gain insight into fundamental matters via what is called gallows humor, the kind of sour humor that sometimes makes the rounds. Recently I was reading an anthology of gallows humor that was circulating in Russia. One of the stories concerned the May Day Parade. At the end of this long parade of military might and weaponry, there was a little truck with three men riding in the back. Brezhnev is alleged to have turned to the chief of staff and said, "What is the meaning of this joke? We've had this inspiring display of destructive power and then you have this little truck here at the end?"

The chief of staff is alleged to have responded, "Ah, Mr. Chairman, the three men you see there are our top economists, and you have no idea how much destructive power they represent!"

In all seriousness, I wonder how many people could identify the world's largest wheat exporting country at the turn of the century. It was Russia. And today they are having to import massive quantities of wheat in order to take care of their food requirements.

Here is a quotation: "Those who are bursting to give the world advice are less clear in their own minds, or at all events, less unanimous than they might have been thirty years ago." To me this pretty well captures the change from a prior period when we thought we knew how to manage the economy. That confidence has evolved into substantial uncertainty as to whether we really know what to say and what advice to give. That quotation was from a paper written fifty years ago by D. H. Robertson, a distinguished English economist. This is not the first time the human race has confronted economic uncertainty.

If one were to look back over the long course of our history, one could identify three major parameters measuring what we might call the par-for-the-course performance for the American economy. If we want to measure economic performance in very broad terms, the three basic overall measures would be the unemployment rate, the rate of inflation, and growth in real income—the extent to which our economic system has demonstrated its capability to deliver rising material levels of living widely defused throughout our economic system. Par for the course for the American economy for the first two-thirds of the twentieth century was something like this:

Unemployment—4.8 percent, leaving out the world wars and the Great Depression

Inflation—2.1 percent annual compounded rise in the consumer price index, 1900-1967.

Growth in real income—25 percent to 30 percent per decade during the same period, the most important measure of all.

I cite these figures to offer some perspective on our current problems. The problem we face now is not the usual one of economic stabilization—of stimulating the economy when it is a little weak or cooling it down when it is getting above the trend. We have found ourselves here with some fundamentally very difficult economic maladjustments that must be corrected.

Now, what was the strategy of the current government in Washington to try to deal with these problems? It is not my objective here to give any kind of partisan panegyric about the occupants of the White House. Standing back and looking at the basic strategy that seems to be underpinning their actions and the program that the president put forward, I would identify three or four basic axioms. One of these is that the administration clearly has embraced supply-side economics in what I would call the vernacularized form. Supply-side economics in the fundamental sense of being concerned about the quantity of output that an economy can deliver has been a concern of economists since there has been a discipline of economics. The full title of Adam Smith's book was *An Inquiry Into the Nature and Causes of the Wealth of Nations*. If the term gross national product (GNP) had been invented then, the title might have been *An Inquiry Into the Nature and Causes of the Growth in Real GNP*. Supply-side economics, however—in the vernacularized form that we use—means something different. It means that if we had a tax reduction this would so release the creative energy in our economy that the economy would move forward much more rapidly, and the result of tax rate reduction would be that the economy would speed up and the treasury would reap even more revenues.

The second basic philosophical underpinning of the Reagan economists was a good deal of confidence in what economists have called the doctrine of rational expectations. A lot has been written on that subject but it can be summarized in two words: "people learn." But what it really means is this: after a period of price stability such as, for example, the period leading up to or ending about 1966 or 1967, you can pursue inflationary policies and for a while all good things seem to happen. Demand picks up, production picks up, and employment picks up. Only as those pressures finally move through the economy and hit the price level do you start to see the rate of inflation rise. But even then, the rise in the rate of inflation at the outset seems to be a rather small price to pay for the goodies that you are getting in terms of employment and output.

The trouble is that people learn, and after a while they see that when government starts to pursue inflationary policies it is going to lead to inflation. And therefore the interlude of good things gets shorter and shorter. As government pursues inflationary policies, unions start to demand more in wages, and businesses raise their prices. So end the good things.

Finally, there was the conviction of the administration that we had to pursue a much more restrained and moderate demand management policy.

Here we are two years later. How are we doing? Obviously, the track that the economy has followed in real terms over the last two years is not what the administration had projected. If you look back on the economic projections for the economy in February 1981, you wouldn't find 9 percent unemployment and the kind of shortfall in real output and real income that we now see in the economy. What's gone wrong? I think in many respects what probably went wrong had more to do with unrealistic expectations than the wrong policies. After a long period of inflation, you can't assume that people are going to believe you when you say we are now going to pursue steadily and persistently disinflationary policies. After all, we have been hearing that from presidents, Democratic and Republican, for fifteen years. Now a new man comes into the White House in January 1981 and says we are going to persist and stabilize the price level. Too much faith was placed in an almost immediately favorable response to a reduction in tax rates. There was never any hard analytical evidence that such a tax-rate reduction would produce good results.

In spite of all this, however, we do, I think, have to recognize that there are some positive things. It is possible now to see at least some of the things that we should be seeing in the economy before getting on a track of more enduring and persistent and stable economic expansion. I will indicate a few of those.

Possibly the most obvious favorable development of the last two years is that we have made far more rapid progress against inflation than most economists would have predicted. The rate of inflation had risen to 12 percent to 14 percent per year by the end of the 1970s. It is now down basically in the area of about 5 percent. That is extraordinary progress.

Moreover, we are also finally seeing some progress in what has really been the hard-core problem of inflation—the wage inflation problem. There has not been a response on the wage side for the last twenty years. We are starting to see somewhat more moderate wage settlements than we had a year ago, and this, of course, is essential if we are to have any hope of stabilizing the price level in general. Labor costs are a large proportion of general price levels. So, we've made some progress there.

In terms of monetary policy we have made a little progress. Progress here, however, has been disappointing. I recently proposed in a paper that the time has come for this country once again to have what we would call a national commission (what the British would call a royal commission) to explore the problems involved in the management of monetary policy.

Recently we have been seeing signs that the economy may not be very far from its low point and that an upturn in business activity is not far away. I would cite here quickly two things. One of these is that if you look at the net balance between the percentage of companies reporting an increase in new orders and a percentage of companies reporting a decline in new orders for themselves, you would find that the net balance is starting to shift in a favorable direction. I was also much encouraged by the report indicating that for the first quarter of 1982, businesses were selling products significantly faster than they were producing them. Why is that encouraging? Simply because you cannot indefinitely continue to sell more than you produce without ultimately having to step up production schedules and employment in order to service the current volume of sales. On the other hand, as production schedules and employment are stepped up, retail sales should then pick up, becoming part of the normal cumulative process of economic expansion.

Finally, I want to identify one unresolved issue, and how this issue is resolved will importantly influence the way the economy is going to go: the budget problem. There is no doubt but what we have to have some kind of compromise between the two ends of Pennsylvania Avenue to get us on a track so that the deficit in the federal budget will be declining in the years ahead rather than rising, as would probably be the case if we just rocked along with essentially the current program.

There is obviously an impasse between Congress and the White House. We have a government structure with a clearly delineated separation of powers, and Congress has its role to play just as the president does. There is, therefore, always a certain game of chicken played out every year. We're seeing that once again, but it's particularly important that this impasse be resolved. If it is, I think we have the best chance that have had for well over a decade to get the U.S. economy moving toward 5-percent unemployment, and 2-percent inflation per year, and delivering gains in real income.

APR 27 1989
MAY 18 1989

MAY 15 REC'D

JUN 1 4 1993
MAY 2 RECD
R 2 2 1994
AR 2 RECD

MAY 17 1996

MAY 05 REC'D